PROFILE OF AUTHOR

Mr. Seth E. Terkper is currently an Adviser on the Economy to the President of the Republic of Ghana. He was the Minister for Finance [2013 to 2016] and Deputy Minister for Finance [2009 to 2013].

He is a Lecturer in Public Policy, Public Financial Management [PFM], and Taxation at the University of Ghana Business School [UGBS]. He is a consultant and founding and continuing member and lecturer at the African Development Bank PFM Academy.

Prior to holding these positions, Mr Terkper was a Senior Economist at the Fiscal Affairs Department [FAD] of the International Monetary Fund [IMF] in Washington DC [1999-2009]. While there He taught at the IMF Institute.

He was the National Coordinator for the introduction of the Value Added Tax [VAT] in Ghana [1993-1999] and Deputy Commissioner of the VAT Service [VAT] before joining the IMF. He held pioneer roles in the National Revenue Secretariat [NRS]--now the Ghana Revenue Authority [GRA] from 1986 to 1998--under the Ministry of Finance [MOF] in Ghana.

Mr Terkper has worked in consulting positions in the IMF and World Bank. As well as part-time, visiting, and adjunct lecturer positions in various universities that include Harvard, Duke, Georgetown, and Strayer in the United States.

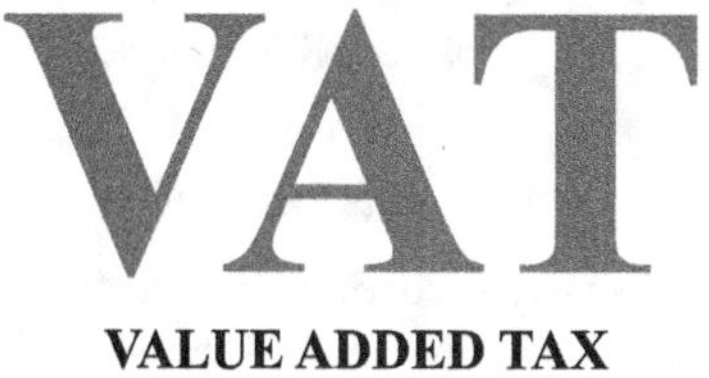

VALUE ADDED TAX

IN AFRICA

THE GHANA EXPERIENCE

Retrospections And Introspections

Seth E. Terkper

VALUE ADDED TAX (VAT) IN AFRICA; THE GHANA EXPERIENCE

Copyright © Seth E. Terkper, 2024

All Rights Reserved

This book is sold subject to the condition that it shall not, by way of trade or otherwise, be lent, re-sold, hired out or otherwise circulated without the publisher's prior consent, in any form of binding or cover other than that in which it is published and without a similar condition including this condition being imposed on the subsequent purchaser.
No part of this book may be reproduced in any form by photocopying or by any electronic or mechanical means, including information storage in a retrieval system, without the written permission of both the copyright owner and the publisher of this book.

ISBN: 979-8-9939162-9-3 (Paperback)
ISBN: 979-8-9960228-0-9 (Hardcover)

Cover Design and Book Layout

Nana Kwame Amoah

Tel: +233 557 555 317 | +233 207 845 105

Published by

Dawn Publishers

P O Box 7465, Accra North, Accra, Ghana

Tel: +233 264 339 066 | +233 244 704 250 | +233 247 896 375

Email: info@dakpabli.com

DEDICATION

This book is dedicated to my family, whose unwavering support has been my foundation; to my colleagues in taxation and fiscal management, whose work inspires continuous learning; and to the countless students I have had the privilege to teach across various educational institutions, whose curiosity and dedication have fuelled my passion for sharing knowledge.

TABLE OF CONTENTS

FOREWORD

This book, "VAT in Africa: The Ghana Experience" is the second of two books on VAT to have been written by Hon. Seth Terkper. The author who has distinguished himself as Ghana's Deputy Minister of Finance (2009 – 2012) and Minister of Finance (2013 – 2016). He was the National Coordinator for the VAT Project from 1993 to 1999, as well as a pioneering force behind its conception and implementation in Ghana. This second Book is specific to the VAT experience in Ghana and Africa where the change of many general consumption taxes to a single VAT regime started in the early 1980s.

I was the Minister for Finance in Ghana when the VAT was re-introduced in 1999 after the first attempt under my predecessor, Hon. Dr. Kwesi Botchwey was "suspended" in 1995. I had the privilege of working closely with the author Seth and the VAT Team under Mr. Ferdinand Asamoah—the Director of the Project and first Commissioner of the VAT Service.

Ghana's initial effort to implement the VAT between 1993 and 1995 was unsuccessful mainly because in addition to the universal abhorrence of citizens to new tax increases, the political environment was not conducive at the time. This attempt was at a time when the country had just transitioned to a multi-party Constitutional rule with its 4-year General election cycle. This was at a time when Ghanaians were generally fatigued by a decade-long, IMF inspired corrective ERP/SAP austerity measures of the Provisional National Defence Council (PNDC) era.

The opposition, as expected in this partisan environment, exploited this ready-made election issue by organising demonstrations against the introduction of the VAT and succeeded in halting its implementation. With just a year-and-half to the 1996 General elections, the cancellation of the newly introduced VAT considerably diminished its impact as an election issue. Immediately after the General elections which returned the NDC to power, and following widespread stakeholder consultations a'slimmed-down' model of the rejected version was successfully introduced in 1999.

Throughout this period, Seth continued to play a key role as the National Coordinator and, after the establishment of the VAT Service, as its first Deputy Commissioner of Finance and Administration.

Seth's leadership and commitment to this course were exemplary and contributed significantly to making VAT central to our fiscal policy.

Between 1999 and 2008, Seth left Ghana to the Fiscal Affairs Department (FAD) of the International Monetary Fund (IMF) where he participated in, and also led missions to, several countries on VAT and other fiscal assignments. In This was after Seth had returned to Ghana as Deputy Minister, at the instance of President Evans John Atta-Mills who, together with Hon. Ato Ahwoi, led the comprehensive tax policy and administration reforms under the PNDC's ERP/SAP Program. It was upon his return that Seth started working again to implement the recent widespread fiscal policy and administration measures, including the GIFMIS and debt repayment mechanism (Sinking Fund) that are widely associated with his name and period in office.

"VAT in Africa: The Ghanaian Experience" exhaustively chronicles the frustrations or challenges, triumphs, and experiences gained along a circuitous VAT route in Ghana. It offers valuable lessons on the intricacies of tax policy and administration that are valuable even beyond our borders. It covers the common program and legislative framework for introducing and administering the VAT in any country.

The author shows how in Ghana and other African countries VAT continues to be distorted notably with the re-introduction of many secondary taxes or levies that affect its smooth administration and compliance. This, the author asserts, is the cause of the failure of the VAT regime to realize its buoyant revenue potential, as many countries continue to wrestle with making VAT the ideal general consumption tax. This Book covers every primary and secondary VAT law, including repeals and amendments, that Ghana's Parliament has passed since 1995.

The Book is also a historical record and resource for policymakers, academics, and practitioners across the continent and beyond. Seth captures the very essence of a transformative era in Ghana's economic history. His personal experience, combined with expert analysis, brings rich and deeper insights to readers interested in the impact and importance of VAT in economic growth and development.

"VAT in Africa: The Ghana Experience" is a simple account of events in history and a beacon for a bright future in tax policy and administration. This book is a treasure of knowledge and inspiration for practitioners, academics and scholars. It is my expectation that it will inspire future generations to pursue bold and courageous reforms to improve the African condition.

Hon. Kwame Peprah
Former Minister for Finance,
Republic of Ghana

ACKNOWLEDGEMENT

I would like to express my heartfelt gratitude to the numerous individuals and organizations whose contributions have been instrumental in the publication of this book. First, I acknowledge the unwavering support of my family, who have endured my physical absences while I immersed myself in research, often transforming our dining table into a makeshift workspace.

I also extend my appreciation to the generations of students I have had the privilege of teaching since the 1980s, both in Ghana and abroad, with the longest tenure being at the University of Ghana Business School (UGBS), Legon, Accra. From my earliest students to my most recent, many have participated in my physical and virtual classes on taxation, public financial management (PFM), Value Added Tax (VAT), public policy, and budgeting. I am particularly grateful to the participants in the African Development Bank (AfDB) Public Financial Management Academy (PMFA) and other programs. I must also recognize my colleague lecturers and advisers at the Academy, as well as the officials of the AfDB's African Development Institute (ADI), led by Professors Kevin Urama and Eric Ogunlaye. Additionally, I am indebted to Professor Ubogu, who served as my mentor and headed the ADI during the 1980s.

The lectures at UGBS and AfDB spanned both the pre- and post-COVID-19 era, with the lockdown in Accra providing the inspiration and solitude necessary to begin writing this second book—VAT in Africa: The Ghana Experience. During that period, I was away from my family in the United States, whose encouragement and interest in my progress motivated me to persevere. I am also grateful for the uncoordinated but invaluable encouragement of two professional colleagues and friends, Messrs. Felix Addo and Vish Ashiagbor, the immediate past and current Senior Partners of PwC, Accra, respectively.

I acknowledge the contributions of my colleagues from the VAT Project (1993), whose dedication laid the groundwork for many of the concepts explored in this book. Special thanks to Messrs. George Kuntu-Blankson, Azaglo, Ezekiel Asamoah, and Nii Aryee, who were seconded from the then Customs, Excise and Preventive Service (CEPS) and the Internal Revenue Service (IRS). The technical assistance provided by Crown Agents, under the leadership of

Messrs. Steve Lowthorpe (London) and Isaac (Ike) Duker (Accra), was invaluable, while administrative support was ably handled by Ms. Liza Obeng.

I also want to acknowledge Messrs. Herbert Morisson and James Otieku of Morisson and Associates for their public education and training efforts. Mr. Otieku, a childhood friend from my hometown, Somanya, was also an early colleague at UGBS, then the School of Administration (SOA). In my first VAT book, I noted the roles of H.E. President J.D. Mahama, who served as Deputy Minister for Information during VAT's reintroduction in 1998, and Hon. Ekwow Spio-Garbrah, then Minister for Information and the first Chairman of the substantive VAT Service (VATS) Board.

I am grateful to Messrs. Abeku Gyan-Quansah of PwC and Felix Ampedu Sumdey of the Ghana Revenue Authority (GRA) for reviewing the initial and final drafts of the manuscript. Finally, I extend my deepest thanks to Mr. Kofi Akpabli and his team of publishers for their efforts in bringing this book to print and for their involvement in organizing the technical seminars and launch of *VAT in Africa: The Ghana Experience*.

PROLOGUE

25 YEARS OF VAT IN GHANA

Introduction

Since the successful re-introduction of the Value Added Tax (VAT) in Ghana, under the VAT Act 1998 (Act 486), the setting up of the VAT Project office in 1993 and earlier launches of the VAT in many states, forty-five (45) African countries have introduced similar versions of the *VAT based on the invoice-credit method*. Currently, VAT remains the main broad-based, indirect consumption or expenditure tax on the continent.

The VAT initiative, which was part of Ghana's tax reforms in the 1980s through the 1990s, followed a worldwide trend that started in the late1960s in the European Union (EU) after it was adopted as the *EU's 6th VAT Directive*. The African spread was part of a global trend that also followed the progress made in selected South American countries. The general goal was to consolidate several sales and service tax regimes under *a single general indirect tax structure.*

In his book (Modernizing VATs in Africa, 2019), Professor Sijbren Cnossen cites Ghana as the *only African country that ever cancelled or suspended the VAT implementation*, about three months after its introduction in 1995. However, the country reinstated the VAT within three years in 1998. Ghana holds this rare failure to introduce VAT with Malta and Grenada, Belize and Vietnam, all of which also reintroduced the VAT after earlier failed attempts.

It is important to note that the initial failure to introduce VAT in 1995 and subsequent success in 1998, after the 1996 elections, are *major political-economy outcomes* that continue to affect the smooth implementation of the tax in Ghana. This is because the VAT initiative became a major topic in the first two elections that followed Ghana's transition from military to civilian rule in 1992, which was barely a year before it set up the VAT Project in 1993.

Ghana's First Attempt and Failure to Introduce VAT

The opposition parties were against the new tax regime because of *the clear fatigue from and, opposition to, major reforms,* including

IMF Adjustment Programs, under a broader *Economic Recovery Programme (ERP) or Structural Adjustment Programme (SAP)*—in short, ERP/SAP. The discussion of VAT issues became virulent and fuelled frequent demonstrations against the government across the country.

Hence, in 1995, the *VAT implementation was suspended* following the violent "Kumepreko" demonstrations that resulted in many casualties in Accra. However, as noted above, the suspension was short-lived, as the ruling National Democratic Congress (NDC) successfully relaunched the VAT from 1996 to 1999, upon passage of a new VAT law in 1998 and after it won the 1996 national elections.

Further, the series of VAT or "Preko" demonstrations, especially "Kumepreko" (which translates as "kill me now"), appear to sow the *seed for the politicization of VAT and other tax reforms in Ghana.* This is because, as this book later notes, the victory of the opposition National Patriotic Party (NPP) in the third 4th Republican elections in 2000 started the significant, frequent and ongoing policy changes in the *substantive Value Added Tax (VAT) Act, 1998 (Act 546)—that replaced the original and aborted VAT* Act, 1994 (Act 486).

VAT remains a *heated political-economy tax instrument.* After the election of the NDC to power again in 2009, it passed a comprehensive replacement law, namely, the *VAT Act, 2013 (Act 870).* Unsurprisingly, perhaps, many of the VAT Act 870 updates were promptly reversed when the NPP took power again in 2017.

Summary of Parts of the Book

Within the context of the preceding summary, this book is structured into the following major parts, each encompassing some chapters:

Part 1—Background (Chapters 1 to 5) covers taxation and the fiscal framework, tax and revenue administration, the theoretical and policy context of VAT and other consumption taxes. It focuses on the mechanics of collecting the tax under the popular *Invoice-Credit VAT method* that has widely replaced the old Sales (and Service) taxes that preceded the VAT reforms in many countries. It summarizes the basic features and methods of collecting these earlier taxes.

Part II—Legislation (Chapters 6 to 7) covers the VAT structure under the initial or original VATA 1998 (Act 546)—which is the law that repealed VAT Act 1994 (Act 486), after the cancellation of VAT in 1995 (see a summary of the contents in Appendices 1.1 and 1.2). The chapter also provides a summary of the several amendments and repeals of the VAT Act 546 that preceded and followed the passage of the third comprehensive VAT law, the VAT Act 2013 (Act 870)

Part III—VAT Implementation Challenges (Chapters 8 to 11) covers the changes in VAT policy, base and structure in the form of amendments and repeals from 1998 to 2022. Most changes or distortions to both VAT Act, 1998 (546) and VAT Act 870 (2013), including detailed extracts and analyses, are found in Schedule 1 (Exemptions), Schedule 2 (Reliefs) and Schedule 3 (Zero-rating).

Administration of VAT

In a forthcoming and related publication on General Revenue Administration in Ghana, the Book cites several changes to the administration of VAT and the other direct and indirect taxes. These include the following:

(i) *Revenue agencies as part of the Civil Service*—up to 1987, the tax agencies that were part of the Civil Service, under the Ministry of Finance and Economic Planning (MOFEP) were the Central Revenue Department (CRD) and the Customs and Excise Department (CEP).

(ii) *Establishment of National Revenue Secretariat (NRS)*—in 1984, the NRS was established to exercise supervisory administrative powers over the CRD and CED to improve revenue policy and administration, within context of an overall Economic Recovery Program (ERP)—also known as the Structural Adjustment Program (SAP) or simply ERP/SAP.

(iii) *Semi-autonomy for revenue institutions*—in 1987, the status of CRD and CED changed to semi-autonomous institution under the Internal Revenue Service (IRS) Act 2000, (Act 592); and the Customs, Excise and Preventive Service (CEPS) Act respectively—and each with a separate supervisory board.

(iv) *Third revenue agency*—as part of the replacement of sales (CEPS) and service (IRS) taxes with the Value Added Tax (VAT), a third agency with a separate supervisory Board, was established under the Value Added Tax (VAT) Service (VATS) Act.

(v) *Replacement of NRS with RAGB*—the separate supervisory boards of NRS were merged into a single *Revenue Agencies' (Governing) Board (RAGB)* under the *RAGB* Act, 1998 (Act 558).

The second generation of tax or revenue administration reforms in Ghana occurred in 2009 with (a) the setting up of the Ghana Revenue Authority (GRA) as an apex semi-autonomous agency; and (b) the integration of IRS, CEPS and VATS as operational Departments of GRA. The main elements are summarized as follows:

(i) *Ghana Revenue Authority (GRA) Act 2009 (Act 791)* to replace the Revenue Agencies (Governing) Board *(RAGB)* Act, 1998 (Act 558) as well as the merger of the Internal Revenue Service *(IRS)* and the VAT Service *(VATS);*

(ii) Under the GRA Act, the *IRS and VATS* became the Domestic Tax Revenue Division (DTRD)while the Customs, Excise and Preventive Service (CEPS) became the Customs Division (CD);

(iii) Further, the separate administrative support units for IRS, VATS and CEPS were combined into GRA's Support Services Division (SSD); and

(iv) Finally, a consolidated *Revenue Administration Act (RAA), 2016 (Act 915)* was passed to merge the administrative provisions for all the direct and indirect taxes since GRA had become the apex body for all direct and indirect taxes.

(v) Another important development was the establishment of a *Tax Policy Division (TPD)* in the Ministry of Finance (MOF) to separate the policy and administrative aspects of tax and revenue management.

Further, in 2013, the Ministry of Finance and Economic Planning [MoFEP] became the Ministry of Finance (MoF) after its physical planning function was moved to the National Development Planning Commission (NDPC).

Political Economy of VAT

In conclusion, it must be noted that launch of VAT was part of the Structural Adjustment Program (SAP)—also called the Economic Recovery Program (ERP)—that (a) covered significant macroeconomic, monetary, fiscal and real sector reforms; and (b) became embroiled with transition from military rule to civilian administration under the PNDC and NDC. Unfortunately, Ghana continues to struggle with separating VAT policies from its politics, with significant changes occurring whenever the National Democratic Congress (NDC) or New Patriotic Party (NPP) takes power.

As a result, businesses and consumers bear the brunt of an unstable, inefficient VAT system. Like other African nations, Ghana has yet to fully tap into the revenue potential of VAT, largely due to frequent exemptions, zero-rating of "basic" goods and services, and sub-optimal VAT rates since its introduction.

Frequent technical changes to VAT regimes further hinder the ability to maximize VAT revenue. This disrupts the efficiency of the invoice-based Input Tax Credit (ITC) method, known for its streamlined credit and refund processes, which prevent the cascading effect of consumption taxes and enhance the benefits of zero-rating exports.

Conclusion—fiscal implications

In a *broader fiscal context,* despite VAT's reputation as a reliable revenue "spinner," Ghana's politicized and distorted VAT regime has stagnated in realizing its full potential. As a result, its positive impact on addressing high deficits, debt distress, and default has been minimized. This comes two decades after Ghana's declaration as a Highly Indebted Poor Country (HIPC) and is compounded by ongoing domestic and external public debt restructuring following the significant default on debt obligations in 2022. These unfortunate outcomes are partly the result of schemes such as

(i) the sub-standard rate classification of some registered entities under the VAT Flat Rate Scheme (VFRS); and

(ii) conversion of the GETFund Levy and NHIL to so-called excise-type "straight" levies.

The latter has effectively blocked 5% of the original 17.5% VAT rate from being eligible for Input Tax Credits (ITC), leading to significant instances of multiple taxation or "cascading.

These changes have blurred the revenue and non-revenue objectives that the Economic Recovery Program (ERP) and Structural Adjustment Program (SAP) restructuring aimed to achieve in the 1980s and 1990s. To build resilience into the tax system, it is essential to allow major tax handles to mature over time, fostering stability and generating the necessary inflows.

While this book focuses on Ghana, it offers valuable lessons for other African countries and nations that have similarly distorted the relatively efficient VAT invoice-credit method. It provides numerous examples of VAT policy and legislative changes that have led to excessive VAT burdens, rampant evasion or avoidance, and ultimately made the perception of VAT as a "money spinner" elusive.

PART I

VALUE ADDED TAX (VAT): FISCAL, TAX POLICY & ADMINISTRATION CONTEXT

Chapter 1

BACKGROUND: TAXATION AND THE FISCAL FRAMEWORK

Introduction to the Fiscal Framework

Tax or broader revenue policies and administration are major elements in the public finance or the public financial management (PFM) framework for both central (unitary or federal) governments and sub-national governments (SNGs). This chapter summarizes the elements or components of the fiscal framework including revenue, expenditure, budget deficit or fiscal balance, financing or borrowing, and public debt.

The fiscal framework has outcomes that affect the efficient mobilization of revenue, use of budget resources approved by Parliament, management of the entire economy, prospects for development and the welfare of its citizens. Examples include:

- critical macro-fiscal management performance (e.g., revenue-to-GDP, deficit-to-GDP, and public debt-to-GDP);
- the efficient management of monetary and financial policy (e.g., heavy reliance on the central bank to monetize the deficit and escalation of inflation);
- efficient allocation of budget resources to real sector projects (e.g., roads, power plants, airport and harbour facilities, running the government); and
- macroeconomic outcomes (e.g., growth, job creation, social intervention programs.

An important aspect of these fiscal analyses and performance is that the actual and projected performance have become part of the 2015 as well as 2023 International Monetary Fund (IMF) Enhanced Credit Facility (ECF) Programs under Ghana's two (2) separate governments. A second twist is that 2013 marks the year in which the Ministry of Finance (MOF) was formally notified by the World Bank and African Development Bank (AfDB) that Ghana had become a Lower-Middle-Income Country (L-MIC).

Summary Analyses of Components of the Fiscal Framework

The ensuing paragraphs summarize the revenue, expenditure, deficit or fiscal balances, borrowing or financing, and public debt components as the nation's Fiscal Framework. Hence the macro-fiscal performance analyses of the budget begin with the actual current and prior year cash flow performance as well as the annual and medium-term budgets or fiscal forecasts, estimates or projections.

The first fiscal outcome of the cash inflows (revenues) and outflows (expenditures) is the budget deficit or Fiscal Balance (FB) on Commitment Basis. The next step adds the short-term liabilities—also called arrears or commitments—to the "cash" deficit to produce the Overall Fiscal Balance (FB) or Fiscal Balance (FB) on Cash Basis. The Public Accounts are prepared from actual fiscal outcomes while the Budget is based on projections of estimates.

The final components of the Fiscal Framework include Financing or Borrowing and Amortization—in which net sum is an increase or decrease in the national or Public Debt. When borrowing exceeds the repayment (i.e., amortization), the rate of Public Debt accumulation increases while a positive outcome reduces the rate of growth of the national or public debt.

Components of the Fiscal Framework: A critical analysis suggests that the Fiscal Framework has four (4) components, namely, the Cash Inflows & Outflows; Short-term Liabilities (variously called arrears, accruals or commitments); Financing or Borrowing; and the Public Debt Stock. These are shown in high-level summaries from Tables 1.1 to 1.5.

(i) **Component I—Revenue, Expenditure and Budget (Cash) Deficit:** The cash inflows and outflows of the framework include revenues and expenditures or spending which, when offset against each other, result in the budget deficit. It is the most accurate element in Low-Income Countries (LICs) and Lower-Middle Income Countries (L-MICs). Table 1.1 further shows the H-L Tier 2 components comprising domestic revenues and grants as well as recurrent and capital expenditures.

Table 1.1: Cash Component—Revenue, Expenditure & Budget Deficit

GHANA: OVERAL FISCAL FRAMEWORK (ECONOMIC CLASSIFICATION]			
HIGH-LEVEL REVENUE, EXPENDITURE, DEFICIT & FINANCING (1)			
S/N	HEADING	POLICY GOALS OR OBJECTIVES	COMMENTS
1	Revenue & grants	Annual tax & non-tax revenue and grants	While these are current year inflows and outflows, the national budgets normally include medium-term forecasts (on rolling basis)
1.1	Domestic Revenues	Tax and non-tax (fees/charges) revenues	
1.2	Grants	Grants or aid from Development Partners (DPs)	
2	Expenditure	Total expenditure	
2.1	Recurrent Expenditure	Current-year budget spending	
2.2	Capital Expenditure	Current-year spending	
3	Budget (cash) Deficit	Revenue less Expenditure (Fiscal Bal. Commitment)	Deficit (or surplus); fiscal identity

The Budget (Cash) Deficit is equal to the Fiscal Balance (on Commitment Basis) because they are fiscal identities. Hence, this Fiscal Balance I is also brought forward (b/f) or carried forward (c/f) as the first element in Table 1.2.

(ii) Component II—Accrual or Commitment and Fiscal Balances: The short-term liabilities that are also called accruals, arrears or commitments increase the cash budget deficit. After accounting for any discrepancy, this becomes what is often called the Fiscal Balance (Cash) Basis. Table 1.2 summarizes the "accrual" component.

Table 1.2: Short-term Liabilities (Accrual or Commitments) Component

GHANA: OVERAL FISCAL FRAMEWORK (ECONOMIC CLASSIFICATION]			
HIGH-LEVEL ACCRUAL AND FISCAL BALANCES (2)			
S/N	ITEM	EXPLANATION	
4	Arrears or Commitments	Annual Short-term (Routine) & Exceptional Liabilities	Also called accruals
4.1	Fiscal Balance I (Commitment)	Fiscal identity (same as Budget Deficit above)	Neutral effect. In prin
4.2	Add: Routine Net Arrears	Typical current year unpaid bills (Item 1.2 above)	The control of exceptional (also termed unbudgeted & unpaid) lies in effective budget buffer policies.
4.2.1	Current Year Net Arrears	Estimate of arrears or commitment from previous fiscal year	
4.2.2	Less: Previous Year Net Arrear	Net Arrears from immediate past fiscal year	
4.3	Add: Exceptional expenditure	Expenditures that do not recur annually	
4.4	Add/Less: Discrepancy	Rounding-up and unexplained differences	These requires process improvements
5	Fiscal Balance II (Cash or Over	The budget deficit (cash) plus arrears to be funded	Also Fiscal Balance (Cash Basis)

Under the full-accrual or semi-accrual rules, the arrears or unpaid bills owed to suppliers, contractors, and others at the end of the fiscal year [FY]) are passed through ledger records that include the following—

- balances brought forward (b/f)—including arrears or commitments from the previous or prior year(s);
- amount of the current fiscal year's unpaid bills, invoices, or vouchers—after payments in the fiscal year—Item 4.1 (routine) and Item 4.2 (exceptional) in Table 1.2) above; and
- the difference or the balance of arrears that is carried forward (c/f) to the ensuing fiscal year (FY).

The routine or normal arrears, covering wages, expenses, and other recurrent and capital expenses recur annually and are the result of credit or repayment terms that overlap the fiscal year. In contrast, the exceptional arrears are the result of occasional expenditures such as domestic and global shocks that are difficult to predict and, therefore, are periodic and, often unplanned, outstanding items in annual budgets.

(iii) Component III--Financing or Borrowing: As noted in Table 1.3, the arrears increase (and rarely decrease) the Budget Deficit or Fiscal Balance I to become Fiscal Balance II (Cash Basis). The latter is equal to the loan amount that Parliament approves for the ensuing fiscal year (FY).

Table 1.3: Financing of the Fiscal Balance

GHANA: OVERAL FISCAL FRAMEWORK (ECONOMIC CLASSIFICATION]			
HIGH-LEVEL FINANCING OR BORROWING (3)			
S/N	HEADING	POLICY GOALS OR OBJECTIVES	COMMENTS
6	Financing (Borrowing)	Financing Fiscal Balances (net of amortization)	Appropriation is by the Parliament
6.1	Short-term loans	These classifications reflect the duration it will take to repay	The alternative classification is by
6.2	Medium-to-long term loans	the loan.	source, namely, domestic or foreign.
6.3	Amortization	Repayment of past borrowing (i.e., principal)	May include interest, if not a bullet loan
7	Ghana Petroleum Funds	The balances depend on PRMA rules-based flows 1/	A Sovereign Wealth Fund (SWF)
7.1	Stabilization Fund	The use of Stabilization Funds require Parliamentary	Budget buffer or loan reduction
7.2	Heritage Fund	approval; withdrawal from Heritage Funds is "frozen"	Freeze lift subject to Parliament

The repayment period for loans or borrowing to finance the fiscal balance may be short-term (e.g., treasury bills and notes) or medium-term loans and bonds (e.g., sovereign bonds), with sources from either domestic or external financial markets. The Sources of loans, which are also the classification of the public debt, are discussed in the next component of the Fiscal Framework.

(iv) **Component IV--Public Debt Component:** As Table 1.4 shows (a) the current year borrowing, financing or loans; and (b) repayment or amortization—which often includes borrowing to refinance or rollover existing loans that the government cannot repay. The difference between the annual borrowing (i.e., Component III above) and repayment determines the rate of debt accumulation and net increase (i.e., negative) or decrease (i.e., positive) in the Public Debt.

Table 1.4: Impact of Annual Items on Public Debt Stock

GHANA: OVERAL FISCAL FRAMEWORK (ECONOMIC CLASSIFICATION)			
HIGH-LEVEL PUBLIC DEBT (4)			
S/N	HEADING	POLICY GOALS OR OBJECTIVES	COMMENTS
8	Debt stock	Public Debt stock at the beginning or end of the year	Cumulative from previous years
8.1	*Balance brought forward (b/f)*	*Balance outstanding from previous year*	*Amount outstanding from start of FY*
8.2	*Add: Financing*	*Fiscal identity, same as Item 6*	*Part of annual budget approvals*
8.3	*Less: Amortization*	*Repayment from budget, sinking fund, others*	*Based on terms of loan contracts*
9	Balance carried forward (c/f)	Balance outstanding at the end of the current year	Net (financing v repayment) position
1/ Petroleum Revenue Management Act (PRMA)			

Sources of the loans: These are the same as the *borrowing or financing sources* in Component III and may be incurred *directly* through the same intermediaries or lenders. However, they may be offered through intermediaries that are agencies of the primary lenders and through the financial markets. They include

- **official lenders or creditors**: these include loans from relatively advanced sovereign governments and international institutions that typically give development assistance loans to low-income countries—with concessional or soft terms and conditions;
- **other bilateral sources:** the governments may include governments and/or its entities and their lending arms or agencies such as USAID, DfID and the commercial and Export-Import (i.e., EXIM) Banks;
- **multilateral sources:** the typical ones are global financial institutions such as the African Development Banks (AfDB); World Bank; and International Monetary Fund (IMF) that lend on soft or concessionary terms and conditions.

The multilateral and bilateral governments and institutions are also the ones that provide the bulk of *aid or grants* to low-income countries (LIC). The loans may also be classified by *duration* or *maturity* period as *short-term* (i.e., mainly for *liquidity management*) as well as *medium-term and long-term* (i.e., *project or programme-oriented*),

The Chapter continues with a summary explanation of the Fiscal Framework comprising (a) the primary and secondary *tax and non-tax revenues* which (b) together with the expenditure flows, gives (c) the annual or multi-year budget deficits (but rarely surpluses). Further, it gives the actual and projected performance for the annual and medium-term Fiscal Framework from FY2024 to 2027.

Revenue Performance—High-Level Primary and Secondary Tax Instruments

The fiscal strength or ability of a country to meet its expenditure and debt service needs depends on its *core or primary* tax handles or instruments and complementary *minor or secondary* instruments. It is the strength or resilience of the tax handles that makes the tax regime buoyant and makes the fiscal regime sustainable and sound.

As discussed later, fiscal performance also depends on prudent expenditure policies and measures to achieve low levels of fiscal deficits, borrowing or financing public debt. The following is a summary of Ghana's principal or major and secondary direct and indirect tax handles or instruments.

Primary Tax Instruments: These generate substantial revenues that may amount to about 80 per cent or more of total tax revenues. A high-level breakdown includes—

- **Direct Taxes (Income & Property)**: These are taxes imposed on the taxable income or earnings from employment and self-employed persons, doing business as corporate entities; and owning property.
- **Taxes on employment:** These are payable on the total taxable emoluments comprising salaries, wages and allowances of employees. The income tax on emoluments in many countries is based on progressive (zero, low and high) tax rates that are published in tax tables or schedules.
- **Taxes on income from property:** These are imposed on the taxable elements that include (a) rent and property tax from ownership; and (b) profits or gains made from the disposal of both tangible (e.g., house) and intangible (e.g., investment securities) assets. It is necessary to note that in many jurisdictions, including Ghana, property taxes are imposed and collected by

sub-national governments (SNG) that are called Metropolitan, Municipal and District Assemblies (MMDAs).

- **Indirect Taxes (Consumption Expenditures)**: These are taxes imposed on taxable consumable expenditures by individuals and households—and, therefore, also called consumption taxes.
    - **Value Added Tax (VAT):** The VAT or general consumption tax has the widest tax base and, in principle, is imposed on taxable goods and services at a single or flat rate. However, the law may (a) exempt or exclude the taxation of some items; and (b) impose lower rates on social or economic grounds. VAT is neutral since it is imposed on both domestic and international trade.
    - **Excise Duty:** The two (2) aspects of excises are that it is (a) a punitive tax that is imposed on harmful commodities including alcohol, tobacco and petroleum; and (b) neutral because, as with VAT, it is imposed on both taxable imports and domestic supplies. Though the taxable import and domestic bases are narrow, they tend to generate high and buoyant tax revenues because of the relatively high rates.
    - **Tariffs or Import Duties:** These general consumption taxes are restrictive because they are imposed on only taxable supplies of imported goods. Hence, they are also called a protective tax because it is not imposed on domestically produced goods and, therefore, not as neutral as the VAT or excise duty. Import duty rates also vary with the type of supply: (a) consumer goods—highest rate; (b) raw materials—lower rate; (c) semi-produced or "knocked-down" parts—also lower rates; and (c) exempt (general or end-user) at a nil rate.
- **Secondary Tax or Revenue Instruments:** these are normally (a) external grants or aid; (b) "levies" or taxes; and (c) fees and charges—both of which are given other names.
    - **Grants or aid:** These are budget assistance from multilateral and bilateral sources that include the World Bank, African Development Bank (AfDB) and the IMF. As with Upper- and Lower-Middle Income Countries (U-MICs and L-MICs), this source of revenue tapers with that transition from a Low-Income Country (LIC).

- **Levies or taxes:** These may be complete or partial tax instruments that are often imposed to complement the expenditure reforms that countries use in austerity **programs** to manage both domestic and external economic crises.
- **User fees and charges:** These fiscal impositions are restricted to the beneficiaries or users of specific public goods or services—including vehicle renewal, registration of land, and road tolls. Hence, (a) those who do not use the supply do not pay the charges or fees; and (b) in principle, they may be classified as tax when the levels of fees or charges are too high as compensation for the supply.

The imposition of both direct and indirect taxes (a) relies on businesses as agents for collecting the taxes: and (b) the base of the various taxes on only the taxable elements of the income or supply. One reason for a narrow taxable base is the exemptions and incentives that are granted to individuals and businesses for specific social or economic policies.

As is usually the case, these actual and projected fiscal analyses and performance are included part of the 2015 as well as 2023 International Monetary Fund (IMF) Enhanced Credit Facility (ECF) Programs under Ghana's two (2) separate governments, Next, we discuss the nature and actual performance, at the upstream or primary level, for the various elements of the fiscal framework, namely revenue, expenditure, fiscal balance as well as borrowing and debt—as shown in Ghana's Annual Budgets and the 2024 Medium-Term projections.

High-Level Revenue Performance—Annual Budget and Medium-Term (2013 to 2024)

The ensuing paragraphs discuss Ghana's *actual tax and non-tax revenue performance* from 2013 to 2017 fiscal years (FY 2013-17), based on (a) MOF historical data from FY 2013 to FY 2022 fiscal years (FY); (b) the FY 2024 annual estimates; (c) the 2022 probable actual; and (d) the medium-term projections from FY2025 to FY 2027).

These analyses start with Table 1.5, which repeats and concisely explains the high-level (HL) domestic taxes and external aid or grants, including—

- **total revenues:** at the apex of the framework, this includes domestic revenue (i.e., tax and non-tax revenues) and grants or aid;
- **domestic revenues:** these include **tax and non-tax revenues**, social security contributions, and other tax revenues; and
- **grants or aid:** these include the **external** (i.e., non-domestic) resources that the multilateral and bilateral institutions, including foreign governments and their agencies, give to support the budget.

The tables that follow continue show a more detailed breakdown or hierarchy of these main revenue and tax instruments or handles.

Table 1.5: Total and Domestic Revenues and Grants

GHANA: TAX & NON-TAX REVENUES [BUDGET FRAMEWORK]					
ITEMS	**HEADING**	**CATEGORY**	**SUB-CATEGORY**	**SUB-ITEM**	**POLICY OBJECTIVES**
1	**Revenue & grants**				Total revenues
1.1		Domestic revenue			Local sources of income
1.1.1			Tax Revenue		Tax (direct/indirect) & Non-Tax Revenues
1.1.1.1				*Taxes on Income & Property*	Direct taxes
1.1.1.2				*Taxes on Domestic Goods & Svcs*	Indirect [domestic] taxes
1.1.1.3				*International Trade Taxes*	Indirect [foreign] taxes
1.1.2			Social contributions		SSNIT contributions to NHIL
1.1.3			Non-Tax Revenues	*Income and fees*	Part is Internally-Generated Funds (IGF)
1.1.4			Other revenues	*Taxes, incomes & fees*	Exceptional & non-reccurrent
2		Grants/Aid	Foreign income or budget support other than loans		Mostly from multilateral & bilateral sources

High Level (HL) Revenue Performance: Table 1.6 shows the headline nominal values of the Total Revenue and its second-tier Domestic Revenue, with third-tier elements, in nominal (Ghc m) values. It highlights the *Electronic Transactions Levy (e-Levy)* as the most recently failed pivotal revenue policy measure that will boost revenue and fiscal performance significantly.

The tax was promoted as a major *general or consumption* (e.g., VAT) or *special* (e.g., excise duty) tax on goods or services. In reality, as a tax imposed on a narrow base, the electronic money transfer tax or e-Levy is a *minor* sub-sector service tax on savings or investment and cascades because it does not allow registered entities to claim Input Tax Credit (ITC) or refund.

Table 1.6: High-Level Revenue Summary (with Offsets)—Nominal (Ghc m)

Tax Revenue (Ghc Million)															
	Provisional Actual										Proj	Budget	MTBF		
	2013	2014	2015	2016	2017	2018	2019	2020	2021	2022	2023	2024	2025	2026	2027
Total Rev	19,471.6	24,745.5	32,040.4	33,678.2	41,497.9	47,636.7	52,974.1	55,138.2	70,096.5	98,080.4	133,875.1	143,956.4	171,757.4	206,532.0	232,366.25
o/w e-Levy										[illegible]	[illegible]	[illegible]	[illegible]	[illegible]	[illegible]
Dom. Rev.	18,732.1	23,931.3	29,351.7	32,537.4	39,963.0	46,501.9	51,988.0	53,909.5	68,914.3	95,532.7	131,400.9	141,552.7	169,465.7	204,655.2	231,448.2
Tax Rev.	14,307.7	19,229.8	24,140.9	25,728.7	32,227.6	37,784.2	42,355.5	44,447.8	56,533.1	75,548.2	107,648.6	112,357.9	139,974.9	170,425.7	193,296.0
Grants	739.4	814.1	2,688.8	1,140.7	1,534.9	1,134.8	986.1	1,228.7	1,182.2	1,503.81	2,474.19	2,403.7	2,291.7	1,876.8	918.1

Table 1.7 repeats Table 1.5 in *percentage (%) of Gross Domestic Product (GDP)* to reflect the real value performance. It shows that *Ghana now relies less on external aid or grants* to finance the budget because of three (3) factors—namely, the end of HIPC/MDRI inflows, the rebasing of the GDP and the strong boost from the services and petroleum (energy) sectors.

Table 1.7: High-Level Revenue Summary (with Offsets)—Percent (%) of GDP

Revenue: Percent (%) of GDP															
	Provisional Actual										End-Aug	Budget	MTBF		
	2013	2014	2015	2016	2017	2018	2019	2020	2021	2022	2023	2024	2025	2026	2027
Total Rev	15.7	15.9	17.8	15.7	16.2	15.8	15.3	14.4	16.2	16.1	15.7	18.0	18.0	18.9	18.7
o/w e-Levy										0.1	0.1	0.3	0.3	0.3	0.3
Dom. Rev	15.1	15.4	16.3	15.1	15.6	15.5	15.0	14.1	15.9	15.7	15.4	17.7	17.8	18.7	18.6
Tax Rev.	11.6	12.4	13.4	12.0	12.6	12.6	12.2	11.6	13.0	12.4	12.7	14.0	14.7	15.6	15.5
Grants	0.6	0.5	1.5	0.5	0.6	0.4	0.3	0.3	0.3	0.2	0.3	0.3	0.2	0.2	0.1
Nom. GDP (13' Base)	123,650	155,433	180,139	215,077	256,671	300,596	345,946	383,305	433,686	610,222	850,656	800,921	953,578	1,094,354	1,244,226

Figure 1.1 expresses Table 1.7 in *graphical or visual terms* and highlights the ambitious goal of increasing the performance in the expressed medium-term. They show the *stagnant and slightly declining* revenue performance that, among other fiscal measures, was expected to rise significantly in the medium-term (2024 to 2027) under an IMF Program.

Figure 1.1: Revenue Performance

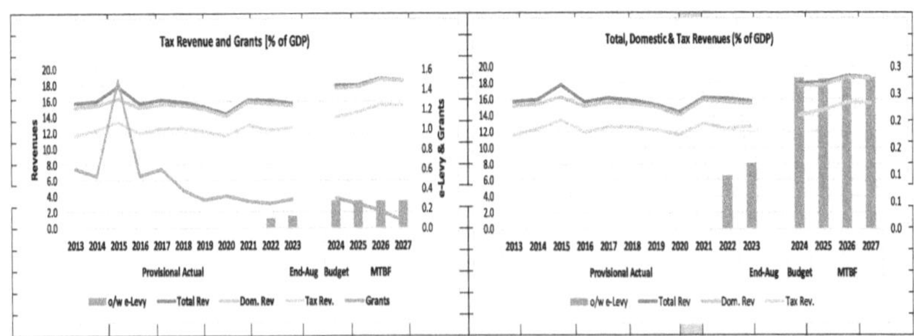

Nature of domestic non-tax revenues: In contrast, the underlying charges and fees that result in non-tax revenues are linked directly to the benefits of goods and services provided by central and sub-national governments. An explanation of the fees and charges that accumulate to become non-tax revenues includes the following—

User fees: usually, this is a generic term used for services that offices belonging to MDAs and MMDAs render to citizens—the typical example being one-time or renewable fees paid for operating licenses (e.g., to trade or process a permit).

- **Charges:** governments classify these as part of fees but related to payments made in exchange for the supply of tangible goods or property.
- **Incomes:** these are earnings (i.e., price or profits) made by MDAs and MMDAs for selling goods and services related to administering the Customs Tariff.
- **Levies:** these have features of taxation since they may be paid compulsorily, in whole or in part for services that are not the result of being a direct beneficiary of a commodity or service.

External grants or aid: grants and aid are non-tax revenues but represent direct external inputs to the budget. Typically, they are from multilateral and bilateral sources, including institutions such as the World Bank, and African Development Bank (AfDB) and external national development institutions such as USAID or DFID.

- **Declining share of total revenue**: the share of grants has been declining since (a) officially, Ghana became an L-MIC in 2010; and (b) most of Ghana's aid is now channelled through Non-Governmental Organizations (NGOs) or Civil Society Organizations (CSOs).
- **Tracking aid flows to the real sector:** a serious effort to track flows outside the Budget began with the coding and classification of such budgetary (and non-budgetary) contributions under the comprehensive reporting or declarations under the Revenue Modernization Program (RMP) under GRA; and (b) the overall PFM or GIFMIS reforms under the Ministry of Finance (MOF).

Table 1.13 summarizes the elements of **Non-Tax Revenues** and the difference between the total amount collected and lodged into the Consolidated Fund. The difference is derived from the **retention policy and law** (Revenue Agencies (Retention of Part of Revenue

Act, 2002 (***Act 628***). that allows MDAs and MMDAs to keep part of the fees and charges for specific expenditure needs.

Table 1.13: Non-Tax Revenues—Nominal (GHC million)

	Provisional Actual										Proj	Budget	MTBF		
	2013	2014	2015	2016	2017	2018	2019	2020	2021	2022	2023	2024	2025	2026	2027
Total Revenue	20,313.6	24,588.8	32,667.5	35,123.3	43,301.3	47,636.7	52,974.1	55,138.2	70,096.5	96,651.2	133,876.1	176,414.1	211,035.1	249,535.7	281,088.1
Non-Tax Rev.	4,265.4	4,483.4	4,921.4	4,882.4	5,325.2	6,523.7	7,567.6	6,667.3	7,908.9	14,561.0	17,595.4	22,565.2	25,898.5	29,306.3	32,274.0
Retentions	2,516.3	2,497.3	2,530.6	3,367.8	2,848.5	3,164.8	3,952.7	4,003.2	4,708.1	7,018.2	10,606.6	12,339.4	13,840.4	15,607.1	17,610.4
Lodgements	1,749.1	1,986.1	2,390.8	1,514.6	2,476.7	3,358.9	3,614.9	2,664.1	3,200.8	7,542.8	6,988.8	10,225.7	12,058.1	13,699.1	14,663.7
Fees & Charges	372.2	329.8	662.7	465.6	552.5	554.6	623.0	565.1	768.9	774.4	930.1	1,625.5	1,761.4	1,958.4	2,470.9
Div, Int, Profits (Other)	500.0	217.8	725.6	555.5	330.7	139.2	105.9	275.5	474.8	473.8	233.5	644.1	879.6	1,026.7	1,220.9
Div, Int & Profits (Oil)	875.4	1,434.7	994.5	490.5	1,585.6	2,530.8	2,691.1	1,695.8	1,816.6	6,082.4	5,537.3	7,716.7	9,151.4	10,437.1	10,667.2
Surface Rent (oil)	1.3	3.7	5.9	2.9	7.9	11.8	19.5	7.3	5.6	25.1	53.5	10.6	14.0		

Table 1.14 shows the elements of Table 1.3 (non-tax revenue) in percentage (%) of GDP.

Table 1.14: Non-Tax Revenue Lodgements—Percent (%) of GDP

Non-Tax Revenues: Percent (%) of GDP

	Provisional Actual										Proj	Budget	MTBF		
	2013	2014	2015	2016	2017	2018	2019	2020	2021	2022	2023	2024	2025	2026	2027
Total Revenue	16.4	15.8	18.1	16.3	16.9	15.8	15.3	14.4	16.2	15.8	15.7	22.0	22.1	22.8	22.6
Total Non-Tax Rev.	3.4	2.9	2.7	2.3	2.1	2.2	2.2	1.7	1.8	2.4	2.1	2.8	2.7	2.7	2.6
Retention	2.0	1.6	1.4	1.6	1.1	1.1	1.1	1.0	1.1	1.2	1.2	1.5	1.5	1.4	1.4
Lodgements	1.4	1.3	1.3	0.7	1.0	1.1	1.0	0.7	0.7	1.2	0.8	1.3	1.3	1.3	1.2
Fees & Charges	0.3	0.2	0.4	0.2	0.2	0.2	0.2	0.1	0.2	0.1	0.1	0.2	0.2	0.2	0.2
Div, Int, Profits (Other)	0.4	0.1	0.4	0.3	0.1	0.0	0.0	0.1	0.1	0.1	0.0	0.1	0.1	0.1	0.1
Div, Int & Profits (Oil)	0.7	0.9	0.6	0.2	0.6	0.8	0.8	0.4	0.4	1.0	0.7	1.0	1.0	1.0	0.9
Surface Rent (oil)	0.001	0.002	0.003	0.001	0.003	0.004	0.006	0.002	0.001	0.004	0.006	0.001	0.0	0.0	0.0
Capping (Yield)						0.034	0.033	0.031	0.031	0.031	0.028	0.029	0.029	0.025	0.024

Figure 1.3 shows the contents of **Table 1.13, Table 1.14** and **Figure 1.3** as graphs. They show the **declining feature of the non-tax revenues**—like the trends depicted by the tables and graphs relating to total revenues.

Figure 1.3: Non-Tax Revenues—Percent (%) of GDP

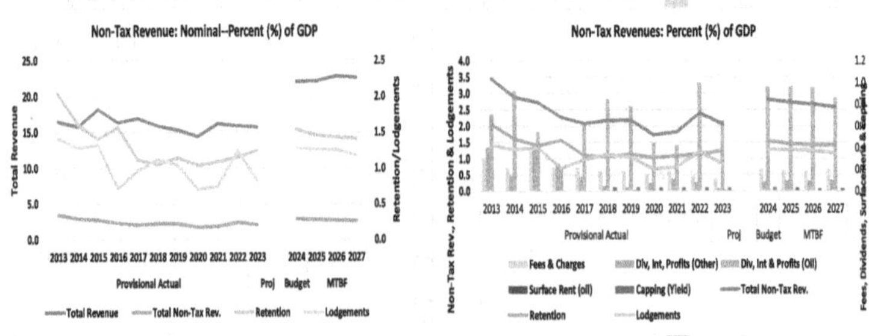

Expenditure Performance (2013 to 2024): Annual Budget and Medium-Term

The state uses the total tax and non-tax revenues generated, as discussed in the preceding section, to meet its expenditure or spending commitments which include the following two major categories at a high level (HL).

- **Recurrent expenditures:** these are typical spending or appropriations for the current fiscal year (FY) on recurring costs for which the state prepares an annual budget.
- **Capital expenditure:** these project-oriented or developmental expenditures are multi-year in nature and, therefore, span more than the current year. **Table 1.8** and **Table 1.9** show the expenditure performance in terms of nominal (Ghc million) value and as percentages (%) of GDP over the last decade.

A key feature of the expenditure performance during the period is the fiscal space taken by compensation and interest payments—the result in increasing civil and public sector employment and borrowing beyond the capacity to repay, which led to excessive debt and default. Secondly, as discussed in earlier sections, they show the odd nature of fiscal "offsets" that have also been referred to as "fiscal engineering"—a factor that gave a false picture of positive fiscal performance.

Table 1.15: Headline Expenditure Performance (Nominal Ghc million)

Rev & Expenditure Breakdown: Nominal (Ghc million)															
	Provisional Actual										Proj.	Budget	MTBF		
	2013	2014	2015	2016	2017	2018	2019	2020	2021	2022	2023	2024	2025	2026	2027
Tot Expdx (w/ offset)	25,701.1	30,744.5	36,713.3	43,827.7	50,182.6	58,618.0	68,244.7	88,931.6	106,349.6	146,370.7	172,968.5	190,996.5	235,443.4	253,214.0	285,350.41
o/w Offset [Out'sd Cmmt)				*5,031.6*						*(22,091.2)*					
Tot Exp [w/o offset)	25,701.1	30,744.5	36,713.3	38,796.1	50,182.6	58,618.0	68,244.7	88,931.6	106,349.6	168,461.9	172,968.5	190,996.5	235,443.4	253,214.0	285,350.4
Cmpnsx	9,479.1	10,466.8	12,111.2	14,164.8	16,776.2	19,612.0	22,033.4	28,268.9	31,663.3	39,434.1	51,211.9	63,683.2	73,146.6	82,483.8	92,898.8
Int Pmts	4,397.0	7,080.9	9,075.3	10,770.4	13,572.1	15,821.8	19,756.1	24,599.3	33,522.6	45,687.4	34,772.8	55,932.4	65,840.4	73,529.3	60,483.5
Gds & Svcs	1,513.6	1,776.6	1,570.2	3,277.8	2,482.1	5,548.9	6,743.4	8,031.7	7,804.2	7,926.2	11,811.3	11,065.4	11,343.2	14,535.2	17,591.5
Subsidies	1,158.1	473.7	25.0	0.0	0.0	125.3	124.2	168.1	135.9	167.0	211.2	426.1	495.0	559.2	631.7
Transfers	4,547.9	4,850.8	6,798.0	7,733.7	9,197.1	10,789.2	11,423.6	11,882.0	13,315.2	24,550.3	28,867.9	39,588.9	46,902.6	54,737.4	61,669.2
CapExp	4,604.4	6,095.7	7,133.6	7,678.1	6,331.4	4,738.3	6,151.8	12,082.9	16,967.1	18,688.7	18,613.7	28,719.8	24,202.7	44,763.1	49,931.6
Memo:															
GDP (Nominal)	*123,650*	*155,433*	*180,139*	*215,077*	*256,671*	*300,596*	*345,946*	*383,305*	*433,686*	*610,222*	*850,656*	*1,050,978*	*1,216,845*	*1,372,186*	*1,548,313*

Table 1.15 and Table 1.16 as well as Figure 1.4, highlight an aberration that is termed fiscal "offsets" where an accrual (i.e., Outstanding Commitments) is shown in the cash component of the fiscal framework in 2016 and 2022 only. The counterpart "offsets" are in the Accrual component of the Fiscal Framework (see next section).

Table 1.16: Headline Expenditure Performance (Percent (%) of GDP)

High-Level Expdx (w/ or w/o Outstanding Expenditure): Percent (%) of GDP															
	Provisional Actual										Proj.	Budget	MTBF		
	2013	2014	2015	2016	2017	2018	2019	2020	2021	2022	2023	2024	2025	2026	2027
Tot Expdx (w/ offset)	20.8	19.8	20.4	20.4	19.6	19.5	19.7	23.2	24.5	24.0	20.3	18.2	19.3	18.5	18.4
o/w Offset				2.3						(3.6)					
Tot Exp [w/o offset)	20.8	19.8	20.4	18.0	19.6	19.5	19.7	23.2	24.5	27.6	20.3	18.2	19.3	18.5	18.4
Cmpnsx	7.7	6.7	6.7	6.6	6.5	6.5	6.4	7.4	7.3	6.5	6.0	6.1	6.0	6.0	6.0
Int Pmts	3.6	4.6	5.0	5.0	5.3	5.3	5.7	6.4	7.7	7.5	4.1	5.3	5.4	5.4	3.9
Gds & Svcs	1.2	1.1	0.9	1.5	1.0	1.8	1.9	2.1	1.8	1.3	1.4	1.1	0.9	1.1	1.1
Subsidies	0.94	0.30	0.01	0.00	0.00	0.04	0.04	0.04	0.03	0.03	0.0	0.04	0.04	0.04	0.04
Transfers	3.7	3.1	3.8	3.6	3.6	3.6	3.3	3.1	3.1	4.0	3.4	3.8	3.9	4.0	4.0
CapExp	3.7	3.9	4.0	3.6	2.5	1.6	1.8	3.2	3.9	3.1	2.2	2.7	2.0	3.3	3.2

Figure 1.4: Headline Expenditure Performance

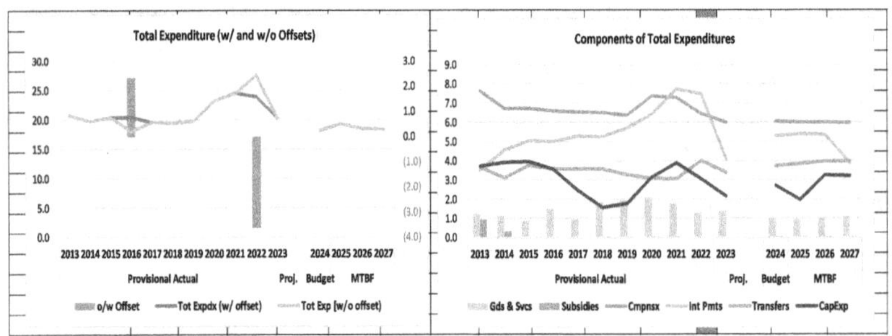

The graphs clearly show the "odd bars" that describe the periods of the offsets, when both entries were under the control of a new administration, the entries were likely to be deliberate acts of **fiscal "engineering"** to (a) **negatively** increase the fiscal deficit for a predecessor government in FY 2016; and (b) likewise, **positively** reduce its own expenditures in FY 2022.

Budget Deficit Component (Fiscal Balance [Commitment Basis])

As shown in **Table 1.17** the difference between the total tax revenues and total expenditures or spending determines the initial fiscal gap that is called the Budget (cash) Deficit. As a fiscal identity, this budget deficit is carried forward (c/f) to the Accrual component in the next section to become the Fiscal Balance (Commitment).

Table 1. 17: Revenue & Expenditure Summary (w/ & w/o Offsets)—Nominal (Ghc m)

Budget Deficit: Nominal (Ghc m) and Percent (%) of GDP

Nominal Deficit *(w/o offset)*

	Provisional Actual										Proj.		Budget	MTBF		
	2013	**2014**	**2015**	**2016**	**2017**	**2018**	**2019**	**2020**	**2021**	**2022**	**2023**		**2024**	**2025**	**2026**	**2027**
Rev	19,027.9	22,835.6	29,829.6	34,502.3	42,758.0	46,840.7	52,045.6	54,469.5	68,916.3	94,942.3	133,875.1		173,412.8	208,206.7	244,857.3	275,828.5
o/w E-Levy										***592.1***	***1,032.2***		***2,102.0***	***2,433.7***	***2,744.4***	***3,096.6***
Exp (w/ offset)	25,701.1	30,744.5	36,713.3	**43,827.7**	50,182.6	58,618.0	68,244.7	88,931.6	106,349.6	146,370.7	172,968.5		190,996.5	235,443.4	253,214.0	285,350.4
o/w Exp Offset				***5,031.6***						*(22,091.2)*						
Exp (w/o offset)	25,701.1	30,744.5	36,713.3	38,796.1	50,182.6	58,618.0	68,244.7	88,931.6	106,349.6	168,461.9	172,968.5		190,996.5	235,443.4	253,214.0	285,350.4
Deficit (w/ offset)	(6,673.2)	(7,909.0)	(6,883.7)	(9,325.4)	(7,424.6)	(11,777.3)	(16,199.1)	(34,462.1)	(37,433.4)	(51,428.4)	(39,093.4)	##	(17,583.8)	(27,236.7)	(8,356.7)	(9,521.9)
Deficit (w/o offset)	(6,673.2)	(7,909.0)	(6,883.7)	(4,293.8)	(7,424.6)	(11,777.3)	(16,199.1)	(34,462.1)	(37,433.4)	(73,519.6)	(39,093.4)		(17,583.8)	(27,236.7)	(8,356.7)	(9,521.9)

Table 1.18 shows Table 11.17 in percentage (%) of GDP and with real value impact of the e-Levy (i.e., projected peak at only 0.3 per cent) and the fiscal offsets at relatively substantive values of 2.3 per cent in 2016 and 3.6 per cent in 2022.

Table 1.18: HL Revenue & Expenditure (w/ & w/o Offsets)— Percent [%] to GDP

Deficit *(w/o offse)* ***: Percent (%) of GDP***

	Provisional Actual										Proj.		Budget	MTBF		
	2013	**2014**	**2015**	**2016**	**2017**	**2018**	**2019**	**2020**	**2021**	**2022**	**2023**		**2024**	**2025**	**2026**	**2027**
Rev	15.4	14.7	16.6	16.0	16.7	15.6	15.0	14.2	15.9	15.6	15.7		16.5	17.1	17.8	17.8
o/w E-Levy										0.1	0.1		0.2	0.2	0.2	0.2
Exp (w/ offset)	20.8	19.8	20.4	20.4	19.6	19.5	19.7	23.2	24.5	24.0	20.3		18.2	19.3	18.5	18.4
o/w Exp Offset				2.3						(3.6)						
Exp (w/o offset)	20.8	19.8	20.4	18.0	19.6	19.5	19.7	23.2	24.5	27.6	20.3		18.2	19.3	18.5	18.4
Deficit (w/ offset)	(5.4)	(5.1)	(3.8)	(4.3)	(2.9)	(3.9)	(4.7)	(9.0)	(8.6)	(8.4)	(4.6)		(1.7)	(2.2)	(0.6)	(0.6)
Deficit (w/o offset)	(5.4)	(5.1)	(3.8)	(2.0)	(2.9)	(3.9)	(4.7)	(9.0)	(8.6)	(12.0)	(4.6)		(1.7)	(2.2)	(0.6)	(0.6)

Table 1.18 further shows the related Budget Deficits, with the real value impact of the with or without the "offsets", more clearly. These cash offsets are discussed later, together with other anomalies such as memoranda or footnote treatments or "fiscal engineering," in the "accruals" component of the fiscal framework.

Figure 1.5 depicts the Cashflow Deficit or the Fiscal Balance (Commitment Basis) as the difference between Total Revenues (including e-Levy) and Total Expenditure or Spending as the Fiscal

Gap (without "arrears"). They are shown "with" and "without" the fiscal "offsets" to show their unusual effect or difference between the Fiscal Balances on a commitment basis and, as discussed later, cash basis.

Figure 1.5: Cashflow Deficit

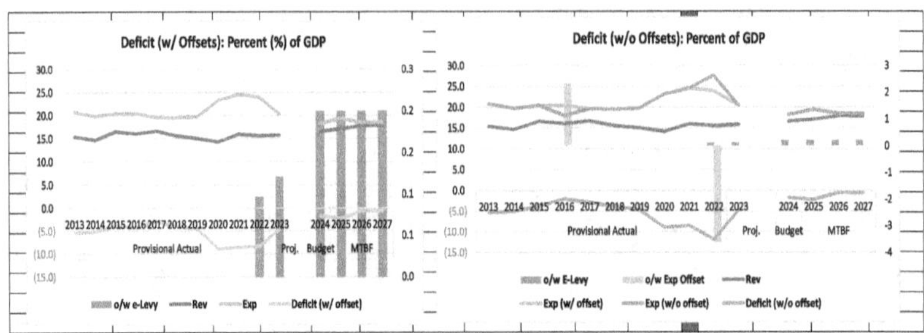

To clarify the impact of the "fiscal offsets," Table 1. 19 shows only the Budget (i.e., Cashflow) Deficit as the difference between total expenditures and total revenues. It shows the effect of the 2016 and 2022 fiscal "offsets" (with or without) more vividly. Table 1.20 also shows only the high-level deficits or the difference between total revenues and expenditures or spending as well as their reported fiscal "offsets" (in per cent of GDP).

Table 1.19: Budget (Cash) Deficit (w/ & w/o Offsets) — (Ghc m/% of GDP)

Summary of Budget Deficits (nominal)																
	Provisional Actual										Proj.		Budget	MTBF		
	2013	2014	2015	2016	2017	2018	2019	2020	2021	2022	2023		2024	2025	2026	2027
Deficit (w/ offset)	(6,673.2)	(7,909.0)	(6,883.7)	(9,325.4)	(7,424.6)	(11,777.3)	(16,199.1)	(34,462.1)	(37,433.4)	(51,428.4)	(39,093.4)		(17,583.8)	(27,236.7)	(8,356.7)	(9,521.9)
Deficit (w/o offset)	(6,673.2)	(7,909.0)	(6,883.7)	(4,293.8)	(7,424.6)	(11,777.3)	(16,199.1)	(34,462.1)	(37,433.4)	(73,519.6)	(39,093.4)		(17,583.8)	(27,236.7)	(8,356.7)	(9,521.9)
Diff. = Offset				(5,031.6)						22,091.2						
Summary of Budget (% of GDP)																
	Provisional Actual										Proj.		Budget	MTBF		
	2013	2014	2015	2016	2017	2018	2019	2020	2021	2022	2023		2024	2025	2026	2027
Deficit (w/ offset)	(5.4)	(5.1)	(3.8)	(4.3)	(2.9)	(3.9)	(4.7)	(9.0)	(8.6)	(8.4)	(4.6)		(1.7)	(2.2)	(0.6)	(0.6)
Deficit (w/o offset)	(5.4)	(5.1)	(3.8)	(2.0)	(2.9)	(3.9)	(4.7)	(9.0)	(8.6)	(12.0)	(4.6)		(1.7)	(2.2)	(0.6)	(0.6)
Diff. = Offset				(2.3)						3.6						
Nom. GDP ('13 Base)	123,650	155,433	180,139	215,077	256,671	300,596	345,946	383,305	433,686	610,222	850,656	0	1,050,978	1,216,845	1,372,186	1,548,313

Figures 1.6 and 1.7 show how Ghana's recent rapid fiscal meltdown is partly due to excluding the fiscal offsets most macro-fiscal reporting.

- a false high negative "offset" and fiscal decline that occurred in FY2016;
- the opposite positive impact in 2022, as higher fiscal "offset"; and
- the two (2) vivid "offset" graphical bars in the two respective fiscal years.

Figure 1.6: Fiscal Balance (Commitment) with Impact of Offsets (% of GDP)

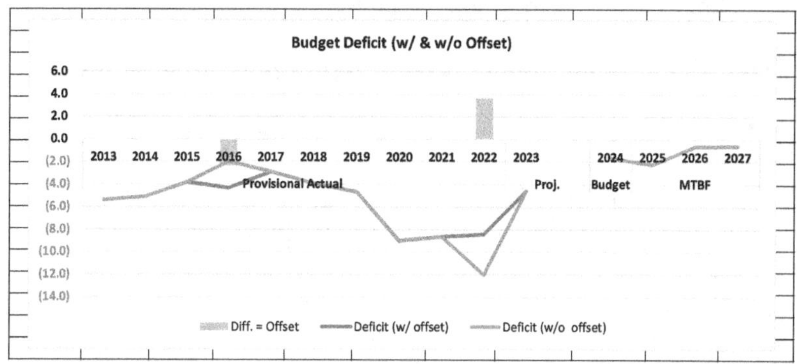

Figure 1.7: Revenue & Expenditure Summary (w/ & w/o Offsets) —Nominal (Ghc m)

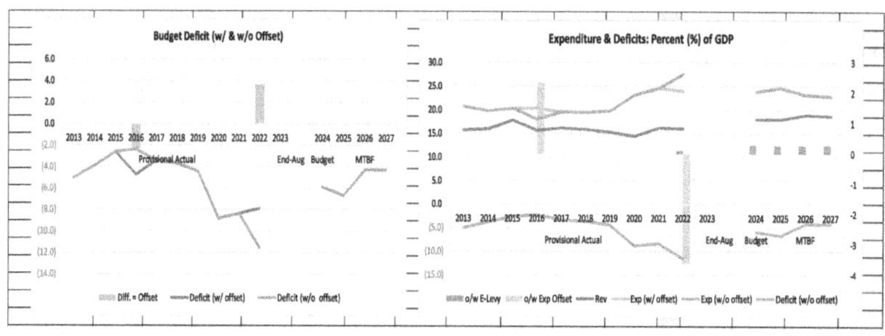

Arrears (Accruals) and Fiscal Balance (Commitment Basis)

Table 1.20 shows the elements of the fiscal framework that are short-term liabilities—that are described in other ways as unpaid bills, arrears, accruals or commitments—at the end of the fiscal year. It begins with the Fiscal Balance (Commitment Basis) as a fiscal identity that becomes the Overall Fiscal Balance (on Cash Basis).

In principle, the difference between the two (2) Fiscal Balances includes two abnormal items, namely Fiscal "Offsets", involving the misrepresentation of short-term and medium-term arrears or liabilities, and Bailout Costs that also involve another type of arrears owed to the energy and banking sectors.

Table 1.20 shows the positive numbers—in a negative part of the Fiscal Table, the Ghc 4.3 billion and Ghc 0.74 billion (i.e., approximately Ghc 5 billion) that neutralise or complete the "fiscal offset" discussed in paragraph 6 above.

Table 1.20: Deficit (Fiscal Balances) and Arrears in Numbers (nominal {Ghc m})

Fiscal Framework: Fiscal Balances and Accrual Component (with & without "offsets")															
Nominal Fiscal Balance (w/ "offset")															
	Provisional Actual										End-Aug	Budget	MTBF		
	2013	2014	2015	2016	2017	2018	2019	2020	2021	2022	2023	2024	2025	2026	2027
FB 1: Commitment Basis	(6,673.2)	(7,909.0)	(6,883.7)	(9,325.4)	(7,424.6)	(11,777.3)	(16,199.1)	(34,462.1)	(37,433.4)	(51,428.4)	(39,093.4)	(17,583.8)	(27,236.7)	(8,356.7)	(9,521.9)
Road arrears	(205.1)	(231.7)	(322.3)							***18,683.9***		(14,435.3)	(7,300.0)	(7,300.0)	(8,052.8)
Non-road arrears	(1,965.8)	(3,848.8)	(2,087.2)	*(5,869.3)*	(1,758.0)	(858.5)	(730.0)	(1,443.2)	(3,700.0)	*(11,643.3)*	*(6,000.0)*	*(20,795.3)*	*(15,332.2)*	*(16,985.2)*	*(18,278.2)*
Unpaid commitments				***4,292.3***											
Outst'ding pmts/Payables				***743.3***	(510.8)				(3,700.0)		(6,000.0)	(14,435.3)	(7,300.0)	(7,300.0)	(8,052.8)
Clearance: Oust cmtms				*(2,320.3)*	(1,247.2)	(858.2)	(730.0)	(1,443.2)	(3,700.0)						
Tax Refunds	(182.0)	(157.0)	(627.0)	(1,445.2)	(1,803.4)	(1,816.7)	(2,470.2)	(2,586.7)	(2,777.0)	(4,116.2)		(6,359.9)	(8,032.2)	(8,785.2)	(10,225.4)
FB 2: Cash Basis	(9,026.1)	(12,146.5)	(9,920.2)	(15,194.7)	(10,986.0)	(14,452.5)	(19,399.3)	(38,492.0)	(43,910.3)	(48,504.0)	(45,093.4)	(59,174.3)	(57,901.1)	(40,527.2)	(46,078.2)
Disc/DivestX	889.3	(96.6)	886.5	1,685.6	1.4	(254.1)	(1,300.0)	(2,182.7)		(3,793.6)	0.0				
FB 3: Cash (Incl. dicrp/divstx)	(8,136.8)	(12,243.1)	(9,033.7)	(13,509.1)	(10,984.6)	(14,706.6)	(20,699.2)	(40,674.7)	(43,910.3)	(52,297.6)	(45,093.4)	(59,174.3)	(57,901.1)	(40,527.2)	(46,078.2)
Note: Fiiscal "offset" were in Arrears (2016) and Fiscal Balances (2022)															
Memo/Checks:															
Road + Non-Road Arrears	*(2,170.9)*	*(4,080.5)*	*(2,409.5)*	*(5,869.3)*	*(1,758.0)*	*(858.5)*	*(730.0)*	*(1,443.2)*	*(3,700.0)*	***7,040.7***	*(6,000.0)*	*(35,230.6)*	*(22,632.2)*	*(23,385.2)*	*(26,331.0)*
Unpd, outsd+Clearance	*0.0*	*0.0*	*0.0*	***2,715.3***	*(1,758.0)*	*(858.2)*	*(730.0)*	*(1,443.2)*	*(7,400.0)*	***0.0***	*(6,000.0)*	*(14,435.3)*	*(7,300.0)*	*(7,300.0)*	*(8,052.8)*
Offset (ref: HL Expdx)				***5,031.6***						*(22,091.2)*					

Table 1.21 shows the same fiscal offsets of Ghc 4.3 billion (i.e., 2.0 per cent) and Ghc 0.74 billion (i.e., 0.3 per cent) or total of Ghc 5 billion (i.e., 2.3%) that neutralise or complete the "fiscal offset" discussed earlier as percentages of GDP.

Table 1.21: Deficit (Fiscal Balances) and Arrears in Numbers (Percent {%}) of GDP

Percent (%) of GDP: Deficit & Fiscal Balance (w/ offset)															
	Provisional Actual										Proj	Budget	MTBF		
	2013	2014	2015	2016	2017	2018	2019	2020	2021	2022	2023	2024	2025	2026	2027
FB 1: Commitment Basis	(5.4)	(5.1)	(3.8)	(4.3)	(2.9)	(3.9)	(4.7)	(9.0)	(8.6)	(8.4)	(4.6)	(1.7)	(2.2)	(0.6)	(0.6)
Road arrears	(0.2)	(0.1)	(0.2)							3.1		(1.4)	(0.6)	(0.5)	(0.5)
Non-road arrears	(1.6)	(2.5)	(1.2)	(2.7)	(0.7)	(0.3)	(0.2)	(0.4)	(0.9)	(1.9)	(0.7)	(2.0)	(1.3)	(1.2)	(1.2)
Unpaid commitments				2.0											
Outst'ding pmts/Payables				0.3	(0.2)				(0.9)		(0.7)	(1.4)	(0.6)	(0.5)	(0.5)
Clearance: Oust cmtms				(1.1)	(0.5)	(0.3)	(0.2)	(0.4)	(0.9)						
Tax Refunds	(0.1)	(0.1)	(0.3)	(0.7)	(0.7)	(0.6)	(0.7)	(0.7)	(0.6)	(0.7)		(0.6)	(0.7)	(0.6)	(0.7)
FB 2: Cash Basis	(7.3)	(7.8)	(5.5)	(7.1)	(4.3)	(4.8)	(5.6)	(10.0)	(10.1)	(7.9)	(5.3)	(5.6)	(4.8)	(3.0)	(3.0)
Disc/DivestX	0.7	(0.1)	0.5	0.8	0.0	(0.1)	(0.4)	(0.6)		(0.6)					
FB 3: Cash (Incl. dicrp/divstx)	(6.6)	(7.9)	(5.0)	(6.3)	(4.3)	(4.9)	(6.0)	(10.6)	(10.1)	(8.6)	(5.3)	(5.6)	(4.8)	(3.0)	(3.0)
Note: Fiiscal "offset" were in Arrears (2016) and Fiscal Balances (2022)															

Table 1:22: Summary: Fiscal Balances on Commitment (w/ & w/o Offsets & Bail Out) Nominal (Ghc million)

A) Nominal FB 3: w/ "Offset" & w/ "Bailout" costs															
	Provisional Actual										End-Aug	Budget	MTBF		
	2013	2014	2015	2016	2017	2018	2019	2020	2021	2022	2023	2024	2025	2026	2027
FB 3: w/ offset & w/ B-O	(8,136.8)	(12,243.1)	(9,033.7)	(13,509.1)	(10,984.6)	(14,706.6)	(20,699.2)	(40,674.7)	(43,910.3)	(52,297.6)	(45,093.4)	(59,174.3)	(57,901.1)	(40,527.2)	(46,078.2)
Diff. (= Offset)				(8,580.6)						22,091.2					
GOG: FB 3 (w/ Offset & BO)	(8,136.8)	(12,243.1)	(9,033.7)	(13,509.1)	(13,184.6)	(24,507.9)	(23,914.2)	(48,754.7)	(56,010.3)	(52,297.6)	(45,093.4)	(63,780.0)	(62,434.8)	(44,965.2)	(50,516.2)
BOG: FB 3 (w/ Offset & BO)	(8,136.8)	(12,243.1)	(9,033.7)	(13,509.1)	(10,984.6)	(24,306.6)	(30,759.2)	(55,974.7)	(58,810.3)	(52,297.6)	(45,093.4)	(59,174.3)	(57,901.1)	(40,527.2)	(46,078.2)
IMF: FB 3 (w/ offset & BO)	(8,136.8)	(12,243.1)	(9,033.7)	(13,509.1)	(10,984.6)	(24,507.9)	(30,325.9)	(58,858.7)	(61,473.3)	(52,297.6)	(45,093.4)	(65,154.3)	(64,583.1)	(48,026.2)	(53,577.2)

Table 1:23: Summary: Fiscal Balances on Commitment (w/ & w/o Offsets & Bail Out) Nominal (Ghc million)

A) Fiscal Bal (FB 3)--*Percent (5) of GDP : Including "Offset" and "Bailout" costs*															
	Provisional Actual										End-Aug	Budget	MTBF		
	2013	2014	2015	2016	2017	2018	2019	2020	2021	2022	2023	2024	2025	2026	2027
FB 3: w/ offset & w/ B-O	(6.6)	(7.9)	(5.0)	(6.3)	(4.3)	(4.9)	(6.0)	(10.6)	(10.1)	(8.6)	(5.3)	(5.6)	(4.8)	(3.0)	(3.0)
o/w offset				(4.0)						3.6					
GOG: FB 3 (w/ Offset & BO)	(6.6)	(7.9)	(5.0)	(6.3)	(5.1)	(8.2)	(6.9)	(12.7)	(12.9)	(8.6)	(5.3)	(6.1)	(5.1)	(3.3)	(3.3)
BOG: FB 3 (w/ Offset & BO)	(6.6)	(7.9)	(5.0)	(6.3)	(4.3)	(8.1)	(8.9)	(14.6)	(13.6)	(8.6)	(5.3)	(5.6)	(4.8)	(3.0)	(3.0)
IMF: FB 3 (w/ offset & BO)	(6.6)	(7.9)	(5.0)	(6.3)	(4.3)	(8.2)	(8.8)	(15.4)	(14.2)	(8.6)	(5.3)	(6.2)	(5.3)	(3.5)	(3.5)

Figure 1:8: Summary: Fiscal Balances on Commitment (w/ & w/o Offsets & Bail Out)

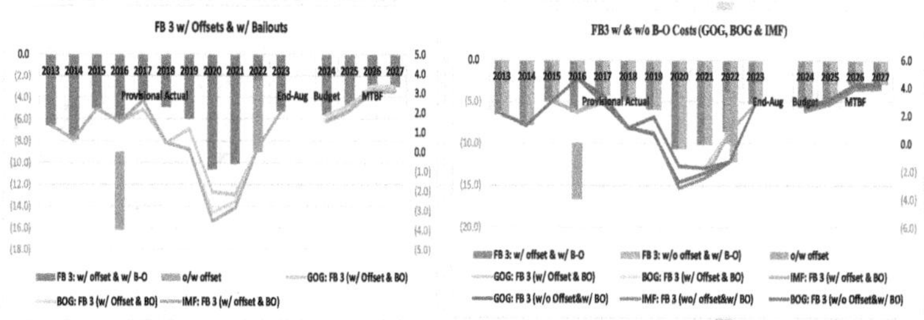

The following bullet points from the Tables and Figures above describe the key elements of the semi-accrual components of Ghana's actual fiscal performance since FY 2013.

Fiscal Balance I (Commitment Basis): this is a fiscal identity because it is the same as the Budget Deficit comprising actual cash inflows and outflows.

- **Arrears (routine or normal):** unpaid bills, invoices and approved warrants for wages, supplies and contracts that are outstanding at the end of the fiscal year.
- **Arrears (exceptional);** these are **typically large** fiscal impairments from imprudent fiscal measures and unbudgeted arrears from domestic or external **crises or shocks**—such as the global financial crisis (GFC), drought or floods, COVID-19 health crisis.

Fiscal Balance II (Cash Basis): this is the final element of this component, after adding both routine and exceptional arrears.

- **Fiscal Offsets:** the FY2016 and FY2022 fiscal data show exceptional standalone items that distort the standard reporting. First, they appeared as "accrual" items in Part 1 of the Fiscal Framework even though it is the Cash Component.

  The second anomaly is their related appearance of "negative" items in Part II, which are "negative" arrears and increase the "Fiscal Balance" on a cash basis. The two (2) items are clearly offset and that neutralizes their effect but increases (FY2016) and lowers (FY2022) the Fiscal Balances (commitment and cash basis).
- **Bailout Costs as "Footnotes":** The second major anomaly shows the arrears owed contractors and suppliers in the energy sector as "footnotes" or "memoranda" items. The effect is a lower Fiscal Balance (Cash Bais) or the Overall Fiscal Balance. The non-payment of the energy sector arrears, especially the ESLA that was designed to clear related banking sector arrears by the suppliers, resulted in higher non-performing loans and the "big bang" shutdown of banks that affected depositors.

In summary, the budget deficit before adding arrears or commitments is the Fiscal Balance (Commitment Basis), a fiscal identity. Consequently, the Fiscal Balance (Cash Basis) includes both routine and exceptional arrears and represents the gross amount that Parliament approves in the Appropriation Act.

Financing the Overall Fiscal (Cash) Balance

Overview of Borrowing by GOG: The extent of borrowing from the domestic or external bilateral, multilateral and financial markets to support the Overall Fiscal Balance (i.e., Fiscal Balance on Cash Basis) or fiscal gap is determined by various public financial management (PFM) rules. The fiscal balances indicate the amount of borrowing by the government from domestic and external or foreign sources, including the government and financial markets to finance the deficit or overall fiscal balance.

Borrowing is typically from loans, including the sale of government securities such as treasury bills, notes or bonds. The repayment or maturity period for the principal amount and interest may be short-term, medium-term or long-term.

Sources for loans: the sources from which the government, borrows to finance the budget may be classified as

- **official** or **bilateral** loans from foreign governments or their agencies that often have offices in the country:
- **multilateral**—World Bank, International Monetary Fund (IMF) and African Development Bank (AfDB) etc.; and
- **commercial**, which may be domestic (e.g., local bonds) or external money markets (e.g., sovereign bonds) and include banks (including the central bank), stock exchanges, and non-bank financial institutions.
- **Amortization or repayment:** the extent of financing or borrowing also depends on the annual budget allocation for amortization or debt repayment of the balance or outstanding principal or loan. Hence, the annual financing or borrowing minus amortization or repayment results in the annual net increase (i.e., borrowing being higher) or net decrease (amortization being higher) of the national or public debt.

The amount of **new borrowing** may be used to re-finance or roll over the amount of principal or interest due existing debt, but which cannot be covered by the provision made in the Annual Budget for amortization or repayment.

Numerical performance of Financing The performance and changes in financing the Budget and projection into the medium-term, on an annual rolling basis in **nominal cedi values** are shown in Table 1.23.

Table 1.24: High-Level Financing of Overall Fiscal Balance (Ghc m)

Summary: High-Level Financing (Ghcm)															
	Provisional Actual										Proj	Budget	MTBF		
	2013	2014	2015	2016	2017	2018	2019	2020	2021	2022	2023	2024	2025	2026	2027
Total Financing	9,454.6	11,550.6	8,760.3	13,144.9	12,244.7	11,672.7	16,726.7	44,897.9	42,354.7	65,156.3	45,093.4	61,879.7	59,421.7	65,467.5	50,705.0
Foreign (net)	3,212.0	5,874.1	5,877.9	2,960.3	(47.4)	2,724.2	4,837.7	31.2	20,082.1	9,600.0	8,498.5	463.5	(22,863.8)	(22,700.3)	(23,512.3)
Domestic (Net)	7,057.9	6,142.7	2,982.4	11,264.5	11,969.8	9,800.1	13,125.4	45,643.0	21,987.8	54,169.9	37,438.5	62,690.6	83,628.1	89,768.3	75,889.5
o/w BOG	1,166.3	1,581.5	(201.2)	2,392.0	(3,563.7)	884.3	(5,889.7)	22,562.4	(1,681.5)	53,150.2	0.0	0.0	0.0	0.0	0.0
Ghana Petrol. Fund	(677.7)	(175.9)	390.3	(113.1)	(231.0)	167.2	(148.0)	1,104.1	(835.9)	(2,787.0)	(684.0)	(1,033.3)	(1,088.6)	(1,297.7)	(1,355.9)
Sinking Fund	0.0	0.0	(178.5)	(760.9)	879.9	(947.1)	(996.0)	(572.9)	0.0	42.5	159.6	241.1	254.0	302.8	316.4
Contingency Fund	0.0	(50.0)	(89.3)	0.0	0.0	0.0	0.0	(1,203.7)	(658.8)	0.0	0.0	0.0	0.0	0.0	0.0

Table 1.25 shows the financing items in Percent (%) of Gross Domestic Product (GDP)

Table 1.25: Financing—Percent (%) of GDP

Summary: High-Level Financing (% of GDP)															
	Provisional Actual										Proj	Budget	MTBF		
	2013	2014	2015	2016	2017	2018	2019	2020	2021	2022	2023	2024	2025	2026	2027
Total Financing	7.6	7.4	4.9	6.1	4.8	3.9	4.8	11.7	9.8	10.7	5.3	5.9	4.9	4.8	3.3
Foreign (net)	2.6	3.8	3.3	1.4	(0.0)	0.9	1.4	0.0	4.6	1.6	1.0	0.0	(1.9)	(1.7)	(1.5)
Domestic (Net)	5.7	4.0	1.7	5.2	4.7	3.3	3.8	11.9	5.1	8.9	4.4	6.0	6.9	6.5	4.9
o/w BOG	0.9	1.0	(0.1)	1.1	(1.4)	0.3	(1.7)	5.9	(0.4)	8.7	0.0	0.0	0.0	0.0	0.0
Ghana Petrol. Fund	(0.5)	(0.1)	0.2	(0.1)	(0.1)	0.1	(0.0)	0.3	(0.2)	(0.5)	(0.1)	(0.1)	(0.1)	(0.1)	(0.1)
Sinking Fund	0.00	0.00	(0.10)	(0.35)	0.34	(0.32)	(0.288)	(0.15)	0.00	0.01	0.02	0.02	0.02	0.02	0.02
Contingency Fund	0.00	(0.03)	(0.05)	0.00	0.00	0.00	0.000	(0.31)	(0.15)	0.00	0.00	0.00	0.00	0.00	0.00

Figure 1.9 (a) & (b) shows a graphical representation of Table 1.23 of the high-level external and domestic sources from which the government borrows to finance the Budget. Figure 1.9(a) includes the Petroleum Funds—which are strictly foreign exchange reserves—and therefore reflect "negatives" or "positives" to show the extent of their depletion (i.e., "positive") to fulfil budget needs.

Figure 1.9 (a) & (b): Financing

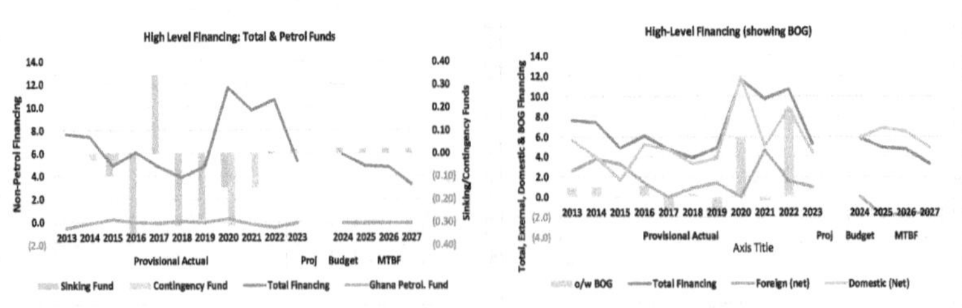

Public Debt stock:

The **annual debt stock increases or decreases** by the **"net amount"** that is the **difference** between the **annual borrowing** and the **debt repayment or amortization.** Typically, the sources from which the government borrows also determine the **classification of the public debt**—reflecting inflows, outflows and balances at the beginning and end of the fiscal year.

- *Refinancing and roll-overs*: It must be noted that some of the funds raised may be used to re-finance or roll over the portion of existing public debt that is not repaid or amortized.
- *Multi-year (3-year) "rolling" budget*: The elements of this include the current year's budget, which is often called the Medium-Term Expenditure Framework (MTEF) even though it covers projections of revenues, expenditures, and financing.
- *Memoranda or Footnote Items*: Table 6 shows the Appendix Memorandum items, notably the energy sector costs, bank bailout costs, and arrears—particularly, road contractors.
    - The treatment of exceptional items as footnotes, memoranda or appendix items is a significant departure from the convention underlying the framework that has been in use since the Economic Recovery Program (ERP) or Structural Adjustment Reforms (SAP).
    - The Fiscal Balance (Commitment and the Fiscal Balance (Cash) Basis are also described as deficits or fiscal balances on a narrow and broad basis, with the difference being short-term liabilities or arrears.
    - Basically, the impression of fast fiscal consolidation does not reflect (far exceeds) the rate of borrowing and debt accumulation—often resulting in off-budget or off-GIFMIS treatment of expenditures and arrears.

It gave rise to the phenomenon of "parallel" reporting, notably to the IMF—which used Article IV (2019) and RCF Loan (2020) Reports to the Board of Directors.

The Section stresses the need to shift to semi-accrual through a combination of (a) electronic databases for contracts awarded, showing; (b) the respective adjustments in the value and work-in-progress (WIP); and (c) the components of certified amounts that remain outstanding after the payments made in the fiscal year.

Public Debt Management: It is apparent that, at any given time or period, the Public Debt situation is the outcome of the quality of its management as well as the other elements of the Fiscal Framework, including revenues, expenditures, arrears and amortization or repayment. It is important because if the management of these elements of the Fiscal Framework is not managed efficiently, the critical public debt situation can topple the entire edifice of the Framework.

Table 1.26 as well as Figure 1.10 of the GDP Table show the nominal (Ghana cedis) and real (Percent {%} of GDP) from 2013 to 2023. Figure They explain the rapid increases in the public debt that led to the default of Ghana's commitments in the last 3-to-5 years.

Table 1.26: Public Debt (Nominal & Percent {%} of GD

Ghana: Public Debt: Nominal (Ghc million)												
`	2012	2013	2014	2015	2016	2017	2018	2019	2020	2021	2022	2023
Domestic	18,792.7	27,254.0	44,530.0	59,912.8	68,859.6	75,787.2	86,169.0	112,509.4	149,833.9	181,777.2	282,501.4	259,700.0
External	17,206.9	25,827.3	35,040.2	40,322.1	53,403.4	66,768.9	86,899.7	105,481.2	141,796.8	170,009.8	261,809.8	350,300.0
Total	35,999.6	53,081.3	79,570.2	100,234.9	122,263.0	142,556.1	173,068.7	217,990.6	291,630.7	351,787.0	544,311.2	610,000.0

Ghana: Public Debt (% of GDP)												
	2012	2013	2014	2015	2016	2017	2018	2019	2020	2021	2022	2023
Domestic	25.0	22.0	28.6	33.3	32.0	29.5	28.7	32.5	39.1	41.9	46.3	41.2
External	22.8	20.9	22.5	22.4	24.8	26.0	28.9	30.5	37.0	39.2	42.9	30.5
Total	47.8	42.9	51.2	55.6	56.8	55.5	57.6	63.0	76.1	81.1	89.2	71.7

Figure 1.10 represents the Percent of GDP version of the two tables above. They include two (2) graphs that show the same outcomes—the rapid rise in Ghana's debt in the latter years

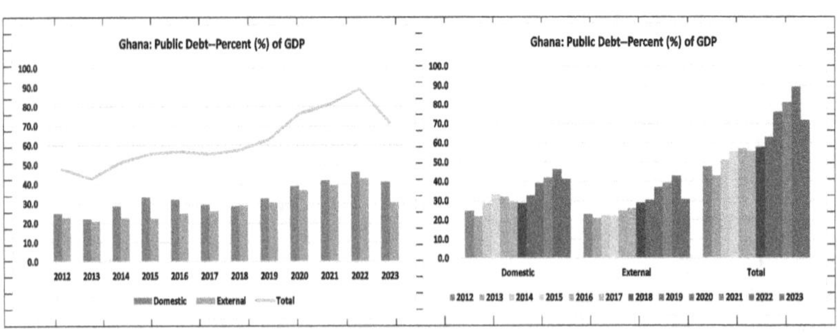

Fiscal Performance and Debt Stock: The deterioration in fiscal performance includes other features such as high levels of Central Bank financing of the Budget and renegotiation of its loan with all categories of lenders, including citizens as well as government and financial market institutions.

As noted in the next Section, where the budget provision for debt repayment or re-financing is not adequate, the country heads towards default, as in the current situation in Ghana. As summarized in Box 1 later, this is Ghana's worst post-HIPC debt and fiscal situation facing the country since it declared Highly Indebted Poor Country (HIPC) status in the early 2000s.

Financial markets: these are individuals, firms and organizations that meet in a fixed domestic or external location (e.g., Stock Exchange) and virtually to trade in or exchange marketable short-term and long-term loan instruments, including bonds, bills and notes.

- **Primary markets**—these markets are for new issuances or sales of equity or loan instruments to governments (central and local), businesses and households.
- **Secondary markets** (e.g., Stock Exchanges etc.,)—the local or external markets for repayment or retirement and refinancing or exchange.
- **Economic entities as both buyers and sellers**: The households, businesses and the government are the sources of savings to the financial markets but often through intermediary public and private sector institutions (e.g., equity funds, mutual funds). They offer and buy the debt instruments and keep the markets active, with the **government also buying and selling to stabilize the "booms and busts" of the market.**

Public Debt Management Office for Ghana (PDMO)

Many Low-Income Countries (LICs) and, as Ghana has now become, Lower Middle-Income Countries (L-MICs) have gone through periods of debt forgiveness, reliefs such as suspension of debt repayment, and default in the last three decades. It is against this background that Ghana's PFMA provides for the establishment of the PDMO.

Functions of the PDMO: Section 54 of the PFMA provides for the following specific functions for PDMO.

Section 54(1): The Ministry of Finance (MOF) shall have an office that is responsible for public debt management, and which shall be under the supervision of the Chief Director in accordance with the Civil Service Act, 1993 (PNDC L 327).

Section 54(2): The Public Debt Management Office (PDMO) shall—

a. handle debt management operation of the Government;
b. assess risks for government guarantees and lending;
c. assess all forms of credit agreements, including suppliers' credit, buyers' credit; mixed credit and finance lease agreements to be entered into by the Government;
d. assess the feasibility of borrowing requirements implied by the path for the fiscal deficit in the Fiscal Strategy Document (FSD);
e. formulate the Medium-Term Debt Management Strategy (MTDMS); and
i. perform any other functions that may be determined by the Minister.

Options for a DMO unit: since MOF has a Debt Management Division already, it may be necessary to include stand-alone options with a larger measure of semi-autonomy—either (a) as a separate agency or office; and (b) an additional unit within, and expansion of, the Controller and Accountant-General's Department (CAGD)—which currently handles most of the post-Budget operational functions for the Ministry and also interfaces with BOG on deposits and payments.

Ghana's recent public debt experience: As Box 1.1 notes, in summary, the causes of debt accumulation, crisis and default are from multiple factors, including low levels of revenue collection relative to high levels of expenditure and arrears. It is these factors and the low provision for Debt Repayment (Amortization) in Part IV of the Framework that has resulted in Ghana's unsustainable budget deficits, borrowing and, eventually, debt default and negotiation with creditors.

Box 1.1: Strengthening PFM Institutions Proposed Public Debt Management Office

Strengthening PFM reforms: the Public Financial Management Act requires Ghana to set up a ***Public Debt Management Office (DMO)*** under the **Public Financial Management Act (PFMA), 2016 (Act 920).** The purpose of the Act was to focus more on the nation's debt challenges, including ***advanced debt management techniques and investor relations***—against the background of the following key factors--

a) the ***unstainable debt levels*** that led to the declaration of a ***Highly Indebted Poor Country (HIPC)*** status in 2002; together with Ghana joining the ***Multilateral Debt Restructuring Initiative (MDRI);***

b) as ***bilateral and multilateral debt reliefs***, the HIPC/MDRI initiative provided significant budgets support to Ghana until 2013 when the government declared an end to these HIPC/MDRI flows; and

c) ***a post-HIPC/MDRI debt rise*** due to (i) ***wage and salary overruns*** caused by a 2008 ***Single-Spine Salary Scheme (SSSS)***—also called Single Spine Pay Policy (SSPP); which implementation from 2009 led to major deviations from the pilot or design; and (ii) the ***disruption in gas supply*** from Nigeria that, in turn, caused major power outages that affected the budget and economy; and

d) efforts to ***leverage on the discovery and sale of petroleum and gas*** in commercial quantities to manage the public debt through ***debt repayment mechanism (i.e., Sinking Fund)*** under the 1992 Constitution and derived from the ***Stabilization Fund*** under the ***Petroleum Revenue Management Act (PRMA), 2011 (Act 815).***

Recent factors that make it necessary to enhance the capacity of the debt management office in MOF include (i) continued access to the Capital Markets, on the back of two(2) new oil fields and borrowing heavily through the issuance of domestic and external Sovereign Bonds; (ii) depletion of the Stabilization Fund and stopping to fund the Sinking Fund—despite the discovery of two (2) additional Petroleum Fields; (iii) stalled revenue and expenditure reforms to support the expansion of fiscal projects and stagnant revenues; and ***inability to service the public debt*** and, ***ultimately defaulting*** on the borrowing commitments made to all categories of domestic and external lenders.

The deterioration in fiscal situation includes other features such as high levels of Central Bank financing of the Budget and renegotiation of its loan with all categories of lenders, including citizens as well as government and financial market institutions. As noted in the next Section, where the loan for repayment and re-financing is inadequate, the country may default, as in the current situation in Ghana. Box 1 summarizes this worst public debt and fiscal performance situation facing the country since it declared Highly Indebted Poor Country (HIPC) status in the early 2000s.

Conclusion

Revenue policy, mobilization and administration are important fiscal functions that underwrite the ability of countries to achieve relatively high levels of recurrent and capital expenditures, and low deficits as well as borrow and maintain positive ratings that support activity on capital markets sustainable public debt performance levels. Two of Ghana's important fiscal initiatives were the setting up of the Stabilization Fund (as a budget buffer) and the Sinking Fund (as debt repayment mechanisms to keep the deficit and public debt low.

The lesson from Ghana's debt default and negotiations with domestic and external creditors suggests that (a) positive and periodic high levels of growth that are due to (b) new natural resource finds and expansion of the services sector are not sufficient to ensure prudent borrowing to maintain sustainable fiscal balances and debt levels. Another factor is the development of budget buffers to manage unusual domestic and external crises as well as a debt repayment mechanism to keep the public debt within sustainable floors and ceilings.

The Ghana Government's loss of access to the domestic and foreign financial markets was also due to its inability to maintain a good credit score from the Ratings Agencies, notably, Standard and Poor's (S&P), Fitch and Moody's. Hence its debt strategy must include the revamp of the Debt Management Division (DMD) of MOF or setting up the Public Debt Management Office (PDMO) under Section 54 of the Public Financial Management Act (PFMA).

Chapter 2

TAX AND REVENUE ADMINISTRATION: REFORMS, PRINCIPLES AND PRACTICE

1. Introduction

The terms *"tax"* and *"revenue"* are often used interchangeably but, in principle, revenue is a wider term that includes both tax or taxation and *non-tax revenues*. In principle, *taxation* refers to the *compulsory deduction or payment* of part of the earnings from employment, profit or income from doing business or engaging in an enterprise; or (b) the sale of property. Ghana implemented many tax policy and administration reforms as part of the Economic Recovery Program (ERP) or Structural Adjustment Reforms (SAP).

This Chapter discusses some elements of tax administration reforms and legislation, including (a) the setting up of a separate VAT Service (VATS) in 1998; and (b) later, in 2009, the integration of the management of the Internal Revenue Service (IRS) and VATS as the Domestic Tax Revenue Division (DTRD) of the Ghana Revenue Authority (GRA).

> **1984 to 1986:** Setting up a semi-autonomous administrative body called the National Revenue Secretariat (NRS) to lead the tax policy and administration component of SAP/ERP. NRS took over the functions of the Revenue Administration Division (RAD) of the MOF.
>
> **1986 to 1999:** Under their semi-autonomous laws, separating the Income Tax Department (ITD) and Customs and Excise Department (CED) from the core Civil Service and, respectively, replacing them with the semi-autonomous Internal Revenue Service (IRS) and Customs, Excise and Preventive Service (CEPS).**1986 to 1999:** Placing IRS and CEPS under two separate supervisory Boards of Directors, prior to setting up a third semi-autonomous VAT Service (VATS), with the introduction of VAT, under a third Board—with all these structures under the administrative direction of NRS, which reverted to MOF under the special civil service administrative arrangements.

2000 to 2008: Replacing NRS with the Revenue Agencies' [Governing] Board (RAGB) with (a) an Executive Secretary, and (b) replacing the three (3) separate Boards of Directors with a single supervisory Board of Directors for VATS, CEPS, and IRS.

2009 to 2016: Setting up the Ghana Revenue Authority (GRA) to replace the RAGB under the Ghana Revenue Authority Act, 2009 (Act 791).

Apex Body: GRA continues to be a semi-autonomous apex body but with unambiguous operational and executive authority vested in a Commissioner General (CG) under a unified Board for tax and customs administration.

Integration of Domestic Tax Agencies: The GRA Act merged the IRS and VATS under a Domestic Tax Revenue Division (DTRD); replaced CEPS with a Customs Division (CD); and consolidated all the previous IRS, VATS, and CEPS administrative functions under a Revenue Administrative Division (RAD).

Segmentation of Tax Offices: The original restructuring of DTRD's domestic tax field offices under the Large Taxpayer Office (LTO); Medium Taxpayer Office (MTO); and Small Taxpayer Office (STO) have now been regrouped under single Taxpayer Service offices (see Box 1 and a discussion of the issue Section 9 below). The Customs Division (CD) offices continue to be at Ghana's land, sea and air entry or border points.

2015: MOF Tax Policy Division (TPD) to separate the tax administration or operations function under GRA from the formulation of tax policy and legislation, as macro-fiscal activities. In 2018, TPD was placed under a new Resource Mobilization and Economic Relations Division (RMERD), which focuses on both domestic and external (i.e. grants) revenue mobilization. Later, a Revenue Policy Division (RPD), continues to have responsibility for both tax and non-tax revenues, including fees and charges.

2016: Passage of the Revenue Administration Act, 2016 (Act 915) to merge all common direct and indirect tax administration functions, including registration and taxpayer services; tax accounting (i.e., recordkeeping, filing and payment);

compliance and enforcement (i.e., debt management, audits, and prosecution); and taxpayer appeal.

The changes from 2009 to 2016 settled the status of the apex body as an executive unit with powers for all revenue administration or operations. This follows the global tax reform trends in integrating VAT and income tax administration and focusing on the special needs of taxpayers under the LTO, MTO, and STO tax office structure.

Chapter 11 continues Part IV with a discussion of key stakeholders and their registration and assessment obligations under Act 915 while Chapter 12 ends Part IV with a coverage of payment obligations, enforcement and appeals. Part V covers Chapter 13 and discusses the political economy of VAT which, as discussed in Chapter 14, form part of fiscal and macroeconomic reforms under the ERP-SAP reforms of the 1980s and 1990s.

2. Trends in Tax Administration Reforms

In a macroeconomic context, the fiscal aspects of structural adjustment programs (SAPs) in many African countries from the 1980s to the early 2000s included significant reforms of tax policy and administration. They resulted in streamlining or rationalizing the policy objectives of tax instruments and the functions of tax administration—organization, voluntary compliance and enforcement.

Organization: The basis for modern tax administration is to set up semi-autonomous agencies for taxpayers to *comply voluntarily* with the obligations under the tax law, with broad operational powers. However, if taxpayers fail to meet this obligation, then the tax agency can take various *enforcement* actions against them.

Voluntary compliance: The main obligations of taxpayers are to register, as well as assess the tax due, which then results in their filing a tax return and paying the self-assessed or official assessment or tax calculated by GRA for any given tax period. The voluntary assessment of taxes due is what gives voluntary compliance an alternative description called *self-assessment*.

Enforcement: If taxpayers do not meet these obligations, the law empowers tax agencies to take *enforcement* actions. These include registering and assessing them officially as well as recovering arrears or tax owing, inspection and audit, and prosecution. The law also allows taxpayers to appeal against these administrative and legal actions.

As noted in the next Section, tax offices design *taxpayer assistance programs* to support voluntary compliance actions (i.e., registration, assessment, filing, and payment) but also take enforcement actions (i.e., audit, recovery of arrears, prosecution and appeals). It is these actions that also define the *functions* performed by tax agencies and tax offices.

3. Functions of Tax Administration

The functions performed by tax offices globally are standard and only differ according to the level of advancement of the country—particularly, the extent of expertise of tax officials and automation of tax processes and systems.

Registration: All eligible taxpayers are required to apply for registration, in a standard format, to a tax office that is normally the closest to their employment or business. Following the integration of the tax administration functions, many countries now issue a *single taxpayer identification number (TIN)* to taxpayers to meet all their tax obligations, including customs.

***Assessment, filing and payment*:** Upon registration, taxpayers regularly (e.g., monthly, annually or quarterly) perform the standard activities of (a) assessing the amount of tax due; (b) filing a tax return (called a declaration for customs); and (c) paying the tax assessed upon submission of the return to the tax office where they are registered.

***Taxpayer education and assistance*:** all tax offices have a unit to assist taxpayers in making enquiries and to comply with this basic and other obligation, including their right of administrative or legal appeal whenever an issue is in dispute.

The first two functions above fall under the *voluntary compliance and self-assessment* responsibilities of registered taxpayers. The goal of taxpayer education and assistance is to help these taxpayers perform this obligation—it is when they fail to do so willingly that the tax office uses its powers of enforcement described below.

Compulsory registration and assessment: registration and assessment are fundamental obligations of a tax system and, therefore, the law allows tax offices to use best judgement methods (e.g., determination of annual turnover) to compel taxpayers to register and to raise official assessments of tax due for a tax period or periods.

Recovery of arrears (debt): where taxpayers delay in making tax payments due, they may make acceptable arrangements with the tax office to pay, often in instalments; otherwise, the tax office can resort to garnishment and other methods to compel payment.

Audit, examination, and inspection: even when taxpayers comply voluntarily, the tax office is empowered to conduct audits and examinations of business records (e.g., invoices and ledgers, including automated systems) and physical assets (e.g., stocks) to ensure that they are dealing fairly with the tax administration.

Administration sanctions: under these administrative processes, prior to prosecution and appeal, the law permits tax agencies to impose fines and penalties for non-compliance, including non-registration, non-filing, non-payment, and keeping of improper records.

Prosecution**:** in addition to these main administrative measures, the tax laws permit the tax office or agency to take enforcement actions through the courts, which often result in forfeiture and sale of property, fines, and imprisonment.

Taxpayer appeal**:** finally, the law allows taxpayers to appeal against actions taken by tax offices or the courts—the latter being the final arbiter of all conflicts. Typically, in both cases, appeals begin in tax offices and may end at the Head Office or in lower courts to the Supreme Court.

These topics are interrelated with the *taxpayer obligations* forming the basis of the functions of administration, both of which determine the arrangements for tax processes and systems as well as the organization of tax offices.

4. Systems and Processes

The purpose of setting up effective, efficient, and integrated management information systems (MIS) for tax processes is to improve performance in tax offices. Compared to manual and semi-manual processes, technology helps to improve enforcement and the services that tax offices render to registered taxpayers, the fiscal authorities, and the general public.

Partial automation: many developing countries use a mix of manual or unintegrated basic electronic systems and processes to achieve their goals and assist taxpayers in meeting their obligations under the relevant tax and fiscal laws, regulations, and guidelines.

Substantive automation: in contrast, the tax agencies and taxpayers in advanced and emerging [EM] states use processes and systems that are predominantly electronic or digital to perform all the tax functions and obligations.

Integrated MIS systems: as with the case of organizational structures discussed earlier, modern tax systems and processes are not designed for separate tax-type agencies but, following integrated tax reforms, they are uniform for the tax functions.

Typically, the joint or common systems apply to "integrated" domestic tax (i.e., income tax and VAT) agencies, such as GRA's Domestic Tax Revenue Division (DTRD) of GRA. In the GRA context, the common domestic tax systems and processes also integrate or interface with the customs system. The contrast is when the institutions that DTRD replaced (i.e., VATS and IRS) had separate tax processing systems, which is a less efficient architecture.

5. Organization of tax offices

Tax agencies and offices have gone through three basic or hybrid forms of organizing tax offices and processes, including the units in head office, to assist taxpayers in complying with their obligations and also take enforcement action.

Tax-type organization: Under this structure, the field offices are set up as separate tax institutions with responsibility for the separate tax types. Hence, invariably in the same location or town, the defunct IRS and VATS had independent offices that often did not work in common. Hence, they often duplicate the activities that underlie the functional administration structure in the next bullet.

Functional organization: In terms of processes, the independent tax offices duplicate or perform the same functions that were described earlier—registration and taxpayer; tax accounting (assessment, filing and payment); and enforcement (debt or arrears, audit, prosecution, and appeals). In contrast, in an integrated environment, the functions are set up to administer and enforce multiple tax structures (e.g., VAT, income tax and excise).

Segmented organization: The *integration and segmentation* by taxpayer category—under large, medium, and small taxpayer offices was initiated after the integration of IRS and VATS. However, as discussed in Section 9, it was *short-lived* under a new political administration and replaced with single taxpayer service centres in various localities around the country.

The main focus of administration offices includes functional structure to effective compliance as well as efficient use of limited budget resources. This is often because both registered taxpayers and tax offices use the same documents (e.g., invoices etc.) to meet and enforce their tax obligations, respectively.

6. Ghana: Tax administration reforms

This section focuses in more detail on the extent to which the tax administration reforms in Ghana were consistent with the reforms discussed above. Ghana was among many countries that applied the philosophy behind these reforms, as designed and implemented through technical assistance (TA) from the Fiscal Affairs Department (FAD) of the International Monetary Fund (IMF) in the 1980s and 1990s.

Besides the IMF, the World Bank and other multilateral agencies such as the African Development Bank (AfDB) and OECD as well as Development Partners (DPs) such as USAID, Harvard Institute for International Development (HIID), Department for International Development (DFID), and Germany's GIZ also provided funding, logistics, and expertise for the joint TA efforts. These resources were used by countries to improve their tax policy and administration structures.

The remaining sections discuss the *initial administration reforms* that resulted in setting up the National Revenue Secretariat (NRS) and the removal of the revenue agencies, namely the Central Revenue Department (CRD) and Customs and Excise Department (CED), from the core civil service. It also discusses the special relationship between NRS and MOF in the ensuing Section.

General nature of the administration reforms: the general nature of the initial nature of the administration reforms included the following specific elements.

Semi-autonomy: the National Revenue Secretariat (NRS), together with the IRS and CEPS, was set up between 1984 and 1986 by the PNDC Government as autonomous *bodies* to implement very major tax policy and administration reforms. The status of NRS and its notable achievements include the following—

Non-executive status of NRS: The Secretariat was *administratively detached* under a Minister or Secretary of State and a Chief Director. It was a lean body that replaced the Revenue Division (under a director), in MOF. As a *fiscal management unit,* NRS did not exercise full executive or operational powers over IRS and CEPS.

These initial reforms were implemented alongside tax policy reforms that rationalized and streamlined the goals and objectives of the tax instruments, notably the Income Tax (both corporate, employment and self-employed), customs duty, excise duty and the introduction of VAT to replace the sales and service taxes.

Legal backing for semi-autonomy: While, as an administrative body, NRS lacked legal backing, in 1986, NRS successfully presented draft bills that became laws for the semi-autonomies for tax and customs administration. The operational autonomies from the core civil service remain to date.

Internal Revenue Service (IRS): The IRS was set up under the *Internal Revenue Service (IRS) Act, 1986 (PNDC Law, 143)* with a separate supervisory Board of Directors that reported to a *Minister (Secretary) for Revenue.* IRS had a commissioner who was in charge of collecting the *direct taxes on income and property*—an operational function that was previously under the Internal Revenue Department (IRD) of MOF.

Customs Excise and Preventive Service (CEPS): CEPS was set up under the *Customs Excise and Preventive Service (CEPS) Law, 1986 (PNDC Law 144)*—and, later, *CEPS Management Law 1993, (Act 330).* It also had a separate Board and Commissioner that were charged with collecting the import duties (tariffs), sales tax and excise duties. CEPS replaced the Customs and Excise Department (CED) that was previously under MOF.

VAT Service (VATS): In 1994, under the first VAT episode that was suspended in 1995 and the second VAT episode that led to its reintroduction in 1998, Ghana set up VATS as a third revenue agency to collect the VAT until 2009. It had similar supervisory and operational structures as the IRS and CEPS. While VAT was suspended between these two (2) laws, the staff of the VAT Project were on secondment to the IRS or CEPS.

Given the wider spread of its offices, the IRS collected the *indirect domestic service tax* on selected professional and other services, which was later added to the sales tax as Value Added Tax. The VAT Service also collected the excise duties on behalf of CEPS just, as the latter was responsible for collecting the import VAT.

Supervisory and operational structures: Hence, IRS, VATS, and CEPS had similar but separate supervisory Boards of Directors and Chief Executives (i.e., Commissioners) that, at various times, reported to NRS, RAGB and MOF.

Boards of Directors: IRS, CEPS and VATS had three (3) separate Boards of Directors under the operational authority of separate Commissioners even though several of their functions overlapped. These Commissioners were also the only Executive Directors on their respective Boards.

Functions of the Board of Directors: the functions of the Board included—

Administration: "ensuring the effective assessment and optimum collection of all taxes and penalties to the State under the relevant laws administered by the Department before the coming into force of this Law and any other tax laws that may be introduced from time to time;"

Policy recommendations: "making recommendations to the Minister on tax policy, tax legislation, tax reform, tax treaties and exemptions as may be required from time to time;

Transfer to Consolidated Fund (CF): "ensuring that all amounts collected by the Service are paid into the CF unless otherwise provided in this Law;"

Supervision: "generally controlling the management of the Service on matters of policy, subject to the provisions of this Law;"

Staffing: "appointing, promoting, and disciplining (including dismissing) employees of the Service;" and

Scheme of service: "drawing up a scheme of service prescribing the terms and conditions of service as well as the remuneration of the employees of the Service."

Eventually, under the GRA structure, the Boards of Directors of IRS, VATS and CEPS were unified as part of the creation of a unified GRA supervisory board that continues to report to the Minister for Finance.

7. Supervisory Body Reforms: NRS, RAGB and GRA

In a reversal in 1991, the government moved NRS back to MOF under an MOF Director (Mr. Odartei-Laryea) while keeping some of its autonomy. Officially, however, it did not revert fully to its former status as a civil service Division of MOF because the staff continued to be on secondment from NRS, IRS and VATS. As noted later, eventually, NRS was replaced by the Revenue Agencies' Governing Board (RAGB) in 2001.

Status: NRS continued to be physically and operationally separate from MOF, but the reporting lines were to the MOF Chief Director and the Minister for Finance. Further, the designation or position of Secretary (as was used at the time for Ministers) for Revenue was also abolished.

Fiscal policy: NRS was accountable to, and took directions from, the Ministry of Finance on overall fiscal policy and budget formulation. However, it continued to exercise tax policy and administration powers.

Supervisory Boards: the separate Boards of IRS, VATS, and CEPS continued to supervise the operations of their respective agencies without change to the laws that created them.

Staffing: NRS was under a Secretary (Minister) of Revenue and Chief Director of Revenue while its full-time senior and junior public officers were on secondment from IRS and CEPS. The staff of the VAT Project were also under NRS.

Legacy of NRS: The legacy of NRS is that it was the trailblazer for semi-autonomous revenue agencies in Africa, notably through initiating the legal backing it secured for IRS and CEPS in 1986. However, it was neither autonomous nor an apex institution.

Hence, the Uganda Revenue Authority (URA) became the first semi-autonomous institution that combined a semi-autonomous apex body and downstream revenue agencies. It was set up in 1988 under Ghana's first Chief Director of Revenue in NRS (Mr. Odame Larbi-Siaw), who also became the first Commissioner-General for the Rwanda Revenue Authority (RRA).

Revenue Agencies' Governing Board (RAGB): **NRS** remained in MOF from 1991 until its replacement by the Revenue Agencies' Governing Board (RAGB) in 2001.

> ***Single Supervisory Board:*** RAGB was also *an administrative body,* similar to NRS but it *consolidated the Board of Directors of IRS, CEPS and VATS* into a single supervisory body under one chairman.
>
> ***Executive Directors of the Board:*** the Commissioners of these three (3) revenues agencies became Executive Directors on the new Board.
>
> ***Executive Secretary:*** RAGB had an Executive Secretary but had fewer powers since the three (3) revenue agencies continued to operate under the operational authority of their commissioners who also remained on the Board.

The *RAGB concept did not clearly resolve the outstanding question of separating the supervisory fiscal nature of NRS from the headquarters of an autonomous* revenue agency or authority. It took another decade for the government to settle the issue convincingly by the setting up Ghana Revenue Authority (GRA) in 2009.

Ghana Revenue Authority (RA): Many African countries have set up revenue authorities as *apex bodies* to exercise full executive powers over their tax operations. As discussed, the traditional functions include the registration of taxpayers, education to enable them to comply with their obligations voluntarily and, failing which, tax offices are empowered to take enforcement actions.

Later in the book, we discuss the application of the revenue authority model under the GRA Revenue Authority Act, 2009 (Act 791) and the revenue processes under the Revenue Administration Act (RAA), 2016 (Act 915), which followed the consolidation of tax administration in Ghana.

Revenue Policy Division (RPD): In 2013, MOF set up RPD to merge (a) the *policy functions* of the Revenue Policy Unit (TPU) under the Economic Research and Forecasting Division (ERFD); with (b) those of the Non-Tax Revenue (NTRU) that was under the Budget Division (BD)

Scope of responsibility: it separated the Responsibility for tax administration or operations under CG and GRA officials from tax policy and legislative functions, which are deemed to be macro-fiscal activities.

Policy advice: the head of RPD offers tax policy advice as part of the overall fiscal policy formulation. The GRA's research units often collaborate in this exercise, in revenue estimation and revenue performance analyses.

Legislation: This involves regular consultation and collaboration by RPD with MOF's Legal Division, GRA's research units and the Attorney-General's (AG's) Department in preparing Bills for approval by Cabinet and passage by Parliament.

Collaboration with GRA: the aspects that involve GRA take various forms, including tax estimation, research, and performance evaluation for each of the tax instruments.

Budget preparation: the GRA collaboration extends to the preparation of the medium-term and annual Budgets by MOF and includes regular exchanges of view on forecasting and the implications of tax policy changes by the government.

As noted earlier, in 2018, MOF combined the domestic revenue policy and external resource mobilization under a single directorate called the Resource Mobilization and Economic Relations Division (RMERD).

8. Summary of Legislative Reforms

A notable aspect of the tax reforms is the update of legislation to make them consistent with the policy and administration reforms as well as the development of the country that changed the composition of its GDP and made lower middle-income country (L-MIC) status.

Revenue legislation reforms: There was a significant and comprehensive tax policy, administration, and legislation review by the NDC II government. Under the Agenda, Parliament passed several laws between 2009 and 2016 that include—

Ghana Revenue Authority (GRA): As noted, the GRA Act, 2009 (Act 791) is the apex for tax and customs administration in the country.

Excise Duty: Excise Duty Act, 2014 (Act 878) introduced a new law on excise duty, from provisions in the customs and VAT legislation.

Excise Tax Stamp: The Excise Stamp Tax, 2013 (Act 873) is a compliance or enforcement arrangement for taxable goods, whether imported or produced locally.

Customs Duty or Tariffs: Customs Act, 2015 (Act 891) comprehensively replaced the Customs, Excise and Preventive Service (Management) Act, 993 (PNDC Law 330).

Income Tax: The Income Tax Act, 2015 (Act 896) comprehensively replaced the Internal Revenue Act, 2000 (Act 592).

Revenue Administration: Revenue Administration Act, 2016 (Act 915), which consolidates the revenue administration provisions from the old VAT, Income Tax, and Customs laws.

The effects of the RAA include the uniform application of virtually all operational and legal processes to all taxpayers and placing all the operational support functions and activities under the GRA's Support Services Division (SSD). Where necessary, the book uses Tables or Boxes to cite relevant portions of the substantive laws to explain the principles and practices discussed in the book.

Ghana Revenue Authority Act, 2009 (Act 791): The following is a summary of the principal law on the organizational structure of Ghana's tax agencies and is discussed in further detail in the next Chapter.

Preamble: "An Act to *establish the Ghana Revenue Authority (GRA) to replace* the Internal Revenue Service (IRS), the Customs, Excise and Preventive Service (CEPS), and the Value Added Tax Service (VATS) for the *administration of taxes* and to *provide for related purposes.*"

Summary of the Legislation: the law is divided into four major parts for the effective *administration of all the tax and customs laws*—under *three (3) GRA Divisions,* namely Domestic Tax Revenue Division (DTRD), Customs Division (CD), Support Services Division (SSD), and any other Divisions determined by Parliament.

Parts of GRA Act, 2009 (Act 791): The parts include *(a) Part I:* Establishment and Governing Body; (bi) Part II: Administrative Matters; *(c) Part III:* Finances of the Authority and Miscellaneous Matters; and *(d) Part IV:* Transitional and Final Provisions.

In summary, the GRA law *replaces* the supervisory and operational structures of the *tax-type agencies with a single Authority* that could potentially enhance the operations or operations of GRA along *functional* lines. This followed the *tax administration reform trends* in many countries at the time of the enactment.

Revenue Administration Act (RAA), 2016 (Act 915): Following the "integration" of VATS and IRS under the Act, the GRA's DTRD removed several duplications under the "tax-type" administration structures. Hence, the passage of the RAA, 2016 (Act 915) is to give legislative meaning to the unified administration of the tax functions under GRA's DTRD—and, to an extent Customs administration under the Authority's CD.

Purpose of RAA: The Act combines "the administration and collection of revenue by the Ghana Revenue Authority (GRA) and for related matters." The common direct and indirect tax functions are (a) taxpayer assistance [i.e., registration and services]; (b) tax accounting [i.e., keeping records, assessment, filing and payment]; and (c) compliance or enforcement [i.e., debt collection, audits, prosecution and appeals].

Nature of legislation: Table 2.1 shows the various parts of the Revenue Administration Act (RAA) for managing all the direct and indirect taxes.

Table 2.1: Part of the Revenue Administration Act (RAA)

Parts	Descriptions
1	Stakeholders—revenue authority, taxpayers, and tax consultants
2	Official communications and documentation
3	Retention and provision of information—maintaining documents and provision of information.
4	Primary tax liability
5	Dispute resolution
6	Payment and recovery of tax
7	Interest, penalties, offences, and proceedings

8	Other provisions: tax laws and miscellaneous provisions
Schedules	1. Transactions for which TIN or TCC is required); (2) Tax Returns and Assessment); Third Schedule (Consequential Amendments and Repeals).

The remaining Chapters discuss these elements of the RAA in detail and as they relate to the substantive tax or revenue laws that now define the purposes of and indirect tax instruments in the country. They show the underlying importance of the provisions of the RAA 915 to the administration of the technical or substantive laws.

Tax regulations, and fiscal and financial laws: These tax laws derive from policies that formed part of the fiscal regime—as complemented by the banking and other financial laws.

Tax regulations: Parliament passes the requisite Regulations, as subsidiary legislation, to support the implementation of the primary laws.

Other fiscal laws: the revamp of tax policies and passage of the revenue laws are also part of the updates of all fiscal and financial sector legislation such as the Public Financial Management Act, 2016 (Act 921)—to replace the Financial Administration Act (FAA), 2003.

9. Conclusion

This chapter covered the trends in tax administration reforms that started with the creation of the National Revenue Secretariat (NRS) in 1985. The Secretariat was under a Cabinet-level Minister for Revenue and a Chief Director of Revenue as civilian head. It became the trailblazer for the semi-autonomy of revenue administration in Africa—a trend that virtually removed revenue or tax administration from the core civil service and placed them under the Revenue Authority (RA) concept.

While the role in the non-autonomous NRS also did not vest his office with direct executive control over operations, Ghana's first Chief Director of Revenue became the first Commissioner-General (CG) of a unified and semi-autonomous Uganda Revenue Authority (URA). The vague NRS status continued with the Revenue Agencies' Governing Board (RAGB). Hence, URA became Africa's first revenue authority with full operational and executive power over tax (i.e., customs and income tax administration as well as some non-tax revenues). He also became the first CG of the Rwanda Revenue Authority (RRA) and advised widely on revenue administration in Africa.

Ghana delayed in setting up a full Revenue Authority (RA) until 2009 when it also started to *integrate* the domestic direct and indirect tax agencies as well as *segment* the tax offices as Small Taxpayer Offices (STOs), Medium Taxpayer Offices (MTOs) and Large Taxpayer Offices (LTOs). While belated, these moves were consistent with the main themes of rationalizing the tax and non-tax revenue objectives of tax instruments and tax offices. They were also consistent in moving tax organizations, systems and processes *from tax-type to functional structures*—which were the emerging tax reform trends during the ERP-SAP period.

Ghana's review of tax administration was part of its macroeconomic and fiscal reforms, including tax policy, under the PNDC/NDC's ERP/SAP reforms from the mid-1980s until 2000 when the NPP took over from the NDC. The main reason for Ghana's delay in setting up an RA and adopting other revenue administration reforms, such as segmentation and integration, is attributed to the transition to civilian rule and politicization of economic reforms and its first attempt to introduce the VAT between 1993 and 1995.

Chapter 3

VALUE ADDED TAX (VAT): THEORETICAL AND POLICY CONTEXT

1. Introduction

The main laws under which the Value Added Tax (VAT) was *introduced, cancelled and reintroduced in Ghana* were (a) *VAT Act, 1994 (Act 486)* and (b) ***VAT Act, 1998 (Act** 546).* A comprehensive review of these laws came under the *VAT Act, 2013 (Act 870).* The enactment of the *Ghana Revenue Authority Act, 2009 (Act 791)* also consolidated the operations and administration of the VAT with other direct and indirect tax types under the Authority.

VAT is among the *indirect taxes* that, in principle, *final consumers* (including individuals and households) pay as part of the price for goods or services. Hence, they are called *consumption or expenditure taxes on domestic supplies and imports.*

> ***Value Added Tax (VAT):*** The VAT, which is also called the Goods and Services Tax (GST) in some countries, refers to the *uniform tax regime* that many countries use to replace different types of sales and service tax regimes.
>
> ***Other indirect or consumption taxes:*** The other main indirect taxes are *customs duties or tariffs on only imports and excise duties* that, like VAT, fall on both domestic supplies and imports.

Where tax policy options and legislation require that these taxes should not apply to specified entities or supplies, countries adopt *exemption, waiver or deferral; zero-rated; and credit or duty-drawback* schemes to remove or minimize the potential tax burden on consumers. Typically, zero rates target foreign consumers because they make exports cheaper and more competitive because the country does not "export" its domestic taxes.

> ***Direct taxes***: In contrast with indirect taxes, taxpayers pay *direct taxes on incomes* from employment, including wages, salaries, and allowances; *profit* from doing business as companies, partnerships, and sole proprietorships; and *rent or capital gains* from owning or disposing of property respectively. Profit is the difference between purchases and sales of goods and services.

Non-tax revenues: These include fees, charges, and levies—which, unlike the compulsory nature of taxes, affect the *only beneficiaries* of goods sold or services rendered by relevant government agencies.

In principle, the element of any fees or charges that are *not commensurate with the goods bought or services rendered* is deemed to be involuntary and, therefore, similar to an imposition of tax.

Taxable individuals: The law classifies individual taxpayers as *"persons"* who are natural or adopted citizens of a state, with taxable incomes from employment or self-employment. However, under *indirect tax* regimes, including VAT, the term "taxpayer" also refers to the "agents" that the law obliges to register and collect the tax at the point of sale, from final consumers or intermediaries.

Artificial persons: The other category of taxpayers is *artificial entities* that register under the **Companies Act 2019 (Act 992)**. In Ghana, *partnerships* are also corporate entities under the *Incorporated Private Partnership Act,* **1962 (Act 152, as amended**. However, the *natural partners or owners* are individually and severally liable for the tax on their shares of profits earned.

Part I (Chapters 1 to 3) on the Background to General Consumption Taxes [GCTs] deals with the ascendancy of VAT to replace the old sales and services tax regimes from the 1980s to date. This Chapter looks at the policy and administrative measures underlying the old form of consumption or expenditure taxes. Chapter 2 explains the relatively more efficient VAT Invoice-Credit mechanism while Chapter 3 compares the GCTs with the old sales and service tax structures that the VAT replaced in many countries.

2. Global Ascendancy of VAT

As already noted, VAT is a uniform tax that replaced different forms of sales and service taxes and is also the most recent successful and effective retooling of an existing tax handle in the 21st century. In some instances, such as the former Soviet Union economies, in some of these cases, VAT came into force as a virtually new tax initiative. Currently, the domestic and import VAT or GST has the widest indirect tax base and generates the most revenues for national budgets in many countries.

VAT and the European Union: From the 1960s, the European Union (EU) made VAT popular as one of the criteria for membership, under its 6th Directive for old and new members. As noted later, during the 1980/1990s, the IMF worked with the EU and other bilateral technical assistance (TA) providers to assist the former Soviet Union states to adopt VAT among the EU *"accession criteria"*. In the 1980s and 1990s, the IMF also led the drive to use VAT to replace different sales or service taxes in developing and middle-income countries (MIC) as well as emerging economies (Ems).

Early VAT theories: Before the EU era, Cnossen notes that Siemens (1919 & 1920) promoted VAT in Germany as the *multi-stage tax structure* that "improved turnover tax". Adam (1921) devised a US version of a *"modified gross income"* VAT that imposed the tax on the difference between sales and purchases.

Maurice Laure (1953 & 1957) is often called "the father of VAT" *"le père de la TVA (taxe a la valeur ajointee)"* in France. Further, Cnossen cites James (2015) as the promoter of the recent worldwide trend and perspectives.

IMF's push for VAT as a global tax phenomenon: By the mid-2000s, the IMF estimated that over 140 states had introduced VAT—a number that has now risen to 175 countries as of June 2023. The Fund was instrumental in achieving this feat, as a feature of the tax, fiscal and macroeconomic reforms that it has been promoting vigorously since the 1980s. These include the launch of VAT in small island states and land-locked economies, a task that was deemed difficult [Tate, 1988].

Indeed, the IMF even assisted in overcoming the setbacks that saw the re-introduction of VAT, after failed attempts, in Grenada, Malta, Belize, Vietnam, and Ghana. These countries had repealed their VAT laws because of political unpopularity and a general lack of proper planning and implementation.

3. VAT in Africa

In Africa, some experts credit Cote d'Ivoire with introducing a credible VAT regime in the 1970s [Cnossen] but the wave of consumption or expenditure tax reforms for VAT came in the 1980s. However, during this latter period, many African states replaced existing single-stage Sales and Service Taxes with VAT in the 1980s and early 1990s—along with the *deferral or suspension* of the tax payable on inputs for registered businesses.

The lesson from Ghana is that, while it had a reputation for reforms in the 1980s and 1990s, it delayed and, consequently, failed to introduce VAT until 1995, about a decade behind many of its counterparts in Africa. As was well known at the time, Ghana's two-year VAT plan from 1993 to 1995 to introduce VAT failed but it reintroduced the tax successfully in 1998/99. Thus, at the time, Ghana joined Malta, Grenada, Belize and Vietnam, as the only states that introduced the VAT, cancelled it and reintroduced it again.

> ***VAT and structural reforms:*** The VAT and, in general, tax policy and administration reforms in Africa, were *part of the fiscal and macroeconomic reforms* that the IMF, World Bank and other bilateral agencies launched in the 1980s to 2000s. These structural and austerity programs started in the Washington Consensus era in the 1980s and were known as Economic Recovery Programs (ERP) or Structural Adjustment Programs (SAP).
>
> ***VAT and fiscal reforms:*** The categorization and rationalization of tax instruments, as *part of overall fiscal reforms,* aimed at streamlining their tax and non-tax revenue objectives. Unlike the compulsory nature of taxes, the beneficiaries of the supply of goods and services by governments pay for them directly as fees and charges. The other parts of fiscal reforms were wide-ranging expenditure, budget, and debt management measures that improved the overall fiscal situation.
>
> ***VAT and tax reforms:*** In line with this overall rationalization of the goals of tax instruments, VAT *had a predominantly revenue-generation goal.* In contrast, excise duties were *punitive;* customs duties or tariffs were *protective* while income taxes served *multiple goals,* including revenue, investment incentive, and redistribution roles. In general, however, as part of the design of fiscal policies, all the taxes have elements of revenue and non-revenue goals—notably, social intervention.
>
> ***VAT as a replacement tax:*** Compared to their French-speaking counterparts, VAT replaced the sales tax regimes that were under Customs departments in the English-speaking countries (as was the case in the UK) and the service taxes that were virtually non-existent or ineffective counterparts to the sales tax

regimes. Many countries also had excise and tariff or customs regimes that they streamlined to serve protection, revenue and other goals.

VAT and semi-autonomy: In Africa, the continent-wide VAT initiatives preceded the *"semi-autonomy"* or *"revenue authority"* models that removed tax agencies from the core Civil Service—but as part of the general public sector. As a *pioneer*, Ghana set up the National Revenue Secretariat (NRS) in 1984, which pushed for two (2) separate autonomy laws in 1986.

These were *PNDC Law 143* for the Internal Revenue Service (IRS) and *PNDC Law 144* for Customs, Excise and Preventive Service (CEPS)—both repealed by Internal Revenue Act, 2000 (Act 592) and CEPS Act, 1993 (PNDC Law 330). As noted in the ensuing section, a third agency, the VAT Service (VATS) was established along with the introduction of the tax.

Ghana cedes leading the lead tax reforms: Ghana *ceded its pioneer semi-autonomy role* in setting up the National Revenue Secretariat (NRS) by not passing a law for a single apex executive body over IRS, CEPS and VATS. Hence, the honour for Africa's first Revenue Authority (RA) went to Uganda in 1991, with its first Commissioner-General (CG), Dr. Edward O. Larbi-Siaw. He was Ghana's first Chief Director (CD) of the semi-autonomous National Revenue Secretariat (NRS). As noted in the ensuing section, after many iterations of this fiscal or tax administration experiments, Ghana switched fully to the semi-autonomous Revenue Authority (RA) option in 2009.

4. VAT in Ghana

Ghana's VAT initiative was part of a broad reform of fiscal and tax policy as well as tax administration reforms under the 1983 SAP Program. Hence, while the period marked other significant reforms, including a major tax policy overhaul, discussed later in Chapters 13 and 14, the *decade's delay in setting up the VAT Project Office in 1993 made the VAT program isolated and difficult to implement.* Further, as noted later, it was a year after the 1992 Constitution was promulgated to make the transition from military to constitutional rule, under multi-party democracy.

This section summarizes the progress on major reforms and the political, social, and economic context in which the VAT project was launched. It also covers the reasons for the failure to introduce VAT successfully in 1995 and the enhanced activities that led to a relaunch in 1996 and the successful reintroduction of the tax between the end of 1998 and early 1999. The book discusses these political-economy issues in more detail in the final Chapters 13.

4.1 Apex Revenue Administration Reform Context

Ghana's VAT administration, policy, and legislative reforms, including automation of tax processes, fell under various Tax Modernization Projects (TMPs) led by NRS. As noted, they resulted in semi-autonomy from the core Civil Service for the Internal Revenue Service (IRS) and the Customs, Excise and Preventive Service (CEPS)—and later, the VAT Service (VATS). However, these *tax-type Services* were under separate supervising Boards until the passage of the RAGB and GRA laws.

NRS was not an "apex" body: The National Revenue Secretariat (NRS) developed the initial overall tax administration and policy framework for VAT and other tax reforms between 1984 and 1995. During the period VAT was introduced and cancelled or suspended after implementation for about three months. NRS was also instrumental in setting up IRS and CEPS as semi-autonomous agencies but, unlike the Revenue Authority (RA) model, they fell under separate supervising Boards and Commissioners—not as integrated institutions under NRS.

Complex fiscal developments: The initial NRS tax reform initiatives were substantive since they were under a Cabinet minister, Mr. Ato Ahwoi, to whom the Chief Director, Dr. E. O. Larbi-Siaw reported directly. However, overall fiscal policy remained under MOF, with Dr Kwesi Botchwey (later Mr. Kwame Peprah) as well as Messrs K.B. Amissah-Arthur and Victor Selormey as Ministers and Deputy Ministers. As Box 1.1 notes, these resulted in significant personnel as well as tax and reform policy overlaps.

Box 1.1: Ghana: VAT, Tax Reform and Political Personality Profile

During the period that the VAT initiative remained suspended between 1995 and 1998/99, the Project was placed under IRS, whose Commissioner (Prof. J.E.A. Mills) would become the Vice President. By this time, Dr. Kwesi Botchwey had resigned as the Minister for Finance and, therefore, Prof. Mills and Mr. Kwame Peprah (as the new Minister for Finance) who led the successful reintroduction.

As Vice President, HE Mills served under HE President J.J. Rawlings, whose Presidency launched the ERP/SAP reforms in 1983). As President, H.E Prof. Mills also assented to the GRA Act while his Vice President HE John D. Mahama, as Deputy-Minister for Information, led the revamped VAT Education initiatives during the VAT re-launch from 1996. Mr. Ekwow Spio-Garbrah (then Minister for Information), chaired the VATS Board while Mr. Ezekiel Asamoah became the Commissioner for VATS.

The author of this book (as VAT National Coordinator) and his colleague on the Project Team at the time, Mr. George Kuntu-Blankson, became Deputy Minister and Minister for MOF and first Commissioner-General (CG) respectively during the more recent reforms that started in 2009.

NRS reverts to MOF: as an administrative *reform measure* without legal backing, the two (2) IRS and CEPS Boards chipped away at most of the NRS's supervision role over operations or administration. Further, since *fiscal policy remained entirely with MOF*, the tax policy reform role of NRS also waned after the rationalization of direct and indirect tax regimes in the mid-1980s to the mid-1990s. Eventually, *all NRS functions reverted to MOF* under the Director of Revenue by the time VAT was reintroduced in 1996.

***Collection of sales and service taxes*:** As discussed earlier, at the time of introducing the VAT, Ghana's two (2) revenue agencies had become *semi-autonomous*. Hence, the *old sales tax regime*, on only goods at the import and manufacturing stages, was under CEPS. In contrast, the *service tax* on *selected* professional services was under the IRS since it had a larger number of domestic tax offices than the CEPS limited domestic offices. These old arrangements were restored as part of the VAT cancellation and reintroduction between 1995 and 1998.

VAT Service as 3rd tax agency: The VAT Project was set up administratively in 1993 and followed by the *VAT Service (VATS)* under the *VAT Act, 1994 (Act 486)*—thus, deepening the *tax-type* *structure* that was common during the period. After its retention under the **VAT Act, 1998** *(***Act** *546),* the VAT Service took charge of the VAT reforms until its merger with the IRS under the *GRA Act, 2009 (Act 791).*

This move aligned Ghana with trends that changed tax-type agencies to functional, integrated, and segmented forms of tax administration. The varieties of tax-type and functional administration of tax processes—registration and taxpayer service, tax accounting (assessment, filing and payment), enforcement and appeals —were in vogue at the time but also undergoing various reforms in developing countries.

RAGB replaces NRS: A Revenue Agencies [Governing] Board (RAGB) Act, 1998 (Act 558) was passed *to substantively replace NRS.* This move was a substantive part of the *VAT introduction (1995), cancellation (1996) and reintroduction (1998/99).* The RAGB Act *merged the IRS, VATS and CEPS supervisory Boards* and, partially, placed their operations under a single *Executive Secretary*—a *confusing compromise* that also retained most of the powers on the Commissioners for IRS, CEPS and VATS.

GRA as ultimate "apex" tax administration body**:** The Revenue Agencies [Governing] Board *(RAGB) Act, 1998 (Act 558)* was passed *to replace NRS.* However, after a decade, the *Ghana Revenue Authority Act, 2009 (Act 791)* repealed Act 558 and *GRA replaced RAGB* as the "apex" body. Hence, belatedly, these moves legislated Ghana's semi-autonomy program under the RA model—with various other changes that are discussed in the ensuing paragraphs.

GRA Commissioner-General (CG): the GRA Act, 2009 (Act 791) had a *single supervisory Board* and, unlike the RAGB Executive Secretary, a CG who now exercises *full executive or operational powers,* with the Commissioners as subordinates. The GRA law belatedly *merged IRS and VATS* into a single Domestic Tax Revenue Division (DTRD), while CEPS became GRA's Customs Division. A third *Support Services Division (SSD)* took over all the auxiliary GRA technical support activities or services that were under three (3) separate agencies, as listed under Schedule 3 of the GRA Act.

Revamp of technical laws: Until the repeal and replacement of the old laws, including a new *Excise Duty Act, 2014 (Act 878)* and *Revenue Administration Act (RAA) 2016 (Act 915),* the consolidation of support services occurred under repeals to the old technical laws under the *GRA Act (Act 791)*. The new laws were the *VAT Act 2013, (Act 870)*, which replaced the VAT Act 1998 (Act 546); the *Income Tax Act, 2015 (Act 896)*, which replaced the Internal Revenue Act, 2000 (Act 592); and the *Customs Act, 2015 (Act 891)*, which replaced the CEPS (Management) Act, 1993 (PNDC Law 330)

Strengthening legislation and supervision under RAA: As earlier mentioned, GRA's Support Services Division (SSD) took over all the auxiliary technical support services with a repeal of the existing tax and customs laws. Besides the consolidation, the *RAA, 2016 (Act 915)*, (a) updated the administrative and judicial sanctions under various tax offences; (b) set up a Tax Appeals Board—under *RAA (Amendment) Act, 2020 (Act 1029)*; and (b) paved way for the rearrangement of GRA's tax offices, as discussed below.

Tax process and tax office arrangements: Part IV (VAT Administration) discusses the role of the Support Service Division (SSD) in strengthening the customs and domestic tax offices under the *RAA 2016 (Act 915)*. Earlier, following the passage of the GRA Act, the Authority started to *integrate* [i.e., IRS and VATS] and *segment* [i.e., size of taxpayer] DTRD offices under targeted Small Taxpayer Offices (STOs), Medium Taxpayer Offices (MTOs) and Large Taxpayer Offices (LTOs). However, by 2018, the concept changed to the setting up of domestic Taxpayer Services Centres (TSCs) to perform administration functions.

Hence, VATS kept its separate semi-autonomous tax-type organization or agency status, as were older IRS and CEPS, from 1998 until the setting up of GRA in 2009. During this period, the setting up of VATS became an important element of the comprehensive revenue or tax administration reforms under the ERP/SAP initiatives that started in 1983.

4.2 VAT and the Revenue Administration Reform Context

Since 2009, together with the IRS, Ghana's third tax-type VAT Service (VATS) became part of GRA's Domestic Tax Revenue Division (DTRD). The core VATS staff were from the VAT Project (1993) and retained VATS Phase 1 staff (1995)—who became substantive employees of MOF, CEPS and IRS during the period of VAT suspension from 1995 to 1998.

VATS as part of GRA reforms: GRA was set up with *three (3) Divisions*: (a) merger of IRS and VATS under a single Domestic Tax Revenue

Division (DTRD); (b) restructuring CEPS as Customs Division (CD); and (c) integrating all IRS, CEPS, and VATS administration functions under a Support Services Division (SSD).

Financing and technical assistance (TA): The Revenue or Tax Modernization Programs (TMPs) and other reforms were financed with soft loans and grants from the World Bank and other donors as well as TA providers, including bilateral partners and IMF. The Project got substantive support from the UK's Department for International Development (DfID), with the Crown Agents supporting the VAT Project with TA.

Across Africa, the trend was initially the establishment of separate VAT agencies, but later, there was a shift toward merger or integration with the IRS, as exemplified by the case under GRA in 2009. It is important to note that some staff of IRS and CEPS opposed the setting of a separate VAT agency in Ghana, including testimonies made to Parliament and its Committees.

4.3 SAP/ERP, Reform Fatigue, and Political Transition

The following is a summary of the launch of the VAT project in 1993, the failed effort to introduce the tax in 1995, and its successful relaunch between 1998 and early 2000. As has been noted, these developments were major twilight elements of the *launch and implementation of several tax, fiscal, sector and macroeconomic reforms in 1983* under the Structural Adjustment Programme (SAP)—which was also called the Economic Recovery Program (ERP).

Delay in launching VAT: There is a strong view that Ghana should have introduced VAT earlier in the mid-to-late 1980s, with the other major macroeconomic, monetary, fiscal, and real sector reforms under the SAP-ERP. Particularly, this would have avoided the disconnect between the VAT initiative and related reforms in tax administration, rationalization of tax instruments and fiscal policy changes.

VAT Project: The funding and TA for the VAT Project from 1993 was from the UK's DfID and Crown Agents, respectively It was based on a feasibility study by Harvard Institute for International Development (HIID), Harvard University (USA), from 1984 to 1986. The Government contemplated *a two-stage* VAT program, involving (a) *a pilot* to replace the "ring" method for sales tax on goods with a "credit" mechanism at the manufacturing and import stages; and

(b) the full invoice-credit VAT method, compared to the addition or subtraction methods, for all sectors after this pilot phase.

Launch of VAT: The Government shelved the HIID study for a decade until DFID funded Crown Agents long-term, peripatetic, and short-term experts to support the VAT launch between 1993 to 1995. After three months of continuous "Kumepreko" demonstrations by the opposition New Patriotic Party (NPP), the Cabinet suspended the VAT until its successful relaunch from 1996 to 1998. Nonetheless, the National Democratic Congress (NDC) lost the 2000 elections and, on taking over, the NPP launched several amendments that entrenched the politicization of the technical aspects of VAT in Ghana.

Inter-agency rivalry: An obstacle to VAT was the inter-agency rivalry that pitched some senior staff and board members of CEPS and IRS against the VAT Project/Service. It followed earlier opposition to removing the tax and customs agencies from the core civil service, under the NRS *semi-autonomous* program. The tipping point for VAT was the testimony in Parliament to oppose aspects of the VAT plan by these tax officials.

VAT as main revenue source: VAT was part of a comprehensive domestic resource mobilization (DRM) agenda involving tax (i.e., direct and indirect) and non-tax revenues.

> ***Direct taxes:*** the incidence of direct taxes is on income earners, including profits under the corporate income tax (CIT); personal income tax (PIT) on employment (i.e., salaries and allowances) and the share of profits for self-employed persons and partnerships; and rent and capital gains tax on property and investments.
>
> ***Indirect taxes:*** the taxes on consumption expenditure, including customs duties or tariffs as protection to discriminate against imports; excise duties as punitive or "sin" taxes; and VAT, which replaced various sales and service tax or general consumption tax regimes.
>
> ***Non-tax revenues***: the levies, charges and fees that fall under the generic description of non-tax revenues are imposed in exchange for sales of goods or services rendered to citizens directly by various central government ministries, departments and agencies (MDAs) and sub-national government metropolitan, municipal and district assemblies (MMDAs).

First, unlike the *compulsory nature of taxes,* income and fees are deemed optional. Secondly, all the tax and non-tax instruments or handles serve *revenue and non-revenue goals,* notably in line with the social intervention or progressive agenda of the state.

VAT and structural adjustment fatigue: the delayed VAT implementation made the VAT plan a victim of citizen's fatigue and protests by civil society, professional groups, and students—following two decades of economic reforms and many counter-cyclical or austerity measures that Ghana and other SSA states use as counter-cyclical measures to correct economic crisis and realign the economy.

Exogenous triggers: Most domestic factors have exogenous triggers such as droughts that affected agricultural output and caused power shortages and bushfires, and difficulty in sustaining subsidies and other social intervention programs from depleted budget resources. Others include frequent falls in demand in advanced economies that affect the export price for primary commodities. This leads to shortages of foreign currency reserves, precipitous depreciation of the local currency, and higher prices for imports.

The main *goal of corrective austerity measures* is higher revenues and lower expenditures to reduce the adverse impact of high fiscal deficits, borrowing or financing, and debt. It is also to stem falling foreign exchange reserves; loss in value of the local currency; high import bills and commodity prices.

Ultimately, they lead to downturns in productivity and a fall in GDP growth that perpetuates the instability. They are easy to exploit in the political arena even though they often follow periods of economic crisis that may be rooted in non-economic causes.

4.4 Registration of Numerous Small Entities

In many instances, the opposition to VAT succeeded because of deliberate distortions of the goals of fiscal policies. A notable example is scaring small entities that did not even qualify to register for VAT to overwhelm the VAT media and public relations strategies.

VAT registration threshold: the new VAT regime had a significantly high conventional turnover registration threshold, the equivalent of US$50,000 that potentially removed many small entities in the informal sector from the VAT registration.

Non-registration for sales and service tax: nonetheless, it was difficult to educate many small entities that VAT would not affect them directly, as prevailing under the pre-existing registration for sales and service taxes.

Number of VAT registrants: with only 15,000 persons registered after three (3) months of VAT implementation, the opposition view persisted that the VAT register had many small entities that could not comply. For the VAT relaunch, VATS undertook a new round of registration with a higher threshold that was equivalent to US$75,000.

A major point that is overlooked is that the reintroduction of VAT in 1998 resulted in more, not less, VAT registrants, compared to 1995. The success of the VAT relaunch may be due to two factors: lowering the VAT rate from 17.5 per cent to 10 per cent and honouring all VAT credits, including the payment of all VAT refunds, under the aborted 1995 VAT.

4.5 Public Perceptions of Inadequate Preparations

Another criticism was inadequate preparation for launching VAT, resulting in less time for its implementation. On the contrary, as the summary below shows, Ghana had devoted sufficient time and resources to the task.

Financial and TA support: As noted, for the period of implementation, the UK's DfID and Crown Agents supported the VAT initiative. The IMF and HIID also led on policy prescription and implementation advice. Besides being familiar with the reforms in Ghana, these agencies were part of the global effort to use VAT to replace existing Sales Taxes or implement VAT as a new tax handle.

Period of preparation: Ghana's initial VAT implementation plan from 1993 to 1995 was consistent with the 18-to-24-month timelines proposed by the IMF, HIID and other TA providers. The staff of the VAT Project Office were drawn from NRS/MOF, IRS, and CEPS, with most of them involved in ongoing tax policy and administration reforms. They were "seconded" to work full-time and exclusively on the VAT implementation.

Setting up the VAT Service: VATS took over the VAT Project and continued to plan and manage the VAT exclusively *under the VAT Act 1994 (Act 486) and the VAT Act 1998 (***Act** *546)* until the GRA Act was passed in 2009. The VATS permanent staff, including new staff and those from IRS, CEPS and NRS who worked under the conditions of service approved by the RAGB Board and either maintained their analogous grades or were promoted into new roles. The main high-level elements of the *VAT Act 486, since repealed,* are summarized in Table 3.1.

Table 3.1 Main "Parts" of original VAT Act 1998--repealed

VALUE ADDED TAX ACT, 1994 (ACT 486)	
Summary of Main Parts	
Parts	
I	Imposition of Value Added Tax (VAT)
II	Returns, Remittances and Recovery
III	Administration of VAT
IV	Offences, Penalties and Miscellaneous Provisions
Schedules	
1	Exempt supplies [Section 5(1)]
2	Zero rate supplies [Section 5(2)]
3	Relief supplies [Section 5(3)]
4	Repeals [Section 54]

The complement to the VAT Act is the VAT Regulations, 1995 (LI 1598), whose main parts are summarized in Table 3.2.

Table 3.2: Main Parts and Schedule in VAT Regulations

VALUE ADDED TAX REGULATIONS, 1995 (LI 1598)	
Summary of VAT Regulations	
Parts	
I	Regulations
II	Apportionment of Input Tax between Taxable and Exempt supplies
III	Tax Invoices
IV	Tax Returns and Tax Payments
V	Recovery of Sales Tax
VI	Retail Sales
VII	Distraint Procedure
Forms	
A	Application for Registration for VAT
B	Certificate of Registration for VAT
C	Example of Tax Invoice
D	VAT Returns
E	Claim for Refund of VAT
F	Form of Warrant of Distress

VAT Academy and staffing: The VAT Project training unit became the VATS Academy and staff included those who had attended various "train-the-trainer" courses in the UK. Eventually, the VATS, IRS and CEPS academies were combined into the GRA Academy in 2009.

Experience in tax reforms: As noted, the staff from existing revenue agencies in the VAT Project were engaged in various ongoing tax and customs reforms under the ERP-SAP agenda. Second, every new senior or support staff undertook the mandatory VAT and overall tax training before taking up their training or as part of on-the-job training. Hence, it is untrue that the VAT Project did not have qualified staff.

Communications strategy: An improved communications plan was key to the successful relaunch of the VAT and seems to buttress the view that public awareness was inadequate in 1995. Nonetheless, as noted in paragraph 3.2, the overwhelming factors appear to be public demonstrations, due to adjustment fatigue and a bid to win the 1996 elections.

In conclusion, while no major tax or fiscal reform can be perfect, the factors that undermined the VAT process in Ghana include political ambition, misperceptions, and distortions. Ghana had sufficient funds, tax implementation experience, and a comprehensive timetable that was consistent with 18-to-24 months for VAT implementation. It must be noted that some tax officials from Ghana, under Dr. E. O. Larbi-Siaw, assisted in the launch of the Uganda Revenue Authority (URA in 1991 and the successful launch of VAT in 1996.

4.6 Erroneous view of VAT as a new form of tax

A persistent view from 1995 to 1996 was that VAT would be a "new" form of tax that would add to existing direct and indirect tax burdens. This was in sharp contrast with the following points that explain the nature of the taxes that VAT replaced.

Sales and service tax regimes: CEPS charged sales tax on taxable imports, at the uniform rate that *replaced the multiple rates* (i.e., standard, super, and sub-standard) for the *sales tax*. IRS collected a complementary *service tax on selected services,* including entertainment, betting, and professional services, from its registered entities. IRS was a direct tax agency that administered this indirect tax because it had a wider network of domestic tax offices.

Repeals and amendments under substantive laws: Table 3.3 shows the sections that (a) repeal the old sales and service tax laws; (b) extend ITC benefits to pre-VAT stocks of taxable supplies; and (a) preserve several enforcement and administrative provisions of the old law under the VAT Act, 1994 (Act 486).

Table 3.3: Repeals and rights to ITC relating to old laws

Value Added Tax Act, 1994 (Act 486)		
Section	**Item and Description**	**Comments**
54	**Repeals and transitional provisons**	
(1)	The ***enactment specified*** in paragraph 1 and 2 of ***Schedule 4*** to the Act shall on the date of the imposition of the tax ***be deemed to be repealed or amended*** to the extent indicated.	Contrary to general view, ***VAT consolidated several existing sales & service taxes (see Table 1.2)***
	Preservation of enforceable actions under repealed laws	
(2)	Notwistanding subsection (1) of the this section, provisions in the repealed enactments ***shall remain in force for the purpose of*** verifying the relevant tax returns and claims and for assessing and recovering any arrears or penalties payable under the enactments prior to the date of imposition of the Value Added Tax (VAT).	***Enforceability*** of admistrative & compliance provisions ***under old laws***
(3)	Taxable persons in ***possession of goods on 1st March 1995*** on which ***sales taxes has been paid*** shall be eligible for ***repayment of the sales tax***, subject to compliance with regulations made under the act; for the purpose of verifying claims for repayment, an officer shall hold all the powers appropriate to the sales tax held by the CEPS.	In effect, the ***VAT law was used to allow the equivalent of Input Tax Credit*** for taxable supplies held under the old laws

Repeals of specific acts, laws and decrees in Schedule 4: The two specific categories of the taxes in these laws are *(a) Service taxes collected by IRS*—entertainment duty, betting, hotel and restaurants, and advertising; and *(b) Sales tax collected by CEPS.*

Rates of tax: The pre-existing tax structures required only a few manufacturers to register and charge the Sales tax of 15 per cent on taxable supplies while the IRS levied the Service Tax at variable rates—without recourse to ITC or tax deferral. Therefore, it was also not true that VAT, with its relatively efficient and unconditional "credit" and "refund" mechanism, was a new tax that increased prices.

Sales and service tax schemes: Registered manufacturers were *put in a fictional or compliance "ring"* that allowed CEPS to "waive", "defer" or "suspend" the sales tax on inputs. These are importations or domestic supplies of raw and semi-produced materials related to the taxable supplies. IRS charged the service tax without recourse to ITC or "ring" suspension, which is an alternative scheme to invoice-based ITC.

Hence, at the time, the proposed design and implementation of VAT implied a *shift to a more comprehensive and uniform taxable supply base than the pre-existing service and sales taxes*. Besides the cascading effect of non-ITC, the multiple rates and narrow scope of sales taxes are unfair to final consumers and make its administration and compliance complex.

4.7 Successful VAT Relaunch after the 1996 Elections

Upon winning the 1996 elections, the NDC administration decided to relaunch the VAT project and reintroduce the VAT. Eventually, this resulted in replacing the various interim laws—including the CEPS (Management) (Amendment) Act, 1995 (Act 500), Service Tax Act, 1995 (Act 501) and The Service Tax (Amendment) Act, 1997 (Act 529)—as used to manage the old sales and service taxes during the suspension of VAT implementation in 1995.

Substantive suspension, not cancellation: *elements of* the three laws on VAT point to a suspension and an *inherent goal of reintroducing VAT after the 1996 election.* As noted later, the reform imperative and *fiscal necessity of VAT* led to saving the obligations and rights of VAT-registered taxpayers, notably the right to ITC claims or refunds for the three-and-half months of VAT operations in 1996.

Table 4.4 lists the specific general consumption tax laws that were replaced in Schedule 4 of Value Added Tax and subsumed under the provisions of the VAT Act, 1994 (Act 486).

Table 4.4: List of existing laws repealed by the VAT Act 486 (Schedule 4)

	Value Added Tax Act, 1994 (Act 486)
	Schedule of Repealed Legislation
Schedule 4	**Repeals (Section 54)**
List 1	**Entertainment Duty Act, 1962 (Act 150)**
	Entertainment Duty (Amendment) Decree 1972 (NRCD 105)
	Entertainment Duty (Amendment) Decree 1978 (SMCD 44)
	Entertainment Duty (Amendment) Law, 1985 (PNDCL 132)
	Entertainment Duty (Amendment) Law, 1987 (PNDCL 175)
	Entertainment Duty (Amendment) (No. 2) Law, 1987 (PNDCL 186)
	Betting Act, 1965 (Act 268)
	Hotels and Restaurants (Taxation) (Amendment) Decree, 1976 (SMCD 50)
	Hotels and Restaurants (Taxation) (Amendment) Decree, 1977 (SMCD 131)
	Hotels and Restaurants (Taxation) (Amendment) Decree, 1978 (SMCD 193)
	Hotels and Restaurants (Taxation) (Amendment) Decree, 1979 (SMCD 393)
	Hotels and Restaurants (Taxation) (Amendment) Decree, 1988 (PNDCL 197)
	Advertisement Tax Decree 1976 (SMCD 43)
	Local Government Act 1993 (Act 462) 6th Schedule, Items 1 and 3
List 2	Customs, Excise and Preventive Service (Management) Law, 1993 (PNDCL 330) is ***amended*** as follows--
	(a) by the ***repeal of--***
	(i) section 24(2)(c)
	(ii) section 24(4)(a)
	(iii) sections 60 to 63; and
	(b) by the ***deletion of the words "sales tax"*** wherever they appear in the Law

Lower VAT rate: the reduction of the VAT rate from 17.5 per cent to 10 per cent helped to make the VAT re-launch successful. However, this did not help to lower the budget deficit nor made the tax regime efficient. Hence, in less than 5 years, the rate was increased by 2.5 per cent (GETFund levy) and 2.5 per cent (NHIL).

Benefits of ITC and refunds: another factor in the successful VAT relaunch from 1998 to 1999 was allowing registered entities to apply for ITC and refunds for the three (3) months that VAT had been effective in 1995. It showed the superiority of the VAT credit method and resulted in more business entities and civil society organizations (CSOs) lending their support to the VAT relaunch in 1998/99.

Reorganization of VAT Project and Service: the key elements of the decision to retain the VAT project and VATS between 1995 and 1998 include the following:

Reinstatement of VAT Service [VATS]: at the apex of the reinstated VATS was the Board of Directors which had a Minister as Chairman and members belonging to different professions.

Facilities and staff: the staff, assets, and logistics for the earlier VAT effort were retained under the IRS and returned to ensure a smooth reintroduction of the program; a Deputy Commissioner was assigned by the IRS to head the VAT Project, as Director (became the first Commissioner of VATS)—thus separating the Chief Executive position from that of the National VAT Coordinator.

Conditions of Service: given the autonomy of operations, the team of VATS staff (i.e., from the VAT Project, NRS (MoF), IRS, CEPS and recruits) were placed on the same conditions of service as IRS and CEPS. Besides basic salaries and allowances, these include annual bonuses and welfare schemes.

Technical assistance (TA): the original design of Ghana's VAT was by the (now defunct) Harvard Institute for International Development (HIID) in 1992 while the Crown Agents provided technical assistance (TA) for the initial introduction of VAT in 1995 and its relatively smoother relaunch in 1998, with the effective date in 1999.

Higher VAT threshold: VATA 1998 increased the turnover or sales threshold amount for registering to charge Output VAT and claim ITC. This was meant to remove many SMEs from the old register but the number rather increased. This is due to several positive impacts of the VAT ITC and refunds to taxpayers.

Improved communications strategy: Given the misinformation and distortions that led to the inability to continue with the VAT implementation, the Government took a decision to elevate the revamping of the VAT communication strategy to the national level. The Deputy Minister for Communications became Chairman of the sub-committee for Public Information and led the team to significantly enhance the strategy.

With the failure to introduce the VAT at the first attempt in 1995, Ghana became only one of three countries at the time, after Malta and Grenada, to introduce a VAT and withdraw it from full implementation. While Ghana and Malta reintroduced the VAT successfully in 1999, with the latter as a condition for EU accession, Grenada's reintroduction occurred in 2010, along with several Caribbean Island States.

4.8 Major Consumption Tax Transitions To-Date

Technically, due to the protests, Ghana "suspended" its VAT implementation in 1995, although the contrary and common view is that it "cancelled" the program. This section summarizes the VAT "transition" policies and laws, including the new VAT Act in 2013, that have characterized VAT policy and implementation in Ghana.

VAT political "tug-of-war": It is easy to associate the milestones in VAT policy and legislation to Ghana's return to civilian or 4th Republican administrations under the 1992 Constitution. As noted earlier, the VAT design and implementation, which was meant to replace the sales and service taxes from 1993 to 1998, includes (a) the transition to constitutional rule from 1992; and (b) the period of demonstrations and turmoil against VAT and its ultimate "suspension" between 1995 and 1996.

Sales tax (1960s to 1992): Before the 1995 attempt and successful 1998 VAT sagas in the 4th Republic, Ghana had three (3) civilian and four (4) military administrations, with the last being the PNDC that implemented the ERP/SAP program. The general indirect or expenditure taxes were the (a) sales tax at a single stage on specified goods at the import and manufacturing points; and (b) later, service tax on selected services.

Sales and service taxes (PNDC—1983 to 1992): The ERP/SAP reforms also included delays in replacing the sales and services taxes with VAT. Ghana missed a good opportunity to introduce VAT as part of major tax administration and policy reforms, and part of major fiscal and macroeconomic reforms in the late 1980s to early 1990s.

VAT introduction (NDC I—1992 to 2000): The VAT introduction (1994), suspension (1995), and reintroduction (1998) under NDC also marks the transition to the 4th Republic's civilian rules that also led to the inevitable politicization of VAT to date. Specifically, VAT was often cited in the "preko" demonstrations, the peak of which was the "Kumepreko" protests in 1995, with casualties, before the second general elections in 1996.

VAT changes (NPP I—2001 to 2008): the VAT protests that contributed to the NPP's win seem to embolden it to make policy changes that continue to compromise the VAT structure and its collection and compliance. The distortions include the VAT Flat Rate Scheme (VFRS) and expansion of the scope of exempt domestic supplies—

and later, zero-rating of, and reliefs for, supplies made by registered entities at various upstream, midstream, and downstream stages.

VAT revamp (NDC II—2009 to 2016): In 2009, the NDC government continued with major tax reforms and reviews of all tax laws, including VATA, 2013 (Act 870). Unlike past changes to reflect policy, VATA 870 was a complete rewrite of the Act, as was the case with the income tax, excise (new), and customs laws. The reforms were part of overall tax reforms that led to the setting up of GRA and its Divisions in 2009.

VAT reversals by NPP II from 2017 to date: as discussed in Parts II and III, the NPP reversed many of the updated VAT Act 870 provisions, with the most significant being the reversal of the VFRS changes and introduction of several levies, including the conversion of GETFund Levy and NHIL to *so-called "Straight" levies.*

The summary of macroeconomic and fiscal reforms in Part V (Chapters 13 and 14) covers the socio-political context of VAT under the NDC and NPP—with a legacy of distortions that persist to date and affect the smooth administration of the VAT regime.

5. VAT cancellation and transition laws

This section summarizes the substantive policy decisions and legislative steps that led to the cancellation of the VAT implementation—*not through a direct repeal of VATA 1994 (Act 498).* These policy and legislative moves include;

- a very *abrupt increase in the VAT rate,* during a difficult implementation, from 15 per cent to 17.5 per cent under *VATA, 1994 (Act 498);*
- *re-enactment* of sales tax provisions under CEPS (Management) Law, 1990 (PNDCL 330)—as *CEPS (Management)(Amendment) Act, 1995 (Act 500);*
- passage of a *Service Tax Act, 1995 (Act 501);* and later enactment of the *Service Tax (Amendment) Act, 1999 (Act 529)* to expand the service tax base at various rates;
- Acts 500 and 501 were designed to *retain the VATS staff, assets and liabilities,* as the Minister may decide, under IRS, CEPS or the Ministry; and
- *expansion of STA 501's taxable services* base under the *Service Tax (Amendment) Act, 1997 (Act 529)*—but still keeping the tax base to specified services only.

An important measure of confidence by the business community in the invoice-credit mechanism was in the power vested in the Minister to honour liabilities, including VAT credits and refunds, for the approximately three months that VAT was implemented in 1995.

Abrupt increase in VAT rate: An important point that is often missing among the reasons for unsuccessfully introducing the VAT was an abrupt amendment to *increase the rate from 15 per cent to 17.5 per cent.* The only logical reason was the *fiscal pressure that underestimated and, therefore, aggravated the anti-VAT sentiments* that were fuelling the anti-VAT public protests. *Table 3.5* summarizes the amendment.

Table 3.5: Abrupt increase in VAT rate (VATA 498)

Value Added Tax (Amendment) Act. 1995 (Act 498)			
An Act to amend the VAT Act, 1994 (Act 486) to provide for the rate of tax chargeable.			
Section	**Item**	**Description**	**Comments**
1	**Act 486 Amended**		
	The VAT Act, 1994 (Act 486) is amended by the ***repeal of s6***		*An abrupt increase in VAT rate from 15 percent to 17.5 percent may have contributed to thefailure to introduce the VAT successfully*
	Rate of tax	The tax chargeable shall be ***17.5 percent*** of the value of the taxable supply or import determined under s7 or 8 of this Act	
2	**Commencement**	This Act shall ***come into force*** on the ***1st day of March 1995***	
(a) ***Assent:*** *February 2, 1995; (b)* ***Gazette notification*** *: February 10, 1995*			

CEPS (Management)(Amendment) (No. 2) Act, 1995 (Act 500): this was the *"re-enactment"* law that *restored the Sales Tax* and allowed CEPS to collect the old sales tax again between 1996 and 1998/99. *Tables 3.6 to 3.8* show the *restored sections* of *PNDC Law (PNDCL 330 of 1993*—with Table 1.6 below dealing with the imposition of tax at *"various rates"*.

Table 3.6: Restoring the rules for collecting the old Sales Tax—1

Customs, Excise and Preventive Service (CEPS) (Management) (No. 2) (Amendment) Act, 1995 (Act 500)			
An Act to amend the CEPS (Management) Law 1993 (PNDC L330) by *re-enacting* therein, provisions on sales tax and to provide for related purposes			
Section	**Item**	**Item and Description**	**Comments**
1	**Section 24 of PNDC Law 330 amended**		
	The CEPS (Management) Law, 1993 (PNDC L330) referred to in this Act as the principal enatment is amended in section 24–		
(a)	by the insertion in sub-section (2) of paragraph (c) as follows–"(c) sales tax";		
(b)	by the insertion in sub-section (4) of paragraph (a) as follows–"(a) for the ***imposition of various rates of sales tax*** on such goods as may be prescribed";		*Note s4 below gives a 15% standard rate*

Rules for collecting sales tax: Again, Table 3.7 (Act 500(2) also restored various rules under the collecting the old sales tax but *with some enhancements from VATA 1995 (Act 486)*. To reiterate, however, the Amendment Act *restricted or retained the taxable base for the domestic sales, upstream at* the manufacturing stage.

Table 3.7 Restoring the rules for collecting the old Sales Tax—2

Customs, Excise and Preventive Service (CEPS) (Management) (No. 2) (Amendment) Act, 1995 (Act 500)			
An Act to amend the CEPS (Management) Law 1993 (PNDC L330) by re-enacting therein, provisions on sales tax and to provide for related purposes			
Section	**Item**	**Item and Description**	**Comments**
2	**Section 60-63 of Principal Enactment Re-Enacted**		
	The principal enactment is amended by the insertion of the following sections--		
	60	**"Imposition of Sales Tax"**	
(1)	Sales tax shall be payable on ***all locally manufactured*** or produced goods as well as goods imported into the country, ***unless the goods are exempt***.		*"Upstream", not "downstream" at consumer stage as VAT.*
(2)	Sales tax shall be payable on goods given as gifts or used for protocol and sales promotion purposes.		*Same "in-kind" provision as VAT*
	61	**Calculation of Sales Tax**	
	Sales tax shall be calculated on the cost of production and profit margin		*Application of the "addition" method, in principle*
	62	**When Sales Tax is Payable**	
	Time, place, value etc., rules relating to manufacturing, ex-factory, warehousing & import supplies, hire purchase/instalment payment etc., delivery or supply.		*In many instances, same as VAT rules.*
	63	**Rates of Sales Tax and Exemptions**	
	Regulations by Minister to specify rates for taxable supplies and those to be exempted		*Note s4 below gives a 15% standard rate*

Transition clauses to facilitate VAT reintroduction: CEPS (Amendment) Act 500, together with the *Sales Tax Act (STA) 1995 (Act 501)*, the ensuing provisions seemed designed to facilitate the reintroduction of VAT—as occurred later in 1998/99 after the 1996 elections. In this regard, *Section 5, sub-sections 3 and 4* from *Table 3.8* below are repeated for emphasis.

> *"Notwithstanding the repeal under s2 and of s5, any person employed for VATS who was in the said employment immediately before the coming into force of the Act may be assigned to CEPS to assist with the collection of sales tax after consultation by the Minister with the CEPS Board."—s5(3).*
>
> *and*
>
> *"Except as otherwise provided in this Act and the Service Tax Act, 1995 (Act 501) any assets, credits or liabilities existing in favour of or against the VATS immediately before the coming into force of this Act shall on the coming into force of the Act, be dealt with and managed as the Minister may direct."—s5(4).*

Table 3.8: Repeals, savings and transitional provisions

Customs, Excise and Preventive Service (CEPS) (Management) (No. 2) (Amendment) Act, 1995 (Act 500)		
An Act to amend the CEPS (Management) Law 1993 (PNDC L330) by ***re-enacting*** therein, provisions on sales tax and to provide for related purposes		
Section	**Item and Description**	**Comments**
3	**The words "Sales Tax" to be Re-Inserted"**	
	The principal enactment is amended by the insertion of the words "sales tax" wherever they appeared before their repeal under s54 of the VATA 1994 (Act 486).	*Effectively substitutes the words "sales tax"for "VAT" with the repeal ofthe VATA*
4	**Rate of Sales Tax**	
	Notwithstanding any rate of sales tax provided for in any other law, the rate of sales tax chargeable under the principal enactment and any other law shall be 15%	*Standard rate ofsales tax at 15% is lower than 17.5% VAT*
5	**Repeal, savings and transitional provisions**	
(1)	The VATA 1994 (Act 486) and VATAA 1995 (Act 498) ***are hereby repealed***.	
(2)	The VAT Regulations 1995 (Ll 1598) ***are hereby revoked***.	
(3)	Notwithstanding the repeal under ss2 and 2 of s5, ***any person employed for VATS*** who was in the said employment immediately before the coming into force of the Act may be assigned to CEPS to ***assist with the collection of sales tax*** after consultation by the Minister with the CEPS Board.	*Preservation of employment (similar clause in Service Tax Act 501)*
(4)	Except as otherwise provided in this Act and the Service Tax Act, 1995 (Act 501) any ***assets, credits or liabilities existing in favour of or against the VATS*** immediately before the coming into force of this act shall on the coming into force of the Act, be dealt with and managed as the Minister may direct.	*Preservation of liability was useful for meeting outstanding VAT refunds and ITC, despite repeal ofthe Act*
(a) ***Assent***: June 14, 1995; (b) ***Gazette notification*** : June 14, 1995		

Transition provisions: In summary, Table 1.4 shows that the provisions affect former *employees of the VAT Service* (whose appointments were not terminated); and *protection of the Service's assets and liabilities* (including ITC and refunds due to taxpayers).

> ***employment:*** subject to consultations between the Minister and the RAGB Board, both new and seconded employees of VATS preserved their jobs through re-assignment to CEPS (and IRS) as well as a few in the VAT Project;
>
> ***assets and liabilities:*** the law saved the assets and liabilities of the VAT Service which, in particular, enabled the Minister for Finance to meet the VAT ITC and refund commitments for the period that the VAT had been implemented.

Sales tax rate: the standard rate was reduced from 17.5 per cent, enacted in only February 1995, to the original sales tax rate of 15 per cent under the old CEPS legislation—made provision in other sections for exemptions and, likely, sub-standard rates.

Winding down VAT implementation: while Parliament spent a lot of time on these laws, from February to June 1995, the Presidential

Assent and Gazette notifications were on the same day (June 14, 1995). This latter action suggests the extent of political pressure under which these actions were made.

Service Tax Act (STA), 1995 (Act 501): as with the CEPS Act, STA 501 restored the charging and collection of the limited services tax by the IRS—a direct tax institution that collected an indirect tax. *Table 3.9* begins a discussion of various aspects of the *imposition* of the service tax under Act 501, starting with Section 1, imposition of tax.

Table 3.9: Restoration of service tax and taxable supply base

Service Tax Act, 1995 (Act 501)—1			
	An Act to provide for the imposition of tax on specified services rendered to others and to provide for related purposes.		
Part	Section	Item and Description	Comments
I	IMPOSITION OF SERVICE TAX		
	1	Imposition of Service Tax	
		Subject to the provisions of this Act, there shall be charged and paid on services rendered to any person, a tax to be known as service tax.	*Changed VAT to Service Tax, as before the VAT cancellation.*
	2	Liable persons	
	(1)	The tax shall be *paid by* the person to whom the service is rendered and shall be *collected* by the person or business rendering the service, who shall be *liable to pay* the tax to the Commissioner.	*The person charging the VAT is also liable for the tax though the incidence is on the buyer*
	(2)	The tax shall *be on service rendered in Ghana* and payable to the person rendering the service at the time of receipt of payment or issue of invoice or receipt for the service.	*Responsibility of the beneficiary to pay the tax to the person rendering the service*
	3	Services subject to this Act	
		The tax payable shall apply to the provision of the *following services*:	
	(a)	entertainment;	*Compared to VAT, re-limits the scope of taxable supplies on which the Service Tax is to be imposed*
	(b)	betting;	
	(c)	accommodation and food in hotels;	
	(d)	food in restaurants and snack bars; and advertisements; and	
	(e)	such other service as the Minister may by regulations prescribe.	

Unlike the *"all-inclusive"* approach of the VAT rule—all supplies are taxable unless exempted—the new law reverts to *"taxing only specified services"* to augment the sales tax under Act 500, also restricted to the import and manufacturing stages.

As noted in *Table 3.10,* in relation to the scope of coverage, in 1997 the list of taxable transactions was expanded under *The Service Tax (Amendment) Act, 1997 (Act 529).* The Service Tax Act, 1995 (Act 501) continues in *Section 4* with the *value* for determining supply; *Section 5* on the *rate of tax;* and *Section 6* on the *administration* of the tax by IRS, concurrent with the collection of sales tax by CEPS.

Table 3.10: Value of supply of services, rate of tax and administration

Service Tax Act, 1995 (Act 501)–2 (continued)			
An Act to provide for the impositionn of tax on specified services rendered to others and to provide for related purposes.			
Part	**Section**	**Item and Description**	**Comments**
I	**IMPOSITION OF SERVCICE TAX [cont'd]**		
	4	**Value for determining tax**	
	(1)	The value for determining the tax payable on services rendered shall–	
		(a) wehre the service is ***for a monetary consideration***, be the amount of the consieration exluding the tax	*These value of trransaction rules are similar for all cosumption or indiret taxes.*
		(b) where the service is ***not for a monetary consideation*** or is only partly for monetary consideration, be the open market value of the service excluding the tax itself.	
	(2)	For the purposes of this Act, the ***open market value(OMV)*** of the service means the value determined under paragraph (a) of this section, if the person rendering the service or any other person concerned in the transaction were completely independent of each other and did not in any way influence the transaction.	*This proviso for the value of trransaction rules are similar for all cosumption or indiret taxes.*
	5	**Rate of Tax**	
		The rate of the service tax payable under this Act shall be ***15 percent*** of the value of the service rendereed.	*Same as the Sales Tax (note:* ***without ITC****, as under VAT)*
	6	**Administration of the tax**	
		The tax shall be ***collected and administeed by the Internal Revenue Service*** and for that purpose, except as otehrwise proved in this Act, the laws and regulations, including penalties applicable for the time being to the other taxes by the IRS shall, with such modication as may be ncessary, apply	*IRS had more domestic tax office to collect the domestic indirect tax on service, unlike CEPS*

Restoring the old service tax regime: In general, the old service tax was restored by STA 1995 (Act 501) at a lower rate of 15 per cent, compared to the controversial VAT rate of 17.5 per cent. However, the service tax was without the ITC and refunds for input VAT which made the VAT more efficient because it did not result in the "cascading" associated with turnover taxes.

IRS retains management of the service tax: The STA 501 also made the IRS responsible for administering the Service Tax, restoring the situation where a direct tax institution collected a consumption tax. This is an expedient move that makes it possible to use a larger number or network of IRS domestic offices to charge and enforce the collection of the service tax.

Service Tax Returns and Remittances: Table 3.11 reflects the common accountability provisions of consumption tax collection and payment every month, with most of the administrative responsibility being discharged by the registered businesses that collect the tax.

Table 3.11: Service Tax returns and remittances

Service Tax Act, 1995 (Act 501)--3 (continued)			
An Act to provide for the impositionn of tax on specified services rendered to others and to provide for related purposes.			
Part	**Section**	**Item and Description**	**Comments**
II	**TAX RETURN AND REMITTANECES**		
	7	**Tax returns and tax payment**	
	7(1)	Unless otherwise directed in writing by the Commissioner, a taxable person shall account for tax each calendar month	*Similar rule as the Sales Tax or other indirect taxes*
	(2)	The returns shall be submitted not later than the last working day of the month immediately following the month to which the returns relate.	
	(3)	The Commssioner may where he considers it ncessary, the the protection of revenue request a taxable person in writing to provide such securiy=ty as the Commissioner considers adequate.	
	(4)	The tax return shall be in such form as the Commissioner shall prescribe	
	(5)	The payment for any tax due shall reach the Commissioner not later that the last working day of the month immediately following the month to which the returns r relates	

Registration and records for Service Tax: As applies under the *general voluntary compliance rules for all taxes,* Table 1.12 obliges eligible taxpayers to register to collect the tax, keep proper records of all transactions, and pay the tax due under the relevant sections of tax laws.

Table 3.12: Obligation to register and keep proper records

Service Tax Act, 1995 (Act 501)--4 (continued)			
An Act to provide for the impositionn of tax on specified services rendered to others and to provide for related purposes.			
Part	**Section**	**Item and Description**	**Comments**
II	**TAX RETURN AND REMITTANECES**		
	8	**Keeping and production of records**	
	(1)	Every taxable person shall keep such records and books of accounts as the Commissioner may direct and ***shall produce them at such place and time*** as the Commissioner may by general notice published in the Gazette or any national newspaper or in writing to a taxable person, require.	*All registered entities are required to keep appropriate records*
	(2)	All records and books of account relating to tax payable under this Act ***shall be retained by the taxable person for at least six years*** from the date of the creation of the records or such other period as the Commissioner may allow.	*A similar primary obligation applies to the keeping of records for a specified period.*
	9	**Registration of taxable persons**	
	(1)	Any taxable ***person who is liable to pay service tax to the Commissioner shall apply*** to be registered by the Commissioner on such form as the Commissioner shall prescribe	*The obligation to register rests on the potential taxpayer--in voluntary compliance terms.*
	(2)	All persons who, ***on the coming into force of this Act, are registered with the Value Addd Tax Act, 1994 (Act 486)*** for the tax specified in this Act ***shall, on the coming into force of this Act, be deemed to have been registered for service tax under this Act***.	*This section of the law implicitly applies the VAT registration threhold as condition for the Service Tax registration.*
	(3)	For the purposes of subsection (1) of this Section, an ***application for registration shall be made within 30 days*** of the person becoming liable for	

Notification of registration and invoicing: Table 3.13 relates to general tax administrative provisions that require the Commissioner of IRS to acknowledge and confirm the registration. Similar general provisions apply to a change in business ownership as well as the invoicing.

Table 3.13: Notification of registration and invoicing

Service Tax Act, 1995 (Act 501)--5 (continued)			
An Act to provide for the impositionn of tax on specified services rendered to others and to provide for related purposes.			
Part	**Section**	**Item and Description**	**Comments**
II	**TAX RETURN AND REMITTANECES**		
	10	**Notification of registration**	
	(1)	The Commissioner shall notify a taxable person when he has been registered for Service Tax and shall issue a certificate of registration to him	*These are general tax administration provisions that require the Comssioners to acknowledge and confirm the registration. Similar general conditions apply to the change of business ownership, tx invoices and registration.*
	(2)	A taxable person shall keep exhibited in a conspicuous position at the principal place of his business , the certicate of registration.	
	11	**Change of business**	
	(1)	A registered taxable person shall notify the Commissioner in writing if the business ceases or if ownership of the business changes	
	(2)	The notifiation shall be made within thirty days of the cessation or change of ownership.	
	12	**Issue and content of tax invoice**	
		A taxable person shall on rendering service to a customer issue to the customer, a tax invoice in a form specified by the Commissioner	
	13	**Retention of tax invoice**	
		A taxable person who issues tax invoices shall retain a copy of each tax invoice issued in a serial number order	
	14	**Notification of registration**	
		Where any doubt arises as i=to whether this Act is applicatble to any business or person, the doubt shall be resolved by the Commioner without prejudice to any	

Miscellaneous provisions—exemption and regulations: Table 3.14 covers Part III of STA 501, which deals with the power to grant exemptions and issue Regulations under the substantive Act.

Table 3.14: Miscellaneous provisions

Service Tax Act, 1995 (Act 501)–6 (continued)			
An Act to provide for the impositionn of tax on specified services rendered to others and to provide for related purposes.			
Part	**Section**	**Item and Description**	**Comments**
III	**MISCELLANEOUS PROVISIONS**		
	15	**Exemption**	
		The Ministrr may by leegislative insttument provide for bodies, organizations, and individuals exeempted from the provisions of this Act	
	16	**Regulations**	
		The Minister may by legislative instrument make regulations providing for–	
		(a) other exemptiosn; (b) issue of tickets or recreipt bookd; and © generally giving full effet to the implementation of this Act.	
	17	Interpretation	

Miscellaneous and transitions: Table 3.15 continues with the miscellaneous provisions that deal with savings and transitional provisions that ensured a smooth suspension as well as the careful preservation of rights and obligations previously registered taxpayers of under the repealed VAT Act law. These provisions, notably the right to VAT ITC and refunds under the repealed law, contributed to a better understanding of the benefits of VAT and, subsequently, its reintroduction.

Table 3.15: Miscellaneous—savings and transition provisions

Service Tax Act, 1995 (Act 501)--7 (continued)			
An Act to provide for the impositionn of tax on specified services rendered to others and to provide for related purposes.			
Part	**Section**	**Item and Description**	**Comments**
III	**MISCELLANEOUS PROVISIONS [details as in the Act]**		
	18	**Savings and transition provisions**	
	(1)	Notwithstanding the repeal of the VAT Act, 1994 under the CEPS (Management) (Amendment)(No.2) act, 1995 (Act 500), any person employed for the VAT Service and who was in the said employment immediately before the coming into force of this Act, may be	*These deal with the various amendments and repeals that restored the VAT to its current scheme after the cancellation in 1995.*
	(a)	assigned to the IRS to assist with the collection of the service tax by the Minister, after consultation with by the Minister with the IRS Board; or	
	(b)	assigned to the Ministry of Finance in consultation with the Civil Service Council to monitor the collection of taxes and perform such functions as the Minister may determine.	
	(2)	Notwithstanding the repeal of the VAT Act, 1994 (Act 486) and the regulations made thereunder by section 5 of the CEPS (Management) (Amendment)(No.2) Act, 1995 (Act 500), the provisions in the repealed enatment shall remain in force for a period of not more than four months--	

	(a)	for the purpose of verifying the relevant tax returns; and	
	(b)	for the assessment and recovery of any arrears or penalties payable	
		under the repealed enatmenets immediately before the oming into force of this Act	
	(3)	Without prejudice to the provisions in subsection (2) of this section, the Commissioner shall issue guidelines for the determination of claims and payments under the VAT Act before the repeal	
(a) ***Assent:*** *June 14, 1995; (b)* ***Gazette notification*** *: June 14, 1995*			

Service Tax (Amendment) Act, 1997 (Act 529): The amendment Act extended the scope of the services tax but not to the extent of the "all-inclusive" and comprehensive base of the VAT, unless specified otherwise by law. The full scope of Act 529 is shown below in Table 3.16

Table 3.16 Addition of more taxable services under STA 501

The Service Tax (Amendment) Act, 1997 (Act 529)			
An Act to amend the STA, 1995 (Act 501) ***to extend*** the tax to the provision of additional services.			
Section	**Item and Description**		**Comments**
1	**Section 3 of Act 501 amended**		
	The Service Tax Act, 1995 (Act 501) is amended by the ***insertion immediately after paragraph (e) of of Section 3*** of the following new paragraphs		*Note that it extends the scope of selected taxable supplies under The Service Tax Act, 1995 (Act 501). Noneless, the service tax remains selective and not as comprehensive as VAT.*
	(f)	management services;	
	(g)	services provided by financial analysts, financial advisers, tax practitioners and economic consultants;	
	(h)	accounting services (including any types of auditing, book-keeping and related services;	
	(i)	legal services where the fee charged exceeds Ghc200,000;	
	(j)	services provided by architects (including services provided by lanscape designers and draughtsmen)	
	(k)	services provided by land, building and quantity surveyors;	
	(l)	services provided by insurance brokers, insurance assessors, fire and marine insurance loss adjusters and similar service;	
	(m)	services provided by consulting engineers and similar technical services;	
	(n)	courier services;	
	(o)	mobile cellular phone service.	
2	**New Section 5(A) inserted**		
	The Service Tax Act, 1995 (Act 501) is further amended by the insertion immediately after paragraph (e) of of Section 5 of the following new section		
	5A	Notwithstanding s5, the rate of service tax payable under the Act in respect of (f) to (p) of s3 shall be 10 percent of the value of the service rendered.	*Recall that the STA standard rate is 15 percent.*
(a) ***Assent:*** *May 6, 1997; (b)* ***Gazette notification*** *: May 23, 1997*			

Implicit plan to retain features of invoice-credit VAT: The nature of amendments in these laws suggest an intention to reintroduce VAT after the 1996 elections since they retained the VATS organization and staffing but under the IRS. They also kept the right to ITC and refund VAT collection between 1995 and 1996. This was achieved under VATA 1998 (Act 546), as discussed below.

The decision to cancel or suspend the VAT implementation led to various repeals of VATA, 1994 (Act 486) and, substantively, restoration of the old service and sales tax regimes under IRS and CEPS respectively. The Sales Tax was on manufactured and imported goods while the Service Tax was on selected services. VATA 486 took effect in January 1995, at a rate of 15 per cent when, within two months, it increased to 17.5 per cent.

6. VAT reintroduction law: VATA 1998 (Act 546)

VATA 546 was Ghana's second VAT Act that was also used to reintroduce the VAT in 1998/99. It covers the underlying principles of VAT and became the subject of several amendments that distorted the original VAT structure. The Parent Act and its amendments are summarized in this chapter and discussed in more detail in subsequent chapters.

Several of the distortions remained in operation until VATA 2013 (Act 870) was passed to adopt a more efficient VAT structure. However, in tune with the apparent political-economy treatment of VAT issues discussed in Chapter 14, several of these clean-ups and enhancements were reversed again after another change in government in 2017, resulting in the restoration of the distortions to the VAT regime.

Elements of VATA, 1998 (Act 546)

The main sections of VATA 546, which was Ghana's original VAT law, are summarized at a high level in this section in terms of (a) key elements that defined the VAT invoice-credit mechanism; (b) the amendments that began to distort the VAT regime; and (c) its relevance for the *first major review* of the VAT regime in VATA 2015 (Act 870).

The next chapter discusses the features of the invoice-credit VAT regime while Section 5.2 discusses the amendments to the Act. The elements of VATA 870 are discussed in Part II, Chapter 5—which latter Act also being a major review of the Value Added Tax Act [VATA], 1998 (Act 546). Table 3.17 shows the Parts of VATA 546 while the specific Sections under the Parts are reproduced in Appendix 1.1.

Table 3.17: Summary of VAT Act 1998 (Act 546)

Be it enaɔted by Parliament as follows:		
Parts	**Descriptions**	**Sections**
I	Imposition of Value Added Tax	**1 - 3**
II	Taxable person	**4 - 8**
III	Suppliy of goods and serviɔes	**9 - 12**
IV	Taxable supplies	**13 - 17**
V	Time and plaɔe of supplies	**18 - 21**
VI	Taxable value	**22 - 23**
VII	Deduɔtion of input tax and refunds	**24 - 27**
VIII	Tax returns, reɔords and assessment	**28 - 30**
IX	Reɔovery of due tax, interest and other liabilities	**31 - 35**
X	Administration of Value Added Tax	**36 - 53**
XI	Obæɔtions and appeals	**54 - 55**
XII	Offenɔes and penalties	**56 - 72**
XIII	Misɔellaneous provisions	**73 - 79**
Schedules		***1 - 5***

The ensuing sub-section highlights the *main tax policy changes and related legislative amendments to VATA 546* that caused significant distortions in the implementation of VAT between 1998 and 2013 before the major review was undertaken in the form of VATA 870.

7. Summary of Major Amendment to VATA 1998 (Act 546)

The sub-section shows that *the substantive amendments* were exemptions and domestic zero-rating of *pharmaceutical and agricultural supplies*. It reflects the ability of business groups to effect changes to policy and legislation. The zero-rating of domestic supplies is often administered poorly because of a lack of adequate funds to pay refunds.

The sub-section also summarizes the amendments that led to the imposition of a *flat 3 percent VAT sub-standard rate,* without recourse to ITC, under the *VAT Flat Rate Scheme (VFRS).* It continues to apply to *"retailers of goods"* since a recent extension to wholesalers was rescinded. The VFRS is discussed in detail in Part II (Chapter 4).

Pharmaceuticals (Schedule 1): Table 3.18 shows the summary of amendments relating to specified pharmaceutical supplies with the concessions being mainly granted on social intervention grounds.

Table 3.18: Exempt pharmaceutical supplies

Amendments: Exempt supplies (Schedule 1–Pharmaceuticals)					
Year	VATA (#)	Section	Content or Change	Book Chapter	Comments
2000	579	14/16	Exempt supplies	6	Pharmaceuticals [Schedule 1 and new Schedule 1A]
2001	595	14/16	Exempt supplies	6	Pharmaceuticals
2004	670	14/16	Exempt supplies	6	Pharmaceuticals (New Schedule 1B)
2008	765	14/16	Exempt supplies	6	Pharmaceuticals [HS Code/Minister]
2010	810	14/16	Exempt supplies	6	Pharmaceuticals

The additional *pharmaceutical exemptions* fell under a new Schedule 1A while the *domestic zero-rated supplies* showed as amendments to Schedule 2 (zero-rating, which is normally reserved for exports) as well as Schedule 3 (reliefs, usually for the President of the Republic and diplomats).

Agricultural supplies (Schedule 1): Agricultural supplies also attract concessions in many countries because of the favourable social and economic view of peasant or small-holder farming and food security for low-income persons. *Table 3.19* shows the scope of amendments for final, primary, or intermediate supplies. In particular, the *upstream and midstream* exemptions lead to cascading and high consumer prices but fail to increase tax revenues, due to tax evasion and avoidance.

Table 3.19: Exempt Agricultural supplies and inputs

Amendments: Exempt supplies (Schedule 1–Agriculture)					
Year	VATA (#)	Section	Content or Change	Book Chapter	Comments
2002	629	14/16	Exempt supplies	6	Agriculture supplies and inputs
2004	671	14/16	Exempt supplies	6	Fishing inputs; musical instruments [HS Code Chapter 92]
2008	765	14/16	Exempt supplies	6	Agricultural inputs

Other exempt supplies (Schedule 1): Table 3.20 shows the *addition of more products* to the VAT Schedule 1 exemption, which results in complex VAT administration and compliance difficulties.

Table 3.20: Other exempt supplies

Amendments: Exempt supplies (Schedule 1–Others)					
Year	VATA (#)	Section	Content or Change	Book Chapter	Comments
2002	629	16	Exempt imports	6	Clarifies nature of exempt supply
2002	629	14/16	Exempt supplies	6	Buildings; mosquito & salt
2003	639	14/16	Exempt supplies	6	Compact Flourescent Lights (CFL); Fully-assembled computers (imports/domestic]
2006	696	14/16	Exempt supplies	6	Correction
2008	752	14/16	Exempt supplies	6	Telephone/cellular phone
2008	765	14/16	Exempt supplies	6	Repeal and consolidation of Schedule 1, 1A & 1B as new Schedule 1
2010	810	14/16	Exempt supplies	6	Definition: coverage of "transportation"
2010	810	14/16	Exempt supplies	6	Textbooks and agricultural machinery

Zero-rated (Schedule 3) supplies: By convention, the original VATA Act 546 restricted zero-rating to exports and ship supplies, which led to refunds because it offsets zero (0) Output Tax against positive Input VAT at the standard rate. In contrast, the amendments in Table 3.21 extend the exemptions to domestic supplies (i.e., educational materials and locally manufactured inputs).

Table 3.21: Additions to zero-rated supplies

Amendments: Zero-rated supplies (Schedule 2)					
Year	VATA (#)	Section	Content or Change	Book Chapter	Comments
2006	696	15	Zero-rated supply	6	Locally produced text/exercise books
2006	696	15	Zero-rated supply	6	Locally manufactured agricultural machinery & implements
2008	765	15	Zero-rated supply	2 & 6	Zero-rating pharmaceuticals

The main obstacle to the smooth implementation of zero-rated domestic supply is that it worsens the effects of inadequate budgetary provisions to support the payment of tax refunds to a larger number of taxpayers.

Relief supplies (Schedule 3): the scope of conventional exempt relief supplies is limited and, in the case of diplomats, they are subject to reciprocal rules under the Vienna Convention. As with income tax, reliefs also apply to the Office of the President, as with the income tax.

Table 3.22 worsens the distortions by extending the concession to members of the Association of Ghana Industries (AGI), who may also buy imported inputs from non-members "midstream" and "upstream". The concession is likely to lead to distortions since the cash-flow advantage to members of the Association will not extend to importers that are not members and are often small and medium-scale entities.

Table 3.22: Additions to exempt relief supplies

Amendments: Relief Supplies [Schedule 3)					
Year	VATA (#)	Section	Content or Change	Book Chapter	Comments
2004	671	17	Relief for regular supply	8	Relief from payment of VAT on raw materials, at importation to members of Association of Ghana Industries (AGI)
2010	810	LI 1817	Revoked	2	GIPC VAT powers to grant reliefs; deletions

VFRS and registration threshold: The original VAT Act 456 was not based on the conventional approach of registering only entities that have annual sales or turnover above a given threshold. Instead, it restricts the non-registration of small entities to only "retailers of goods". As Table 3.23 shows, the VAT Act 2001 (Act 595) continued to apply this provision to a *lower registration threshold amount* of GH₵ 10,000, instead of GH₵ 20,000 in the VAT Act 546. This had the potential of roping in many smaller entities than required, which cannot keep proper records in the VAT base.

Table 3.23: Changes in VAT registration threshold policy

Amendments: Sections [Registration]					
Year	VATA (#)	Section	Content or Change	Book Chapter	Comments
2001	595	s5(1)	Registration threshold	2 & 9	Lowers and restricts annual ***VFRS registration threshold*** to only a "retailer of goods"
2010	810	5	Registration threshold		Restores conventional VAT registration threshold [Ghc90,000] & 3% VFRS to entities with annual turnover between Ghc10,000 & Ghc90,000.

Further VFRS changes: Table 3.24 shows the distortionary effects of the VFRS sub-standard rate of 3 per cent, which continued to apply to only *"retailers of goods"* at a lower registration threshold of GH₵ 10,000 and with no recourse to ITC claims. This "retail" qualification was stopped with the enactment of the VAT(Amendment) Act, 2010 (Act 810), which *made the registration threshold applicable to all entities.* Table 3.20: VFRS and alongside the conventional VAT threshold.

Table 3.24: Further VFRS Laws and Provisions

Amendments: Sections [VAT standard & VFRS rates]					
Year	**VATA (#)**	**Section**	**Content or Change**	**Book Chapter**	**Comments**
2000	579	s3	Standard rate	3	Increase from 10% to 12.5% for GET-Fund
2007	734	s3	VFRS (3%)	9	Applicable to taxabler person who is **"retailer of goods"**
	734	s76	VFRS (3%)		Definition VFRS as approximate margin between Output VAT and Input VAT
2010	810	s3	Standard rate	3	Taxable supplies above threshold of Ghc90,000 p.a.
2010	810	s3	VFRS (3%)	9	Rate applicable to **all entities, not "retailer of goods"** only, with annual turnover between Ghc10,000 and Ghc90,000

***Denial of VAT ITC and VAT refunds*:** Table 3.25 - it must be noted that the new flat rate of 3 per cent in the amendments:

i. does not allow taxpayers to claim ITC for the taxes paid on inputs or purchases;

ii. *zero-rates locally produced* textbooks and exercise books as well as *locally manufactured* agricultural machinery and other agricultural implements or tools (under Schedule 3 [reliefs], are not under the general Schedule 2 zero-rating); and

iii. lowers the excess value of total supplies exported from 70 per cent to 25 per cent

iv. but adds a provision that makes the *right to refunds subject to proving that the taxpayer has repatriated the export proceeds to a bank in Ghana.*

Table 3.25: Denial of ITC

Amendments: Sections [Input Tax Credit or ITC]					
Year	**VATA (#)**	**Section**	**Content or Change**	**Book Chapter**	**Comments**
2006	696	s25	Input Tax Credit [ITC]	2 & 8	Discretion for Cgto offset rather than grant automatic ITC/refunds
2007	734	s24(6a)	VFRS & ITC		Disallows ITC for VFRS
2008	765	s24	ITC		Power of Commissioner to make offsets rather than refunds for excess credit

VAT offences and penalties: As noted in Part IV Table 3.26 shows amendments that affected offences and penalties—before the consolidation under RAA, 2016 (Act 915).

Table 3.26: Offences and penalties

Amendments: Sections [Offences and penalties]					
Year	**VATA (#)**	**Section**	**Content or Change**	**Book Chapter**	**Comments**
2008	765	68(3)	Seal Off	2	New Warrant of Seal Off as Schedule 5B
2010	810	62	Obstruction of Officer	12	Penalty for obstruction of Officer

In summary, the cumbersome changes to the exempt and zero-rating VAT supply rules that the amendments in Tables 1.12 to 1.21 make it difficult for business entities to meet their obligations smoothly and for the tax agency to administer and enforce the law effectively. It is these distortions and the advances in VAT structure and administration that gave rise to the passage of a third substantive enactment of the VAT Act, 2013 (Act 970).

8. VAT Revamp: VAT Act, 2013 (Act 870) and amendments

The VAT Act 870 and, later VAT Act 890, *are unique as complete rewrites, not amendments,* of VATA 546. They clarify and *restore the exempt status* of domestic supplies, *as opposed to zero-rating*. However, as if to give effect to the political-economy nature of VAT in Ghana, a change of Government in 2017 to NPP II reversed many of the enhanced provisions of VATA 870.

Two of the changes affect the structure of VAT substantively and restore past complex provisions that led to cascading and distortion—namely, the blocking of ITC through the VAT Flat Rate Scheme (VFRS) and the change in status of GETFund Levy and NHIL from *de facto VAT regimes* to so-called Straight Levies. Table 3.27 summarizes the various rewrites of VAT Act 870 and later Amendment Acts that are discussed in detail in Chapters 4 and 5.

Table 3.27: Summary of VAT Act, 2013 (Act 870) and Amendments

Year	VATA	Description/Comments
2013	870	Comprehensive review and replacement of VATA 1998 (Act 546); update VAT rules and principles for Ghana's new economy.
2015	890	The exempt status of pharmaceuticals, paper, and steel; also imposed a flat 5% VAT on real estate development, without recourse to input tax credit (ITC).
2017	948	Restores exempt status of real estate, domestic air travel, hydrocarbon, and immovable property; introduces VFRS at 3 per cent for both retail and wholesale sectors
	948	Various specific changes to VAT Schedules, including exemptions, domestic zero-rating and reliefs
	954	Exemption for Lotteries Authority and gaming products
		Change in definition of communication; clauses on *Withholding Agents & VAT Credit Certificate*
2018	970	Decoupled NHIL & GETFund Levy, as "Straight" levies (i.e., 2.5%+2.5% = 5%, without recourse to ITC. Hence, lowers the standard VAT rate to 12.5 per cent.
2018	980	Exemption of locally manufactured textiles
2019	1005	Exemption from the payment of VAT on imports of plant and machinery designed specifically for use in the automobile industry, management fees for private equity, venture capital and mutual funds.
2021	1072	Applied a limitation of the flat rate to retailers with a turnover not exceeding five hundred thousand Ghana Cedis and extended the VAT zero-rate on African prints for local textile manufacturers by a period of two years
2022	1082	Provided and up-front payment of Value Added Tax by an Un-registered importer, taxation of electronic commerce, electronic issuance of tax invoice, zero-rating of the supply of locally assembled vehicles
2022	1087	Increased the standard VAT rate to 15%

9. Conclusion

The fiscal measures that lead to *national progress, development and stability* for nations include sound and incremental tax policy and administration reforms. Though *systemic in hindsight,* they include setbacks as well as consistent, and contradictory measures that follow domestic and global or external trends, experiences, and initiatives. Over the *medium term,* tax policy measures such as VAT tend to show *significant policy and legislative measures and reviews* that have far-reaching consequences for their administration and compliance.

The *wider political, social and economic context and exigencies* require policymakers and politicians to take *pragmatic steps and measures that may be less ideal or optimal*. This is the background to the topics covered in Part II (Legislation), Part III (Policy Review), Part IV (Administration Framework) and Part V (Political Economy Context) including amendments to the two substantive VATA 546 (1998) and VATA 870 (2013) laws.

They show that within the context of Ghana's charged two-party (NDC and NPP) political environment, the country often enacted laws that reverse and distort many previous sound tax policies, principles and structures. The case of VAT was its most obvious, with ambivalent and progressive measures that improved or reversed both good and bad policies. The trend occurs in other African countries where some reversals restore previously flawed sales and service tax regimes that VAT was designed to replace.

Some of these states, including Ghana, have attained Lower Upper Middle-Income Country (L-MIC) and Upper-Middle-Income Country (U-MIC) status. Hence, they need stable tax structures, with efficient administration and enforcement elements, to *generate sufficient revenues to replace the inevitable loss of grants and concessional loans*. These are relatively soft funds from multilateral agencies such as the World Bank and African Development Bank [AfDB] and aid or grants from bilateral advanced countries and non-governmental sources.

The countries in this transition mode are not able to raise sufficient revenue from these traditional sources, they resort to the capital markets where *non-performance can easily lead to public debt distress and possible default*. The outcomes include further resort to even more *costly debt and ratings downgrade* that worsen the *impact of the global and domestic crises* that have occurred frequently in the last two decades.

The chapters use a standard *value addition table* to assess the underlying policy changes that distort the VAT regime at the downstream (distribution); upstream (manufacturing and imports); and midstream (wholesale) stages. In future, policymakers can use the format to predict the likely impact of politically motivated policy changes.

Appendix Chapter 1

Appendix Table 1.1: Parts and Sections of Value Added Tax 1998 (Act 546)

<table>
<tr><th colspan="4">Parts and Sections of VATA</th></tr>
<tr><td colspan="4">VALUE ADDED TAX ACT [VATA] 1998 (Act 546)</td></tr>
<tr><td colspan="4">An Act to provide for the imposition of Value Added Tax (VAT) and to provide for purposes related to the tax.</td></tr>
<tr><td colspan="4">Be it enacted by Parliament as follows;</td></tr>
<tr><td>Part</td><td>Section</td><td>Item and Description</td><td>Comments</td></tr>
<tr><td>I</td><td colspan="3">IMPOSITION OF VALUE-ADDED TAX</td></tr>
<tr><td rowspan="3"></td><td>1</td><td>Imposition of tax</td><td rowspan="3">The persons or business entities that must register to charge VAT at the rate in the law.</td></tr>
<tr><td>2</td><td>Persons liable to tax</td></tr>
<tr><td>3</td><td>Rate of Tax</td></tr>
<tr><td>II</td><td colspan="3">TAXABLE PERSON</td></tr>
<tr><td rowspan="5"></td><td>4</td><td>Taxable person</td><td rowspan="5">Persons also refer to "taxpayers" in some laws but are not confused with final consumers who pay the tax VAT. Small entities are not required to register and charge Output VAT.</td></tr>
<tr><td>5</td><td>Registration of taxable person</td></tr>
<tr><td>6</td><td>Register and particulars of taxable person</td></tr>
<tr><td>7</td><td>Change of business</td></tr>
<tr><td>8</td><td>Cancellation of Registration</td></tr>
<tr><td>III</td><td colspan="3">SUPPLY OF GOODS AND SERVICES</td></tr>
<tr><td rowspan="4"></td><td>9</td><td>Supply of goods</td><td rowspan="4">Some goods and services, called supplies, are excluded from the VAT base on various grounds (e.g., basic goods to benefit low-income citizens)</td></tr>
<tr><td>10</td><td>Supply of services</td></tr>
<tr><td>11</td><td>Mixed supply</td></tr>
<tr><td>12</td><td>Supply by agent</td></tr>
<tr><td>IV</td><td colspan="3">TAXABLE SUPPLY</td></tr>
<tr><td rowspan="5"></td><td>13</td><td>Taxable supply</td><td rowspan="5">Part IV describes the different types of supplies, including zero-rated supplies that typically apply to exports (to avoid imposing the tax on foreigners who buy the exported supply).</td></tr>
<tr><td>14</td><td>Exempt supply</td></tr>
<tr><td>15</td><td>Zero-rated supply</td></tr>
<tr><td>16</td><td>Exempt import</td></tr>
<tr><td>17</td><td>Relief supply</td></tr>
</table>

<table>
<tr><td>V</td><td colspan="3">TIME AND PLACE OF SUPPLY</td></tr>
<tr><td rowspan="3"></td><td>18</td><td>Time of supply</td><td rowspan="3">The time and place of supply vary among different types of businesses' practices.</td></tr>
<tr><td>19</td><td>Issue of tax invoice</td></tr>
<tr><td>20</td><td>Place of supply</td></tr>
<tr><td>VI</td><td colspan="3">VALUE OF SUPPLY</td></tr>
<tr><td rowspan="3"></td><td>21</td><td>Value of Supply</td><td rowspan="3">The value of supply also depends on a variety of business terms and conditions.</td></tr>
<tr><td>22</td><td>Value for determining the tax on imported supply</td></tr>
<tr><td>23</td><td>Adjustments</td></tr>
<tr><td>VII</td><td colspan="3">DEDUCTION OF INPUT TAX AND REFUNDS</td></tr>
<tr><td rowspan="4"></td><td>24</td><td>Credit for deductible input tax</td><td rowspan="4">These sections deal with the right of registered entities to "offset" the VAT paid on purchases (inputs) against the VAT charged on sales (output).</td></tr>
<tr><td>25</td><td>Refund or credit for excess tax paid</td></tr>
<tr><td>26</td><td>Deductible tax for mixed taxable and exempt supply</td></tr>
<tr><td>27</td><td>Time of payment of refund</td></tr>
<tr><td>VIII</td><td colspan="3">TAX RETURNS, RECORDS, AND ASSESSMENT</td></tr>
<tr><td rowspan="3"></td><td>28</td><td>Submission of tax returns and date of payment of the tax</td><td rowspan="3">Administrative provisions that require the registered taxpayer to meet their obligations "voluntarily"</td></tr>
<tr><td>29</td><td>Records to be kept for purposes of the tax</td></tr>
<tr><td>30</td><td>Assessment of the tax and correction of return</td></tr>
<tr><td>IX</td><td colspan="3">RECOVERY OF DUE TAX, INTEREST AND OTHER LIABILITIES</td></tr>
<tr><td rowspan="5"></td><td>31</td><td>Recovery of tax due</td><td rowspan="5">Basic administration and compliance provisions that are found in many direct and indirect tax laws.</td></tr>
<tr><td>32</td><td>Payment of interest and outstanding tax</td></tr>
<tr><td>33</td><td>Garnishment</td></tr>
<tr><td>34</td><td>Restraint of liability</td></tr>
<tr><td>35</td><td>Recovery in respect of persons under liquidation</td></tr>
</table>

X	ADMINISTRATION OF VALUE ADDED TAX (VAT)		
	36	Establishment of Value Added Tax (VAT) Service	The Act was used to *create the VAT Service* under the oversight *Board of Directors*. It also gives significant operational powers to the *Commissioner* (now the Commissioner-General [CG]) and officials of the now defunct VAT Service to manage the tax.
	37	The functions of the Service	
	38	Members of the Service	
	39	Governing body of the Service	
	40	Qualification of members	
	41	Functions of the Board	
	42	Tenure of the Board	
	43	Meetings of the Board	
	44	Commissioner of VAT and his functions	
	45	Deputy Commissioners and their Functions	
	46	Secretary to the Board	
	47	Internal Auditor	
	48	Other staff of the Service	
	49	Delegation of Powers of Appointment	
	50	Expenses of the Service	
	51	Accounts and Audit	
	52	Payment of tax into the Consolidated Fund	
	53	Annual reports	
X1	OBJECTIONS AND APPEALS		
	54	Objections to decisions of an officer other than the Commissioner	Taxpayer's right of *appeal* to the Courts
	55	Appeal to court	

<table>
<tr><td>XII</td><td colspan="3">OFFENCES AND PENALTIES</td></tr>
<tr><td rowspan="17"></td><td>56</td><td>Failure to register</td><td rowspan="17">The Act requires taxpayers to comply voluntarily, as with the obligation under other forms of direct and indirect taxes. Consequently, the CG is also vested with powers of enforcement under the law. However, taxpayers have recourse to appeal to the Courts where they disagree with the decision of the CG or tax officials.</td></tr>
<tr><td>57</td><td>Failure to issue a tax invoice</td></tr>
<tr><td>58</td><td>False or misleading statement</td></tr>
<tr><td>59</td><td>Falsification and alteration of documents</td></tr>
<tr><td>60</td><td>Evasion of tax payment</td></tr>
<tr><td>61</td><td>Failure to maintain proper records</td></tr>
<tr><td>62</td><td>Obstruction of Officer of the Service</td></tr>
<tr><td>63</td><td>Offences relating to officers</td></tr>
<tr><td>64</td><td>Protection of officers</td></tr>
<tr><td>65</td><td>Relationship of the Service and other public services</td></tr>
<tr><td>66</td><td>Taking of Samples</td></tr>
<tr><td>67</td><td>Power of inspection and warrants</td></tr>
<tr><td>68</td><td>Power to seal off premises</td></tr>
<tr><td>69</td><td>Provision of information</td></tr>
<tr><td>70</td><td>General penalty</td></tr>
<tr><td>71</td><td>Penalty for unauthorized collection of the tax</td></tr>
<tr><td>72</td><td>Compounding of offences</td></tr>
<tr><td>XII</td><td colspan="3">MISCELLANEOUS PROVISIONS</td></tr>
<tr><td rowspan="7"></td><td>73</td><td>Evidence in proceedings</td><td rowspan="7">Various other provisions to (a) make the VAT regime efficient and effective; and (b) ensure a smooth transition from the old sales and service taxes as well as administration, including the date on which the tax should commence or start.</td></tr>
<tr><td>74</td><td>Regulations</td></tr>
<tr><td>75</td><td>Directives and other powers of the Commissioner</td></tr>
<tr><td>76</td><td>Interpretation</td></tr>
<tr><td>77</td><td>Consequential amendments</td></tr>
<tr><td>78</td><td>Repeals, savings and transitional provisions</td></tr>
<tr><td>79</td><td>Commencement</td></tr>
<tr><td colspan="4">SCHEDULES</td></tr>
</table>

Chapter 4

BASIC MECHANICS OF THE VAT INVOICE-CREDIT METHOD

1. Introduction

The Value Added Tax (VAT), which is also called Goods and Services Tax (GST) in countries such as Canada, is the main method for collecting general consumption taxes. Other methods include sales and turnover taxes that increase costs and prices at multiple stages. While VAT is collected at multiple stages, its impact on costs is minimized by the input tax credit (ITC) and refund for the VAT paid on inputs by registered business-to-business (B2B) entities.

> *Value Added Tax (VAT):* As noted in Chapter 1, since the 1980s, advanced, emerging and developing countries have used the VAT as a new form of general consumption tax or to refine existing turnover, service and sales taxes.
>
> *Credit method:* This Chapter discusses its ***Invoice-Credit or Input Tax Credit (ITC) attribute***, which is more effective in ensuring that the burden falls on final consumers and not on businesses or foreign consumers.
>
> ***Sales and turnover taxes:*** Chapter 3 discusses the more distortionary ***turnover and sales taxes*** that did not have an "offset" method for taxes paid by registered firms on inputs. To mitigate its adverse impact, countries implemented various ***suspension or deferral schemes*** for such input taxes.
>
> *Coverage of services:* It was common for countries to augment the sales tax on goods with service tax regimes on selected services—usually, professional services such as law, accounting, and architecture.
>
> ***Point of collection:*** These constraints resulted in tax agencies collecting the ***sales tax*** at the distribution or consumer stage only while some developing states restricted it further "upstream" to the manufacturing and import stages.

The goal of suspension schemes is to ensure that only the final consumer pays the tax as an increase in the price of goods or services.

However, the VAT invoice-credit scheme is more efficient since it is better at imposing the general consumption tax as a ***business-to-consumer (B2C)*** tax and not a ***business-to-business (B2B)*** tax. It allows ***registered VAT entities*** to offset or claim a credit for VAT paid on inputs related to taxable supplies.

2. Invoice-Credit VAT Method

The ***ideal Invoice-Credit VAT method*** imposes the ***Output VAT*** on all taxable supplies of goods and services. Since it is a tax on consumption, not businesses, it allows ***registered*** entities, taxpayers or persons to ***offset the Input VAT*** paid against the Output VAT collected. The main features of the invoice-credit VAT mechanism include the following—

> ***Value addition:*** Ideally, transactions start with ***domestic supplies*** at the farm gate or agricultural stage and ***externally*** with ***importers*** paying the initial VAT since the country of origin applies a zero (0) rate to exports. ***Value addition*** means that many ***registered (and unregistered) business entities,*** manufacturers, wholesalers, and distributors add to production and distribution costs until a final sale is made to a consumer.
>
> ***VAT destination rule:*** In essence and principle, VAT is imposed on domestic supplies and imports at a standard and, exceptionally, lower or higher positive rates (now ideally assigned to excise tax regimes). Hence, by applying a ***zero (0) rate to exports,*** VAT became a destination-state tax that ***alleviates its burden on exporting or origin-state businesses*** and consumers—except under the special supply rules for services.
>
> ***Taxable and exempt supply:*** The supply of goods and services are classified as taxable and exempt for purposes of VAT administration, with only the taxable supplies attracting Output VAT. In contrast, the exempt and relief supplies do not attract VAT on grounds of social intervention, technical difficulties and special dispensation that includes diplomats.
>
> ***Non-registration:*** In general, VAT laws oblige entities making ***annual total sales or turnover*** above a given "threshold" amount to register and charge VAT on t***axable supplies***. Hence, they exclude small entities with sales below the threshold from registering for VAT, filing a return and making payment. However, the VAT regime became more complex with the

implementation of the VAT Flat Rate Scheme (VFRS) that was extended to larger retailers and wholesalers.

ITC and reverse invoicing: The ***ITC*** process allows a registered entity to offset the ***Input VAT*** on purchases against the ***Output VAT*** on sales and pay only the ***Net VAT*** to a tax office. Hence, until a final consumer receives goods or services, the Output VAT on a sales invoice for sellers represents the Input VAT on a purchases invoice for the buyer. This reverse sales and purchase invoicing feature is a key feature of the VAT mechanism.

Invoices as prerequisites for ITC: The right to ITC or refunds is subject to (a) VAT registration; and (b) producing a VAT invoice during audits or examinations to prove that the Input VAT was paid by registered entities along the production-distribution chain. Only ***registered entities*** can charge VAT on sales and claim ***input tax credit (ITC)*** on purchases. Hence, the ITC paid by ***non-registered VAT entities*** adds to costs and prices.

In summary, the ***"value addition"*** process ends at the consumption stage, where a final buyer consumes the goods or services. The book uses the ***same "value addition" table*** in all the Chapters to show how importers, producers or manufacturers, wholesalers, and retailers build the value for the goods and services that end with consumers.

3. Importance of supplies and invoices

VAT is a tax on the "additional value" that business entities "add" to the cost of ***supplies*** at each stage of the production-distribution process. The ***Output VAT*** charged by sellers appears explicitly on ***sales invoices*** and is the opposite of the ***Input VAT*** on the buyer's ***purchase invoice***. Under the ***Invoice Credit VAT method***, registered entities claim a VAT "credit" by offsetting the Input VAT against the Output VAT and paying the difference ("net" VAT) to the tax office.

Supplies: the term supplies refer to ***both goods and services*** under VAT regimes and may fall into the following categories:

taxable supplies refer to goods and services that attract Output VAT, including zero-rate (0) and on which registered entities are eligible to claim ITC or refunds;

non-taxable supplies usually basic or special goods and services that do not attract Output VAT and make the business entity ineligible to claim ITC—which, as discussed later, are normally grouped as exempt or relief supplies; and

mixed supplies: which refer to registered taxpayers making combinations of taxable and non-taxable, usually exempt, supplies—leading to apportionment of ITC claims (Chapters 4 and 8).

Invoice-Credit VAT process: The following features of the mechanism embody the obligation to charge VAT and the right to claim ITC.

Output VAT: the VAT charged on the turnover or sales to consumers of taxable supplies by registered business entities.

Input VAT: the reverse of Output VAT is the VAT on purchases of taxable supplies by registered and non-registered entities as well as consumers.

Input Tax Credit (ITC): the key element of the Invoice-Credit VAT method is the right of registered entities to offset the Input VAT (paid) against the Output VAT (charged).

Payment of tax due: registered entities pay the net amount (i.e., Output VAT less Input VAT) to their registered tax offices.

Refunds: some registered taxpayers may claim refunds, not credits, where the Input VAT exceeds Output VAT, in zero-rated exports and input VAT is paid upfront on investments at an early phase of doing business and prior to making sales or turnover.

VAT invoices and ITC: registered entities claim ITC when they possess a *VAT invoice,* as evidence of paying the Input VAT—with the same sales invoice issued by the seller being the purchase invoice for the buyer making the ITC claim.

To reiterate, VAT is a form of general consumption tax (GCT), together with turnover and sales taxes while the invoice-credit method compares with other methods of collection such as the *addition or subtraction* methods. These alternatives of consumption or expenditure taxes are discussed and compared with the VAT credit method in more detail in the ensuing Chapters 3, 4 and 5.

4. Registration for VAT

The envisaged criterion for voluntary or compulsory registration for VAT as a taxpayer, at the time of introducing the VAT in 1995 and at its reintroduction in 1998, was the domestic currency (cedi) equivalent of minimum annual turnover or sales of US$50,000. To date, Ghana has not enacted a threshold at this level despite two increases in the cedi amount to GHȻ 200,000 (reference: VAT Act 904 {Act 904).

Registered VAT entities: all businesses that make sales or turnover above a given minimum annual amount or threshold must register, charge Output VAT, and claim ITC, subject to having a VAT invoice.

Non-registered VAT entities: the grounds for excluding small entities (e.g., retail outlets and cottage industries) from registration include (a) making ***annual sales or turnover below the registration threshold,*** (b) operating in the ***informal sector***; and (b) practical difficulties in keeping VAT records and meeting other VAT obligations.

Small entities and imports: Typically, under customs rules, goods are classified only as taxable or exempt and, therefore, small non-registered entities pay the VAT (together with import duty, excise etc.,) on imports without recourse to credit or refunds. This is the same principle as the VAT on domestic supplies.

Voluntary VAT registration: VAT laws allow small entities to ***register voluntarily*** when they show that they can keep proper records and meet their VAT obligations. Usually, small firms opt to ***register voluntarily and claim ITC*** because they (a) make supplies to larger entities that insist on VAT invoices; and (b) are aware of the benefits of ITC and strive to comply—usually using tax agents or preparers.

The ensuing sections show how registered VAT entities—either as standalone entities or a chain of entities that run through the entire economy—charge Output VAT on sales; reclaim, credit or reclaim input VAT on purchases; and pay the difference or Net VAT to the tax office.

5. VAT rate and exemption structure

Countries impose VAT at specific rates while also making provisions for exemptions and reliefs—often on account of social intervention, incentives for business and special rights. It is important to note that until 2018, when they changed to ***"straight" levies,*** the standard

GETFund Levy (2.5 per cent) and NHIL (2.5 per cent) were part of the effective VAT rate of 17.5 per cent.

> ***VAT rate structure:*** The ideal VAT regime has a ***two-rate structure,*** namely standard and zero (0) rates on taxable supplies—and with non-rate Output VAT application for exemptions and reliefs. However, some countries add ***sub-standard*** (lower) and ***super-standard*** (higher) rates to the standard rate.
>
> ***Standard VAT rate:*** the positive standard rate applies to taxable imports and domestic supplies—and is often the only preferred option for making the VAT operations effective and efficient.
>
> ***Multiple "positive" VAT rates:*** some VAT laws impose ***lower or substandard*** and ***higher super rates*** on certain categories of taxable supplies. These were imposed as concessional or punitively, respectively, to achieve fiscal policy goals.
>
> ***Zero (0) VAT rate:*** this non-positive rate is imposed on exports of goods while, as an exception to the destination rule, the ***VAT on services*** in international business is charged in the country where the service is rendered at the positive rate.

To simplify VAT administration and distinguish among the goals of tax instruments, VAT experts advise countries to use ***exemptions*** (without the option of ITC) and punitive ***excise duty*** rates, respectively, instead of sub-standard and super-standard rates. Part III (Chapters 9 to 13) discusses these policy options in detail.

> ***Exemptions and reliefs***: In addition to the standard and other rates, countries grant exemptions and reliefs for social intervention and other reasons.
>
> ***Exemption (non-taxable supplies):*** means a ***non-rate for specific supplies*** that attract Output VAT but makes it ineligible for registered entities making the supply to claim the related ITC on the transaction.
>
> ***Exemption (entity registration):*** in most VAT laws, the exclusions that result in the non-registration of small entities are based on an annual turnover or sales threshold—resulting in ***payment of Input VAT but without the right to charge Output VAT and claim ITC.***

Reliefs (entities and supplies: these are the same as exemptions but often apply to non-business entities or persons (e.g., diplomats and office of the Head of State) rather than types of supplies to registered entities.

In summary, it is ***incorrect to view exemptions and zero rates as interchangeable*** since the former does not allow registered entities to take credit or refunds for input VAT. Some countries require beneficiaries of exemptions and travellers leaving the country to pay the Output VAT and then file for refunds, upon producing the VAT invoice or receipt as proof of payment.

6. VAT Input Tax Credit (ITC) mechanism

GRA's Domestic Tax Revenue Division (DTRD) and Customs Division (CD) collect the domestic import VAT respectively ***as though they were a customs duty or tariff.*** The latter also administers the zero-rating regime for exports. As noted below, registered VAT importers can claim ITC by using the ***customs entry or declaration as the de facto VAT invoice*** to support the ITC or refund claims for imports and exports.

Value addition (VA): Table 2.1 shows a ***simple "value addition" format*** for calculating the value of final products in an economy or the production-distribution chain. It assumes the involvement of an importer, manufacturer, wholesaler and retailer in a transaction or the economy.

In principle, beneficiaries of services from non-registered taxpayers operate at any stage under the same rules—including the "reverse-charge" rules for imported services. In other words, registered entities can claim ITC and credits through this special "self-assessment" (i.e., reverse charge) scheme.

Table 4.1: Value Addition (VA) process

Value Addition Process					
	Business Entity	**Value (ex-VAT)**	**Cumulative Value Added**	**Explanation**	**Comments**
	1	2	3	4	5
a	Importer	1000	1000	a3 = a2	Value added [VA] at origin
b	Manufacturer	800	1800	b3 = a2 + b2	Cumulative VA at manufacturing, wholesals and retail stages
c	Wholesaler	600	2400	c3 = b2 + c2	
d	Retailer	400	2800	d3 = c2 + d2	
e	Consumer	2800			Final [total] VA or price to consumer
f	Tax/VAT rate [standard]		17.5%		

Ideal VAT regime: Table 4.2 shows the ideal invoice-credit VAT which obliges registered entities to charge Output VAT along the value chain but also allows them to offset or claim ITC against the Output VAT, paying only the Net VAT to the tax office.

Table 4.2: Ideal VAT regime

Value Added Tax [All Entities Registered]								
	Business entity	Value ex VAT	Value Added	Output VAT	Input VAT	Net VAT	Price [VAT-plus]	Comments
	1	2	3	4	5	6	7	8
			2+[{b/f]	(3 x f3)		(4 - 5)	(3 + 4)	
a	Importer	1000	1000	175	0	175	1175	B2B [ITC]
b	Manufacturer	800	1800	315	175	140	2115	
c	Wholesaler	600	2400	420	315	105	2820	
d	Retailer	400	2800	490	420	70	3290	
e	Consumer	2800				490	3290	B2C [final; no ITC]
f	Rate [standard]		17.5%					

B2B and B2C transactions: Two ***registered entities*** selling to, and buying from, each other (with right to ITC) are involved in a ***business-to-business (B2B)*** transaction, compared to a ***business-to-consumer (B2C)*** one (with no right to ITC). Also, the right to ITC is blocked where a business entity is unregistered.

Single-stage Sales Tax methods: The VAT regimes in many countries replaced the ***single-stage sales tax*** (and the consumption ***taxes*** on selected services). Table 4.3 is an example of sales tax collection at the distribution point (i.e., the final B2C stage) only.

Table 4.3: Ideal single (distribution) state sales tax

Fair and efficient [single-stage sales or GCT regime					
Items	Taxpayers	Value ex-GST	Ideal Tax & Price		Comment [single-stage tax]
			GCT Due	Collection	
	1	2	3	4	5
a	Importer	1000	175	na	B2B supplies [non-registered]
b	Manufacturer	800	140	na	
c	Wholesaler	600	105	na	
d	Retailer	400	70	490	B2C supply
e	Total/Price	2800	490	3290	e4 = total VA + GCT
g	Standard rate		17.5%		

A comparison of ***ideal VAT and single-stage (distribution)*** Sale Tax leads to the following policy and quantitative outcomes—

i. ***Tax rate and burden or incidence of tax***: ideally, the burden of tax and revenue (GH₵490) at 17.5 per cent under the single-stage sales tax regime ***is equal to*** the multi-stage VAT-ITC; and

ii. ***cumulative VA and consumer price:*** both regimes impose the VAT on a ***cumulative VA*** of GH₵2,800 and at a consumer price of GH₵3290—without *cascading* or "tax-on-tax".

Sales tax collection at the distribution stage: Only registered retailers collect the sales tax directly from consumers at the final stage where it is difficult to impose and collect GCT because of informal operations and inadequate records at the distribution stage.

Weaknesses of final-stage tax regimes: the VAT credit method is superior to the final-state sales tax and VAT for the following administration and compliance reasons:

weak business and accounting records: many entities, doing business as small distribution outlets in the informal sector downstream, lack administrative and accounting structures to meet their legal obligations; and

weakest link in the value addition chain: the final stage in the value addition process is the weakest because distribution outlets often deal with consumers who may not have a business incentive to keep proper records for tax purposes.

The difficulty in enforcing tax laws against informal sector SMEs leads to the ***special registration threshold*** and collection (e.g., presumptive income tax) policies and rules. It is also the reason why many developing countries restricted the collection of the old sales tax regimes to the manufacturing and import stages—with service taxes at the distribution stage on limited supplies, including professional services (e.g., legal, accounting, architecture etc.,) as well as formal activities such as telecommunications and restaurants.

7. Superior features of the ITC-VAT method

Under the invoice-credit VAT method, registered entities charge Output VAT on business-to-business (B2B) supplies at every stage of the value-added chain and claim ITC until a B2C transaction occurs, typically at the distribution stage. In theory, the efficiency of the method in ensuring compliance also makes it serve as the ***fiscal "money-spinner"***.

Attributes of effective VAT regime: VAT experts cite the following three reasons why the administrative structure of the VAT invoice-credit (ITC) method is deemed to be superior among consumption tax regimes.

VAT invoice requirement: the conventional strength of the VAT credit method is in the obligation of registered entities to produce VAT sales or purchase invoices to validate their ITC claims.

Self-policing: the need to keep VAT invoices, as an accounting record, to claim ITC implies that registered entities will be keen on securing the invoice for tax audits—thus making the "purchase-cum-sales" VAT invoice ***"self-policing" among buyers and sellers.***

VAT invoices and audit trail: the sales and purchases invoices produce an audit trail that, implicitly, enhances tax administration and tax compliance—given the use of the same document as evidence for Output VAT (on the seller's invoice) and Input VAT or ITC (on the buyer's invoice).

Hence, tax offices rely heavily on this feature of the VAT ITC method to improve tax compliance and administration. The need to generate and keep VAT invoices manually or electronically is the most common feature of VAT regimes in all countries.

8. VAT as fiscal "money-spinner"

Tax experts regard VAT as the ***"money-spinner"*** of the fiscal regime but this is only possible with simple VAT structures, notably, a broad-based taxable supply regime.

Broad-base VAT regime: the taxable supply base comes close to the total value of supplies by not allowing the zero-rating and exemption of domestic supplies;

Single VAT rate: a single standard rate lessens the manipulation of multiple VAT standard, sub- or super-standard, and zero (0) rates, typically in apportioning input VAT under the ITC/ refund scheme to achieve favourable outcomes; and

Focus on large and medium entities: ideally, all business entities must register to charge Output VAT and claim ITC but countries *exclude* small business entities from registering for VAT to improve administration and compliance.

Invoices enhance compliance: As noted in the preceding section, the VAT invoice is evidence for charging Output VAT (by the seller) and claiming ITC (by the same registered entities as buyers).

The ideal VAT features that generate maximum revenue also led to serious objections to having a VAT regime that minimizes social intervention elements. In the absence of exemptions for basic supplies and use of other tax handles (e.g., high-income tax thresholds), the VAT is considered to be regressive by tax and fiscal experts. Hence, as noted in the ensuing section, VAT regimes have non-revenue goals that can distort and compromise its efficiency.

9. Non-revenue goals of tax regimes

VAT is basically neutral and, in principle, has few exceptions to the general rule. Hence, the preferred tax policy option is to implement a tax regime that predominantly and effectively attributes non-revenue goals to other tax instruments. Part V (Chapter 13) discusses the revenue and non-revenue goals of the various tax handles including the following—

punishment: the use of ***excise duties or "sin" taxes***, as preferred policy choice to influence behaviour, excises are imposed on a narrow supply base and at high rates on harmful or dangerous products such as alcohol, tobacco and petroleum;

protection: this role is assigned to ***customs duties or tariffs*** but with a broader base because they apply to all taxable imports and, therefore, "protect locally-produced" supplies by discriminating in their favour;

investment incentives: many countries use income tax regimes to attract investments, through measures such as accelerated depreciation and tax holidays;

progressivity (social intervention): the main mechanism of relieving the burden of tax on low-income persons includes graduated income tax rates and exemption of basic goods and services from the VAT base.

Many tax, economic and social experts argue that these policies blunt the impact of VAT, as a ***pure "money-spinner"***, on low-income persons and to serve other fiscal goals, an argument which the VAT regimes also do not escape in practice (i.e., exemptions and reliefs). The examples in the Tables that form part of the ensuing sections show the ***extent to which policies on exemptions and reliefs can compromise or distort the ideal VAT structure.***

10. Zero-rating exports

The application of a zero (0) rate to exports is an important VAT policy because VAT is a domestic tax and its imposition on foreign buyers will make the origin state non-competitive unless the ***destination state*** unilaterally waives the VAT at importation.

Conventional zero-rating of exports: As Table 4.4 shows, the ***country of origin*** (i.e., domestic state) becomes neutral and competitive by applying a zero rate to exports going to ***destination*** *(i.e., foreign)* states. Hence, the final price and tax burden to overseas buyers depends on the nature of their VAT regime.

Table 4.4: Conventional Application of Zero-rating to Exports

Zero-rated supplies [Conventional Application to Exports]								
Items	Business entity	Value ex Tax	Value Added	Output VAT	Input VAT	Net VAT	Price [tax plus]	Comments
	1	2	3	4	5	6	7	8
			2+[{b/f]	(3xf3)		(4 - 5)	(3 + 4)	
a	Importer	1000	1000	175	0	175	1175	B2B [ITC]
b	Manufacturer	800	1800	315	175	140	2115	
c	Wholesaler	600	2400	420	315	105	2820	
d	*Exporter 1/*	*400*	*2800*	0	*420*	(420)	*2800*	*Exporter claims ITC*
e	Consumer	2800				0	2800	B2C [final; no ITC]
f	Rate [standard]		17.5%	Zero-rate	0.0%	Conventional VAT rate for exports		
1/ The beneficiary of the supply is in a foreign jurisdiction								

Uniform or different policies: The main outcome is that the burden of VAT is zero and the total value addition remains at GH₵2,800. However, this outcome depends on the ***similar or the same VAT destination and origin rules,*** in addition to other attributes.

The ***burden of tax on foreign buyers is zero or neutral*** but the destination government, which imported the goods, begins to impose domestic VAT when the imported commodity enters the value-addition chain on the domestic market.

The origin and destination states apply the same export rules, notably the standard and zero VAT rates. However, these may vary in practice and, therefore, policymakers need to scan the trade and business environment carefully in formulating VAT rules.

Similar origin and destination VAT rules: Table 4.5 is based on the same rules—standard rate of 17.5 per cent, zero (0) rate on exports (to the destination state), and the same level of business efficiency.

Table 4.5: Uniform origin and destination stage VAT assumptions

Same VAT assumptions in Origin and Destination States								
Items	Entity	Value ex Tax	Taxable Value	Output VAT	Input VAT	Net VAT	Price (tax plus)	Comments
	1	2	3	4	5	6	7	8
Domestic (Origin) State activities								
a	Importer	1000	1000	175	0	175	1175	Manufacturer is a registered importer & exporter
b	Manufacturer (Exporter)	800	1800	0	175	(175)	1800	
External (Destination) State activities								
c	Wholesaler/importer	600	2400	420	0	420	2400	Business entities subject to foreign country tax regime
d	Retail/distributor	400	2800	490	420	70	2800	
e	Consumer (non-resident)	2800		490			3290	
f	Rate (Standard)	17.5%	The same rates in both countries					
g	Export tax rate (zero)	0.0%						

The outcome of the import-export mechanism in the two states with similar VAT rules (Table 4.5) does not change the conventional ***single-state VAT*** zero-rate outcome discussed in earlier sections and the chapters in this book.

VAT values: cumulative value added or VA (2,800), price (3,290) tax burden-cum-fiscal revenue (490)—assuming that the VAT rates do not vary between the two (2) states; and

Recapture of VAT waived: the outcome is the same since the VAT waiver and recapture in the origin and destination states make the impact of VAT neutral.

Since the importers in the destination state did not pay Input VAT [i.e., zero-rated in the origin state], the Net VAT is equal to the Output (Import) VAT (420). Hence, the VAT invoice and ITC mechanism continue smoothly in the two states.

Different origin and destination state VAT rates: Table 4.6 assumes that the cumulative value added is still GHȻ 2,800.

The destination and origin states allow their registered exporters to apply a zero (0) rate to shipments overseas.

However, the standard rate in the destination state of 10 per cent is lower than the 17.5 per cent in the origin state.

Table 4.6: Different origin and destination state VAT assumptions

Different VAT assumptions in Origin and Destination Countries [States]								
Items	Entity	Value ex Tax	Taxable Value	Output VAT	Input VAT	Net VAT	Price (tax plus)	Comments
	1	2	3	4	5	6	7	8
Domestic (Origin) State VAT activities								
a	Importer	1000	1000	175	0	175	1175	Manufacturer is a registered
b	Manufacturer (Exporter)	800	1800	0	175	(175)	1800	importer-cum-exporter
External (Destination) State activities								
c	Wholesaler/importer	600	2400	240	0	240	2400	Business entities subject to
d	Retail/distributor	400	2800	280	240	40	2800	foreign state tax regime
e	Consumer (non-resident)	2800		280			3080	
f	Rate (Standard)	17.5%	Country of Origin					
g	Rate (Standard)	10.0%	Country of Destination					
h	Export tax rate (zero)	0.0%	Both countries					

The cross-border values are unchanged but the ***difference in VAT rates*** in the origin and destination states changes the outcomes—a substantial reduction in ***consumer price (GHȻ 3080)*** and ***tax burden*** and fiscal revenues (GHȻ 280). The ensuing paragraph discusses the situation where some states use zero-rating, not exemptions, as social intervention policy and deal with technicalities in the banking, housing, and other sectors.

11. Exemption of VAT supplies

As noted earlier, the goal of granting exemptions for basic supplies (e.g. basic food and health and education services) under VAT regimes is to support low-income persons and help resolve some technical difficulties.

Social intervention: the *"basic supplies"* or necessities that take up a large part of the income of poor or low-income persons include foodstuff, education (e.g., textbooks) and health (e.g., analgesics) services and public transportation; and

Technical reasons: exemptions may be on technical grounds, including financial services (e.g., interest earned on savings is an investment, not consumption) and resident or owner-occupied first homes. As implied, the ***preferred mechanism is an exemption (section 9.1), not zero-rating (section 9.2) or multiple taxes (Section 9.3),*** to avoid complexity and high administration and compliance costs.

Exemption of domestic supplies: As Table 4.7 shows, exemptions cascade and their extent depends on their occurrence on the value chain. It is minimal at the distribution stage, compared to upstream and midstream exemptions on ***B2B transactions.***

Table 4.7: Exempt VAT supply at distribution stage

Exempt VAT supply of Textbooks									
Items	Business entity	Value ex VAT	Value Added	Output VAT	Input VAT		Net VAT	Price [tax plus]	Comments
					Recv'ble	Non-Rec			
	1	2	3	4	5	6	7	8	9
			2+[{b/f]	(3xf3)			(4 - 5)	(3 + 4)	
a	Importer	1000	1000	175	0	0	175	1175	B2B [ITC]
b	Manufacturer	800	1800	315	175	0	140	2115	
c	Wholesaler	600	2400	420	315	0	105	2820	
d	*Retailer 1/*	*400*	*2800*	*na*	0	*420*	*0*	*3220*	*Retailer adds Input VAT*
e	Consumer	2800					420	3220	B2C [final; no ITC]
f	Rate [standard]		17.5%						
1/ Supply (e.g., textbook) is exempt. No Output VAT is paid but Input Tax added to price because ITC is blocked									

The ***"cascading" and other outcomes*** depend on the exemption occurring midstream, upstream or downstream on the VA chain.

Exempt supply: the final output (e.g., specified school textbooks) is exempt but the registered entity paid Input VAT on the supplies used to manufacture and distribute the product.

Input Tax Credit (ITC): the exemption option blocks the registered entity from claiming ICT for the Input Tax paid on supplies.

Consumer price: the ***blocked, denied or irrecoverable Input Tax*** "cascades" and increases the final price by GHȻ 420 or cumulative VAT charged from the import to wholesale stage.

Tax relief: given that the Input Tax is irrecoverable, the only "***tax relief***" is equivalent to the VAT on the value added at the retail stage (GHȻ 70 = GHȻ 400 x 17.5 per cent).

The exempt supplies may make "***mixed***" (i.e., taxable and exempt supplies) that require apportionment of ITC, with the Input Tax on the exempt element being irrecoverable.

Zero-rating domestic supplies: If the VAT law zero-rates, rather than exempts domestic supplies, the outcome will be substantive. The assumption in Table 4.8 is that a zero (0) rate replaces the exemption of textbooks at the distribution stage, with an ITC claim that offsets a positive Input VAT against zero (0) Output VAT.

Table 4.8: Zero-rated domestic supply

Zero-rated domestic VAT supply (Textbooks)								
Items	Business entity	Value ex Tax	Value Added	Output VAT	Input VAT	Net VAT	Price [tax plus]	Comments
	1	2	3	4	5	6	7	8
			2+[{b/f]	(3xf3)		(4 - 5)	(3 + 4)	
a	Importer	1000	1000	175		175	1175	
b	Manufacturer	800	1800	315	175	140	2115	B2B [ITC]
c	Wholesaler	600	2400	420	315	105	2820	
d	*Retailer 1/*	*400*	*2800*	0	*420*	(420)	*2800*	*Retailer claims Input VAT*
e	Consumer	2800				0	2800	B2C [final; no ITC]
f	Rate [standard]		17.5%	Zero-rate	0.0%	Relief from VAT at zero (0) rate		
1/ Supply (e.g., approved textbooks) is taxed at zero (0) and results in "refund" after ITC claim								

The following are the ***main outcomes*** of zero-rating basic domestic supply, instead of exempting them, to grant relief from VAT on socio-economic grounds:

Tax relief: zero-rating waives the entire Output VAT of GHȻ 490, given that a positive Input VAT (GHȻ420) is offset against zero (0) Output VAT.

Price: the final price is neutral—without Output or Net VAT and with the same outcome as zero-rating exports.

Zero rates ***may add to the inefficiency of VAT*** where registered entities add the gross Output VAT to price because of inadequate budget provisions for refunds. This often results after taxpayer complaints about long delays in the verification and payment process.

Multiple domestic VAT rates: So far, the discussions assume that the VAT law imposes a single standard VAT rate of 17.5 per cent. In practice, besides zero-rating and exemptions, some countries impose other lower or higher VAT rates on supplies.

Table 4.9 assumes ***multiple VAT-rate regimes, reflecting a complex policy option*** for textbooks and other publications, covering zero (0) rate (pre-school), exempt (primary), lower 5 per cent (secondary/tertiary), 25 per cent punitive (adult), and standard 17.5 per cent (all others).

Table 4.9: Multiple domestic (standard, exempt & lower/higher) rates.

Multiple (or variable) Output VAT rates														
Item	Business entity	Value ex Tax	Value Added	Output VAT [multiple regimes]						Input VAT		Net VAT: Output - Input VAT	Price [tax plus]	Comments
				Stan-dard	Zero	Exempt	Lower	Higher	Total	Deduc-tible	Non-deductible			
	1	2	3	4	4	5	6	7	8	9	10	11	12	13
a	Importer	1000	1000	175	na	na	na	na	**175**	0	0	175	**1175**	External "inputs" activity
b	Manufacturer	800	1800	126	0	na	14	90	230	175	0	55	**2030**	Assumes no domestic inputs
c	Wholesaler	600	2434	170	0	na	18	122	310	195	34	115	**2745**	Starts ITC apportionment
d	*Retailer*	*400*	2881	202	0	na	22	144	367	264	47	103	**3248**	*Continues ITC apportionment*
e	Consumer	2800								634	81	448	3248	B2C [final; no ITC]
f	Rates			17.5%	0.0%	na	5.0%	25.0%			Effective VAT rate		13.8%	
g	Ratio of sales			40.0%	10.0%	15.0%	15.0%	20%	100.0%					

The main outcomes of this mix of concessionary (zero/exempt), punitive, and standard rates are pronounced and can be summarized as follows—

lower price and VAT burden of GH₵ 3,248 and GH₵ 448 respectively—which is due to the weights of the supply favouring zero (0) and exemption; and

compared to an ideal price VAT burden of GH₵ 3290 and GH₵ 490 respectively

The downside is that, as with all exempt and multiple rate regimes, VAT administration and compliance become complex and costly. Clearly, in this example, the VAT regime becomes a proxy for other tax instruments such as excise duty.

12. VAT Threshold—exclusion of entities from registration

VAT regimes use low annual turnover amounts to limit the eligibility of entities to register, charge Output VAT and claim ITC. The main provisions of VAT laws include:

annual turnover: the primary rule to register is achieving a minimum level of ***annual turnover or sales of "taxable supplies"***—for example, local currency equivalent of US$50 million, as envisaged in the planning for VAT in the early 1990s;

quarterly and monthly targets: taxpayers are required to assess their eligibility to register by checking proportionate amounts of actual or projected monthly or quarterly turnover; and

voluntary registration: small entities can register at the discretion of the tax authorities, often by proving that they can keep adequate VAT and tax records.

As discussed below, some VAT jurisdictions including Ghana, allow small entities to ***pay presumptive or estimated taxes*** in lieu of income tax and VAT or separately for the two (2) taxes to meet all tax obligations under the law.

Non-registered retail outlets (downstream): Table 4.10 depicts the non-registration of ***small entities at the distribution (downstream) stage*** in the informal sector, with improper or inadequate records, and low annual turnover.

Table 4.10: Non-registered retail outlet (downstream)

Non-registered Retailer (Downstream)									
Item	Business entity	Value ex VAT	Value Added	Output VAT	Input VAT		Net VAT	Price [VAT plus]	Comments
					Recoverable	Non-recoverable			
	1	2	3	4	5	6	7	8	9
			2+[{b/f]	(3xf3)			(4 - 5)	(3 + 4)	
a	Importer	1000	1000	175	0	0	175	1175	B2B [no domestic VAT)
b	Manufacturer	800	1800	315	175	0	140	2115	B2B [charge domestic VAT]
c	Wholesaler	600	2400	420	315	0	105	2820	
d	*Retailer 1/*	*400*	*2800*	*na*	*na*	420	*na*	*3220*	*B2B (non-registered)*
e	Consumer	2800					420	3220	B2C [final; no ITC]
f	Rate [standard]		17.5%						
1/ No Output VAT charged; no ITC claim (blocked); prior Input VATs paid added to price									

The outcome is the same as the exemption of supplies at the distribution stage, as discussed in earlier sections;

the revenue loss is equal to Output VAT at the final stage (i.e., GHȻ 400 x 17.5% = GHȻ 70); and

Net VAT is equal to VAT charged to the wholesale stage (i.e., GHȻ 2,400 x 17.5% = GHȻ 420).

Non-registered cottage industry (upstream): As shown in Table 4.11 below, the exemption of small businesses from registration may occur.

upstream, when small manufacturers do not meet the eligibility criteria; but, at the same time, however,

the VAT paid by exempt manufacturers on ***taxable imports*** by registered and non-registered importers, under the Customs Tariff or Code, is irrecoverable.

Table 4.11: Distortions caused by upstream (small manufacturing) non-registration.

Non-registered Manufacturer (Upstream)										
Items	Business entity	Value ex VAT	Value Added	Output VAT	Input VAT		Net VAT	Price [VAT plus]	Comments
					Recove-rable	Non-rec'ble			
	1	2	3	4	5	6	7	8	9
			2+[{b/f]	(3xf3)			(4 - 5)	(3 + 4)	
a	Importer	1000	1000	175	0	0	175	1175	B2B [origin: no domestic VAT]
b	*Manufacturer 1/*	*800*	*1975*	*na*	*0*	*175*	*na*	*1975*	*B2B [not registered]*
c	Wholesaler	600	2575	451	0	0	451	2575	B2B [charges but no ITC invoice]
d	Retailer	400	2975	521	451	0	70	*3496*	*B2B (non-registered)*
e	Consumer	2800					696	3496	B2C [final; no ITC]
f	Rate [standard]		17.5%						
i/ No Output VAT charged; no ITC claim (blocked); prior Input VATs paid added to price									

The Input VAT denied upstream cascades from the wholesale stage, with consequences that include the following–

non-registered manufacturers cannot claim ITC (i.e., import VAT) because they are blocked by the principle or law in doing so;

however, the registered wholesaler can issue an Output VAT invoice but cannot claim ITC because the exempt manufacturer does not issue a purchase invoice.

The outcome is an increase in price (GH₵ 3,496 instead of GH₵ 3,290) and tax burden (GH₵ 696 instead of GH₵ 490).

Non-registered wholesaler (midstream entity): Table 4.12 shows a small exempt or non-registered wholesaler (midstream) buying from a registered manufacturer and adding the VAT on inputs to costs because they are non-registered.

Table 4.12: Non-registered wholesaler (midstream entity)

Value Added Tax [non-registered wholesaler]									
Item	Business entity	Value ex Tax	Value Added	Output VAT	Input VAT Rec'ble	Input VAT Irrec'ble	Net VAT	Price [tax plus]	Comments
	1	2	3	4		5	6	7	8
			2+[{b/f]	(3xf3)			(4 - 5)	(3 + 4)	
a	Importer	1000	1000	175	0		175	1175	B2B [ITC]
b	Manufacturer	800	1800	315	175		140	2115	
c	***Wholesaler 1/***	***600***	***2715***	***0***		***315***	***0***	***3030***	***non-registered***
d	Retailer	400	3115	545	0	0	545	3660	B2B
e	Consumer	2800					860	3660	B2C [final; no ITC]
f	Rate [standard]		17.5%						
1/ No Output VAT charged; no ITC claim (blocked); prior Input VATs paid added to price									

The result is cascading at the retail stage only, where the final distributor adds the blocked Input VAT to the final price. State revenue and ***tax burden*** increase to GH₵ 860 while the ***price*** is GH₵ 3,660.

"Concurrent" exempt supplies and non-registration: So far, the discussions suggest that, as ***separate but non-concurrent*** or overlapping policies, both (a) exemption of supplies and (b) exclusion of business entities from registration often result in the VAT charged increasing costs, prices and tax burden revenues because of blocking ITC.

Table 4.13 is an example of concurrent (a) non-registered manufacturer; and (b) non-taxable or exempt supply at the distribution stage.

Table 4.13: Non-registered manufacturer (upstream) and exempt supply (downstream)

Non-registered Manufacturer (Upstream) and exempt/non-table supply (downstream)									
Items	Business entity	Value ex VAT	Value Added	Output VAT	Input VAT		Net VAT	Price [VAT plus]	Comments
					Recove-rable	Non-rec'ble			
	1	2	3	4	5	6	7	8	9
			2+[{b/f]	(3xf3)			(4 - 5)	(3 + 4)	
a	Importer	1000	1000	175	0	0	175	1175	B2B [origin: no domestic VAT]
b	*Manufacturer 1/*	*800*	*1975*	*na*	*0*	*175*	*na*	*1975*	*B2B [not registered]*
c	Wholesaler	600	2575	451	0	0	451	2575	B2B [charges but no ITC invoice]
d	*Retailer 1/*	*400*	*3426*	*0*	*0*	*451*	*0*	*3426*	*B2B (exempt/non-taxable supply)*
e	Consumer	2800					626	3426	B2C [final; no ITC]
f	Rate [standard]		17.5%						
1/ No Output VAT charged; no ITC claim (blocked); prior Input VATs paid added to price									

The outcomes, compared with the *ideal VAT* situation (Table 4.3) and exemption of a small-entity manufacturer only (Table 4.10) are shown below—

for the combination of policy measures, increase in price (GH₵ 3,426 instead of GH₵ 3,290) and tax burden (GH₵ 626 instead of GH₵ 490); and

compared to the case of non-registered manufacturers only (Section 10.2 and Table 4.10), the increase in price is GH₵ 3,426 (instead of GH₵ 3,496 or GH₵ 3,290 ideal VAT); and

tax burden GH₵ 626 (instead of GH₵ 696 and ideal VAT of GH₵ 490).

The difference of GH₵ 70 is the VAT (17.5 per cent) on the Value Added (GH₵ 400) at the retail or distribution stage—that is not imposed because of the exempt status of the supply.

13. Comparison of General Consumption Tax Methods

Tables 2.14 and 2.15 show a summary of the ***different outcomes between the Ideal VAT regime and variations that are common in various VAT legislation,*** as reflected in Tables 2.2 to 2.13 in the preceding Sections. Table 4.14 shows the nominal and percentage outcomes from these original tables while Table 4.15 shows the deviations between the ideal VAT outcome and other outcomes, based on different consumption taxes and policy measures.

Table 4.14: Comparison between the Ideal VAT and other policies in Tables 1 to 13

Comparative Table (based on Value Added of 2,800)									
Tables	Assumpton/Basis	Total VA+VAT Denied	Tax Burden	Output VAT	Input VAT		Total Net VAT Paid	Final Consumer Price	Effective VAT Rate (%)
					Allowed	Denied			
2.2	**Ideal VAT regime**	**2,800**	**490**	**490**	**420**	**0**	**490**	**3,290**	17.5
2.3	Ideal Single-stage Sales Tax	2,800	490	490	na	na	490	3,290	17.5
2.4	*Export: Conventional zero-rate*	*2,800*	*0*	*0*	*420*	*0*	*(420)*	*2,800*	*(15.0)*
2.5	*Exports: same rate (D@17.5%)*	*2,800*	*490*	*0*	*420*	*0*	*490*	*3,290*	*17.5*
2.6	*Exports: lower rates (D@10%)*	*2,800*	*280*	*0*	*240*	*0*	*280*	*3,080*	*10.0*
2.7	Exempt: downstream	2,800	420	420	315	(420)	105	3,220	3.8
2.8	*Zero-rated domestic supply*	*2,800*	*0*	*0*	*420*	*0*	*(420)*	*2,800*	*(15.0)*
2.9	Multiple supply	2,881	367	264	264	(47)	103	3,248	3.6
2.10	Non-registration: downstream	2,800	420	420	315	420	420	3,220	15.0
2.11	Non-registration: upstream	3,115	545	545	175	(315)	545	3,660	17.5
2.12	Non-registration: midstream	2,975	521	521	451	(175)	696	3,496	23.4
2.13	Non-reg.: mix (up/down stream)	3,426	0	0	0	(451)	626	3,426	18.3

Table 4.15 shows the ***nominal deviations*** between the Ideal VAT regime (Table 4.2) and the other outcomes from the other policy options (Table 4.2 to Table 4:13). They give an early indication of the predominant worsening outcomes or distortions from various policy measures discussed in the ensuing Parts and Chapters.

Table 4.15: Deviations between the Ideal VAT and other policies in Tables 1 to 13

Deviation (Ideal VAT minus other bases)									
Tables	Assumpton/Basis	Total VA+VAT Denied	Tax Burden	Output VAT	Input VAT		Total Net VAT Paid	Final Consumer Price	Effective VAT Rate (%)
					Allowed	Denied			
2.2	**Ideal VAT regime**	**0**	**0**	**0**	**0**	**0**	**0**	**0**	**0.0**
2.3	Ideal Single-stage Sales Tax	0	0	0	na	na	0	0	0.0
2.4	*Export: Conventional zero-rate*	*0*	*490*	*490*	*0*	*0*	*910*	*490*	*32.5*
2.5	*Exports: same rate (17.5%)*	*0*	*0*	*490*	*0*	*0*	*0*	*0*	*0.0*
2.6	*Exports: lower rates (10%)*	*0*	*210*	*490*	*180*	*0*	*210*	*210*	*7.5*
2.7	Exempt: downstream	0	70	70	105	420	385	70	13.8
2.8	*Zero-rated domestic supply*	*0*	*490*	*490*	*0*	*0*	*910*	*490*	*32.5*
2.90	Multiple supply	(81)	123	226	156	47	387	42	13.9
2.10	Non-registration: downstream	0	70	70	105	(420)	70	70	2.5
2.11	Non-registration: upstream	(315)	(55)	(55)	245	315	(55)	(370)	0.0
2.12	Non-registration: midstream	(175)	(31)	(31)	(31)	175	(206)	(206)	(5.9)
2.13	Non-reg.: mix (up/down stream)	(626)	490	490	420	451	(136)	(136)	(0.8)

14. Conclusion

Countries must keep VAT regimes close to the ideal invoice-credit VAT regime to make them efficient by avoiding distortions in price, tax burden and fiscal revenue. The increase in costs and prices from cascading could adversely affect macro-fiscal outcomes such as the cost of doing business, inflation and revenue generation. Complex VAT regimes may appear to increase revenue but the effects of their distortion, notably cascading, as well as complex tax administration and compliance costs also lead to tax evasion and avoidance.

The main socio-political and economic lesson of using the uniform tables throughout the book is that, in general, the extent of distortions caused by policy interventions depends on their impact at the downstream (distribution stage), where "cascading" is often minimal and, alternatively, upstream (manufacturing) or midstream (wholesale)—where distortions result in expensive outcomes Hence, it is possible to use the uniform format to predict the likely impact of policy change.

The cautionary note and conclusion are that the theoretical increase in tax burden and potential increase in fiscal revenue may never be realized, due to complex tax structures, compliance and administration. These result in distortion of tax policies as well as widespread tax evasion and avoidance. This has become a definite outcome of Ghana's revenue and VAT potential, where the blocking of ITC and refunds for NHIL and GETFund Levy (i.e., so-called "straight levies" has not resulted in a substantive VAT revenue increase since the middle of the 2018 fiscal year amendments.

Chapter 5

GENERAL CONSUMPTION TAX (GCT): BASIC METHODS

1. Introduction

Chapter 3 discusses the structure of the sales and service taxes that Ghana replaced with the Value Added Tax (VAT). Apart from their narrow tax bases, the Sales Tax was under the Customs, Excise and Preventive Service (CEPS) and the Service Tax under the Internal Revenue Service (IRS). The general overview is also relevant for recent inefficient VAT policy changes such as separating NHIL and GETFund Levy as Straight Levies without the benefit of Input Tax Credit (ITC),

The chapter is based on a standard ***supply*** originating from (a) a ***domestic*** registered farmer or upstream ***entity,*** with minimal or no VAT on inputs; or (b) ***externally*** by ***importers*** who did not pay VAT on inputs because the country of origin classifies exports as zero-rated. Under an ideal ***"value chain"*** concept, the transactions continue among ***registered entities*** that are manufacturers, wholesalers and retailers or service providers who sell to a final consumer.

In practice, some domestic and foreign ***non-registered entities*** may be involved in the value chain. Where they impact the "value chain" upstream or downstream, their activities may result in cascading and a higher tax burden. ***In principle,*** an aspect of consumption taxes is that, ***until the final supply of a commodity or service reaches the consumer—***

> the ***sales or "output"*** of a particular business entity becomes the ***purchases or "input"*** of the other entity in the transaction—at which point the value increases with additional costs and profit margins by the recipient in the transaction;
>
> for the duration that the transactions involve ***registered businesses, a credit or deferral (i.e., ring)*** mechanism evolves to alleviate the tax paid on the inputs or purchases because ***businesses are not the target*** of consumer or expenditure taxes; and

these intermediate or ***business-to-business (B2B) processes*** of value addition, conversion or exchange continue till they end at the ***business-to-consumer (B2C) stage,*** i.e., to a final consumer or household.

Hence, in summary, the ***premise of VAT*** is that, among businesses, the farmer or importer merely introduces a cost or price into the economy—to which other registered or non-registered entities ***"add value"*** in the form of costs and profit margins. The ***"value addition"*** ends at the ***final consumer stage,*** where buyers consume, not exchange, the supply. Its related ***invoice-credit VAT form*** is deemed to be superior to other consumption tax collection methods.

As noted in Chapter 1, before the VAT Act, 1994 (Act 486) and, from its repeal to the time of passing the replacement VAT Act, 1998 (Act 546) which became effective in January 1999, Ghana's now defunct Customs, Excise and Preventive Service (CEPS) collected the ***sales tax*** on goods while the defunct Internal Revenue Service (IRS) also charged the ***service tax*** on selected services.

This chapter compares these two old tax forms, together with other variants from other jurisdictions, with the VAT (a) as a reminder that VAT replaced inefficient tax regimes in many countries; and (b) some recent proposed VAT solutions that mimic these old sales and turnover tax are not novel.

2. Value addition and taxation

The goal of the ensuing sections is to show the ***differences in the incidence or burden*** we use the outcomes from the ideal VAT mechanism to illustrate the negative or distortionary effect of making various changes to the VAT policy, structure or mechanism, and operations.

Value addition

Table 5.1 shows the incremental or progressive values which each entrepreneur or entity adds to the preceding value before the goods or services reach the final consumer. Column 2 shows the ***value added*** at each stage in the chain or economy while Column 3 the ***cumulative value*** that results at each stage.

Table 5.1: Value Added by Entities in the Economy

Value Addition Process					
	Business Entity	Value	Cummulative Value Added	Explanation	Comments
	1	2	3	4	5
a	Importer	1000	1000	a3 = a2	Value Added (VA) at origin
b	Manufacturer	800	1800	b3 = a2 + b2	Cummulative VA at manufacturing, wholesale and retail stages
c	Wholesaler	600	2400	c3 = b2 + c2	
d	Retailer	400	2800	d3 = c2 + d2	
e	Consumer	2800			Total VA or price ex-Tax
f	Tax rate [standard]		17.5%		

GCT at the Final Distribution and Consumer Stage

As a tax on household expenses (B2C), not on business entities (B2B), the ideal method is to charge the ***general consumption tax (GCT)*** at the final stage of the value addition chain. As Table 5.2 shows, this is the point where distributors make ***taxable supplies*** to consumers since all the earlier stages are B2B transactions. It is ***ideal but not always practical*** because of the relatively weak and diverse links among retailers and consumers at the end of the VA chain.

Table 5.2: Imposition of ideal GST (at the consumer stage)

A fair and efficient tax burden					
	Business Entity	Value ex-GST	GCT Due	Collection	Comments
	1	2	3	4	5
a	Importer	1000	175	na	B2B transactions or supplies
b	Manufacturer	800	140	na	
c	Wholesaler	600	105	na	
d	Retailer	400	70	490	B2C supply [e4 = g4 x e2]
e	Consumer	2800	490	3290	Total VA [Price ex-Tax (e4 = e2 + e3)]
f	Tax rate [standard]		17.5%		

Under the alternative "Addition" method, each business collects the GCT on only the "value added" at each stage of the Value Addition (VA) chain. Table 5.3 illustrates this approach, which is known by its process as the ***"addition" method.***

Table 5.3: GCT Addition Method [Tax on VA only]

A fair and efficient tax burden						
	Business Entity	**Value ex-GST**	**GCT on VA only**	**Cummulative GCT**	**Explanation**	**Comments**
	1	2	3	4	5	6
a	Importer	1000	175	175	a4 = a3	Each business entity charges GCT [Col. 3] on only the value added at each stage
b	Manufacturer	800	140	315	b4 = a3 + b3	
c	Wholesaler	600	105	420	c4 = a3+b3+c3	
d	Retailer	400	70	490	d4 = a3+b3+c3+d3	
e	Consumer	2800	490	3290		
f	Tax rate [standard]		17.5%			

In practice, ***VAT laws require farmers and importers, as well as other intermediaries to register*** for VAT when the total actual or potential annual value of taxable sales, turnover or supplies exceeds the ***minimum registration level or threshold.*** Where the ***turnover falls below the threshold,*** a business does not register. In principle, the law does not require consumers who make ***occasional sales*** to register for VAT because they are not businesses.

As Table 5.4 shows, the ***Input Tax Credit (ITC)*** process offsetting Input VAT against Output VAT is the fundamental difference from other GCT or sales tax regimes.

Table 5.4: Ideal VAT regime (all VAT-registered business entities)

A fair and efficient tax burden								
	Business Entity	**Value ex-VAT**	**Cummulative Value Added**	**Output VAT**	**Input VAT**	**Net VAT**	**Price [tax plus]**	**Comments**
a	Importer	1000	1000	175	0	175	1175	B2B [w/ ITC]
b	Manufacturer	800	1800	315	175	140	1940	B2B [w/ ITC]
c	Wholesaler	600	2400	420	315	105	2505	B2B [w/ ITC]
d	Retailer	400	2800	490	420	70	2870	B2B [w/ ITC]
e	Consumer	2800				490	3290	B2C [w/o ITC]
f	Tax rate [standard]		17.5%					

The main features of Table 5.4 under the ITC-VAT process are as follows:

Importer: initiates the imports on taxable supplies (c1,000), charges and collects Output VAT from the manufacturer but does not claim ITC since the origin exporter zero-rates the supply. Hence, the importer pays gross Output VAT of c175 to the tax office.

Manufacturer: adds the value of c800, sells to the wholesaler for c1800 and charges Output VAT c315—against which the registered entity can claim ITC of c175 (i.e., Input VAT)—paid already on c1000 in the cumulative value of c1800.

Wholesaler: goes through the same cycle as the manufacturer with respect to the output tax, input tax and ITC process.

Retailer: goes through the same process as the manufacturer and wholesaler (above) but cannot claim ITC because it is a final B2C transaction.

Table 5.4 outcomes also depict the ideal outcome but are superior to the single distribution-stage sales tax and the VAT "addition" methods. On the other hand, the vulnerable distribution stage may result in less revenue while the turnover tax results in significant multiple taxation, cascading as well as higher price and tax burden.

Box 3.1: Baseline computations

Tables 3.1 to 3.4 will be used throughout the book, unless stated otherwise, as the baseline to compare the outcomes of different GCT regimes as well as assess the implications of VAT policies and legislation on its administration, compliance and other economic variables.

3. Older sales and service tax regimes

Ghana followed a global trend that saw many advanced, emerging and developing economies make the transition from Sales Tax to VAT regimes. This Section discusses global and Ghana's ***old sales and service tax regimes*** and compares them with the ideal VAT regime. Box 3.2 notes that the United States of America (USA) is the only major advanced state that continues to impose a variety of sales and service tax regimes.

Box 3.2: Sales Tax regimes in USA

The only major OECD or advanced country with this tax regime is the United States of America (USA), a federal state, where the sales and service taxes are charged under various regimes at the sub-national government (SNG) level at the state, county, local and city jurisdictions. A few states have VAT-like input tax credit [ITC] regimes that allow registered entities to get a credit, refund or deferral on sales and service tax paid on inputs.

While the narrations and comparisons are historical, they are progressive in drawing attention to emerging policy measures that lead to distortions of VAT regimes and minimize this inefficient mechanism in many African countries. The essence of the remaining parts of the book is to show that the resulting distortions compromise the ideal VAT regime.

Ideal Sales Tax in VAT format: If the goal is to impose 17.5 per cent GCT on the price paid for a supply, then the *ideal single-stage sales tax and VAT methods should give the same results.* Table 5.5 shows this in an ITC-VAT table format.

Table 5.5 Ideal Sales Tax Regime (VAT format)

Single Stage Sales Tax: fair and efficient tax burden								
	Business Entity	Value ex-VAT	Taxable Value	Output VAT	Input VAT	Net VAT	Price [tax plus]	Comments
a	Importer	1000	1000	na	na	0	1000	Non-registered business entities
b	Manufacturer	800	1800	na	na	0	1800	
c	Wholesaler	600	2400	na	na	0	2400	
d	Retailer	400	2800	490	na	490	3290	Registered
e	Consumer	2800		490		490	3290	Total consumer price
f	Tax rate [standard]		17.5%					

Columns 1 to 3 above are the ***same as in Tables 3.1 to 3.3*** but the law imposes the GST at the B2C point where ***only registered retailers*** can charge GST on taxable supplies to final consumers. Though it produces the same outcomes as the ideal VAT method (Table 5.3), there are challenges under this ideal tax regime that include the following:

in practice, the inputs or purchases at prior stages (e.g., manufacturer or wholesaler buying from a retailer) may inevitably attract GST—and result in ***tax-on-tax*** at multiple stages, a phenomenon called ***cascading;***

it ***lacks an efficient mechanism to alleviate the likelihood of "input tax"*** paid by non-registered entities, which they add to the price; and

usually, the retail or ***final service points*** are diverse, largely informal; and therefore, ***difficult to control or police*** by tax officials.

The main outcome of the ideal methods is that they do not result in any sticking taxes on inputs that increase the prices they charge other businesses or consumers. The remaining sections vary these assumptions and, where input taxes are paid, any ***unclaimed amount "cascades" or multiplies*** at various stages of the "value-added" chain and increases prices, often phenomenally.

4. Cascading Sales Tax Regimes

Besides the "Addition" method, Tables 3.2 to 3.5, assume that the retailer is the only registered entity that charges the sales tax with no ITC or deferral to give reliefs to registered businesses that may pay input taxes inadvertently.

> ***Turnover tax:*** The extreme form of this B2B tax on inputs is the turnover tax which assumes that each entity is registered to charge the GCT but without recourse to reliefs under the ITC or deferral/ring methods. Typically, the tax re-enters the value-added chain as costs and results in tax-on-tax or "cascading".

Table 5.6 shows this extreme form of "cascading", where the GCT on B2B supplies or even those of B2C, cascade or roll down, in domino style, from start to finish.

Table 5.6 Turnover [Full Cascading] Tax Regime

Full cascading to retail stage (no ITC or deferral)									
	Business Entity	Value ex Tax/GST	Taxable Value	Output GCT	Input GCT	ITC	Gross Payment	Price [tax inclusive]	Comments
	1	2	3	4	5	6	7	8	9
a	Importer	1000	1000	175	na	na	175	1175	All business entities pay sales tax but without recourse to ITC [Retailer teminates value addition)
b	Manufacturer	800	1975	346	175	na	346	2321	
c	Wholesaler	600	2921	511	346	na	511	3432	
d	Retailer	400	3832	671	511	na	671	4502	
e	Consumer	2800		4502	671		1709	4502	
f	Rate [standard]		17.5%						

In summary, while the original values in Column 2 are the same as in Table 5.1 to Table 5.4, the following factors cause a divergence in the values of the other columns:

registration—under a full Turnover or cascading tax regime, *all* entities register to charge GST (Column 4) but cannot claim ITC (Columns 5 and 6);

input tax as cost—they add the cumulative turnover tax on inputs (Column 5) to the price they charge for the supply or output made to the next business entity;

gross GST payment—unlike an ITC or deferral regime, the output tax (Column 4) is the same as the GCT paid (Column 7);

blocked ITC—Columns 4 and 8 are equal because no mechanism exists for relieving the input tax paid on B2B transactions (Column 5);

cascading—due to the extreme "cascading" or multiple taxes, the tax paid by final consumers is excessively high; and

tax burden and other outcomes—the GH₵ 490 tax burden under the ideal sales tax regime (Table 5.2) compared unfavourably with GH₵ 1,702 (Column 7), while the price increases to GH₵ 4,502 compared to GH₵ 3290 (Table 5.2).

These are the worst ***outcomes*** that result in theoretically high fiscal yields. In practice, however, they result in high levels of ***tax evasion and avoidance*** and social discontent among consumers and businesses.

5. Ghana's Old Sales and Service Tax Regimes

Ghana had ***two (2) separate and major pre-VAT sales and service regimes*** for charging the GCT, with the sales tax including various relief provisions to alleviate the excessive burdens such as multiple taxation and high prices.

Sales Tax regime: The ***main pre-VAT GST regime*** was the domestic and import Sales Tax under CEPS, which is also responsible for ***excise duties***. The ***secondary regime*** was the domestic Service Tax that the IRS charged and collected.

Sales Tax deferral ("ring") method: Before the introduction of VAT in 1998-99, manufacturers collected the single-stage domestic sales tax while CEPS charged the import stage on eligible goods. The main features include the following:

registration: CEPS registered only ***selected manufacturers,*** most of whom also paid excise duty and special indirect taxes, to charge the domestic sales tax at the production or manufacturing stage;

single-stage domestic sales tax: CEPS collected the domestic sales tax at the manufacturing stage only, thus excluding many large and capable wholesalers and retailers from the indirect tax regime;

import sales tax: CEPS also charged and collected the import sales tax on ALL taxable goods brought into the country—from all importers, not just sales and excise tax registered entities;

"ring" mechanism: CEPS placed its registered manufacturers in a ***fictional deferral or "ring"*** mechanism that waived the sales tax on imports and domestic purchases of basic raw materials and semi-manufactured inputs for production;

customs bonded warehousing: registered entities may place all imports of taxable inputs in (customs) bonded warehouses, which is another form of input deferral, and remove them for manufacturing purposes under the strict supervision of resident customs officials;

exports and duty-drawback: the "duty drawback", which is basically a refund mechanism, allows exporters to reclaim the sales tax as well as other import and excise duties on inputs used to produce exportable goods; and

cascading (tax-on-tax): where registered manufacturers pay tax on taxable final, semi-produced or imported goods, from ***unregistered*** manufacturers and other business entities, the sales tax on these inputs adds to the cost of the final product on which they charge sales tax again.

Comparison of Sales tax and VAT invoice-credit method: Unlike the invoice-credit method, the reliefs under the sales tax regime did not extend to non-primary inputs and, in principle, were available to only registered manufacturers, who may import their own taxable inputs.

The registered manufacturer as importer: Table 5.7 shows the ***ideal manufacturing-stage ["ring'] sales tax*** regime where the registered manufacturer is also the importer of the inputs. The law allowed taxpayers to operate under a combined "ring" waiver, transit, and customs bonded warehouse regime.

Table 5.7: Ideal single-stage (manufacturing) "ring" sales tax

Original Sales Tax Regime (Manufacturing as Importer)								
	Entity	Value ex Tax	Taxable Value	Output Tax	Input Tax (waived)	Net Tax	Price (tax	Comments
a	Manufacturer (Imports)	1000	1000	0	0	0	1000	Manufacturer imports &
b	Manufacturer (Domestic)	800	1800	315	0	315	2115	benefits from "ring" waiver
c	Wholesaler	600	2715	na	na	0	2715	Wholesaler & retailer are not
d	Retailer	400	3115	na	na	0	3115	registered (not in "ring")
e	Consumer	2800		315			3115	
f	Rate (Standard)	17.5%						

The *main outcomes* include lower prices (GH₵ 3,115 versus GH₵ 3290) due to

(a) not covering downstream VA; resulting in

(b) lower tax burden; and

(c) less fiscal revenue (GH₵ 315 versus to GH₵ 490).

Registered manufacturer and unregistered importer: In Table 5.8, the importer is not registered as a manufacturer and, therefore, operates outside the "ring" and adds import taxes to the price of inputs. In principle, however, other entities may operate "bonded" warehouses and place them at the disposal of registered manufacturers.

Table 5.8: Original Sales Tax at Manufacturing Stage only

Original Sales Tax Regime (Manufacturing not the Importer)								
	Entity	Value ex Tax	Taxable Value	Output Tax	Input Tax (waived)	Net Tax	Price (tax plus)	Comments
	1	2	3	4	5	6	7	8
a	Manufacturer (Imports)	1000	1000	175	na	175	1175	importer; under "ring"
b	Manufacturer (Domestic)	800	1975	346	0	346	2321	waiver
c	Wholesaler	600	2921	na	na	0	2921	Wholesaler & retailer are not
d	Retailer	400	3321	na	na	0	3321	registered (not in "ring")
e	Consumer	2800		521			3321	
f	Rate (Standard)	17.5%						

The outcomes are increases in consumer price (GH₵ 3,321) as well as tax burden and revenues (GH₵ 521).

The registered manufacturer as importer and exporter: In principle, under indirect tax regimes, the origin states regard GCT as a domestic tax—not a tax on foreigners who patronize exports. The sales tax works alongside other indirect taxes such as excise and import duties under methods that include:

general waiver methods: they include zero-rating; refunds; transit arrangement (i.e., re-export); bond facilities; free zones; and "duty drawbacks".

offsets: registered entities offset input tax on inputs (and expenses) against output tax on sales or turnover—and pay only the net amount to the tax authorities;

refunds: registered entities apply for refunds of excess input tax—a method that is also popular with VAT paid by individual non-registered travellers at the port; and

customs bonds and warehouses: the main waiver or deferral methods include placing the goods in a bonded customs-registered facility; operating in designated zones for exports; and ring-fencing goods meant for transhipment or transit.

Table 5.9 assumes that the taxpayers were a manufacturer, an importer, and an exporter under a CEPS "ring" (waiver or deferral), drawback, or bonded warehouse program.

Table 5.9: Manufacturer as Importer and Exporter

Original Sales Tax Regime (Manufacturer as Importer & Exporter)								
Items	Entity	Value ex Tax	Taxable Value	Output Tax	Input Tax (waived or offset)	Net Tax	Price (tax plus)	Comments
Domestic (resident) activities								
a	Manufacturer (Imports)	1000	1000	0	0	0	1000	Manufacturer is a registered
b	Manufacturer (Domestic)	800	1800	315	(315)	0	1800	importer & exporter
External (non-resident) activities								
c	Wholesaler/importer	600	2400	0	0	0	2400	Business entities subject to
d	Retail/distributor	400	2800	0	0	0	2800	foreign country tax regime
e	Consumer (non-resident)	2800		0			2800	
f	Rate (Standard)	17.5%						
g	Export tax rate (zero)	0.0%						

The basic point in Tables 3.6 to 3.9 is that ***the registration of taxpayers to charge the ideal single-stage sales tax excludes wholesalers and retailers***. It is also pertinent to reiterate that the "ring" or waiver mechanism covered only direct inputs (i.e., semi-manufactured and raw materials), no other expenses.

6. Service tax regime

IRS registered mostly professional service providers, restaurants and entertainment entities to charge and collect the service tax on its behalf. As the ***summary of Service Tax Act, 1995 (Act 501) and Service Tax (Amendment) Act, 1997 (529)*** in Chapter 1 shows, the service taxes were based on ***selected professional and other services***. The key features of the original and later service tax regimes include the following:

> ***status of IRS:*** IRS is a direct tax agency that collects indirect taxes from business entities, in addition to the personal and corporate income tax because the CEPS domestic tax base covers only registered manufacturers of goods;
>
> ***list of taxable services:*** the tax is not "all-inclusive" but imposed on "selected" services, as specified in a Schedule to the Act;
>
> ***registered entities:*** the entities mainly provide specific professional services, such as accountancy to all taxpayers—importers, manufacturers, wholesalers, and distributors;
>
> ***burden of tax:*** the burden of the tax depends on the point at which any of the entities acquire the requisite professional services; and
>
> ***no recourse to ITC***: the tax is irrecoverable, even in B2B supplies, which means that the sales tax could cascade when registered manufacturers treat it as an expense;

Further, registered entities cannot issue an indirect tax invoice to customers to claim ITC and, unlike the single-stage sales tax, the services tax regime lacked a "ring" deferral scheme, the input (service) tax is reintroduced into the value addition process.

Separate single-stage service tax: CEPS registers businesses to charge sales tax at the manufacturing stage while IRS registered professional firms to charge GST on taxable accountancy consultancies rendered to importers, manufacturers, wholesalers and larger retailers along the value chain.

Box 3.3 notes that the 17.5 per cent used in the examples that follow was not the exact Service Tax rates of 15 per cent and 10 per cent after the cancellation of the VAT.

Box 3.3: Rate of Service Taxes

For ease of reference, the examples in the Tables that follow use a 17.5 per-cent Service Tax rate. However, it is necessary to note from Chapter 2 that, after the cancellation of VAT in 1995, *Service Tax Act 501* services were charged at the Sales Tax *rate of 15 percent (*Act 500) while the ***Service Tax (Amendment) Act 529*** imposed a ***rate of 10 percent*** on the add-on services under that law [Ref. Chapter 1 for details)

Tables 3.10 to 3.12 are idealized examples of the impact of a ***single professional firm that renders services to the entire value chain.*** As with the regime at the time, there is ***no recourse to a "ring" and bonded warehouse waivers for upfront tax payments,*** as applied to the Sales Taxes— ***nor ITC benefits*** under the VAT Invoice-Credit method. The rate of service tax is equated to the 17.5 per cent of VAT used in the book.

Table 5.10: Imposition of Service Tax

Service Tax [Parallel to Sales Tax]							
[Assumed to form part of Value Addition]							
	Entity	Value Added	Ratio of Services (o/w)	Service Tax	Value [Tax-inclusive]	Total Tax Payment	Comments
	1	2	3	4	5	6	7
a	Importer	1000	50	9	59	9	The "Value of Service" (Column 3) is part of value added & the tax base
b	Manufacturer	800	40	7	47	7	
c	Wholesaler	600	30	5	35	5	
d	Retailer	400	20	4	24	4	
e	Total	2800	140	25	165	25	
f	Service Tax Rate		17.5%				
g	Ratio of service		5%	[Percent of value addition]			

The service tax at 17.5 per cent is imposed on 5 per cent of the total VA of GH₵ 140 amounts to GH₵ 25 and increases the price of the services across-board to GH₵ 165. As shown in Table 5.11 in the next section, the tax cascades at each value addition stage and is embedded in costs.

Combined Sales and Service Taxes: The sales and service taxes by CEPS and IRS were ***concurrent but not integrated.*** Hence, since the ***service tax on selected services had no waiver scheme,*** it adds to costs along the value chain. Table 5.11 assumes that 5 per cent of VA at each stage is for services.

Table 5.11: Combined Sales and Service Tax

Combined [unintegrated & concurrent] Sales and Service Tax regimes										
	Entity	Value ex Tax	Ratio of Services (o/w)	Taxable Value	Output Tax/GST Sales Tax	Output Tax/GST *Svc Tax (not waived)*	Sales Tax (Waived)	Net Tax Paid	Price (tax plus)	Comments
	1	2	3	4	5	6	8	9	10	11
				(2+8)				(4+5)	(2+8)	
a	Manufacturer (Imports)	1000	50	1000	0	*9*	na	9	1009	Registered manufacturer-cum-importer
b	Manufacturer (Domestic)	800	40	1809	317	*7*	0	324	2132	benefits from "ring" waiver
c	Wholesaler	600	30	2732	na	*5*	na	5	2738	Wholesaler & retailer not registered (not
d	Retailer	400	20	3138	na	*4*	na	4	3141	in "ring")
e	Consumer	2800	140		317	25		341	3141	Inclusive of Service Tax [all stages]
f	Rate (Standard)	17.5%								Service tax cascades because it is part of
g	Ratio of Services	5.0%								the "ring" regime

Combined Sales Tax (direct & indirect costs) and Service Tax: The sales and service taxes imposed by ***CEPS and IRS were concurrent but not integrated.*** However, in practice, as shown in Table 5.12, the service tax on selected services could be imposed on business entities at any stage of our value chain.

Table 5.12: Combined Sales Tax (direct & indirect costs) and Service Tax

Combined [unintegrated & concurrent] Sales and Service Tax regimes										
	Entity	Value ex Tax	Ratio of Services (o/w)	Taxable Value	Output Tax/GST Sales Tax	Output Tax/GST *Svc Tax (not waived)*	Sales Tax (Waived)	Net Tax Paid	Price (tax plus)	Comments
	1	2	3	4	5	6	8	9	10	11
				(2+8)				(4+5)	(2+8)	
a	Manufacturer (Imports)	1000	50	1000	0	*9*	na	9	1009	Registered manufacturer-cum-
b	Manufacturer (Domestic)	800	40	1809	317	*7*	0	324	2132	importer benefits from "ring" waiver
c	Wholesaler	600	30	2732	na	*5*	na	5	2738	Wholesaler & retailer not registered
d	Retailer	400	20	3138	na	*4*	na	4	3141	(not in "ring")
e	Consumer	2800	140		317	25		341	3141	Inclusive of Service Tax [all stages]
f	Rate (Standard)	17.5%								Service tax cascades because it is
g	Ratio of Services	5.0%								part of the "ring" regime

Tables 3.11 and 3.12 ***have many complex features*** that contributed to the GCT regime in Ghana, the ***combination of sales and service tax regimes,*** being replaced with the uniform invoice-credit VAT regime.

> ***Manufacturer as importer:*** The manufacturer is also the importer and benefits from the sales tax ring or waiver (deferral or suspension) as well as bonded warehouse schemes.
>
> ***Wholesaler and retailer:*** These are non-registered entities that cannot charge sales tax and are ineligible for any tax waivers—hence, taxes paid form part of their costs.
>
> ***Service tax:*** It is assumed that a proportion (5 per cent) of the value added at each stage represents various services rendered to the entities from registered service providers under the IRS scheme—the tax is irrecoverable and forms part of costs.
>
> ***Direct and indirect costs:*** The benefits of the sales tax ***"ring" waiver applied to direct inputs***. Hence, compared to VAT, apart from service tax costs, ***did not extend to sales tax on operational expenses***—such as pens, even paid by registered manufacturers.

Since the ***two cases in Tables 3.10 and 3.11 result in cascading,*** they lead to higher tax burdens and fiscal revenues (GH₵341 and GH₵ 522) and higher consumer prices (GH₵ 3141 and GH₵ 3347)—provided they do not encourage tax evasion and avoidance.

7. Comparison of Sales Tax Methods

The pre-VAT Sales Tax regime was not efficient with respect to the scope of taxation (i.e., manufacturing and import stage as well as selected services) and non-uniform application of the deferral or "ring" method of alleviating the tax paid on inputs. Furthermore, the complementary Services Tax was a separate regime from the Sales Tax and was imposed on only selected services and without relief for taxes paid on inputs.

Table 5.13 shows the ***different outcomes*** in comparison with the Ideal VAT or single-stage distribution Sales Tax.

Table 5.13: Comparison of Sales and Service Tax Methods

Comparative Table (based on Ideal Sales Tax/Value Added of 2,800)								
Tables	Assumpton/Basis	Total VA+VAT Denied	Tax Burden	Output VAT	Input VAT		Total Net VAT Paid	Final Consumer Price
					Allowed	Denied		
3.4	**Ideal VAT regime**	**2,800**	**490**	**490**	**420**	**0**	**490**	**3,290**
3.2	Ideal Single-stage GST	2,800	490	490	na	na	490	3,290
3.3	GST Addition method	2,800	490	490	na	na	490	3,290
3.5	Ideal Pre-VAT Sales Tax	2,800	490	490	na	na	490	3,290
3.6	Turnover [Full Caxcading] Tax	2,800	1,710	1,790	na	na	1,710	4,502
3.7	Deferred ["ring"] Sales Tax	2,800	315	315	na	na	315	3,115
3.8	Manufacturing stage Sales Tax	2,800	521	521	na	na	(420)	2,800
3.9	Manufacturer: Importer/Exporter	2,800	0	315	0	(315)	0	2,800
3.10	Service Tax [proportion]	140	25	25	na	na	25	165
3.11	Combined Sales & Services Tax	2,800	341	341	175	(315)	545	3,660
2.12	Non-registration: midstream	2,975	521	521	na	na	341	3,141

Table 5.14 shows the deviations from the nominal figures in Table 5.13; the zeros (0) are neutral outcome, positives adverse, and the negatives favourable for the final consumer.

Table 5.14: Deviations from Ideal VAT and Sales Tax Regimes

Deviations: Comparative Table (based on Ideal Sales Tax/Value Added of 2,800)								
Tables	Assumpton/Basis	Total VA+VAT Denied	Tax Burden	Output VAT	Input VAT		Total Net VAT Paid	Final Consumer Price
					Allowed	Denied		
3.4	**Ideal VAT regime**	**2,800**	**490**	**490**	**420**	**0**	**490**	**3,290**
3.2	Ideal Single-stage GST	0	0	0	na	na	0	0
3.3	GST Addition method	0	0	0	na	na	0	0
3.5	Ideal Pre-VAT Sales Tax	0	0	0	na	na	0	0
3.6	Turnover [Full Caxcading] Tax	0	(1,220)	(1,300)	na	na	(1,220)	(1,212)
3.7	Deferred ["ring"] Sales Tax	0	175	175	na	na	175	175
3.8	Manufacturing stage Sales Tax	0	(31)	(31)	na	na	910	490
3.9	Manufacturer: Importer/Exporter	0	490	175	420	315	490	490
3.10	Service Tax [proportion]	2,660	465	465	na	na	465	3,125
3.11	Combined Sales & Services Tax	0	149	149	245	315	(55)	(370)
2.12	Non-registration: midstream	(175)	(31)	(31)	na	na	149	149

8. Conclusion

The ***sales and service taxes*** discussed in this Chapter covered only registered manufacturers, selected service providers and taxable imports or supplies. In contrast, the ***ideal ITC-VAT process*** allows all businesses to register and claim a credit or refund for the input tax on taxable purchases against the Output VAT charged on taxable turnover or sales. Hence, the ***amount paid to the GRA is the difference between Output and Input VAT***—which is equal to the VAT on value added at each stage of the value chain.

In practice, however, there are ***several caveats to the ideal VAT mechanism,*** including special provisions for domestic supplies and exports under exempt and zero-rated regimes. VAT regimes also ***limit the businesses that can register*** to charge VAT, based on a minimum annual sales or turnover level to eliminate most small entities from the registration base. Further, the VAT process also has ***special regimes for certain transactions,*** including second-hand goods, financial services, and real estate. The ensuing Chapters discuss these issues in detail.

However, as Table 5.14 shows, ***the efficiency of the Ideal VAT is not in doubt*** even while several policy changes continue to mimic the old sales and service taxes regimes that the VAT replaced. The examples show that the policy distortions delay both administration and compliance. Additionally, ***Ghana and other countries realize that the denial of ITC does not increase revenue (from cascading)*** and, disappointment in the ability to deliver on its fiscal promises and impose a fair tax burden on final consumers.

In Ghana, the distortions include inadequate budget provision for refunds relating to zero-rating; the ***arbitrary denial of automatic ITC by separating the Education and Health Levies as "straight" levies;*** VAT withholding schemes that ignore the fact that the Input Tax is a withholding scheme; and distortion of small-entity registration and exempt supply regimes.

PART II

VAT POLICY AND LEGISLATION

Chapter 6

VAT STRUCTURE AND LEGISLATION

1. Introduction

Value Added Tax (VAT) laws follow a ***standard "all-inclusive" approach to*** impose the tax on ***taxable supplies of goods and services*** but with exceptions for ***non-taxable relief and exempt supplies.*** These exclusions are often based on social intervention or technical policies and in compliance with international treaties—notably, the Vienna Convention that guides the reciprocal imposition of taxes on diplomats and diplomatic institutions.

VAT laws require ***persons, taxpayers or entities*** making turnover or sales above a given annual threshold limit to register and charge ***Output VAT as well as claim Input Tax Credit (ITC) and refunds***—which is a major feature of zero-rated exports. Furthermore, the supplies or activities must relate to a ***commercial or profit-making*** activity—in the ***course or furtherance of a regular or continuous*** business, trade, venture, profession, employment or vocation.

While the ***administration*** of VAT falls under different organizational structures and processes, the trend is to ***integrate*** VAT with income tax collections in ***segmented*** tax offices to serve the needs of taxpayers. Further, ***customs agencies*** administer the ***import and export VAT*** as part of tariff rules while domestic tax agencies administer the ***domestic VAT*** separately or with income tax—with integrated offices becoming the trend in many countries.

VAT-registered entities must meet their registration, filing, and payment ***obligations voluntarily,*** failure of which the VAT authorities may use prescribed legal powers such as fines and prosecution to ***enforce compliance.*** All compliance decisions taken in tax offices are subject to successive administrative or judicial appeals—with the legislation of a ***Tax Appeals Board*** being the latest development and final administrative appeals body in Ghana.

Finally, Box 1 draws attention to the ***currency redenomination*** exercise from July 1, 2007, that resulted in an instant change in the real value of Ghana's currency. Under the programme, approximately GH¢ 10,000 = $1 became GH¢ 1 = $1. This is relevant to giving proper interpretation to the differences in currency values, notably in discussing policy measures such as registration threshold and VAT Flat Rate Schemes (VFRS).

Box 4.1: Redenomination of the currency

It is necessary to note that as of 2007, Ghana introduced new currency notes and coins called Ghana Cedi (GH₵), to replace the cedi (c) as part of a currency redenomination policy. The exercise resulted in "slashing" four (4) zeros from the currency in relation to the benchmark currency, the US Dollar—whose value remained constant. Hence, given an exchange rate of approximately GH₵ 10,000 = GH₵ 1 (precisely GH₵ 9,200=$, a VAT small-entity registration threshold amount of c250,000 before 2007 immediately became GH₵ 25.

2. General VAT structure

Under the ***invoice-credit method,*** the design and implementation of VAT follows certain known ***rules or concepts*** relating to the structure, characteristics, and features of supply. The ensuing sections also discuss the forms of organization and process.

> ***Imposition of VAT:*** VAT laws impose the tax at a specified ***rate or rates*** on ***supplies of*** goods and services, with specified ***exemptions*** and ***reliefs*** that may include persons or entities. Exemptions minimize the ***regressive impact*** of VAT on low-income persons.
>
> ***VAT base:*** the goods and services that are subject to VAT may be ***taxable or non-taxable*** (i.e., exempt and reliefs). While the ***ideal fiscal goal*** is to impose VAT on all supplies, this is practically impossible for technical and policy reasons, such as using tax instruments to redistribute incomes (support low-income persons).
>
> *VAT rate(s)*: these are ***standard*** for domestic supplies and imports as well as ***zero (0)*** for exports—to alleviate the burden of VAT on foreign buyers and to make a country's exports competitive in global markets. Some tax laws adopt ***sub-standard*** or lower rates to lessen the tax burden and ***super-rates*** as part of punitive tax regimes.

During its VAT implementation, Ghana replaced some exempt domestic supplies with a ***zero (0) rate*** and, also, added a ***sub-standard rate*** called the ***VAT Flat Rate Schemes (VFRS).*** It has also changed the *de facto* VAT-based GETFund and NHIL to ***"straight"*** levies, with ***no recourse to ITC claims or refunds***. Hence, the straight levies cascade and are worse than the deferred or "ring" sales tax regime that the VAT replaced in the 1990s.

As guidance between the two (2) major VAT Legislation, that is ***VATA 1998 (Act 546) and VATA 2013 (Act 870)***, the headings or arrangements to various Parts of the laws are compared in Appendix Table 1 to 13 to this Chapter.

3. Nature or structure of supplies

Supplies mean ***goods (and property) or services*** that attract Output VAT unless the law excludes them. Goods and property are ***tangible*** while services are ***intangible*** and are defined as a supply other than goods or property. For VAT accounting purposes, the nature, place, and value (consideration for) of supply falls under a variety of rules.

Nature of supply: as noted, supplies may be ***goods or property*** (tangible) ***or services*** (intangible)—and deriving from above, may be also ***mixed*** or ***composite*** supply.

Goods: goods are described as tangible (compared to services) and of a movable or immovable nature;

Services: services are intangible and described in residual terms as "anything that is not goods or property".

Mixed and composite supplies: the combination of taxable and exempt supplies may result in two sub-classes: ***mixed*** (taxable and exempt) or ***composite*** (reverse primary and secondary taxable and exempt) elements.

Nature of supply: the manner of treating supplies depends on whether they are taxable or non-taxable.

Taxable supplies: this category of supplies attracts VAT at specified rates that are standard or zero (0) but some taxes include super and sub-standard rates.

Non-taxable: this category of exempt and relief supplies does not attract Output VAT—with reliefs often extending to persons or entities (e.g., diplomats).

Place (or origin) of supply: the ***place where*** supplies are ***made available, delivered, or rendered; property is located; and brought into the country***.

Domestic supplies: supplies made within the tax jurisdiction, including imports, may attract VAT, if not exempted.

Foreign supplies: imports become domestic supplies while, typically, the consumption of exports is outside the jurisdiction. The origin country imposes a zero (0) VAT rate and, therefore, the ITC offset often leads to refunds.

Time of supply: these rules relate to the period or when registered persons charge and account for VAT. It is the earliest of when the following occurs.

Invoicing (goods and services): VAT liability arises with invoicing, even when the goods are not delivered or made available and services rendered.

Payment (goods or services): payment is received—even when the supply is not made available, delivered or rendered and invoicing or payment does not occur.

Delivery and availability (goods): these often mean a physical act, including the transfer of right of use of property—even without invoicing or payment.

Rendered (services): completion of the performance of services—even without invoicing or payment.

Value (consideration) of supply: this is the price, value, or amount which a buyer forbears or agrees to pay for supplies under a contract—given in cash or in-kind.

Cash: the consideration or payment is in the form of money—cash, cheque, debit or credit card, and bank transfers.

In-kind: consideration is given in full or partial exchange for goods or services.

Forbearance: promise not to do a specified act made under a contract or failure to engage in a specific act.

Imports and exports: Customs offices use the official ***tariff nomenclature*** and rules on cost, insurance, and freight (CIF) to determine the ***import VAT*** on goods. As noted, imports attract the standard and ancillary VAT rates while ***exports*** are zero-rated.

Services and "reverse-charge" rule: Domestic tax/VAT offices administer VAT under the ***"reverse-charge"*** rules, where the domestic beneficiary accounts for both the Out VAT and "reverse" import VAT amounts.

4. Nature of enterprises or entities

The VAT structure covers "persons" that set up a business; engage in commercial activities, with a profit motive; and form of their ownership—for which the VAT law obliges them to register and charge VAT.

> ***Persons:*** A "person" refers to an individual, entity, enterprise, trader, or business—as a ***natural*** or a ***legal*** (i.e., artificial) person (e.g., company or corporation). A person must be eligible for registration to charge Output VAT and claim ITC.
>
> ***Enterprise:*** conducting a business, trade, venture, or similar endeavour with a ***profit motive***—hence, subject to the provisions of the law, ***"not-for-profit"*** entities are not required to register and charge VAT even if they make taxable supplies.
>
> ***Commercial activities:*** the difference between enterprises and "not-for-profit" entities are performing or not performing *regular or continuous activities,* in furtherance of for-profit or enterprise. ***Non-commercial*** activities include the supply of public goods (e.g., by a government entity, personal or private sales (e.g., house or car), and occasional rentals.

"Non-profit" persons or entities include government entities and charities or similar organizations while non-commercial activities also include wages and salaries; meritorious and cultural supplies; and personal transactions.

5. Scope of policy and legislation

In general, Ghana's VAT Acts follow the structure described above and give credence to the argument that the suspension of VAT was mainly due to general political-economy sentiments—notably ERP/SAP fatigue and the transition from military rule to civilian administration under the 1992 Constitution.

The ensuing sections summarize the discussions in Chapter 1 relating to several VAT issues under the laws passed by Parliament since the first attempt to introduce VAT in 1994—and continuing with the reintroduction of VAT in 1998/99. It also includes the reform of tax policy and administration that started in 2009 with the setting up of GRA and the merger of IRS and VATS as GRA's Domestic Tax Revenue Division [DTRD].

Original VAT laws: These were the VAT Act, 1994 (Act 486) and the VAT Act 1998 (Act 546) that backed the VAT introduction and reintroduction from 1995 to 1998. The State used VATA 1994 to set up a third revenue agency, the ***VAT Service (VATS)***, to collect the domestic VAT while CEPS continued to collect the import VAT.

No substantive role for IRS in VAT: As a direct tax agency, the IRS had no technical or administrative role in VAT collection and compliance, except under coordination programs. This is because the service taxes were part of the VAT-based GCT handle,

The merger of IRS and VATS: together with CEPS, the ***3-agency structure*** continued under separate Boards until the merger of IRS and VATS in 2009 as the Domestic Tax Revenue Division (DTRD), under the Ghana Revenue Authority (GRA) Act;

Repeal of original VAT laws: VATA 1994 and VATA 1998 ***repealed the sales and service tax*** operations under CEPS and IRS, with the following key features—

- the state suspended VATA 1994 between 1995 and 1998, after only two-and-half months of charging VAT under this new law in 1995;
- as part of the VAT reintroduction program, the government replaced VAT 1994 with an enhanced VATA 546 in 1998;
- Parliament passed the CEPS (Management) (Amendment) Act, 1995 (Act 500) and Service Tax Act, 1995 (Act 501) to suspend the VAT in 1995 and revert to the old sales and service tax regimes;
- followed by Service Tax (Amendment) Act, 1997 (Act 529), which expanded the scope of services that were eligible to attract the service tax; and
- repeal of the interim VAT, sales and service tax laws to pave for the successful reintroduction of VAT from 1998 under VATA 546.

The five-year period from 1994 to 1999 was the most difficult for ***VAT administration in the country,*** with Ghana joining only a few countries that introduced but failed to consolidate the VAT initiative that was sweeping through many countries at the time.

Importance of transition laws: The transition laws, Act 500 and Act 501, suspended the implementation of VAT but saved clauses to mop up and reintroduce the VAT from 1998 to 1999. The ***key elements of the various laws*** include—

- restoration of the old sales and service tax regimes under Acts 500 and 501 for CEPS and IRS to restart their collection to protect budget revenues;
- meeting all VAT Service obligations and enforcing those against taxpayers for the three-month VAT implementation in 1995, also under Acts 500 and 501;
- vesting the assets, liabilities and staff in the IRS, CEPS and MOF, with additional powers for the Minister to administer the transition; and
- reinstating the VAT Service, planning for the reintroduction of VAT, and passing a new VATA 1998 (Act 546).

Besides the protection of budget revenues and the VAT Project/ Service structures, the transition laws made it possible for registered entities to appreciate the ***benefits of the VAT invoice-credit, notably the right to ITC and refunds.*** This was a major boost to the reintroduction of the VAT in 1998.

Replacement 1998 VAT Act: The first phase of VAT, including the suspension saga, came to an end when Parliament used VATA 1998 to repeal the suspension laws to pave the way for the reintroduction of VAT in 1998. The second phase happened when the House passed a substantive replacement Act, that also enhanced the VAT structure, under VAT Act, 2013 (Act 870), after many amendments to VATA 1994 and 1998.

Tables 4.1 to 4.5 in the ensuing section summarize the set of legislation that covered the ***narrow-based and, therefore, less buoyant sales and service taxes,*** which were replaced with a comprehensive VAT regime with an unambiguous revenue goal.

Pre-VAT Sales and Services Tax

The original pre-VAT consumption taxes were (a) the sales tax that was administered by CEPS under the CEPS (Management) Law of 1985; and (b) various service taxes managed by IRS under the Income Tax Decree 1975, (SMCD 5). Table 6.1 shows a summary of the two laws as well as the original VAT law that was suspended in 1995 before the 1996 elections.

Table 6.1: Original Sales and Service Tax Laws

VAT Acts: Important Milestones (1)				
Items	**Pre-1994 Legislation**	**Tax Instrument**	**Features**	**Comments**
1	**Pre-VAT Consumption Tax Laws**			
1.1	Customs, Excise and Preventive Service (Management Act), 1985	Sales Tax	Single (manufacturing/import) tax on goods; "ring" as input tax relief	Restricted in scope and eligibility to be GRA tax agent
	Income Tax Decree, 1975 (SMCD 5)	Service Tax	Tax on selected professional services	Tax was collected by the defunct IRS since it had a larger number of offices
2	**1st VAT law (introduction)**			
2.1	Value Added Tax Act 1994 (Act 486)	VAT	Original VAT Act (repealed)	Introduced VAT for the first time; not much change in 2nd VATA

VAT implementation suspension laws

The "suspension" of VAT ended after the 1996 elections and the preparations that ensued resulted in a successful VAT reintroduction in 1998/99. As noted, however,

> The ***cancellation*** or, more appropriately, ***transition laws*** helped preserve *the right of registered entities to claim ITC and refunds* for the three-and-half months of VAT operations in 1995;
>
> these laws also preserved the ***status of VAT staff*** within the uniform conditions of service as staff of IRS, VATS and MOF—indeed, many remained in the VAT Service offices and facilities throughout the suspension; and
>
> these factors were ***major promotions and preparation*** for the new effort since they showed the superiority of the VAT invoice credit mechanism over the sales tax.

Table 6.2 summarizes the VAT legislation and amendments that followed the VAT reintroduction under VATA 1998 and its major amendments until the enactment of VATA, 2013 (Act 870) as well as another round of principal amendments that reversed most of the major enhancements—under a new government.

Table 6.2: VAT suspension and transition laws

VAT Acts: Important Milestones (2)				
Items	**Pre-1994 Legislation**	**Tax Instrument**	**Features**	**Comments**
3	**VAT suspension, pre-VAT restoration, transition**			
3.1	CEPS (Management) (Amendment) Act, 1995 (Act 500)	Sales Tax	Restored previous sales tax under only manufacturers under the "ring" or deferred system.	Made old sales tax effective till 1998/99 and preserved the staffing, asset and liabilities of VATS.
3.2	Service Tax Act, 1995 (Act 501)	Service Tax	Restored previous service tax to the 4 sectors, namely gaming, entertainment, hotel accommodation & restaurant meals, and advertisement.	Act that restored Service Tax under IRS, as existed before the introduction of VAT; also preserved staffing, assets and liabilities of VATS
3.3	Service Tax (Amendment) Act, 1995 (Act 529)	Service Tax	Expanded the base of the services that are subject to service tax from 4 to 11 [ref. Chapter 1)	Among the transition laws between the period of suspending and introducing VAT

Fiscal sustainability: One of the moves that made it easy to reintroduce the VAT was the lowering of the rate from 17.5 per cent in 1995/96 down to a fiscally unsustainable 10 per cent. It also followed the public protests that led to fatalities at the peak of the ***"Kumepreko" demonstrations***. The solutions also started the earmarking that has constrained fiscal administration in Ghana.

VAT reintroduction and further rate increase

The VAT was reintroduced in 1998 at a rate of 10 per cent, far lower than the 17.5 per cent at the time of the failed attempt, and was ***never going to be fiscally sustainable***, even with an expanded VAT or consumption tax base. Hence, the NDC increased the rate by 2.5 per cent to 12.5 per cent and ***dedicated net proceeds (after ITC and refunds) to education***. In a counter-political economy, the NPP followed with a 2.5 per cent increase that it dedicated to Health.

NPP I ***"earmarked"*** the second 2.5 per cent VAT increase to the ***National Health Insurance (NHI) Scheme*** in 2008 and introduced the ***sub-standard VAT Flat Rate Scheme (VFRS)*** of 2.5 per cent. Finally, the NDC II dedicated the proceeds of another 2.5 per cent rate increase in 2014 to the ***Ghana Infrastructure Investment Fund (GIIF)***.

> As discussed in various ensuing Sections, the GETFund Levy and NHIL are now called "Straight Levies", with the related right to ITC denied. The VAT regime flows into the GIIF have also curtailed the amount paid into the general Consolidated

Fund. Nonetheless, it forms part of the VAT base and registered entities are allowed to claim the ITC.

In addition to highlighting the substantive 1998 VAT law (VATA 546), Table 6.3 summarizes the objectives of the various enactments, amendments and originals that are commonly referred to as the ***"statutory" or "earmarked" funds*** in Ghana.

Table 6.3: VAT as Statutory or Earmarked Fund Allocation

VAT Acts: Important Milestones (2)				
Items	**Pre-1994 Legislation**	**Tax Instrument**	**Features**	**Comments**
4	**2nd VAT law (re-introduction)**			
4.1	VAT Act, 1998 (Act 546)	VAT	Reintroduction of VAT (replaced in 2013)	The Act was used to reintroduce VAT successfully
4.2	GETFund Act, 2000	VAT	VAT rate increase by 2.5%; net proceeds dedicated to education sector	GETFund levy is *de facto* VAT; allocation of net proceeds is budgetary allocation
4.3	NHI Act, 2003 (Act 650)	VAT/Levy	VAT rate increse by 2.5% but using the NHI Act	Also allocates net proceeds from 5% to health insurance
4.4	NHI (Amendment) Act, 2008 (Act 753)	VAT/Levy	Amendment of original 2003 NHIL Act	Repealed by NHI Act 2012 (Act 852)
4.5	NHI Act, 2012 (Act 852)	VAT/Levy	An Act that with own taxable, exempt & relief supply schedules, parallel to VATA 456 & 870	Made NHI & VAT complex to administer; repealed by VATAA 2017 (Act 948)
4.6	NHIL (Amendment) Act, 2015 (Act 888)	VAT/Levy	Amended VATAA 852, 2nd Schedule, Item 14	Ensure consistency with VATA 2013 (Act 870)
4.7	GIIF Act, 2014 (Act 877)	VAT	Source of funding includes 15% of VAT revenue (s5)a	Accounted for increase in VAT rate from 15% to 17.5%
4.8	VATA 546 Amendments		Various, often distortionary, amendments	As discussed in detail in Parts III to IV (Chapters 6 to 13)

At the introduction, the earmarked funds were ***charged and collected as though they were VAT***. Hence, registered entities simply charged the VAT at 17.5 per cent and, thereby, claimed ITC and refunds for the general VAT rate as well as the GETFund Levy and NHIL. In 2017, at the instance of the Ministry of Finance, Parliament passed the ***Earmarked Funds Capping and Realignment Act, 2017 (Act 947) to cap the Statutory Funds at 25 per cent***. However, in its ***ruling in 2019, the Supreme Court made an exception concerning the DACF*** (Box 4.2).

Box 4.2: Extract of Supreme Court Decision on Statutory Funds

"To the extent that sections 1(2), 2(b),3(1)(b), 3(5)(a), 7(a) and 8 of the earmarked Funds Capping and Realignment Act, 2017 (Act 947) and Section 126 of the Local Governance Act, 2016 (Act 916) purport to limit the proportion of revenue due for allocation to the District Assemblies Common Fund, as established by Article 252(2) of the Constitution, the same are in contravention of the Constitution and are hereby declared to be null and void".

Further, in 2021, Parliament again ***passed the Ghana Infrastructure Investment Fund (Amendment) Act, 2021, Act 1063*** *to remove the cap placed on GIIF to restore the original allocation and to facilitate its operations. The earmarking of revenues for various purposes remains contentious in Ghana's fiscal and public financial management since it is estimated about 28 per cent of total revenue is allocated to the Earmarked Funds.*

VAT revamp Under VAT Act 870

As Table 6.4 shows, the purpose of VAT Act 2013 (Act 870) is to refine the VAT regime comprehensively has suffered reversals that often bring the VAT regime to its VATA 1998/99 (Act 546) status—particularly, the complementary small entities under the ***VFRS*** and removal of NHIL and GETFund Levy from the VAT base, with their renaming as ***"straight" levies.***

Table 6.4: Post-VATA 870 changes and reversals

VAT Acts: Important Milestones (3)				
Items	**Pre-1994 Legislation**	**Tax Instrument**	**Features**	**Comments**
5	**3rd VAT law (comprehensive review)**			
5.1	VAT Act, 2013 (Act 870)	VAT	Comprehensive review of entire VAT Act	First major review pf VAT since enactment of Act 546
5.2	NHIL/GET Fund "Straight" Levies	VAT/Levy	VATAA, 2018 (Act 970): reduced VAT rate to 12.5%	Rate of 12.5% constitutes VAT (10%) and GIIF (2.5%)
		VAT/Levy	NHI (Amendment) Act, 2018 (Act 971)	Replaces the amendment that reduced the ***de facto VAT*** rate to by 2.5% but in separate Act
		VAT/Levy	GETFund (Amendment) Act, 2018 (Act 972); imposes rate of 2.5% without recourse to ITC	Replaces the amendment that reduced the ***de facto VAT*** rate to by 2.5% but in separate Act
5.3	VATA 870 Amendments	VAT	Various, often distortionary, amendments	VATA 870 forms the basis for the discussions in the entire book

Distortion of simple VAT rate structure: VATA 1998 (546) was based on (a) a two-rate standard and zero-rate regime; and (b) reliefs and exemptions. However, several of the amendments to the Act have also resulted in a VAT rate complexity that includes—

Standard rate: there is confusion as to whether the standard rate remains ***17.5 per cent and has been changed to 12.5 per cent,*** following the amendments that introduced the "straight" levies without recourse to ITC and refunds.

Sub-standard rate: the notable one is the imposition of the ***VFRS at 3 per cent,*** without recourse to ITC or refunds.

Zero (0) rate: while this continues to apply to exports, some complications include—

(a) exports becoming less competitive, given the denial of ITC and refunds for the ***"straight"*** levies;

(b) the same policy effect of denying ITC and possible refunds for ***VFRS;*** and

(c) ***domestic zero-rating,*** which complicates existing inefficiencies in managing the refunds relating to zero-rates, in particular.

Implicit super rates: these are increases that result from denying ITC and refunds, with the cascading effect giving rise to implied rates that exceed the standard VAT rate—even when the VFRS is regarded as sub-standard.

Table 6.5 summarizes the various substantive rate changes that continue to ***complicate administration and compliance with the VAT regime***. Moreover, the notion that these ***ad hoc*** changes will ***generate more revenue has not materialized.***

Table 6.5: VAT and other rates

Original and changes to VAT rate [VATA 546; 579; 734 and 970]			
Section	**Title**	**Description**	**Comments**
VAT Act, 1998 (Act 546)			
3	Rate of Tax	Except otherwise provided in this Act, the rate of the tax shall be ***10 percent*** calculated on the value of the taxable supply of the goods, services or import.	Lowered from the 1995 Act from 12.5 percent
VAT (Amendment) Act, 2000 (Act 579)			
1	Section 3 of Act 546 amended	The VATA, 1998 (Act 546) referred to in this Act as the "principal enactment" is amended in section 3 by the substitution for "10 percent" of ***"12.5 percent"***	Increase of 2.5 percent dedicated to the ***Ghana Eduction Trust Fund (GETFund)***
VAT (Amendment) Act, 2007 (Act 734)			
2	Section 3 of Act 546 amended	The principal enactment is amended in section 3 by the insertion of subsection (2):	Applies to (a) a taxable person; (b) retailer of goods; (c) VAT payable; (d) flat rate of 3 percent; and (e) taxable supply. It seems to apply to ***all large and small retailers***
		"Unless otherwise directed by the Commissioner in writing, a ***taxable person*** who is ***a retailer of goods*** shall account for the ***VAT payable*** under this section at ***a flat rate of 3 percent*** calculated on the value of the ***taxable supply*** ".	
VAT (Amendment) Act, 2018 (Act 970)			
	Section 3 of Act 870 amended	Except as otherwise provided in this Act, the rate of the tax is twelve and half percent and is calculated on (a) the value of the taxable supply of the goods or services; or (b) the value of the import.	Decouples 2.5% GETFund levy as VAT and converting it to "straight levy"

Table 6.6 shows further amendments and original legislation that increases or alters various provisions that relate to the rates associated with the ***NHIS and GIIF*** regimes.3

Table 6.6: Further NHIL and GIIF changes

Original and changes to VAT rate [NHIL Act 650; 852; and GIFF Act 877]			
National Health Iinsurance Act, 2003 (Act 650)			
1	Objective	"The object of this Act is to secure the implementation of a national health insurance policy that ensures access to basic healthcare services to all residents."	the Act that was used to introduce the additonal 2.5% VAT rate that is dedicated to health insurance. Set up a corporate entity with a board to manage the new health insurance scheme.
National Health Insurance Act, 2012 (Act 852)			
47	Levies on supply of goods & services	Substitute Act for 2.5% levy dedicated to National Health Insurance	Collected as though it were a VAT (until changed to "straight" levy
Ghana Infrastructure Investment Fund (GIIF) Act, 2014 (Act 877)			
5	Rate of the tax	5. (1) The sources of money for the Fund are (a) an amount of money equivalentto two and half percentage points of the existing Value Added Tax revenue.	Increase of 2.5 percent dedicated to the ***Ghana Infrastructure Investment Fund***

6. Status of Conventional VAT Registration Threshold and VFRS

The main ***political-economy point*** is the reversal of enhanced provisions in the VAT Act 2013 (Act 870) that was used to correct several anomalies such as substituting the conventional small-entity VAT registration threshold with the VFRS. This is not just political since some of the changes also reflect long-standing differences among *"technical" staff of GRA* on the alternative treatment of small entities under the VAT regime.

NHIL and GETFund Levies as "Straight" levies: This Section discusses two (2) significant changes to the VAT invoice-credit method, through the conversion of the ***GET-Fund Levy and NHIL to so-called "straight" levies*** that results in the blocking of input tax credits (ITC). The implications of the change include–

- ***de facto VAT versus Straight Levy:*** since 2019, the status of NHIL and GET-Fund levy changed from ***de facto VATs*** to so-called ***"straight levies"***.;
- nonetheless, the NHIL and GETFund law still ***"allocate the net/gross VAT/levy"*** by "formula" to the administration bodies;
- ***denial of ITC:*** originally, registered entities charged ALL the "earmarked" levies as Output VAT, which gave them the right to VAT ITC and refunds; and

- ***cascading:*** this contrasts with the outcome of blocking ITC and refunds, which is "cascading" or multiple taxation that increases costs, consumer prices and the tax burden.

Likely impact on potential revenues: the measures may not raise expected revenues because of complex administration as well as audit and other compliance issues arising from tax evasion and avoidance.

VFRS: VFRS adds a sub-standard rate to the single positive standard ***rate regime*** as well as registration and **ITC rules** that result in relatively **complex** small-entity VAT regimes—and, for a brief period, its extension to large (wholesale) entities.

Registration threshold: the ***VFRS*** *continued to apply the registration of small entities* to ***retailers of goods*** until its repeal by the VAT (Amendment) Act, 2010 (Act 810) to apply to all small entities.

Bracket for VFRS: VAT (Amendment) Act, 2010 (Act 810) increased the conventional VAT threshold significantly to GH₵ 90,000 but it also enlarged and placed ***all small entities (not just "retailers of goods"*** within a band of GH₵ 10,000 and GH₵ 90,000.

Presumptive income tax: the Income Tax Act, 2015 linked the basis for presumptive income tax to the VAT Act 2013, as amended, to the VAT threshold of GH₵ 200,000.

Exemptions (Act 1005 (2019): changed many of the VAT Act, 2013 (Act 870) definitions for exemptions under Schedule 2, resulting in a significant expansion in the scope of the concession.

Table 6.7 summarizes the provisions of three (3) VATA amendments that distort the VAT Invoice Credit method by denying the right to ITC and increasing input costs and consumer prices through "cascading".

Table 6.7: Amendments to ITC mechanism

Amendments: Sections [Input Tax Credit or ITC]					
ar	VATA (#)	Section	Content or Change	Book Chapter	Comments
2006	696	s25	Input Tax Credit [ITC]	8	Discretion for CG to offset rather than grant refunds for non-exports.
2007	734	s24(6a)	VFRS & ITC	8	Disallows ITC for VFRS
2008	765	s24	ITC	2	Power of Commissioner to make offsets rather than refunds for excess credit

Table 6.8 summarizes the amendments that oblige a VFRS "person" who is (a) a retailer of goods [VFRS I] with a threshold of GH₵10, 000 to GH₵ 90,000; and (b) retailers or wholesalers [VFRS II] to comply with the scheme.

Table 6.8 Basis for VFRS in amendments

Amendments: Sections [VAT rate]					
ar	VATA (#)	Section	Content or Change	Book Chapter	Comments
2000	579	s3	Standard rate	3	Increase from 10% to 12.5% for GET-Fund
2007	734	s3	VFRS (3%)	8	Applicable to taxabler person who is a **"retailer of goods"**
	734	s76	VFRS (3%)	5	Definition VFRS as approximate margin between Output VAT and Input
2010	810	s3	Standard rate	2 & 7	Taxable supplies above threshold of Ghc90,000 p.a.
2010	810	s3	VFRS (3%)	5	Rate applicable to **all entities, not "retailer of goods"** only, with annual turnover between Ghc10,000 and Ghc90,000

7. Amendments to VAT non-taxable supplies

The VAT Act, 1998 (Act 546) covered the principles of VAT that, eventually, became distorted by several amendments—notably on exemptions and reliefs.

Exempt supplies (Schedule 1): In principle, exempt supplies attract Output VAT without the right to ITC claim. The *Input VAT increases costs* in business-to-business (B2B) contracts and results in ***cascading*** (tax-on-tax). In business-to-consumer (B2C) sales, the ITC denied increases in consumer prices directly.

Pharmaceuticals: Table 6.9 shows the expansion of amendments for pharmaceuticals, making the industry the most active VAT lobby.

Table 6.9: Exempt pharmaceutical supplies

Amendments: Exempt supplies (Schedule 1–Pharmaceuticals)					
Year	**VATA (#)**	**Section**	**Content or Change**	**Book Chapter**	**Comments**
2000	579	14/16	Exempt supplies	6	Pharmaceuticals [Schedule 1 and new Schedule 1A]
2001	595	14/16	Exempt supplies	6	Pharmaceuticals
2004	670	14/16	Exempt supplies	6	Pharmaceuticals (New Schedule 1B)
2008	765	14/16	Exempt supplies	6	Pharmaceuticals [HS Code/Minister]
2010	810	14/16	Exempt supplies	6	Pharmaceuticals

Agricultural Inputs (Schedule 1): Given its favourable social and economic impact, agriculture attracts many concessions, as public policy in advanced and developing economies. The concession may be granted at the final, intermediate, and basic stages. Table 6.10 shows the scope of VAT amendments relating to agricultural supplies.

Table 6.10: Exempt Agricultural supplies and inputs

Amendments: Exempt supplies (Schedule 1–Agriculture)					
Year	**VATA (#)**	**Section**	**Content or Change**	**Book Chapter**	**Comments**
2002	629	14/16	Exempt supplies	6	Agriculture supplies and inputs
2004	671	14/16	Exempt supplies	6	Fishing inputs; musical instruments [HS Code Chapter 92]
2008	765	14/16	Exempt supplies	6	Agricultural inputs

As discussed in Chapter 8, the upstream and midstream exemptions along the value addition chain often led to more cascading and higher prices without the expected increase in tax revenues. This is mainly due to tax evasion and avoidance.

Exempt (miscellaneous) supplies: Table 6.11 shows more products that were added to the VAT-exempt regime under Schedule 1, which led to the complexity in VAT administration and compliance.

Table 6.11: Other exempt supplies

Amendments: Exempt supplies (Schedule 1–Others)					
Year	**VATA (#)**	**Section**	**Content or Change**	**Book Chapter**	**Comments**
2002	629	16	Exempt imports	6	Clarifies nature of exempt supply
2002	629	14/16	Exempt supplies	6	Buildings; mosquito & salt
2003	639	14/16	Exempt supplies	6	Compact Flourescent Lights (CFL); Fully-assembled computers (imports/domestic]
2006	696	14/16	Exempt supplies	6	Correction
2008	752	14/16	Exempt supplies	6	Telephone/cellular phone
2008	765	14/16	Exempt supplies	6	Repeal and consolidation of Schedule 1, 1A & 1B as new Schedule 1
2010	810	14/16	Exempt supplies	6	Definition: coverage of "transportation"
2010	810	14/16	Exempt supplies	6	Textbooks and agricultural machinery

8. Zero-rated domestic and zero-rated supplies (Schedules 2 and 3)

By convention and practice, VAT Act 546 restricts zero-rating to exports and ship supplies while exemption and reliefs (Schedule 1 and 3). However, GOG introduced ***zero-rating as a form of concession for domestic supply*** under Schedule 2

> ***Pressure from cascading:*** As noted in detail in Chapter 8, the cascading effect of the push to expand "midstream" input tax exemptions led to pressure to apply ***"zero-rating" and "relief" provisions*** to the final supplies and inputs.
>
> ***Replace exemption with zero-rating***: The push for *"total input VAT reliefs"* leads to zero rating of domestic supplies.

In general, the pressure to zero-rate domestic supply arises from the disappointing effects of cascading on exemptions—as it blocks the right to ITC and, therefore, increases production costs and consumer prices. Table 6.12 shows the amendments that resulted in putting taxable or exempt supplies (i.e., educational materials and locally manufactured inputs) under the zero-rated mechanism.

Table 6.12 Additions to zero-rated supplies

Amendments: Zero-rated supplies (Schedule 2)					
Year	**VATA (#)**	**Section**	**Content or Change**	**Book Chapter**	**Comments**
2006	696	15	Zero-rated supply	6	Locally produced text/exercise books
2006	696	15	Zero-rated supply	6	Locally manufactured agricultural machinery & implements
2008	765	15	Zero-rated supply	2 & 6	Zero-rating pharmaceuticals

The notion of zero rating is designed to ensure that exporters get a refund for the taxes paid on inputs—given that registered entities are allowed to offset a zero (0) Output Tax against Input VAT at the standard rate under the ITC process.

Relief supplies (Schedule 3): Relief supplies have a limited application which, in the case of diplomats, is subject to reciprocal treaties such as the Vienna Convention. There was ***successful pressure to extend the relief concession to domestic supplies,*** which worsened the VAT distortions. Table 6.13 shows the summary of amendments to Schedule 3.

Table 6.13: Additions to exempt relief supplies

Amendments: Relief Supplies [Schedule 3)					
Year	**VATA (#)**	**Section**	**Content or Change**	**Book Chapter**	**Comments**
2004	671	17	Relief for regular supply	8	Relief from payment of VAT on raw materials, at importation to members of Association of Ghana Industries (AGI)
2010	810	LI 1817	Revoked	2	GIPC VAT powers to grant reliefs; deletions

9. VAT administration and compliance

This section deals with the form in which GRA manages its VAT head office, local offices, and processes with income tax under its single integrated Domestic Tax Revenue Division (DTRD)—which was set up by merging IRS and VATS. This involves the implementation of automated systems and processes to make the mobilization of revenue for the budget effective and efficient

Organization: the responsibility to administer and enforce compliance depends on the VAT supply being domestic or external—

domestic agency: the VAT on ***domestic supplies*** may fall under an ***integrated*** direct tax (i.e., income tax and VAT) or ***separate*** (i.e., VAT-only) agency; and

imports and exports: the external trade element typically falls under the ***customs*** agency, which collects the VAT under the tariff or customs legislation.

Voluntary compliance: tax (administration) laws require all eligible persons to fulfil their obligations ***voluntarily***—also termed *self-assessment*, which narrowly means registering and calculating their own tax liability and filing a VAT return.

registration: the first condition for registration is engaging in an enterprise to make a profit but subject to the annual sales or turnover exceeding a given amount or threshold, as specified in the law;

tax accounting: registered entities must keep proper records of their transactions, including VAT; file a tax return periodically (generally, monthly for VAT); and pay the amount due (Output VAT less Input VAT); and

taxpayer assistance: in return, registered entities can get reasonable help from the tax agency (normally registered tax office) in fulfilling the voluntarily; these include regular visits to seek advice, especially by small entities.

Enforcement and appeal: where taxpayers do not comply willingly, the law empowers the tax agency to take relevant enforcement actions, including;

tax audits: tax officials have powers to examine records and obtain physical evidence that can be used to authenticate the declarations in tax returns and other submissions;

fines, penalties, and other sanctions: tax laws include fines and penalties that tax offices and courts can use to ensure compliance with all tax obligations; and

tax appeals: the law allows taxpayers to launch administrative or judicial appeals against the decisions and actions taken by tax officials or tax offices—a dispensation that the tax office can also use to contest decisions that lower courts take in favour of taxpayers.

Several aspects of VAT administration are the same as other direct and indirect taxes. Hence, Ghana, like other countries, now has a general Revenue Administration Act (RAA), 2016 (Act 915) for all direct and indirect taxes. Part IV discusses the significant changes that occurred in tax administration from 2009.

10. VAT organization

The performance of VAT administration and compliance functions are now under the GRA integrated structure from 2009. GRA performs the domestic indirect tax functions in conjunction with those of income tax under its DTRD while the Customs Division (CD) administers the VAT on imports and exports.

Headquarters and Divisions: GRA's Headquarters is the "apex" of unit, in a pyramid-type structure under the Commissioner-General (CG). There are three (3) GRA Divisions below the Headquarters: Domestic Tax Revenue Division (DTRD), Customs Division (CD) and Support Services Division (SSD).

Scope of duties: DTRD manages the VAT Act, 2013 (Act 870), Income Tax Act, 2015 (Act 896), Excise Duty Act, 2014 (Act 878), and other special direct and indirect taxes. The Customs Division administers the Customs Act, 2015 (Act 891) on all external indirect taxes—and some direct tax duties such as income tax withholding.

Local tax offices: DTRD administers the same substantive systems and processes in the local offices, structured as Large Taxpayer Offices (LTOs); Medium Taxpayer Offices (MTOs); and Small Taxpayer Offices (STOs)—since replaced with Taxpayer Service Centres (TSCS). These offices replaced the tax type, with functional arrangements, and separated local tax offices for IRS and VATS—but have been converted to Taxpayer Services Centres and Area Offices.

Customs offices: The Customs Offices at land, sea and air borders or entry points, administer the external (*import and export)* component of all indirect taxes (and some direct, such as withholding income tax) including VAT, import duties, excise duties, and special taxes under the ECOWAS tariff nomenclature.

The income tax and VAT processes and systems perform functions that include filing, tax accounting (records and payments), routine audit, debt management, and enforcement (investigation, prosecution, and special audits). The administration provisions now come mainly under a comprehensive Revenue Administration Act (RAA) 2016 (Act 915), which is discussed as part of the substantive tax law changes that occurred from 2009 to 2022.

11. VAT administration amendments

The ensuing discussions on administration complete the promulgation to amendments for VATA 1998 (Act 546) that occurred before the passage of VATA 2013 (Act 870)—discussed in detail in the next Chapter 5.

VAT registration threshold: the VFRS I and II have a significant impact on small-entity VAT registration. Apart from the complicated blocking of ITC, as discussed earlier under the VAT structure, the VFRS makes administration and compliance complex. This is because the amendments do not repeal the conventional VAT registration criteria based on annual turnover or sales thresholds. Table 6.14 shows the VATA amendments that periodically varied the nominal currency amount for the traditional registration.

Table 6.14: VAT registration threshold

Amendments: Sections [Registration]					
Year	**VATA (#)**	**Section**	**Content or Change**	**Book Chapter**	**Comments**
2001	595	s5(1)	Registration threshold	2	Restricts & restricts registration threshold to only a "retailer of goods"
2010	810	5	Registration threshold	2	Restoration of conventional VAT registration threshold [Ghc90,000] & 3% VFRS to entities with turnover between Ghc10,000 & Ghc90,000

VAT offences and sanctions: Table 6.15 shows some amendments relating to VAT or tax administration sanctions and penalties

Table 6.15: VAT offices and penalties

Amendments: Offences & Penalties					
Year	**VATA #**	**Section**	**Content or Change**	**Book Chapter**	**Comments**
2008	765	s2(3)	Sealing off	2	New warrant of seal-off as Schedule 5B
2008	765	s2(2)	Registration offences	2	Notice to register & penalty for persistent non-registration
2008	810		Penalty and assistance from Polic	9	Penalty for obstruction of Officer

Major VATA 870 rates: Table 16 provides a summary of the various provisions under the second comprehensive VAT legislation that result in their classification as ***standard, superior, sub-standard, zero-rating and VFRS rates***.

Table 16: Provisions relating to different VAT rates

MAJOR VATA 2013 (Act 870) AMENDMENTS AFFECTING IDEAL INVOICE-CREDIT VAT REGIME	
VATA 870: VAT base (s1[1])	In principle, VAT regimes cover consumer expenditures on all ***taxable supplies*** of goods and services, with the goal of generating revenue for the state. However, as noted below, VAT laws provide for exemptions and reliefs of supplies for certain supplies or persons for technical and policy reasons.
VATA 870: VAT standard rate (s3)	Until 2019, Ghana's VATA 870 imposed a representative ***17.5 percent standard rate*** for the substantive VAT (12.5 percent) and three (3) other levies, at 12.5 percent each, comprising GETFund, NHIL, and GIIF. Since GRA charged the latter as though they were VAT, registered entities could claim ITC relating to any taxable supplies made.
VATA 870: VAT zero (0) rate (s36)	The purpose of ***zero (0) rates*** on exports under VAT laws is to alleviate the burden of domestic VAT on foreign buyers, to make domestic suppliers and their **supplies competitive on regional, continental, and global markets.** It makes the VAT regime efficient and, particularly, relevant to the ECOWAS and Africa Continental Free Trade Area (ACFTA).
Sub-standard rate (VATAA 948)	VATAA 948 restored the ***3 percent sub-standard*** rate and extended it from retailers and wholesalers under the VAT Flat Rate Scheme (VFRS). Originally, however, the VFRS was a ***small entity tax regime***, VFRS applied to only ***small retailers of goods***. The eligibility for VFRS registration was based on a ***lower turnover threshold than the conventional amount***—which continued to apply to larger retailers and entities in other sectors.
VATA 870: Exemptions and reliefs (s35 & s37)	The main purpose of exempting some basic supplies of goods and services is to **redistribute incomes in support of low-income persons or citizens.** In its practical application, registered entities do not to charge VAT on sales of exempt or relief supplies; however, they cannot also claim ITC relating to those supplies—by direct attribution or apportionment.
Zero-rating of domestic supply	Some VAT laws extend the ***zero (0) rate to domestic supplies*** to make the VAT regime ***less regressive.*** However, as noted in various parts, in less efficient refund and fiscal situations, this policy could complicate VAT administration and compliance.
Straight levies [GETFund & NHIL)	Ghana converted the ***de facto*** **VAT levies** called the GET-Fund and NHIA levies to excise-type ***"straight" levies*** at rates of 2.5 percent each and makes the proportionate supplies ineligible for ITC. Obviously, this results in multiple taxation and cascading [Chapter …].

12. VATA 2013: Revamp and Repeal of VATA 1998 (Act 546)

The NDC II's major VAT review law discussed in Chapter 5, VATA 2013 (Act 870), was not isolated since it formed part of a comprehensive agenda to improve the efficiency of fiscal management. A selection of the Tax and PFM laws is shown in Table 6.17 below.

Table 6.17: Selected Tax and PFM Legislation

Selected Tax and PFM Legislations	
1	1992 Constitution [Chapter 13]
2	Public Financial Management Act, 2016 (Act 921)
3	Petroleum Revenue Management Act, 2011 (Act 815)
4	Public Procurement (Amendment) Act, 2016 (Act 914)
5	Ghana Revenue Authority Act, 2009 (Act 791)
6	Fees and Charges (Misc. Prov) Act, 793 (2009)
7	Revenue Administration Act, 2016 (Act 891)
8	Income Tax Act, 2015 (Act 896)
9	Value Added Tax Act 2013 (Act 870)
10	Excise Duty Act, 2014 (Act 878)
11	Customs Act, 2015 (Act 891)
12	Banks & Specialized Deposits Taking Institutions Act, 2016 (Act 930)
13	Bank of Ghana (Amendment) Act, 2016 (Act 918)
14	Securities Industry Act, 2016 (Act 929)

13. Conclusion

The strength of VAT as an efficient tax and revenue tool to support economies depends on a simple ***rule that allows registered entities to claim ITC,*** provided they engage in business-to-business (B2B) transactions or activities. The ***benefit of ITC*** is to minimize cascading or multiple taxation to ease administration and compliance as well as lower costs; final consumer prices and tax burden. In turn, compliance under the simple method increases revenues and minimizes the risk of tax evasion and avoidance.

Ghana's current VAT structure has distortions as well as complex administration and compliance. The most distortionary policy is the ***blocking of ITC under non-creditable levies*** and changes to VAT registration rules, notably under the VFRS—a policy that was extended to wholesalers for a brief period. The levies increase the number of returns and records, leading to complex audit and enforcement methods to avert tax evasion and avoidance.

It is important to note that VAT is part of the major tax, fiscal and macroeconomic reforms that were undertaken as part of the ***Economic Recovery Programme (ERP) and Structural Adjustment Programme (SAP)*** reforms during the 1980s and 1990s. Chapters 13 and 14 summarize these significant economic measures.

Appendix (Chapter 4)

Comparison of VATA 546 and VATA 870

Appendix Table 6.1: Imposition of tax, taxable person & taxable activity

Comparison of Policy and Legislative Changes					
Part I: Imposition of Tax					
VATA 2013 (Act 870)		**VATA 1998 (Act 546)**			**Comments**
Section	**Description**	**Part**	**Section**	**Description**	
1	Imposition of tax	I	1	Imposition of tax	The only substantive changes to these sections is the deletion of the 3% sub-standard rate [VAT Flat Rate Scheme (VFRS)–initially for retailers of goods only but extended to retailers & wholesalers
2	Person liable to pay tax	I	2	Person liable to pay tax	
3	Rate of the tax	I	3	Rate of the tax	
Part II: Taxable person and taxable activity					
4	Taxable person	II	4	Person accountable for VAT	Refers to entity registered to Charge & the VAT
5	Taxable activity	II	5	Activities that attract VAT	Elaborates on s1[2](b) of VATA 870 (2013)

Appendix Table 6.2: Registration

Comparison of Policy and Legislative Changes					
Part III: Registration					
VATA 2013 (Act 870)		**VATA 1998 (Act 546)**			**Comments**
Section	**Description**	**Part**	**Section**	**Description**	
6	Registration requirements	II	5(1)	Registration requirements and obligations [turnover threshold]	These obligation and requirements are not separated in Part III of VATA 870 whiles previously they were part of Part II of VATA 546. It improves administration of, and compliance with, the Act
7	Period of becoming a taxable person				
8	Notice of registration		5(6)	Notification	
9	Certificate of registration			Notification	
10	Notice of cancellation in respect of turnover		5(6)	Notification	
11	Exceptions regarding thresholds		5(6)	Notification	
12	Designation of taxable person in respect of groups and distince divisions		5(8)	Registration of Groups	
13	Application for voluntary registration		5(10)	Voluntary registration	
14	Compusory registration		5(11)	Compulsory registration	
15	Sanctions for failure to register	XII	56	Failure to register	
16	Unregistered, non-resident person who provide telecommunication services or electronic commerce	IV	13	Taxable supply: only reference prior to passage of the CST Act	CST Act, 2008 (Act 754) & CST (Amendment) Act, 2013 (864)
17	Register and particulars of taxable persons	II	6	Register & particulars of taxable persons	
18	Notice of change in business	II	7	Change in business	
19	Cancellation of registration	II	8	Cancellation of registration	

Appendix Table 6.3: Supply of Goods and Services

Comparison of Policy and Legislation					
Part IV: Supply of goods and services					
VATA 2013 (Act 870)		**VATA 1998 (Act 546)**			**Comments**
Section	**Description**	**Part**	**Section**	**Description**	
20	Supply of goods and services	III	9 & 10	Supply of goods (s9); services (s10)	The descriptions in VATA 870 is detailed, where previously they would have had to be in Regulations. ***Some of these supplies are also specified in relation to time, place and value of supply provisions in VATA 546.***
21	Repossession of goods as supply of goods				
22	Lay-away agreement and betting as supply of services	IV	13(1c)		
23	Separate supply				
24	Activities that do not constitute supply of goods or services [employees & representatives]	II	10(2)	Services of employees [representatives not specified]	
25	Effect of denial of input tax				
26	Payment of deposit and receipt of claim as supply of goods or services				
27	Supply of power and others as supply of goods				
28	Disposition of taxable activity				
29	Phone cards and prepayment as supply of services				
30	Regulationsto prescribe for the supply of goods and				
31	Mixed supplies	III	11	Mixed supplies	
32	Supply by agent or auctioneer	III	12	Suppy by agent	

Appendix Table 6.4: Taxable Supplies

Comparison of Policy and Legislative Changes					
Part V: Taxable supplies					
VATA 2013 (Act 870)		**VATA 1998 (Act 546)**			**Comments**
Section	**Description**	**Part**	**Section**	**Description**	
33	Taxable supply	IV	13	Taxable supply	These classifications are similar in the 2 VATAs, except for the imports
34	Payment of tax on imported goods or services	I	1(1)b/c	Tax is imposed on imported goods & services	
35	Exempt supply	IV	14	Exempt supply	
36	Zero-rated supply	IV	15	Zero-rated supply	
37	Exempt import	IV	16	Exempt import	
38	Relief supply	IV	17	Relief supply	

Appendix Table 6.5: Time & Place of Supply

Comparison of Policy and Legislative Changes					
Part VI: Time and place of supply, tax invoice and sales receipt					
VATA 2013 (Act 870)		**VATA 1998 (Act 546)**			**Comments**
Section	**Description**	**Part**	**Section**	**Description**	
39	Time of supply	V	18	Time of supply	The separation of imports is notable
40	Time of import	I	1(3)	Customs rules	
41	Issue of tax invoice or sales receipt	V	19	Issue of tax invoice	
42	Place of supply	V	20	Place of supply	

Appendix Table 6.6: Taxable Value

Comparison of Policy and Legislative					
Part VII: Taxable value					
VATA 2013 (Act 870)		**VATA 1998 (Act 546)**			**Comments**
Section	**Description**	**Part**	**Section**	**Description**	
43	Value of taxable supply	VI	21	Value of taxable supply	
44	Taxable value for determining the tax on imported goods ***and services***	VI	22	Taxable value for determining the tax on imported goods	The addition of "services" is notable
45	Adjustments	VI	23	Adjustments	
46	Adjustments on account of bad debts				

Appendix Table 6.7: Calculation of Tax Payable & Refunds

Comparison of Policy and Legislative Changes					
Part VIII: Calculation of tax payble and refunds					
VATA 2013 (Act 870)		**VATA 1998 (Act 546)**			**Comments**
Section	**Description**	**Part**	**Section**	**Description**	
47	Tax payable for tax period	**na**	**na**	No specific equivalent section	
48	Deductible input tax	**VII**	**24**	Credit for deductible input tax	The two VATAs are comparable
49	Deductible input tax for mixed taxable and exempt supply	**VII**	**26**	Deductible tax for mixed taxable and exempt supply	
50	Refund or credit for excess tax paid	**VII**	**25**	Refund/credit: excess tax paid	
51	Time for payment of refund	**VII**	**27**	Time for payment of refund	

Appendix Table 6.8: Tax Returns, Records & Assessment

Comparison of Policy and Legislative					
Part IX: Tax return, records and assessment					
VATA 2013 (Act 870)		**VATA 1998 (Act 546)**			**Comments**
Section	**Description**	**Part**	**Section**	**Description**	
52	Submission of tax return and date of payment of the tax	**VIII**	**28**	Submission of tax return and date of payment of the tax	
53	Payment of tax on imported services			No specific equivalent section	Specific on "imports"
	No specific equivalent section	**VIII**	**29**	Records to be kept for purposes of the tax	
54	Assessment of the tax and correction of return	**VIII**	**30**	Assessment of the tax and correction of return	

Appendix Table 6.9: Recovery, Interest & Other Liabilities

Comparison of Policy and Legislative Changes					
Part X: Recovery of tax due, interest and other liabilities					
VATA 2013 (Act 870)		**VATA 1998 (Act 546)**			**Comments**
Section	**Description**	**Part**	**Section**	**Description**	
55	Recovery of tax due	**IX**	**31**	Recovery of tax due	
56	Recovery from recipient of a supply	**na**	**na**	No specific provision	New in VAT Act 870
57	VAT Refund Account	**VI**	**69**	[see Revenue Admin. Act, 2016 (Act 915)	Now GRA Tax Refund Account in RAA 915
58	Failure to issue tax invoice	**XIII**	**57**	VAT compliance provisions	Most of these now affected by RAA 915
59	Evasion of tax payment				
60	Power to seal off premises	**XIII**	**68**		

Appendix Table 6.10: Miscellaneous

Comparison of Policy and Legislative Changes					
Part XI: Miscellaneous					
VATA 2013 (Act 870)		**VATA 1998 (Act 546)**			**Comments**
Section	**Description**	**Part**	**Section**	**Description**	
61	Tax-inclusive pricing [with approval of CG]	**VI**	**5**	Value of taxable supply [consideration]	Typically used for retail outlets that issue (cash) sales receipts
62	Declaration of representative			Acting for another person	CG prerogative
63	Person acting in a representative capacity				Definition, responsibility and laibility of a representative
64	Regulations	**XIII**	**74**	Subsidiary legislation	Mininister's prerogative
65	Interpretation		**76**		
66	Repeal, revocation, savings and transitonal provisions		**78**		

Appendix Table 6.11:

Comparison of Policy and Legislative Changes				
Schedules to the Act				
Schedules	**VATA 2013 (Act 870)**	**Schedules**	**VATA 1998 (Act 546)**	**Comments**
First	Exempt supplies	**First**	Exempt Supplies	Note addition of Separate Schedule on Credit and Debit Notes in VATA 870. Also Warrant of Distress in VATA 546
Second	Zero-rated supplies	**Second**	Zero-Rated Supplies	
Third	Exemption for relief supplies	**Third**	Relief supplies	
Fourth	Tax credit note and tax debit note	**Fourth**	Apportionment of input tax	
Fifth	Apportionment of input tax	**Fifth**	Warrant of Distress	
Sixth	Transitional provisions			

CHAPTER 7

VATA 2013 REVAMP OF VAT SUPPLY RULES AND REVERSALS

1. Introduction

VAT policy and administration depend on the effectiveness of its supply rules—since VAT is a tax on ***supplies*** of goods and services. Under the ***all-inclusive rule***, the ***efficiency and revenue potential or buoyancy*** of VAT depends on the classification of supplies as ***taxable*** or ***non-taxable (exemptions and relief) supplies***. Hence, the rampant repeal or amendment of VAT law in ***pursuit of social intervention, trade and investment policies*** can compromise these goals.

The ***first comprehensive review of the VAT Act, 1998 (Act 546)*** occurred in the form of a ***re-written VAT Act 2013 (Act 870)***, which passage followed the enactment of the Ghana Revenue Authority (GRA) Act, 2009 (Act 791). VATA 870 had one major repeal and two (2) amendments, namely, VATAA 2015 (Act 890) and VATAA 2015 (Act 904). In contrast, there were many changes to VATA 1998 (Act 546) that are summarized below.

> ***After the change in Government in 2001***, Parliament enacted amendments for almost each year between Act 546 and Act 870, which include VATAA 579 (2000); VATAA 595 (2001); VATAA 629 (2002); VATAA 639 (2003); VATAA 670 (2004); VATAA 671 (2004); VATAA 696 (2006); VATAA 734 (2007); and VATAA 752 (2008).
>
> Under the ***second NDC administration***, Parliament passed the comprehensive review of VAT under VATA 2015 (Act 870) and two amendments, namely, VATAA 890 and VATAA (No. 2) 904.
>
> ***With yet another change in Government in 2017***, in rapid succession, Parliament passed several amendments to VATA 870 (2013): VATAA 948 (2017); VATAA 954 (2017); VATAA 970 (2018); VATAA 980 (2018); and VATAA 1005 (2019).

Note that, before enacting VATA 870 in 2013, as ***Box 5.1*** shows below, some provisions of Schedule 2 of the VAT Act 1998 (Act 546) and GIPC Legislative Instrument [LI] 1817 were amended by the ***VAT (Amendment) Act 2010 (Act 810).***

Box 5.1 Some pre-VATA 2013 (Act 870) reversals of VATA 1998 (Act 546)

Prior to enacting VATA 870 in 2013, some provisions of Schedule 2 of VATA 1998 (Act 546) and GIPC Legislative Instrument [LI] 1817 were amended by VATAA 2010 (Act 810).

- ***Deletion of Item 3, Item 4, and Item 5: The VAT (Amendment) Act 2010 (Act 810)*** reversed the zero-rating of domestic supplies by stating as follows:
  "Second Schedule of Act 546 amended ... (6) The principal enactment is amended in the Second Schedule by the deletion of items numbered 3, 4, and 5.
- ***GIPC Legislative Instrument (LI) 1817: The VAT (Amendment) Act 2010 (Act 810)*** revokes GIPC LI 1817 as follows:
  "(7) ... The Ghana Investment Promotion Centre (Promotion of Tourism) Instrument 2005 (L.I. 1817) is hereby revoked".

Note: Later, Chapter 7, Paragraph 9 summarizes other provisions of VATA 2010 (Act 810).

Box 5.1 shows some earlier reviews of the VAT Act, 546.

This Chapter ends Part II, which reviews the substantive sections, while Part IV deals with the Schedules, namely, Chapter 6 ***(Schedule 1—exemptions);*** Chapter 7 (***(Schedule 2--reliefs; and Schedule 3—domestic zero-rating).*** Chapter 8 discusses changes to the ***VAT structure and base*** while Chapter 9 focuses on small-entity VAT schemes, including the ***VAT Flat Rate Scheme [VFRS].***

2. Summary of Reasons for the Changes

The finance bills that are tabled in Parliament often give ***technical reasons for the changes.*** However, given the gradual or prompt reversals that occurred with changes in government from 2000, all the VAT repeals and amendments appear to reflect political economy moves. The following is a summary of the reasons given for the VATA 870 changes.

Objectives of change: often, the goal is to further broaden the general consumption tax or VAT base by ***targeting "new economies"*** such as ***financial, construction and electronic*** sectors. However, the use of ***non-VAT tax instruments*** such as excise- or tariff-type regimes leads to more inefficiencies in the ***overall tax structure***.

Nature of distortions to the VAT structure: The main deficiency in the VATA 546 amendments passed was limiting ***the revenue potential of the VAT structure*** through policy changes that affect the taxable (notably, zero-rated) and non-taxable (notably, exempt and relief) supply bases.

Poor fiscal outcomes: Some changes that ***did not realize anticipated revenue*** and ***social intervention goals*** include expansion in exempt supplies, the introduction of sub-standard VAT rate (especially, the VAT Flat Rate Scheme [VFRS]), and expansion of the exempt (Schedule 1); relief (Schedule 2) and zero-rated (Schedule 3) supply bases.

Blocking Input Tax Credit (ITC): These measures deny or block input tax credit (ITC) and aggravate the difficulty in paying VAT refunds—due mainly to replacing exempt domestic supplies with zero-rating as well as ***converting the de facto VAT levies*** (i.e., GET Fund and NHIL levies with ITC rights) to excise-type tax regimes.

Cascading: The repeals that eliminate the right to ITC and refunds lead to extensive cascading (i.e., VAT-on-VAT at multiple stages) and an increase in tax burden and consumer prices. Often, the resulting tax evasion and avoidance hinder the anticipated or commensurate increases in revenue. Consequently, the measures also reverse the goal of implementing simple VAT administration and compliance processes.

Part V (Chapters 13 and 14) covers selected original tax reforms that rationalized the goals of direct and indirect tax instruments—with ***VAT as a uniform and more efficient consumption or expenditure tax regime***. They explain the ***preparation, introduction, suspension, and reintroduction*** of VAT between 1993 and 1998 under a new tax agency, the VAT Service (VATS). The new VAT regime replaced the Sales Tax under the Customs, Excise and Preventive Service (CEPS) and the Service Tax under the Internal Revenue Service (IRS).

Chapter 4 reviewed the related ***VAT policy and structure*** while Chapters 10 to 12 cover the ***changes in VAT administration*** under the Revenue Modernization Program (RMP). Under the RMP reforms, the Ghana Revenue Authority (GRA) law integrated the domestic

VAT and income tax administration under a single ***Domestic Tax Revenue Division (DTRD)*** of the Ghana Revenue Authority (GRA).

In parallel, the ***Customs Division (CD)*** administers the overall import and export tax regimes, including import VAT, customs duty or tariffs, excise duty and, as a compliance tool, the withholding income tax on imports on behalf of DTRD. A third ***Support Services Division (SSD)*** combines the finance, administration, and other supporting or auxiliary functions under the Headquarters as well as the domestic and customs divisions.

3. VATA 870 and classification of VAT supply rules

The VAT structure has several attributes such as the imposition of tax; supply (i.e. taxable and non-taxable [exempt or relief]); rate of tax; and Input Tax Credit (ITC). The most diverse rules relate to the supply of goods and services, with supplies often classified as taxable or non-taxable supplies. Note that the references in the ensuing Sections are to VATA 870 and not VATA 546.

Imposition (chargeability) of VAT (Section 1): refers to the scope of *goods and services* on which registered entities must charge Output VAT—legally or through administrative practice notes that explain the enactments more explicitly.

> ***Exempt supplies****—s1(1a & 1b)*: clarifies or explains that imposition or charging of VAT does not apply to exempt domestic supplies or exports.
>
> ***Taxable activity****—s1(2)*: clarifies that VAT is on the "taxable supplies" of a person and, hence excludes several non-enterprise or non-profit-making activities of natural or artificial persons.
>
> ***Imports****—s1(3):* affirms the imposition of VAT on imports, under the ECOWAS Tariff and as specified on the *import declaration (as de facto VAT invoice)* that registered entities can use to claim ITC or refunds
>
> ***Relief supplies****—s1(4):* clarifies that VAT applies to diplomatic missions, international agencies, organizations, government agencies, or other persons—unless they formally obtain a ***relief*** that excludes the supply upfront or entitles them to a post-sales refund from the tax administration.

Section 1(4) relates to the supply of goods that ***attracted VAT relief at acquisition and are being resold.*** The re-imposition of VAT and customs duties on such dispositions, in the case of imports, is common practice with the diplomatic institutions.

Supply of goods and services: (Section 20): this section relates to the general definitions for goods and services.

Supply of goods: Section 20(1)a: defines this as an arrangement in which the "owner of goods parts with the possession of the goods by way of sale, barter, lease, transfer, exchange, gift or similar disposition".

Supply of services—Section 20(1)b: adopts but expands the conventional *derivative definition* that the supply of services "is *not a supply of goods* or money", including

- performance of service for another person;
- making available a facility or advantage; and
- tolerating a situation or *refraining* from doing an activity.

Going concern*—Section 20(3)b and s4:* describes going concern as a taxable activity that is subject to VAT upon disposal, with a fuller explanation.

Definitions: s20 re-affirms specific conventional definitions, including:

(a) a supply of goods for goods and services is a supply of goods (s20[5]);

(b) a supply of services for services and goods is a supply of services (s20[6]); and

(c) supplies to employees is a taxable supply if it is in furtherance of business activity (s20[7]).

Special supplies—Basically, Sections 21 to 30: these sections remain conventional but they are updated with current developments in the design and implementation of VAT.

Repossession of goods (s21): the repossession of goods under a credit agreement is *a deemed supply by the debtor* if the debtor is a registered person and the supply was purchased in the course or furtherance of a taxable activity.

Layaway or layby agreement (s22): where a lay-away agreement is cancelled or terminated and the supplier retains or recovers an amount under the agreement, the cancellation or termination is a *deemed supply by the seller*.

Supply of power and other as supply of goods (s27): the supply of any form of power, heat, refrigeration, or ventilation is a *supply of goods*.

Phone cards and prepayment as the supply of services *(s29)*: the issuance of a phone card, prepayment on a cellular phone or similar ***scheme of advance payment*** for the supply of goods or services is a ***supply of services*** for VAT purposes.

- ***Supply by an agent or auctioneer*** *(s32)*: deals with the situation in which a supply may or may not be a supply.
- ***Supply by an agent for the principal (s32 [1]):*** supplies made by a person as an agent for the principal is a supply by the principal.
- ***Supply of services by an agent to principle (s32 [2]):*** the supply of services to the principal by an agent is not a supply.
- ***Supply of goods by auction (s32 [3]):*** the supply of goods by an auctioneer is a supply by the auctioneer in furtherance of a taxable activity.

Separate (s23) and mixed (s31) supplies: these *conventional* transactions involve distinct supplies at different rates as well as classifying some related supplies as substantive and/or incidental.

Separate supply: where distinct supplies are made at a positive and (a) zero (0) rate; or (b) as an exempt supply, each part of the supply is treated as separate (where each is reasonably certain to be supplied separately).

Mixed supply: a supply of

- ***service*** that is incidental to a supply of goods is part of the supply of goods;
- ***goods*** that are incidental to a supply of services are part of the supply of services; and
- ***services*** that are incidental to an import of goods are part of the import of the goods.

Despite the first and second types of supply above, a supply of ***real property*** does not include (a) the supply of services or (b) the import of services incidental to that supply.

Non-supply activities: VATA 870 includes ***activities that involve non-payment of VAT*** because the law describes them as non-supplies.

Employee services(s24): the supply of services by an employee to an employer, because of the employment of that employee, is not a supply of services and the "activities do not constitute supplies of goods and services" for VAT purposes.

Effect of denial of ITC (s25): where a registered entity is denied ITC, the supply is a supply of goods or services "***other than*** in the course or furtherance of a taxable supply". The main effect is that the "blocked" input VAT would be added to the cost of providing the supply and cascade, for as long as it takes for the goods to be sold to final consumers.

Taxable supply (s 33 to s38): the sections state that taxable supplies are made by (a) a ***taxable person***; (b) for ***consideration***, *"other than an exempt supply"*; and (c) in the ***course or as part*** of a taxable activity. As noted later, they also cover specific examples of taxable supplies in both VATA 456 and VATA 870.

Imports of goods (s34[a]): emphasizes that VAT is due on imports of goods (a) at the ***time*** of import; (b) according to ***arrangements*** made by the Commissioner-General (CG) of GRA; and (c) under the Customs Act, 2015 (Act 891).

Imports of services (s34[b]): on imports of services, VAT is payable as provided, and as the CG prescribes, under section 53 where for—

- ***filing and payment (s53[1]:*** filing shall be in the form of import declaration and payment made within 21 days; and
- ***import declaration (s53[2])***: the declaration, which is a ***de facto VAT invoice***, state information necessary to calculate the import VAT.

Exempt supply (s35—Schedule 1): s35 states simply that the scope of exempt supply is in *Schedule 1* and it is ***not a zero-rated supply*** (i.e., zero-rate applies to taxable supplies and, unlike exemptions, enables registered entities to claim ITC).

Exempt imports (s37): the scope is regulated by *Schedule 1* and as further classified, as exempt imports in conformity with the Customs Tariff Schedule—alternatively called the Harmonized System (HS) Code.

Impact of variations in supply policies: There are two (2) important areas where the change in supply policies has affected the efficiency of VAT implementation—

Small-entity threshold: as discussed in Chapters 4 and 9, the exclusion of small entities is based on an annual taxable turnover or sales threshold or amount. Hence, the parallel conventional and VFRS amounts complicate administration and compliance.

Schedule 1 to 3 changes: in principle, the expansion of the scope of exempt and relief supplies could limit the taxable supply for registration at the margins while the replacement of exemptions with zero-rating will have the opposite effect.

Streamlining VAT exclusions (VATA 870): Table 7.1 summarizes the amendments in VATA 2015 (Act 870) that restored the use of *exemptions (Schedule 1), as compared with reliefs and zero-rating (Schedules 2 and 3), as the basis for* promoting the government's social intervention programs.

Table 7.1: Pre-2017 changes to exempt supplies (Schedule 1)

VATA (Amendments) Act 2015 (Act 870), Sections [S35 & 37: Schedule 1]					
Year	**VATA (#)**	**Section**	**Content or Change**	**Book Chapter**	**Comments**
2015	890	35/37	Exempt supplies	8	Pharmaceuticals (Essential drugs under Chapter 30 of Customs HS Code, 2012)
2015	890	35/37	Exempt supplies	8	Pharmaceuticals (produced in Ghana; import of ingrediends; import of drugs)
2015	890	35/37	Exempt supplies	8	Supply of paper for production of exercise books
2015	890	35/37	Exempt supplies	8	Import of mild carbon steel for manufacture of machines

VATA 870 reversals (scope of exemptions): surprisingly, some of these VATA 870 changes and restrictions were promptly reversed when NPP II came to office in FY2017. The exemptions are in two (2) categories, as summarized in Table 7.2 and Table 7.3. Table 7.2 summarizes the reversals of the restrictions on the scope of exemptions, as in the VATAA 948 and 954 amendments.

Table 7.2: Post-2016 reversals of Act 870 (Schedule 1)

VAT (Amendments), Act 2017 (Act 948): Sections 35 & 37, Schedule 1					
2017	948	35/37	Exempt supplies	8	Transportation of passenger, including air travel
2017	948	35/37	Exempt supplies	8	Crude oil & hydrocarbon (petrol, diesel, LPG, kerosine, RFO, and natural petroleum gas
2017	948	35/37	Exempt supplies	8	Immovable property including land, used or intended to be used for the purpose of a dwelling
2017	948	35/37	Exempt supplies	8	A supply of financial services
VAT Amendment Act, 2017 (Act 954): Sections 35 & 37, Schedule 1					
2017	954	35/37	Exempt supplies	7	Exempts lotto stakes organized by National Lotteries Authority (NLA)

VATA 870 reversals (domestic zero-rating and relief supplies): Table 7.3 summarizes additional VATA 870 amendment laws that include a mix of exempt, relief, and zero-rated provisions. As in the examples cited previously, they resulted in more distortions that made it difficult to administer or comply with the VAT laws.

Table 7.3: Exempt, zero-rated & relief supplies

Consequential Amendment to Act 852 (NHIL)					
Year	**VATA (#)**	**Section**	**Content or Change**	**Book Chapter**	**Comments**
2017	948	48	Exempt supply of goods & services	8	[48] A supply in respect of any of the matters set out in the 1st schedule of the VAT Act, 2013 (Act 970) is exempt from the levies imposed under S47
2017	948	48	Zero-rated supply of goods and services	8	[49] A supply in respect of any of the matters set out in the 2nd schedule of the VAT Act, 2013 (Act 970) is zero-rated as regards the levies imposed under S47
2017	948	48	Relief from Levies	8	[50] There is granted by this Act, relief from the payment of the levy to the individuals, organizations, and in respect of the matters specified in the 3rd Schedule of the VAT Act, 2013 (Act 870).
VAT (Amendments), 2018 (Act 980); S36 (Schedule 2)					
2018	980	36	Zero-rated supply	8	A supply of locally manufactured textiles by a local manufacturer who has been approved by the Minister for Trade and Industry up to 31st December, 2021

Practical implications: to restate, the practical implications of the policy, as noted in Chapter 4 on the VAT and general consumption tax (GCT) structures include—

> ***Zero-rated supply (s36):*** zero-rated supplies attract a zero (0) rate, according to ***Schedule 2***; and the taxable person shall provide proof of eligibility to the CG.

Relief supply (s38): subject to (a) Regulations for imports and domestic supplies specified in ***Schedule 3***; (b) restrictions by CG; (c) a claim, if it results in a refund; and (d) exclusion of specified components, if not made to manufacturers (Schedule 3, Item 9).

Time of supply (s: 39): Unless provided in VATA 870 or regulations, a supply of goods or services occurs as enumerated below.

Own use—s39(1)a: on the date on which the goods or services are first applied to own use by the registered entity;

Gifts—s39(1)b: where supplies are by way of gift, on the date on which (i) ownership in the goods passes; or (ii) the performance of services is completed;

In any other case—s39(1)c: the time of supply is the ***earliest of dates*** on which

- goods were removed from the premises of the taxable person or other premises where goods are under the control of the taxable person;
- the goods are made available to the person to whom they are supplied;
- the performance of service is completed;
- receipt of payment is made—partly applicable where payment is made for part of the supplies [s39{2}]; or
- a tax invoice or sales receipt is issued—partly applicable where an invoice or receipt is issued for part supplies [s39{2}].

Metered supply—s39(3): where metered supply (e.g., electricity and water supply) is continuous, the time of supply occurs at each meter reading.

Hire purchase and finance lease—s39(4): on the date the goods are made available under the agreement or lease—where for *two or more payments*, each payment is deemed to apply to the separate parts [s39{6}].

Rental or periodic payment agreements—s39(5): the supply is deemed as successively supplied for successive parts under agreement or law—earliest of the date on which payment made or invoice is issued and where for *two or more payments,* payment is deemed to apply to separate parts [s39{6)].

Definition of the term "rental agreement": it means any agreement for the letting of goods other than a hire purchase agreement or finance lease [s39{7}].

Incidental supplies—s39(8): where the supply is incidental to another supply, the time of supply of the incidental supply is the *same as the time of supply for the main or principal goods or services.*

Layaway agreements—s39(9): the supply of goods in line with a layaway agreement occurs when the *supplier delivers the goods to the purchaser.*

Repossessed goods—s39(10): the time of supply is when (a) the goods are repossessed; or (b) the day after reinstatement of the debtor under a law.

Coin-operated machines—s39(11): the time of supply is when the supplier withdraws the consideration from the coin-operated machine.

Forfeiture of deposit—s39(12): other than on a returnable container, the time of supply is when the deposit is forfeited.

Token, voucher, gift certificate, or stamp—s39(13): the time of supply occurs when any of these forms of payment or exchange are issued (note: not when they are used).

Time of import (goods)—s40: an import of goods occurs when the goods are entered for purposes of the Customs Act, 2015 (Act 891).

Time of import (services)—s40(2): an import of services occurs according to VATA 870, section 19 to the import on the basis that the import is a supply of services.

Place of supply—Section 42: subject to any special provisions in VATA 870, the rules for the place of supply depend on whether the supply relates to goods, services, or any other specialized items. It does not always depend on the physical location of the supply.

Place of supply of goods—s42(1): except as otherwise provided in the Act, the place of supply of goods is (a) where the goods are delivered or made available; or (b) if delivery is by transport, the place where the transportation starts or commences.

Intangible flow—s42(2): the supply for certain intangible items is where the buyer receives the supply (such as ***thermal or electrical energy, heating, gas, refrigeration, air conditioning, or water)***.

Place of supply of services—s42(3): the supply of service takes place at the location of the place of business of the supplier where the supply occurs.

Place where the recipient uses the service—s42(4): the ***specific VAT rules*** instances in the VAT Act 870 are as follows—

- a transfer or assignment of a copyright, patent, licence, trademark, or similar right;
- the service of a consultant, engineer, lawyer, architect, accountant or other professionals;
- the processing of data or supplying information, or any similar service;
- an advertising service;
- the obligation to refrain from pursuing or exercising taxable activity, employment, or a right described in this subsection;
- the supply of personnel;
- the service of an agent in procuring for the agent's principal, a service described in this subjection; or
- the leasing of tangible personal property other than transport property.
- ***Exceptions to s42(4) ---4(5):*** unless the service is part of sub-section 4(4) above, the following conditions apply:
  - *where the service is "physically carried out"—s42(5)a & b*:
  - the supply of cultural, artistic, sporting, educational, or similar activities;
  - the supply of services connected with tangible personal property.
  - *where the property is located—s42(6):* rules for the supply of services connected with real property; and

- *place where transportation occurs—s42(7):* rules relating to the supply of services that are incidental to transportation.

Export of services in s42(6)—s42(8): services supplied from a place of business in the country which would be treated as supplied outside the country.

- ***Services connected with real property (ss6):*** unless the service is described in ss4, the supply of services connected with real property takes place ***where the property is located.***
- ***Incidental to transport (ss7)***: unless the service is described in ss4, the supply of services incidental to transport takes place ***where the transportation occurs.***
- ***Services deemed to be exported (ss8):*** services supplied from a place of business in the country which would be treated as supplied outside the country under ss4 to ss7 are considered as exported from the country.

Right to service—s42(9): the ***place of supply*** is the same as the place for the supply of the services made by the supplier to the recipient, whether the right is exercised.

***Definition of right to service—s42(10)**:* includes any right, option or priority with respect to the supply of services and interest derived from a right to service.

Telecommunications service—s 42(11) (ref. s16[2](a): the place of supply is the place where the facility or instrument for the emission, transmission, or reception of the service, in respect of which the invoice for the supply is issued or is to be issued, ***is ordinarily situated.***

Electronic commerce (i.e., e-commerce)—s42(12) (ref. s16[2](b): the place of supply is where the ***effective use or enjoyment of the supply occurs.***

Recharge card or any other similar mode—s42(13): the place of supply is the place where the ***product is supplied.***

As shown in Table 7.4 below, the ***VAT (Amendment) Act, 2022 (Act 1082)*** has expanded on this original VAT Act 2013 (Act 870) concise provision in s42(12)—with more detailed four (2) descriptions, of which the existence of two (2) makes the digital service taxable.

Table 7.4 VAT (Amendment) (No. 2) Act, 2022 (Act 1082)

An Act to amend the VAT Act 2013 (Act 870) to provide for the up-front payment of VAT by an unregistered importer, ***the taxation of electronic commerce***, the electronic issuance of a tax invoice, the zero-rating of the supply of locally assembled vehicles and for related matters		
Section 42 of Act 870 amended		
Section	**Description**	**Comments**
4	The principal enactment is ***amended*** in section 42 by	
(a)	the ***substitution*** for sub-section (12), of	
	"(12) In the case of ***electronic commerce*** under paragraph (a) of subsection (3) of section 16 other than a digital service, the place of supply is the place where the effective use of enjoyment occurs"; and	More elaborate provisions on the taxation of ***electronic commerce***
(b)	the ***insertion*** after subsection (12), of	
	"(12A) In the case of ***a digital service*** under paragraph (a) of subsection (3) of section 16, ***the place of supply is the place*** where the service is supplied, used or enjoyed in the country if any two of the following circumstances exist;	Further expansion on the "place of supply" rule for ***digital services***
	(a) the recipient of the service is a ***resident person***;	The set of ***four (4) conditions, out of which two (2) must prevail*** to trigger the taxation of supplies of electronic commerce and digital services.
	(b) the ***payment***, including mobile money, credit card, debit card or bank account, for the ***supply of a digital service*** originates from a payment platform in the country or a registered or authorized financial institution as provided for under the Bank and Specialized Deposit-Taking Institution Act, 2016 (Act 930);	
	(c) the ***recipient of the supply of a digital service*** has either a business, residential or postal address, internet proxy address or phone number in the country; and	
	(d) the service is received on a ***terminal located in the country***, including a computer, tablet, mobile phone or similar device."	

Value of taxable supply—Section 43: this may be for ***consideration or benefit-in-kind*** and, for VAT purposes, the parties may calculate the value as follows.

Monetary supply—s43(1)(a): the amount of the ***consideration*** with the addition of all duties and taxes excluding the tax.

In-kind supply—s43(1)(b): where the consideration is fully or partly in kind, the value for VAT purposes is the ***open market value*** of a *similar supply*, ***excluding*** the Value Added Tax (VAT).

- ***Open market value (OMV)—s43(2)***: this is the value where the supplier, purchaser or other party in the transaction are completely independent of each other and did not influence the transaction.
- ***Commissioner-General's value—s43(3)***: where the OMV of a taxable supply cannot be determined, the ***OMV*** is determined by the C-G—having regard to all the circumstances of the supply or *similar supply*.

Where "similar supply" (s43[6]), as used in s43(3), ***means*** a supply that is *"identical to or closely, or that substantially resembles the taxable supply—having regard to quality, characteristics, quantity supplied, functional components, reputation of, and materials comprising the goods or service".*

Open market value (OMV)—s43(4): in general, the *OMV at the time* the supplier makes the supply applies to the following—

- ***hire purchase*** or ***finance lease*** excludes any separately stated interest or finance charges—s43(4)a;
- taxable supply of goods by way of an application to a ***different use***—s43(4)(b);
    - a taxable supply for reduced ***consideration***—s43(4)c, or
    - a taxable supply where the ***open market value*** cannot be determined and is there determined by the Commissioner-General under s43(3)—s43(4)d;

Where consideration does not specify a separate amount as VAT—s43(5): where the consideration does not identify a separate amount for payment of the VAT, the taxable value is the consideration paid, excluding the VAT.

No consideration or lower consideration—s43(7): the value for consideration is the OMV, where

- supplier and recipient are ***related persons***; or
- the recipient is an approved ***charitable*** organization—s44(7).

Credit agreement—s43(10): the value of the supply is the ***cash value*** of the supply—implying that it is net of the interest charges.

Value in "special supply" cases (s21 to s32)—s43: VATA 870 discusses the value of supply in relation to specified ***"special supplies"*** under section 43, with references to sections 21 to 32 of the Act).

Repossession under Credit Agreements—s43(8): where *repossession occurs (i.e.,* ***reverse supply*** *by the debtor: reference s21),* the value of supply is the ***lesser of***

- the consideration paid or payable by the taxable person for those goods or services; or
- the open market value (OMV) of the supply.

Note s21 and Regulations by legislative instrument (LI)—s43(9): the ***Minister may prescribe rules*** to determine the value of a supply under ss43(8) where "the taxable person applies less than the entire goods or services to a different use".

Repossession in layaway agreements—s43(11): where repossession occurs *[i.e.,* ***reverse supply*** *by debtor]* under *layaway agreements [reference s22(1)],* the value of the supply is "an amount equal to the ***balance of the cash value of the supply*** of goods to the debtor that has ***not been recovered*** at the time of the supply".

Definition. ***"the balance of the cash value of supply"—s12:*** "... the amount that remains after deducting from the cash value,

(i) "so much of the sum of the payments made by the debtor under the credit agreement as,

(ii) "on the basis of an apportionment in accordance with the rights and obligations of the parties to the agreement,

(iii) "may properly be regarded as having been made in respect of the cash value of the supply".

Betting (s22[2])—s43(12): the value of supply of services [betting] under s22(2) is an amount equal to the ***amount referred to*** in that subsection that is ***retained or recoverable.***

Supply to non-taxable persons—s43(14): where the whole or part of a taxable activity involves supplies to non-taxable persons, the CG may, by notice in writing, direct that the ***value of the supply be equal to its OMV to consumers.***

Token, voucher, gift certificate, or stamp under s29—s43(15): where these are granted in exchange for goods or services for ***monetary value***, the ***"value of the supply*** shall be an ***amount equal*** to the amount by which the *consideration exceeds the monetary value of the token, voucher, gift certificate, or stamp"* (i.e., the intrinsic value of the token, gift, voucher, certificate or stamp).

Token, voucher, gift certificate, or stamp under s29—s43(16): where these are **granted in exchange** for goods or services for ***no monetary value,*** the supplier shall ***include*** in the value of supply of the goods or services, the ***monetary value*** stated on the token, voucher etc., ***less the tax fraction*** of the monetary value.

Definition of "monetary value"—s17: for purposes of s16, monetary value is inclusive of VAT.

Taxable value for imports of goods or services—s44: the Customs Division (CD) of GRA administers the VAT on importation of goods while the DTRD offices administers the VAT on imported services (under the *reverse-charge rules*).

- ***Imports of goods—s44(1):*** the value is the ***"import value" calculated under s29 to s35 of the Customs Act,*** with the ***addition of***
  - the import duties and taxes other than the tax (i.e., VAT); and
  - the cost of insurance and freight, which is not included in the customs value for the import.
- ***Import of services—s44(2):*** the value of imported services is the amount of the ***consideration for the import,*** subject to s44(3), below.
  - ***Import of services at OMV—s44(3):*** the value of imports of services is the ***open market value (OMV),*** where
  - an import of services is made for no consideration or for a consideration that is less than the OMV of that import; and

- the supplier and the recipient are related persons.

VAT-inclusive pricing (imported services)—s44(4): where a portion of the ***price of imported services includes VAT*** under VATA 870, the value is the price reduced by an amount equal to the tax fraction multiplied by that price.

Adjustments to taxable value—s45

VATA 870 ***permits adjustments*** in relation to changes to the agreed value of taxable supplies or correction of mistakes or errors. Adjustments are normal occurrences in carrying out conducting transactions among sellers, buyers, agents and consumers.

Some notable reasons for an adjustment—s45(1): an adjustment applies where in relation to a ***taxable supply*** by a taxable person

- the *supply* is ***cancelled;***
- the nature of the *supply* has been ***fundamentally varied or altered;***
- the ***previously agreed consideration has been altered*** by agreement with the recipient of the supply, whether due to an offer of a ***discount*** *or for any other reason*; or
- the goods or services or part thereof have been ***returned*** to the supplier—normally referred to, in reverse, as returns inwards (for goods received after a sale) and returns outwards (for goods sent out after a purchase).

VAT invoice and VAT return errors—s45(2): where in addition to conditions in s45(1) above, the ***taxable person*** making the supply has

- given ***VAT invoice*** and the VAT shown on the invoice is incorrect because of any one or more of the events mentioned in s45(1); or
- filed a ***VAT return*** for the period in which supply was made and has accounted for the incorrect VAT because of one or more of the events mentioned in s45(1);
- the taxable person making the supply shall make an adjustment, as provided under section 45(3) and section 45(5).

Adjustments through Debit and Credit Notes—s45(3) to s45(7): the ***supplier*** shall issue a Debit Note or Credit Note ***for the adjustments,*** as follows:

- ***Higher Output Tax chargeable—s45(3):*** where the output VAT ***properly chargeable*** ... exceeds the output tax ***actually accounted for*** by the taxable person ... the ***amount of the excess*** shall be ***regarded as tax charged*** by the person in relation to a taxable supply made in the tax period in which the events referred to in s45(1) occurred.
- ***Debit Note—s45(4):*** issued to the ***recipient*** of the supply, where the *Output VAT* ***properly chargeable*** *exceeds* the Output VAT ***actually charged*** *and accounted for* by the taxable person making the supply, as calculated in ***section 45(3).***
- ***Credit Note—s45(6):*** issued to the ***recipient*** of the supply where the *Output VAT actually charged and accounted for exceeds* the Output VAT *properly chargeable* by the taxable person making the supply, as in ***section s45(5).***

It is necessary to note the reverse usage of ***"properly chargeable"*** Output VAT and ***"actually charged"*** in relation to both Debit and Credit Notes above.

Input Tax Credit (ITC)—s45(7): where a deductible ***ITC is not allowed*** under s45(5) where the supply has been made to a non-taxable person, unless the person has actually repaid the excess amount to the taxable person, in cash or as credit.

ITC invoice penalty—s45(8): a person who (a) ***fails to issue*** a Debit or Credit Note; or (b) provides a ***Debit or Credit Note that is not consistent with the law;*** is liable (c) to a penalty of three times the amount of tax involved or 250 currency points, whichever is lower; and (d) penalty in s58 (100 currency unit or 6 months imprisonment or both).

Adjustment on account of bad debt—s46

As with Section 45, ***VATA 870 permits adjustments in relation to bad debt,*** where the consideration in the transaction or supply is not paid by the debtor to the creditor.

Consideration in whole or part of consideration—s46(1): where the ***whole or part of consideration*** on an invoice for goods or services is ***not received,*** the taxable person may deduct ITC (s48) for any amount treated as a bad debt.

Deduction allowed for bad debt—s46(2) and s46(3): the ITC deduction is

- equal to the tax paid in respect of the taxable supply;
- falls due on the date the bad debt was written off; and
- only available if the taxable person satisfies the CG that reasonable efforts were made to recover the tax due.

Bad debt recovered—s46(4): where bad debt is ***wholly or partly recovered,*** the taxable person shall reverse the portion of tax recovered to an amount equal to A x B/C, where—

- A = amount allowed as a deduction under s46(2);
- B = amount of the bad debt recovered; and
- C = amount of bad debt previously written off.

A deduction is allowed under s46(2) only if (a) the taxable supply is made to a taxable person; or (b) the taxable person issued a tax credit note to the taxable purchaser.

Tax Payable, ITC and Refunds—s47 to 51

The ensuing paragraphs deal with the calculation of ***tax payable and claims of input tax credit (ITC) or refunds by a taxable person.*** Recall that the right to ITC or refunds is the main pillar of the VAT invoice-credit method, compared to the other sales and turnover taxes.

Tax payable for tax period—s47: The ***tax payable*** by a ***taxable person*** for a ***tax period*** for ***taxable supplies*** is the total Output VAT ***less*** the total deductible Input VAT. In general, the ***net amount*** is positive and represents the payment made to GRA.

- ***Credit or refund of excess VAT—s47(1):*** where the total deductible Input VAT ***exceeds*** the total Output VAT, the ***excess VAT*** shall be treated as a credit or refund claim.
- ***Imported services—s47(2):*** the *VAT payable on an import of services,* other than as specified in section 31 (i.e., mixed supplies), is subject to s53 of VAT Act 870.

VAT Withholding Agents: The ***VAT (Amendment) Act, 2017 (Act 954)*** includes the following amendments to the VAT Act 870, with respect to the appointment of "VAT Withholding Agents".

These provisions, whose details are shown in ***Table 7.5, seem superfluous and result in cashflow hindrances to registered taxpayers.*** This is because the VAT ***on inputs or purchases represents a de facto withholding scheme***—with the credit or refund in an ITC mechanism being subject to the filing of VAT returns and accounting properly for the Output VAT.

Table 7.5: VAT (Amendment) (No. 2) Act, 2017 (Act 954)—VAT Withholding Agents

<table>
<tr><td colspan="3">An Act to amend the VAT Act 2013 (Act 870) to remove the tax on stakes in the National Lotto, to provide for the withholding from the payment of Value Added Tax to registered Value Added Tax traders and to provide for related matters.</td></tr>
<tr><td colspan="3">Sections 47A and 47B inserted</td></tr>
<tr><td>Section</td><td>Description</td><td>Comments</td></tr>
<tr><td>1</td><td colspan="2">The principal enactment is amended by the insertion after section 47 of</td></tr>
<tr><td></td><td>“Appointment of Value Added Tax Withholding Agent”</td><td rowspan="10">A complex provision that introduces an income tax type “withholding” regime despite the trail of controls embedded in the issuing of VAT invoices for inputs or purchases.</td></tr>
<tr><td>(47A)</td><td>The Commissioner-General may in writing appoint a VAT Withholding Agent for the Authority.</td></tr>
<tr><td></td><td>Duties of the VAT Withholding agent</td></tr>
<tr><td>(47B)</td><td>A VAT Withholding Agent shall</td></tr>
<tr><td></td><td>(a) withhold the payment to a registered VAT trader, seven per cent (7%) of the taxable output value of standard-rated supplies; and;</td></tr>
<tr><td></td><td>(b) at the time of making payment for the standard-rated supplies, issue a Withholding VAT Credit Certificate in the form prescribed by the Commissioner-General to the supplier.</td></tr>
<tr><td></td><td>Scope of VAT Withholding Agent</td></tr>
<tr><td>47(C)</td><td>The scope of a VAT Withholding Agent shall include</td></tr>
<tr><td></td><td>(a) VAT-registered entities whose supplies are zero-rated; and</td></tr>
<tr><td></td><td>(b) Selected Government and other VAT-registered entities.</td></tr>
</table>

Deductible Input Tax (or Input Tax Credit [ITC])—*s48*: subject to s49 [i.e., ITC for mixed and exempt supplies], a taxable person may deduct the following from the total Output VAT due for the period—

- ***Input VAT on domestic supplies and imports—s48(1):*** At the end of the tax period provided in the Act or Regulations, a ***taxable person may deduct the following from the total Output VAT*** charged for the period:

- tax on goods and services purchased ***domestically or imported*** and used wholly, exclusively, and necessarily in the course of taxable activity—
    - i. making taxable supplies;
    - ii. on a tax invoice issued under VATA 870;
    - iii. for imports or supplies from a bonded warehouse, the taxpayer is in possession of relevant customs entries that show the tax paid; and
    - iv. relating to withholding VAT (Act 954)
- the following is an important addition to these rules under the ***VAT (Amendment) (No. 2) Act, 2017 (Act 954) in Table 7.6 below***)
    - i. in respect of supplies made in Ghana, the taxable person is in possession of a ***Withholding VAT Credit Certificate*** issued under this Act.

Table 7.6 VAT (Amendment) Act, 2022 (Act 1082)

An Act to amend the VAT Act 2013 (Act 870) to remove the tax on stakes in the National Lotto, ***to provide for the withholding*** from the payment of Value Added Tax to registered Value Added Tax traders and to provide for related matters.		
Section 48 of Act 870 amended		
Section	**Description**	**Comments**
4	Section 48 of the principal enactment is amended by	
(a)	The insertion after sub-paragraph (iii) of paragraph (a) of sub-section (1) of	
	"(iv) in respect of supplies made in Ghana, ***the taxable person is in possession of Withholding VAT Credit Certificate*** issued under this Act.; and	More elaborate provisions on the taxation of ***electronic commerce***
(b)	the re-numbering of subparagraph (iv) of paragraph (a) of subsection (1) as (v).	

- input tax deduction allowed for ***adjustments*** under s45 and 46 of VATA 870;
- amount of ***tax fraction*** relating to a prize-winning or recipient of a service under s22[2];

- amount of tax fraction paid during the tax period by the taxable person to ***indemnify*** another person under a taxable non-life insurance contract, where—
    i. the supply of the ***non-life insurance*** contract is a taxable supply;
    ii. the ***payment is not in respect of*** the supply of goods and services or their importation;
    iii. the supply of the ***non-life insurance*** contract is not a supply charged with tax at zero per cent under s36 [i.e., provision on zero-rating]; and
    iv. the ***payment does not result*** from a supply of goods or services, where those goods are ***situated outside Ghana*** or are ***physically performed elsewhere than in Ghana*** at the time of the supply.
- an amount equal to the tax fraction of any amount paid to a supplier in respect of the ***redemption*** of a token, voucher, gift certificate, or stamp (s43[16]).
- ***Definition of deductible input tax—s48(2):*** the tax deducted from the output tax under s48(1) is known as deductible input tax or an input tax deduction—also expressed as an input tax credit (ITC) in this book.
- ***Denial of ITC on taxable supply—s48(3):*** unless provided in VATA 870, an input tax deduction or credit shall ***not be allowed*** on purchases or imports of ***exempt*** supplies by the taxable person.
- ***An ITC shall not be made (s48(4):*** (a) ***more than once; and*** (b) after the ***expiration of six (6) months*** after the date the deduction accrued; and
    - on taxable supplies ***not supported by a VAT invoice*** that provides specified details of the transaction; and
    - regular ***resale*** of used goods purchased ***from consumers,*** not approved by the Commissioner-General (CG).
- ***Eligibility for ITC—s48(5) to s48(11):*** unless provided otherwise in VAT 870, a person does ***not qualify*** for ITC, in respect of
    - ***motor vehicles*** and vehicles ***spare parts*** unless as a dealer—s48(5);

    - in respect of ***entertainment***, including hotel, restaurant and meals, unless the person is engaged in these as taxable activities—s48(6);

- ***membership subscription*** for a club, association, or society of a sporting, social, or recreational nature—s48(7);
- proportion of supplies or imports that are ***partly for personal use***—s48(8);
- where ***goods for which ITC was allowed cease to be used for taxable supply or transaction*** before the end of their life and are deemed to be sold at OMV—s48(9);
- for persons ***selling "used" supplies***, the CG may determine the procedure for allowing ITC to the person—s48(10); and
- where a ***taxable person does not have a tax invoice*** that provides evidence of ITC, the CG may allow ITC, in line with Regulations, or is satisfied that;
    - the taxable person took all reasonable steps to acquire a tax invoice;
    - failure to acquire a tax invoice was not the fault of the taxable person; and
    - amount of deductible input tax claimed by the taxable person is correct.
- ***Newly-registered taxable person—s48(12):*** these taxpayers may claim ITC for the ***first tax period*** that registration is effective in the form prescribed by the CG—
- goods acquired or imported within four (4) months before the effective day of registration; and
- capital goods acquired or imported within six (6) months before the effective date of registration.
- **ITC for mixed taxable and exempt supplies—s49(1):** the ITC claim made by a *taxable person* relates to the taxable purchases and taxable imports and, further, they must be directly attributed to the portion of taxable supply only. The following are important rules of the ITC apportionment process.
- ***Apportionment ratio—s49(2)***: where the taxable person ***cannot directly attribute*** the input tax relating to the

taxable and exempt supply elements, the ***apportionment ratio in Schedule 5*** for ITC purposes applies to the taxable supply portion.

- ***Apportionment and denial of ITC—s49(3):*** VATA 870 blocks the ITC claims in s49(1) and s49(2) where the ratio for the period derived is less than 5 per cent.
- ***Attribution of 100 per cent ITC—s49(4):*** VATA 870 allows 100 per cent ITC where the ratio of taxable to exempt supply exceeds 95 per cent.
- ***CG may determine apportionment ratio—s49(5):*** the CG may approve or direct the use of alternative methods where the CG determines that the application of the ratio will result in *unreasonable* calculation of ITC.
- ***Financial institutions—s49(6):*** the right to ITC and apportionment rules to non-core financial services was repealed by VATA 948 in 2017.

- **Refund or credit for excess tax—s50:** the following ***VAT rules shall apply*** where the amount of ***input tax deductible exceeds the amount of output tax*** due for the tax period—
  - ***general rule—s50(1)(a):*** the CG shall credit the excess amount to the taxable person—and carried forward to the next period ***(s50[13])*** but subject to the following conditions;
  - ***exporters—s50(1)(b):*** the CG shall refund the excess where the taxable person is an exporter and the ***export component exceeds 25 per cent*** and export proceeds are repatriated by the exporter's authorized bank into the taxpayer's account;
  - ***textile manufacturers—s50(1)(c):*** in the case of the excess credit directly attributable to locally manufactured textiles subject to zero-rate as provided in the Second Schedule, the Commissioner-General may refund the excess credit attributable to that period upon the receipt of an application for refund of the excess credit—see Table 7.7 below, as per VAT (Amendment) (No. 2) Act, 2018 (Act 980).

Note that as shown in Box 5.1, these provisions are subject to the VAT subsidiary legislation, the VAT Regulation [Legislative Instrument {LI} 2243 Regulation number 42}.

Box 5.1: Repatriation of export proceeds (VAT Regulation 42 of LI 2243)
For the purposes of subsection (1) of Section 50 of the Act, repatriation of total export proceeds is subject to any enactment in force which allows the taxable person to retain part of the export proceeds outside the country.

As noted, Table 7.7 elaborates further on the zero-rating of registered entities that manufacture domestic textiles under the VAT (Amendment)(No.2) Act, 2018 (Act 980).

Table 7.7 VAT (Amendment)(No.2) Act, 2018 (Act 980).

An Act to amend the VAT Act 2013 (Act 870) to zero-rate the Value Added Tax (VAT) on the supply of locally manufactured textiles and to provide for related matters.		
Section 50 of Act 870 amended		
Section	**Description**	**Comments**
1	The Value Added Tax Act, 2013 (Act 870) referred to in this Act as the "principal enactment" is amended in section 50 by the insertion after paragraph (b) of subsection (1) of	Elaborate provision on the taxation of ***electronic commerce***
(c)	"(c) in the case of the excess credit directly attributable to locally manufactured textiles subject to zero-rate as provided in the Second Schedule, the Commissioner-General may refund the excess credit attributable to that period upon the receipt of an application for refund of the excess credit".	

- ***application for refund by the taxpayer—s50(2):*** the eligible taxpayer cannot apply for a refund where the credit is outstanding for more than 3 months or where ITC is denied at the conclusion of an audit.
- ***Excess tax other than ITC claims—50(3) to s50(5):*** where a person has overpaid tax and (i) shows documentary proof or (ii) excess credit arises in circumstances o*ther than s50(1) and s50(2)*, the CG shall comply with the following—
    - ***set-off***: first apply the amount of the excess against the liability of the person for any tax, levy, interest or penalty administered by the Commissioner-General;

  - *refund:* repay any amount remaining to the person within thirty days of being satisfied that the person has overpaid tax—on a specified Refund Claim Form or RCF *(s50[9])* and provide other documentation requested by the CG *(s50[11/12]);*
  - *period for making claim—s50(6):* the period for the taxpayer to make the relevant ITC claims under s50(4) shall be 6 months;
  - *notice of payment—s50(7):* where necessary, the CG shall serve notice of the payment in writing to the beneficiary of the credit or refund;
  - *cancellation of registration—s50(8):* s50(3) to s50(4) applies to specific instances of the cancellation of a business registration for VAT;
  - *rejection of claim—s50(10):* where the CG rejects the claim for a refund, the CG may recover any tax previously refunded under VATA 870; and
  - *penalty—s50(14):* a person entitled to a claim under s50 is liable to a penalty of double the original amount of the refund plus interest.
- **Time for paying refunds—51:** the following provisions apply where a taxable person is entitled to a refund of tax under VATA 870.
  - *Period for payment by CG—s51(1):* the CG shall pay the refund within 30 days after receipt of the application, provided
    - the previous returns have been submitted by the due dates with no tax for any period outstanding; or
    - the amounts of tax, penalties and interest from previous tax periods have been paid by the due dates.
  - *Failure to meet conditions—s51(2):* the failure to meet conditions occur when
    - the taxpayer does not meet the conditions in s51(1)(a), the CG shall reject the claim for refund; and

    - the taxpayer has not paid the amounts specified in s51(1)(b), the CG shall offset any entitlement for a refund against the amounts due; and
    - notify the applicant of the decision in writing within 30 days after the receipt of the application.
- *Failure by CG to pay a refund—s51(3):* where the CG fails to pay a refund of tax relating to an excess under s50 within the period specified in s51(1)—the CG
    - shall pay additional interest at the prevailing BOG discount rate; plus
    - one-quarter of that rate each day commencing on the day after the period within which the CG is required to pay the refund and ending on the date that the payment of the refund is made.

VAT Administration

The passage of VATA, 2013 (Act 870) preceded the Revenue Administration Act (RAA), 2016, (Act 915), which unified several of the procedures for VAT, income tax and customs duty or tariffs. Chapters 10 to 12 discuss the ensuing VATA 870 provisions in conjunction with the relevant general provisions and amendments in the RAA 2016.

Sections 52 to 60 of VATA, 2013 (Act 870) dealt or deal with the administration of, and compliance with, VAT, including (a) tax returns, records, and assessment—s52 to s54; and (b) recovery of tax due, interest and other liabilities—s55 to s60. They are subject to the RAA repeals and amendments.

Miscellaneous provisions—s61 to s66

These provisions of VATA 870 deal with several topics specified in the ensuing paragraphs of this chapter.

- **Tax-inclusive pricing—s61:** the following relate to the general and exceptional rules for pricing taxable products under VAT.
    - *VAT-inclusive pricing—s61(a):* a price advertised or quoted by a taxable person for a taxable supply shall include the VAT chargeable;

- *VAT-exclusive pricing—s61(b):* where a taxable person quotes a price that excludes VAT, the advertisement or quotation must show the VAT separately—subject to any VAT-inclusive price must be "displayed in as prominent a place" as the VAT exclusive price;
- *Price ticket:* these need not include the VAT, if the VAT is indicated by way of notice displayed prominently at the premises of taxable activity; and
- *CG's method:* the CG may approve any other method of displaying prices of goods and services for a person or class of persons.

- **Representation—s62 and s63:** where the CG considers it necessary, the ***CG may declare a person to be a representative of a taxable person*** under section 62. Section 63(1) provides that the term "representative" in s62 means
  - *liquidation:* the designated officer in the case of a company other than a company in liquidation;
  - *unincorporated entities:* a member of the committee of management in the case of an unincorporated association or body under VATA 890;
  - *accounting officer (company):* a person who is responsible for accounting for the receipt and payment of money or funds on behalf of the company, in other cases;
  - *artificial person*: liquidator, other than a company is covered by s63(1)(d);
  - *accounting officer (other):* a person responsible for accounting for the receipts and payments under any other law or appropriation by Government;
  - *partner:* a partner in the case of a partnership;
  - *trustee:* a trustee in the case of a trust; or
  - *non-resident representative:* a person controlling affairs of a non-resident person, including a manager in the country of a taxable activity, as defined in s65.

Definition of Non-Resident [s65]: "Non-resident" means a person who is not a resident of the country and a person referred to in paragraph (b) of the definition of ***"resident person"*** to the extent that the person is not a resident.

Definition of Resident person: paragraph (b) states that a resident person means any other person to the extent that the person carries on in the country, a taxable or other business activity.

Other VATA 870 provisions

VATA 870 ends with the usual provisions for preparing and submitting Regulations to Parliament for approval as well as provisions on interpretation, repeals, revocations, savings and transition, and schedules.

- ***Regulations—s64:*** states the general and specific areas in which the Minister may issue Regulation in the form of a Legislative Instrument (LI).
    - ***Interpretation—s65:*** these must be applied by registered taxpayers unless the context otherwise requires.
    - ***Repeal, revocation, savings, and transition—s66:*** covers the following situations—
    - ***repeals:*** all the VAT legislation from the date of promulgation of VATA 1998 (Act 546) and the effective date of VATA 2013 (Act 870);
    - ***revocation:*** these include LI 21 and 22; and
    - ***savings and transitions:*** VATA 870 were part of the review of several tax laws and their impact of VAT required the savings and transitional provisions in the law.
- ***Schedules:*** the VAT 3012 (Act 870) provisions deal with specific topics and issues that include the following:
    - **Schedule 1:** Exempt supplies (sections 35 to 37)
    - **Schedule 2:** Zero-rated supplies (s36)
    - **Schedule 3:** Exemptions for relief supplies (s38)
    - **Schedule 4:** Tax Credit Note and Tax Debit Note (s45[6])
    - **Schedule 5:** Apportionment of Input Tax (s49[2])
    - **Schedule 6:** Transitional provisions (s66)

Conclusion

This Chapter covered the mechanics of VAT as it relates to the original provisions in VATA 1998 (Act 546) and the extensive review that became part of VATA 2013 (Act 870). Countries design their VAT Acts or laws to reflect best practices and updates that take account of the advances in policy, structure and administration in the design and implementation of VAT. These follow a graduated approach in developing, middle-income, and advanced states.

The reviews under VATA 870 take account of the global trends as well as the political-economy upheavals that have dogged the implementation of the tax since its cancellation in 1995 and reintroduction in 1998. The review of specific VAT policies is treated in Chapters 6 to 10 and followed by changes in VAT and overall tax administration in Part IV (Chapters 10 to 12, which covers the all-inclusive Revenue Administration Act (RAA), 2016 (Act 915).

The RAA 2016 followed the passage of the Ghana Revenue Authority (GRA) Act, 2009 (Act 791), which Act also integrated the VAT Service (VATS) and Internal Revenue Service (IRS)—to create GRA's Domestic Tax Revenue Division (DTRD) and a second Customs Division for tax administration at the borders. Subsequently, under Phase II of the revenue modernization reforms, the tax offices were segmented the field or tax offices into large taxpayer offices (LTO), medium taxpayer offices (MTOs), and small taxpayer offices (STO). However, these have since been reversed under generic Taxpayer Service Centres. Overall, these revenue reforms were part of the tax modernization program under the Public Financial Management (PFM) and, partly, financial sector reforms that were launched from 2010 to 2016.

Finally, as discussed in the latter chapters, while these changes point to progress in updating the respective laws through the Cabinet and Parliament, the political-economy reality of policy formulation in Ghana interfered with the smooth implementation of VATA 870. This is because a new administration rolled back several of its VAT reforms.

PART III

VAT IMPLEMENTATION CHALLENGES

Chapter 8

VAT POLICY REVIEW—1: VAT EXEMPTIONS

1. Introduction

As a form of General Consumption Tax (GCT), the basic elements of the Value Added Tax [VAT] regime and legislation covered in Parts I and II (Chapters 1 to 5), are based on the VAT Invoice-Credit or Input Tax Credit (ITC) method. The following are the underlying rules or principles of the ITC approach that prevent registered entities from adding the tax charged as costs which, thereby increases consumer prices.

> ***Obligation to charge VAT:*** eligible entities that make taxable supplies *must register, charge Output VAT, claim ITC, and pay the difference or net VAT to a tax office.* Where the product or outcome of this process is negative, the entities are eligible for a refund or credit the difference being offset against the Output VAT charged.
>
> ***Right to ITC:*** The right of registered entities or taxpayers to "set off" or "credit" Input VAT paid on taxable purchases and expenses against the Output VAT on taxable sales, turnover or supplies *reduces or ideally eliminates "cascading" or multiple taxation* [i.e., tax-on-tax] on business-to-business (B2B) transactions.
>
> ***Non-cascading:*** Non-cascading or avoidance of multiple taxation means that the *ITC right in the form of credit or refund for VAT paid on inputs by registered entities, at each stage of the "value addition" chain,* is not passed on as higher costs, further taxes, and final price. The denial of ITC is what causes cascading or multiple taxation.

These basic features make the *Invoice-Credit VAT mechanism more efficient and effective to administer and enforce by the tax authorities.* However, after many African and developing countries replaced their inefficient sales and service tax regimes with VAT in the 1980s, some states such as Ghana have made *policy and legislative changes that distort the relatively simple and efficient VAT base and structure.*

However, as reviewed in this Part IV, VAT laws and policies allow for exclusions from the VAT base, usually in the form of exemptions (Chapter 6), reliefs and [domestic] zero-rating (Chapter 7), other changes to the VAT base and structure (Chapter 8)—notably, small-entity exclusions from VAT registration (Chapter 9), based on annual levels of turnover or sales. Part IV (Chapters 10 and 12) discusses VAT administration while Part V (Chapter13 and 14) ends the book by positioning VAT in a macro-fiscal and reform context.

2. Ideal VAT regime and variations

As discussed in earlier Chapters, the ***ideal VAT invoice-credit method*** has certain unique and inherent attributes that make it superior to other general indirect tax regimes, including the VAT addition and subtraction methods. Nonetheless, VAT laws and policies allow exceptions to the ideal VAT base and structure.

Strength of Invoice Credit Method: The efficiency and revenue potential of the limited exclusions and, in general, the VAT mechanism are also associated with certain ***inherent compliance*** features of the invoice-credit mechanism.

- ***self-policing:*** registered businesses that buy inputs *insist on getting a VAT invoice* as proof or evidence of payment of the tax to avoid being denied ITC claims;
- ***audit trail:*** VAT invoices result in an *"audit trail"* that improves compliance since *a seller's sales invoice becomes a buyer's purchase invoice;*
- ***invoice cross-matching:*** auditors from the tax agency can always *cross-check the validity of sales invoices against purchase invoices* among businesses; and
- ***importance of technology:*** given advances in technology, *invoice cross-matching* also occurs on a larger scale to enhance enforcement

The *ITC* process facilitates administration and compliance since eligible entities must show tax invoices as evidence of their inherent ITC benefit to registered entities.

Exclusions from the VAT base: Any ***variation*** from these features ***results in distortions*** to the ideal VAT regime. Nonetheless, VAT laws provide for ***exemptions*** of basic supplies from taxation on social intervention or technical grounds; ***reliefs*** from VAT payment for persons and entities such as the Head of State and diplomats (and diplomatic institutions); and ***non-registration*** of small business entities.

- ***Social intervention policies*** exempt specified ***basic supplies*** from the VAT base because their consumption forms a large proportion of the expenditure of low-income persons although this does not prevent middle and higher-income persons from also benefitting from the exempt supplies.
- ***Technical as well as social considerations*** often result in the exclusion of ***primary residences*** and ***core financial services*** (interest) from the tax base since they are savings or investments (not consumption). Further, the basis of apportionment for ITC purposes may be difficult or arbitrary.
- ***Easing VAT administration and compliance:*** This outcome is achieved through ***non-registration of small entities***—under annual sales or turnover below a given threshold. However, small entities may register voluntarily, providing they meet certain specified conditions, including keeping proper records.
- ***Upfront VAT exemptions in lieu of credits:*** Another practice is the ***exemptions granted for expensive business inputs (e.g., equipment and inputs) in lieu of credits and refunds*** because of delays and non-payment of relatively inefficient VAT refund schemes.

While ***all large or small non-registered entities cannot charge VAT or claim ITC,*** the upfront exemption may perpetuate tax evasion and avoidance, including misclassification and corrupt valuation practices that make audits and other forms of compliance more difficult and expensive.

Justifications for more exceptions to VAT rules: Despite these exclusions or exceptions to ideal VAT regimes, many countries compromise the VAT regime further by adding to exemption and extending VAT zero-rating to domestic supplies.

- ***Distortion of VAT regime:*** Exemptions aggravate the ***distortion of "ideal" VAT*** regimes when granted upstream or midstream—and not at the final distribution stage where it minimizes cascading and eases administration and compliance.

- ***Regressivity of VAT and tax burden:*** other policies that affect the efficiency of VAT regimes are the extension of zero-rating to domestic supplies, against the background of inadequate budget provisions for refunds and legislating lower or sub-standard tax rates.
- ***Complex administration and compliance:*** since most tax agencies are weak, the original and extended scope of exemptions, reliefs and zero-rating makes it more difficult to administer and comply with the VAT regime.

Consequently, the extension of the exempt, relief and zero-rating bases to cover more supplies or entities which depart from the ideal VAT regime makes the tax regime complex and leads to increases in costs and consumer prices. Therefore, a simple VAT regime is the most ideal for compliance, administration and revenue generation.

3. Summary of basic VAT structure

Part I [Chapters 1 and 2] discuss the attributes of the invoice-credit method as ***superior to the alternative VAT addition and subtraction methods.*** The *all-inclusive* ideal VAT regime has a revenue appeal since it is the main tax instrument with the largest indirect or total tax base. Table 8.1 repeats the ***ideal "value addition" process*** from earlier Chapters.

Table 8.1: Value Addition Process

Value Addition Process					
	Business Entity	Value (ex-VAT)	Cumulative Value Added	Explanation	Comments
	1	2	3	4	5
a	Importer	1000	1000	a3 = a2	Value added [VA] at origin
b	Manufacturer	800	1800	b3 = a2 + b2	Cumulative VA at manufacturing, wholesale and retail stages
c	Wholesaler	600	2400	c3 = b2 + c2	
d	Retailer	400	2800	d3 = c2 + d2	
e	Consumer	2800			Final [total] VA or price to consumer
f	Tax/VAT rate [standard]		17.5%		

Table 8.2 also repeats the ideal mechanism from earlier Chapters that obliges eligible entities to register; ***charge Output VAT*** along the production-distribution chain (Table 8.1); and offset or right to

claim ITC for VAT paid on taxable inputs, supplies or purchases. Hence, registered entities ***pay only the Net VAT*** to their registered tax offices.

Table 8.2: Ideal VAT regime

Ideal VAT regime [All Registered]								
Business entity		Value ex-VAT	Value Added	Output VAT	Input VAT	Net VAT	Price [tax plus]	Comments
	1	2	3	4	5	6	7	8
			2+[{b/f}]	(3xf3)		(4 - 5)	(3 + 4)	
a	Importer	1000	1000	175	0	175	1175	B2B [ITC]
b	Manufacturer	800	1800	315	175	140	2115	B2B
c	Wholesaler	600	2400	420	315	105	2820	B2B
d	Retailer	400	2800	490	420	70	3290	B2B
e	Consumer	2800				490	3290	B2C [final; no ITC]
f	Rate [standard]		17.5%					

The ***ideal VAT regime results*** in a tax burden of GH₵ 490, which is also the Net VAT paid, and a final consumer price of GH₵ 3,290 on a cumulative "value added" amount of c2,800. Table 8.2 is the ideal and forms the basis for the comparison of the effects of policies in the ensuing discussions.

4. Expansion of exclusions under VAT Act, 1998 (Act 546)

As noted in earlier Chapters, the main impediment to implementing the original VAT Act, 1998 (Act 546), was the ***expansion to exemption, relief and [domestic] zero-rating regimes*** that made it difficult to administer and comply with the tax.

- ***Schedule 1: Exempt Supply*** (Section 14) and ***Exempt Import*** (Section 16);
- ***Schedule 2: Zero-rated Supply*** (Section 15) exports and ship's stores; and
- ***Schedule 3: Relief Supplies*** (Section 17)—specific end-users, including the President and Diplomats.

This Chapter continues with Schedule I (Exempt Supply) as part of the continuing review of the specific policies and amendments of the "original" schedules while Chapter 7 covers zero-rating and relief supplies.

To re-emphasize, the general effect of all exemptions is that ***registered entities do not charge Output VAT and cannot claim ITC***. Note that this will result in ***"cascading"*** or tax-on-tax that escalates values, when business entities add the input VAT they cannot claim to their costs and increase prices. These get worse with midstream and upstream exemptions.

Exempt supply—Schedule 1 (s14 and s16): Schedule 1 of VATA 546 (1998) combines the exemption of supplies under ***Section 14*** (domestic supply) and ***Section 16*** (imports). ***Section 15*** relates to zero-rating and is discussed in the next chapter, together with reliefs. In addition, the review of Schedule 1 (Paragraph 4), takes note of restrictions such as ***"produced in Ghana"*** that may lead to ***unintended outcomes—such as*** making the ***price of imported goods more competitive than similar domestic supplies***.

- *Exempt [domestic] supply (Section 14):* Section 14 deals with the exemption ***of routine supplies*** of consumer products and the exceptional case of disposing of an entire business entity that continues to operate as a ***going concern***.
    - *Section 14(1) notes: "The supply of the goods and services specified in* ***Schedule 1*** *is exempt supply and not subject to the tax".*
    - *Section 14(2) notes: "Where a supply is an exempt supply under paragraph 19 of Schedule 1, both the transferor and transferee shall notify the Commissioner in writing of the details of the transfer".*

  The essence of Section 14(2) is to exempt the transfer of a business entity as a ***"going concern"*** under Item 19 of the Schedule to avoid paying Output VAT upfront for takeovers, mergers and acquisitions.

- *Exempt import (Section 16):* the customs agencies collect the import VAT on goods under the same rules for charging tariffs (import duty) and other taxes or levies (e.g., import excise) and fees or charges.
    - *Section 16 notes: "An import of goods is an exempt import if the goods are exempt under the Schedule to this Act and classified in conformity with the Harmonized Commodity*

Description and Coding System also known as the 'the Harmonized System".

The extent of ***"cascading" due to denial of ITC depends on whether the exemptions occur upstream, midstream, or downstream*** in the value addition chain. The ensuing section uses examples from the law to test this hypothesis of the nature of exemptions determining the extent of cascading that occurs along the VAT "value addition" chain.

5. Exempt agriculture supplies

The ***Schedule 1 exemption of agricultural supplies*** relates to (a) primary or basic output for consumption or breading and processing; (b) output or supplies ***"produced in Ghana"***; with (c) annual turnover or sales below the VAT *registration threshold.*

- ***Exempt basic agricultural supply upstream:*** The exemptions in Table 8.3 involve the production or imports of basic agricultural, husbandry (animals, livestock, and poultry), and aquatic ***products in their raw state, produced in Ghana*** at the farmgate, river or sea beaches and across land or sea borders.

Table 8.3: Exempt agricultural/aquatic supply

Item	Category	Description	Comments
1	Animal, livestock, and poultry	All live animals.	Exemptions apply to all imports and domestic supplies
3	Animal product in its ***raw state [produced in Ghana]***	Edible meat and offal of the animals ***listed in Item 1, provided*** any processing is restricted to salting, smoking or similar process ***but excluding*** pate, fatty livers of geese and ducks and similar products.	***Note to Schedule 1:*** Products under Items 4 and 5 shall be considered as in their original state even if they have undergone simple processing of preparation or preservation such as freezing, drilling, drying, salting, smoking, stripping or polishing. Also, note "produced in Ghana qualification.
4	Agricultural and aquatic food products in their ***raw state [produced in Ghana]***	Fish, crustaceans, and molluscs (***but excluding*** ornamental fish); vegetable fruits, nuts, coffee, cocoa, shea butter, maize, sorghum, millet, tubers, guinea corn and rice.	

- ***Unprocessed agricultural and aquatic supplies***: the target is supplies made by many ***small farmers or fishers*** and, subsequently sales in ***informal traditional markets*** by small ***traders and processors.***
- ***Materiality of value added.*** It is assumed that there is minimal value added in the traditional form of processing (i.e., smoking) and sales to final consumers or other small entities in the same traditional markets.
    - ***Extent of distortion:*** the policies impede the development of VAT through increases in costs and prices, which depend on whether the exemptions occur ***downstream, midstream or upstream.***

As processing of exempt supplies occurs at any of these stages, cascading occurs and the values for calculating VAT also increase. Generally, as Table 8.4 shows, the exemption of primary agricultural output ***upstream and*** at the farmgate or importation has similar outcomes as the ideal VAT (i.e., Table 2 above) since (a) VAT was not imposed in the origin state; or (b) they ***involve basic processing with virtually no taxable inputs,*** with minimal or no ITC claim.

Table 8.4: Upstream exemption (domestic supply & imports)

VAT Upstream exemptions: domestic supply and imports of live animals								
Business entity		Value ex Tax	Value Added	Output VAT	Input VAT	Net VAT	Price [tax plus]	Comments
	1	2	3	4	5	6	7	8
			2+[{b/f}]	(3xf3)		(4 - 5)	(3 + 4)	
a	Importer/Farmer	1000	1000	n/a	n/a	n/a	1000	B2B [no ITC]
b	Manufacturer	800	1800	315	0	315	2115	B2B
c	Wholesaler	600	2400	420	315	105	2820	B2B
d	Retailer	400	2800	490	420	70	3290	B2B
e	Consumer	2800				490	3290	B2C [final; no ITC]
f	Rate [standard]		17.5%		Exemption	n/a		

The ***Table 8.4 outcomes*** are the same as those under the ideal VAT regimes—*consumer price (GH₵ 3290), tax burden (GH₵ 490), and fiscal revenue (GH₵ 490)* because the exemption occurred upstream (imports or farmgate) with no ITC claim.

- ***Exemption of midstream supplies "produced in Ghana":*** As Box 6.1 notes, the clause ***"produced in Ghana"***, midstream or upstream, may have unintended adverse outcomes for domestic entities in the formal sector.

From a ***political-economy viewpoint,*** the adverse impact of this ***addition*** to the law intensified the debate on whether to keep or cancel similar clauses such as upfront "ring" or tax waivers under the old sales tax methods that the VAT replaced in 1998/99.

> **Box 6.1: Exemption of supplies "produced in Ghana"**
>
> Since most inputs into domestic production are imports, local producers, such as poultry farmers and processors, typically incur irrecoverable input tax when the output is exempt from VAT. Therefore, local entities tend to be uncompetitive since, in theory, the denial of ITC for exempt (non-taxable) inputs results in higher costs, compared to imports.

- ***The "produced in Ghana" qualification*** may result in ***negative "protection" for national agricultural and*** non-***agricultural*** supplies and entities in both the ***formal and informal sectors.*** This anomaly led to policies that zero-rate domestic supplies for the pharmaceutical sector and significant amendments to Item 12 of Schedule 1.

Table 8.5 discusses the outcomes where the ***inputs (e.g., breeders) that occur "midstream" as exempt domestic supplies result in irrecoverable import VAT.***

Table 8.5: Midstream agriculture [breeding] transaction

Midstream exempt agricultural [breeding] domestic transaction										
Business entity		Value ex Tax	Value Added	Output VAT		Input VAT		Net VAT	Price [tax plus]	Comments
				Taxable	Exempt	Recove-rable	Irrecove-rable			
a	Importer/Farmer	1000	1000	131	0	0	0	131	1131	Partly taxable inputs
b	Farm processing	800	1931	0	0	0	131	0	1931	Exempt [breeding]
c	Agro Processor	600	2531	443	0	0	0	443	2974	Taxable
d	Restaurant	400	3374	590	0	0	443	590	3965	Taxable
e	Consumer	2800						1165	3965	Final priɔe
f	Rate [standard]	17.5%			Exempt input ratio		75%	Taxable	25%	

Compared to Table 8.2 and Table 8.6 below (in a similar format as Table 8.5), the denial of input VAT credit or refund *results in cascading and high input costs, VAT burden (GH₵ 490 to GH₵ 590) and final price (GH₵ 3,290 to GH₵ 3,965).*

- ***Agricultural produce as inputs:*** In Table 8.6, Item 2 (animals for *"**breeding**"*) and Item 5 (crops for *"**propagation**"*) are upstream or ***basic agricultural*** inputs—with the emphasis on ***"imported"*** ***in Item 2 making it different from the exemption of both imports and domestic supplies in Item 1 in Table 8.6.***

Table 8.6: Agriculture, fishing, and other inputs

Item	Category	Description	Comments
2	Animals, livestock, and poultry ***[imported for breeding purposes]***	***Live*** asses, mules, and hinnies; bovine animals; swine; sheep and goats; and live poultry	*Local supply or imports of agricultural supplies as inputs, not consumption*
5	Seeds, bulbs, rooting, and other forms of ***propa-gation***	Of edible fruits, nuts, cereals, tubers and vegetables	*Local supply or imports of agricultural supplies as inputs, not consumption*

As Table 8.7 (similar to Table 8.6) shows, in contrast to Table 8.5 and in terms of the final consumer price, the exempt ***imports are cheaper and, therefore, more competitive than equivalent domestic supplies.*** This is because, in the latter case, the upstream exemption does not result in cascading (refer to Box 1 above).

Table 8.7: Upstream exemption of agricultural imported supply (breeders)

Upstream exempt agricultural [breeders] imported supply										
Business entity		Value ex Tax	Value Added	Output VAT		Input VAT		Net VAT	Price [tax plus]	Comments
				Taxable	Exempt	Recove-rable	Irrecove-rable			
a	Importer	1000	1000	0	0	0	0	0	1000	Exempt [breeding]
b	Farm processing	800	1800	0	0	0	0	0	1800	Exempt [live poultry]
c	Agro Processor	600	2400	420	0	0	0	420	2820	Taxable
d	Restaurant	400	2800	490	0	420	0	70	3290	Taxable
e	Consumer	2800						490	3290	Final prioe
f	Rate [standard]	17.5%			Exempt input ratio		0	Taxable	100%	

The outcomes from Table 8.7 are as follows: *consumer price (GH₵ 3290), tax burden (GH₵ 490), and fiscal revenue (GH₵ 490)*—with all forgone Output VAT recovered at the final consumer stage. The following points make the difference—

- taxable "processed" ***imports attract import VAT,*** which results in ITC claims when used to process taxable domestic supplies;

- initially, since the exemption from payment of import VAT appears to be an ***import duty or tariff,*** they are seen as ***"protecting"*** local suppliers; but
- when subjected to ITC and set off against Output VAT on domestic taxable supplies, it eliminates cascading (with the price of 3290), compared to Table 8.5 (with a price of 3965).

In general, these outcomes for exempt supplies "produced locally", with irrecoverable input tax, compare poorly with the VAT exemption on imports—which does not cascade because of the ITC claim. The domestic supply outcome is similar to ***negative tariff protection for domestic producers of downstream exempt supplies*** but remains unresolved.

The relatively inefficient VAT refund schemes delay the benefits of zero-rating inputs registered entities. To date, local producers continue to protest the contrasting outcome where, in terms of price, imported breeders are more competitive and, therefore, partially account for the many amendments to VATA 1998 from 2000.

6. Agricultural and non-agricultural inputs

These supplies refer to a mix of (a) ***agricultural or non-agricultural items*** that may be in the nature of (b) ***capital*** (e.g., equipment) ***or inputs*** (e.g., raw materials). They include **Item 6** (Chemicals), **Item 7** (fishing equipment), **Item 14** (machinery—cross-sectoral), and **Item 15** (crude oil and hydrocarbon products—general application).

Table 8.8: Exemption of inputs: agriculture and non-agriculture

Item	Category	Description	Comments
a) ***Agricultural and other inputs (other non-assets)***			
6	Agricultural ***inputs***	***Chemicals***, including all forms of fertilizers, acaricides, fungicides, nematicides, growth regulations pesticides, veterinary drugs and vaccines, feed, and feed ingredients	The common element is the use of these chemicals to improve production.
15	Crude oil & hydrocarbon products	Petrol, diesel, liquefied petroleum gas, kerosene, and residual fuel oil.	These supplies are subject to high excise duties
b) ***Agricultural and other inputs (capital or assets)***			

Item	Category	Description	Comments
7	Fishing equipment	Boats, nets, floats, twines, hooks, and other fishing gear …	Domestic supplies or imports (see comments below)
14	Machinery	Machinery, apparatus, appliances, and parts thereof, designed for use in (a), veterinary, fishing, and horti-culture; (b) **industry**; (c) **mining** [as specified in the ***mining list***] and dredging; (d) **railway** and tramway.	The mining inputs are in a ***"Mining List"***—not generic as agricultural, dredging, and industry inputs (amended to omit "agriculture" in VATA 2006 (Act 696—Chapter 7).

As discussed in Chapter 7, Item 7 was enlarged to include "Inputs (imported) for fishing nets and twines under VAT (Amendment) (No. 2) Act 2004 (Act 672). Similarly, while omitting "agriculture" in the original Item 14, a separate category for "agriculture" adds "(e) agriculture [excluding manufactured agricultural machinery and other agricultural implements or tools] under VAT (Amendment) (No.2), Act 2008." Finally, the *irrecoverable ITC for local supplies puts* them at a competitive disadvantage to imports.

7. Exemptions as social intervention policy

The goal of ***exempting final supplies*** on redistribution or social intervention grounds is to ***lower prices on expenditures that form a large portion of the earnings of low-income persons or households.*** The exemption for the Items in Table 8.9 ***applies to the final (downstream) stage*** but ***cascades*** when used as input in the value addition process ***upstream or midstream.***

Table 8.9: Final stage (downstream) exemptions

Item	Category	Description	Comments
8	Water	Supply of water, excluding bottled and distilled water.	In general, this applies to only tap water
9	Electricity	Domestic use of electricity up to a minimum consumption level prescribed by the Minister, and, under VATAA 2003, (Act 639),	*De minimis "lifeline"* rule to the exemption—whereby, the supply of power beyond a given amount or limit is taxable.
10	Printed materials ***(books and newspapers)***	Fully printed or produced by any duplicating process, ***including*** atlases, books, charts, maps, music ***but excluding*** newspapers ***(imported)***, plans and drawings, scientific-technical works, periodicals, magazines, trade catalogues, price lists, greeting cards, almanacks, calendars, and stationery	While appearing to be prescriptive, the exemptions may result in tax evasion or avoidance.
11	Education	The supply of ***educational services*** at any level by an educational establishment ***approved by the Minister for Education***. Laboratory equipment for educational purposes and library equipment	The exemption is a mix of services (e.g., teaching) and goods (laboratory equipment).
12	Medical supplies and services (pharmaceutical)	Essential drug lists and medical supplies are ***determined by the Minister for Health*** and approved by Parliament.	Generally, restricted to approved basic drugs.
13	Transportation	Includes transportation by ***bus and similar vehicles***, train, boat, and air but excludes haulage and vehicle hire.	Seems to target mass transport; hence excludes taxi and car rental services (VATAA 810).
18	Goods for the disabled	Articles designed exclusively for use by the disabled.	Social intervention policy. End-user benefit, similar to Reliefs under s17 (Schedule 3) discussed later
20	Postal services	Supply of ***postage stamps***	Stamps are deemed meritorious while other services are taxable.

The Tables above are based on *VATAA 2003 (Act 639)*, which added fluorescent lamps under Item 9 and VATAA (No. 2), 2008 (Act 765) and, hence, expanded the list of exemptions. Further expansions of the exempt health list came under VATAA 2008 (Act 765) and VATAA 2010 (810)—based on the Customs HS Code, 1999. The example in Table 8.10 below shows the exemption in the B2B transaction occurring at the final consumer stage.

Table 8.10: Downstream (final) exemptions

Ideal VAT regime [Downstream exemption]								
Business entity		Value ex-VAT	Value Added	Output VAT	Input VAT	Net VAT	Price [tax plus]	Comments
a	Importer	1000	1000	175	0	175	1175	B2B
b	Manufacturer	800	1800	315	175	140	2115	B2B
c	Wholesaler	600	2400	420	315	105	2820	B2B
d	Retailer	400	2800	0	0	0	2800	B2B [exempt, no ITC]
e	Consumer	2800				420	3220	B2C [final; no ITC]
f	Rate [standard]		17.5%					

The outcomes include ***consumer price (GHȻ 3220), tax burden (GHȻ 420), and fiscal revenue (GHȻ 420)***—a reduction in tax burden and consumer price that is equivalent to the VAT standard rate multiplied by the value added at the final stage (GHȻ 400). The final reduction by GHȻ 70 is also the tax on "value added" at the final retail stage where an exemption applies.

Table 8.11 shows that the extent of downstream cascading depends on the value added at particular points of granting the exemption—usually, on a small margin only on consumer goods. However, there are peculiar issues with some of the items exempted in Table 8.9:

- ***dual use of electricity*** for domestic and business purposes requires apportionment of input tax, with the taxable business element typically falling above the "lifeline" limit;
- ***single use of an electricity meter by multiple households*** in a typical "family" compound makes it difficult for low-income persons to benefit from the exemption;
- newspapers, printed domestically, are exempt from Output VAT (i.e., ITC denied) while ***imports*** by registered entities are eligible for ITC claim and become competitive (discussed in Paragraph 4.2 above);
- the exempt health and education supplies or services are from a list published by the sector ministry—***businesses selling the exempt items cannot claim ITC***; and
- the exempt supplies ***for disabled persons*** are ***user-specific*** while ***postage stamps*** are meritorious—the exemption excludes other postal services, including courier services.

Table 8.11 repeats Table 8.10 but with the exemptions occurring twice at the *downstream and midstream stages,* with registered entities that can make ITC claims.

Table 8.11: Midstream-cum-downstream exemptions

Ideal VAT regime [Midstream & Downstream exemption]									
Business entity		Value ex-VAT	Value Added	Output VAT	Input VAT		Net VAT	Price [tax plus]	Comments
					Allowed	Denied			
a	Importer	1000	1000	175	0	0	175	1175	B2B
b	Manufacturer	800	1975	0	0	175	0	1975	B2B [exempt, no ITC]
c	Wholesaler	600	2575	451	0	0	451	3026	B2B
d	Retailer	400	3426	0	0	451	0	3426	B2B [exempt, no ITC]
e	Consumer	2800					626	3426	B2C [final; no ITC]
f	Rate [standard]		17.5%		Exempt			na	

The outcomes are as follows: higher *consumer price (GH₵ 3426 compared to GH₵ 3290) and higher tax burden and fiscal revenue (GH₵ 626 compared to GH₵ 490).*

8. Exemptions on technical grounds

Table 8.12 shows that the exemptions for supplies of ***land and construction*** activities, including real estate; and ***financial services,*** are narrower because they relate to non-core sector activities. The exemption for the sale of businesses as a ***going concern*** is also technical, where Output VAT and ITC could be substantial and may pose significant but temporary liquidity challenges for buyers.

Table 8.12: Exemption of business inputs

VATA 1998 (Act 546)—Schedule 1 Items (extract)

Item	Category	Description	Comments
16	Land, buildings, and construction	a) land & building; the granting, assignment or surrender of an interest in land or building; ***the right to occupy land or building;***	Exempts all transactions in the sector except professional services.
		b) civil engineering work; and	
		c) services supplied in the course of construction, demolition, alteration, maintenance, to building or other works under (a) or (b) above, ***including*** the provision of labour, ***but excluding professional services such as architectural or surveying***	Also, note the generality of the "right to occupy land or building"—which does not differentiate residential and commercial property (later amended by VATAA 2002 (Act 629).

17	Financial services	a) provision of insurance; b) issue, transfer, receipt of, or dealing with money (including foreign exchange) or any note or order of payment of money; c) provision of credit; *d)* operation of any bank (or similar institution) account; ***but excluding professional advice such as accountancy, investment, and legal.***	Exempts all transactions in the sector except professional services.
19	Transfer of going concern	The supply of goods as part of the transfer of a business as a going concern ***by one taxable person to another taxable person.***	Designed to avoid the payment of substantial input VAT upfront (prior to ITC)

- ***Professional services***: the transactions relating to ***professional services*** may be imports or local supplies that, for imported services, are subject to the ***reverse charge rules***. Secondly, under Section 14(2), the transferor and transferee must both notify GRA about the transaction.

  Land, buildings and construction: after the word "buildings" VATAA 2002 (Act 629) ***excludes the following supplies from the exemption***—meaning it taxes the transactions:

  "... hotel accommodation, warehousing, storage and similar occupancy ***incidental to the provision of the relevant services.***"

  Hence, the amendment expands the scope of the tax and its efficiency as a general consumption tax that also gives the right of ITC to registered entities.

  Technical exclusions: The VATA (1998/99) does not follow other VAT laws in making a difference between (a) core and non-core financial services; and (b) residential and non-residential accommodation, which ***narrows the scope of taxable supplies*** to only selected professional services.

The ***partial recovery of ITC*** for registered entities and specific sectors leads to ***input tax apportionment*** under Schedule 4 (s26[2]—Apportionment of Input Tax). Hence, Table 8.13 assumes that the taxable non-core activity is only 10 per cent (i.e., 90 per cent exempt), with the transaction occurring ***midstream (e.g., banking) services to other business entities [B2B] or downstream to consumers [B2-C].***

Table 8.13: Exemption Midstream at Banking Stage

Ideal VAT regime [Midstream & Downstream exemption]											
Business entity		Value ex-VAT	Value Added	Output VAT		Input VAT		Net VAT	Price [tax plus]	Comments
				Taxable	Exempt	Allowed	Denied			
a	Importer	1000	1000	175	0	0	0	175	1175	B2B
b	Manufacturer	800	1800	315	0	175	0	140	2115	B2B
c	***Banking services***	600	2684	47	423	32	284	15	2730	B2B [exempt, no ITC]
d	Retailer	400	3084	540	0	47	0	493	3623	B2C [final; no ITC]
e	Consumer	2800						823	3623	Consumer [final; no ITC]
f	Rate [standard]		17.5%			Exempt	90%	Taxable	10%	

The outcome of midstream VAT exemption in Table 5.14 shows that consumers pay more (GH₵ 3623), due to the high tax burden (GH₵ 450), which is also the total revenue—*compared to price GH₵ 290, tax burden (GH₵ 490), and fiscal revenue (GH₵ 490) in the ideal VAT situation.*

In contrast, Table 8.14 shows the same transactions underlying Table 8.14 but with the exemption occurring at the retail-to-consumer stage. The midstream ITC on a lower amount of GH₵ 284 still leads to a favourable outcome, given less cascading, despite the denial of a higher ***downstream*** ITC of GH₵ 378 at the final consumer stage, which adds to the price.

Table 8.14: Exemption Downstream at Retail Banking Stage

Ideal VAT regime [Midstream & Downstream exemption]										
Business entity		Value ex-VAT	Value Added	Output VAT		Input VAT		Net VAT	Price [tax plus]	Comments
				Taxable	Exempt	Allowed	Denied			
a	Importer	1000	1000	175	0	0	0	175	1175	B2B
b	Manufacturer	800	1800	315	0	175	0	140	2115	B2B
c	**Wholesaler**	600	2400	420	0	315	0	105	2820	B2B
d	***Banking services***	400	3178	56	501	42	378	14	3234	B2B [exempt, no ITC]
e	Consumer	2800						434	3234	Consumer [final; no ITC]
f	Rate [standard]		17.5%			Exempt	90%	Taxable	10%	

The relative outcomes are lower *consumer price (GH₵ 3234 compared to GH₵ 3290) and lower tax burden and fiscal revenue (GH₵ 436 compared to GH₵ 490).*

Table 8.15 involves ***mixed supplies comprising taxable*** and ***non-taxable*** transactions by registered import, construction [rental real estate] and banking entities in the value chain. It involves a ***relatively complex value addition chain (i.e., mixed supply]*** where all the entities charge Output VAT on only a proportion of taxable supply with the rest being exempt or non-taxable supplies.

Table 8.15: Mix-stream (upstream, midstream & downstream) exemption

Apportionment of Input VAT								
[Exempt construction and core financial & fully taxable professional services]								
Business entity	**Value ex Tax**	**Value Added**	**Output VAT**	**Input VAT**		**Net VAT**	**Price [tax plus]**	**Comments**
				Allowed	**Denied**			
Importer/Farmer	1000	1000	149	0	0	149	1149	No foreign Input VAT
Construction	800	1919	67	30	119	37	1986	Apply apportionment
Real estate	600	2579	45	7	60	38	2625	determined as proportion of
Bank	400	3026	23	2	46	20	3048	taxable & non-taxable supply
Consumer	2800					245	3048	
		Supply		**Importer**	**Constrx**	**R-Estate**	**Bank**	Effect of applying variable
Rate [standard]	17.5%	Taxable ratio		85%	20%	10%	5%	taxable supply (or exempt)
Imports	Exempt	Non-taxable ratio		15%	80%	90%	95%	VAT bases to different sectors

The outcome of the hypothetical multiple midstream VAT policy is that consumers pay more (GH₵ 3124) and incur a high tax burden (GH₵ 324), which is also the amount of revenue—*compared to price GH₵ 3290, tax burden (GH₵ 490), and fiscal revenue (GH₵ 490) to the ideal VAT situation.* Given that they sell different products, the Table also assumes that the transactions apply the apportionment ratios at different rates.

The average ratio for taxable supplies is 30 per cent or GH₵ 840, yielding a hypothetical VAT burden or revenue of GH₵ 147 under an ideal VAT. This contrasts with *a higher price of GH₵ 3290, tax burden (GH₵ 490), and fiscal revenue (GH₵ 490) under the ideal VAT situation.*

9. Zero-rated and resupplies—Schedule 2 (s15)

As discussed in the next chapter, ***Schedule*** 2 of VATA 1998/99 covers the application of a non-positive zero (0) rate of tax (instead of the standard rate) to supplies under Section 15, which notes as follows—

> *"Output tax shall be at zero on the supply of the goods and services specified in Schedule 2 to the Act".*

The Schedule to the original ***VAT and customs laws or Acts with respect to zero-rating*** had a very simple structure and target.

- The ***loading of vessels or ships and aircraft stock is done under customs supervision*** and law and is strictly for consumption on board, hence they are viewed as exports.
- The full VAT refund under the ITC mechanism puts the country in a competitive position because ***the country does not export local or domestic taxes.***

Under an ideal VAT mechanism, the impact of all domestic VAT charges is neutral. This is because the zero (0) value is a tax rate and, therefore, the ITC claim for ***VAT paid on taxable inputs is offset against a zero input VAT—leading to a VAT refund claim.***

10. Relief supplies—Schedule 3 (s17)

Similarly, ***Schedule 3*** of VATA 1998/99 covers the ***relief from Output VAT to specified natural and legal persons*** under Section 17, which notes as follows—

> *"There shall be relief from the tax on taxable supply to the individuals, organizations and businesses specified in Schedule 3 to this Act".*

The reliefs ***may be zero-rated on imports*** but cascade with ***embedded costs for VAT paid on inputs*** at the domestic supply or production stage. This is due to the inability of registered natural or legal persons who charge Output VAT being denied ITC claims.

11. Conclusion

The original VAT Act 1998 (Act 546) exempt supply provisions were liberal to the agricultural sector, with the scope of exclusions to taxable supplies ***affecting supplies and entities at all stages of the value addition chain***—importers, domestic producers, wholesale and retail outlets, and consumers. It results in varying degrees of cascading that may originate with downstream, midstream, or upstream transactions or supply. Secondly, contrary to the general view, exemptions do not result in a total elimination of the burden of VAT.

Hence, in general, exemptions do not achieve the same goal as ***"zero-rating" of exports under Schedule 2***, as they do not result in a complete waiver of the full Output VAT. In a general conventional context, the addition of domestic supplies to the zero-rating regimes results makes tax administration complex because of bottlenecks in paying refunds. This phenomenon also affects the more conventional application to exports.

In the case of Schedule 2, the end-user reliefs were mainly applied to the President and diplomats but were later extended to domestic supplies and imports. Table 8.19 compares the outcomes from the Tables that had a VAT computation in this Chapter.

From a ***political-economy and industry lobby viewpoint, the pharmaceutical sector pushed for the most concessions that led to various amendments under the original VATA but this has had mixed policy, revenue, administration and compliance outcomes.*** The exemption is for Output VAT but given the denial of ITC for registered and non-registered small entities, the input tax adds to cost and minimizes the impact of the exemptions. Finally, besides the agricultural sector, the scope of exemption under the Original VATA was relatively narrow.

These changes also have significance in a political-economy context. After the passage of the Original VAT Act, 1998 (Act 546), the most comprehensive review of the VAT regime that affected supplies, entities and structure occurred under the VAT Act, 2013 (Act 870). Between these periods, with a change in Government, ***Parliament enacted amendments almost every year between Act 546 and Act 870.*** Again, with another change in government, several ***amendments followed the passage of Act 870 (2013)*** to date

Chapter 7 continues to discuss the extension of (a) zero-rating beyond exports to domestic supplies; and (b) reliefs beyond the restriction to specified end-users such as the President and diplomats (on a reciprocal basis). Chapter 8 reviews several amendments that affect the base and structure of VAT, notably the conversion of the GETFund Levy and NHIL to Straight Levies that block registered entities from claiming ITC and refunds.

Chapter 9 deals with the addition of VAT Flat Rate Schemes (VFRS) to the conventional method of excluding small entities from VAT registrations, based on an annual threshold for sales or turnover. Consequently, these entities do not charge VAT and cannot claim

ITC or refunds. In contrast, under the VFRS small retail (and later large retail and wholesale) entities charge a flat VAT rate but without the right to ITC or refunds. Chapters 10 and 11 cover administration while Chapters 12 and 13 deal with macroeconomic and political-economy contexts.

Appendix (Chapter 8)

Appendix Table 8.1

Summary of VATA 1998 (Act 546) and VATA 2013 (Act 870) Amendments

A) **Amendments to VATA 1998 (Act 546)**			
Amend-ment	**Date**	**Preamble**	**Comments**
1. ***An Act to amend the Value Added Tax Act, 1998 (Act 546):***			
VATAA, 2000 (Act 579)	19th April, 2000	… to the ***rate of tax***, to provide for ***exemptions,*** and to provide for ***related matters***.	Exempt imports (Chapter 6) Rate (see Chapter 8)
VATAA, 2001 (Act 595)	4th April, 2001	… by revising the thresholds and removing from the exemption in the Schedule, ***imported finished pharma-ceutical products*** to make them tax-able, except for sale at the retail level.	Exempt do-mestic supply (Chapter 6) Entity (see Chapter 7)
VATAA, 2002 (Act 629)	24th June, 2002	An Act to amend the VATA 1998 (546) … (unspecified preamble)	
VATAA, 2003 (Act 639)	11th April, 2003	… to exempt from VAT, ***Compact Fluorescent Lamps (CFL)*** and ***fully assembled computers imported or pro-cured locally*** by ***educational establish-ments*** that are approved by the Ministry of Education.	This targeted amendment was designed to reduce the cost of education through effi-cient bulbs
VATAA, 2004 (Act 670)	23rd April, 2004	… to include ***pharmaceutical products and expand the list of pharmaceutical raw materials exempt*** from VAT and to provide for related matters.	In addition to the exemp-tion of the basic medical supplies

A) **Amendments to VATA 1998 (Act 546)**			
Amend-ment	**Date**	**Preamble**	**Comments**
VATAA, 2004 (Act 671)	23rd April, 2004	… to ***remove VAT on import*** for VAT ***registered manufacturers on inputs*** for fishing nets, twines, and musical instruments, and for ***connected*** purposes.	An end-user exemption that extends the supply VAT base.
VATAA, 2006 (Act 696)	23rd February, 2006	… to ***zero-rate locally produced*** textbooks, exercise books, locally manufactured agricultural machinery and implements or tools, and related matters.	
VATAA, 2007 (Act 734)	18th May, 2007	… in order to give ***legal backing to a Flat Rate Scheme*** that will ***facilitate VAT collection in the informal retail distribution sector*** and to provide for ***related purposes***.	Entity & rate: VAT Flat Rate Scheme (VFRS)—see Chapter 7 & Chapter 8
VATAA, 2008 (Act 752)	28th March, 2008	… to ***exempt telephone sets*** including ***mobile or cellular phones*** and ***satellite phones*** from the imposition of VAT.	Initiative to cover new technology, which an "all-inclusive" clause does automatically
VATAA, 2008 (No. 2) (Act 765)	17th November, 2008	… to ***zero-rate locally produced pharmaceuticals***, and to provide for ***related matters***	Rate & Supply (Chapter 6 & 8)
B) **VATA 2013 (Act 870) Amendments.**			
Amend-ment	**Date**	**Preamble**	**Comments**
VATAA, 2010 (Act 810)	31st December, 2010	… to ***revise and expand*** the coverage of the ***threshold for registration***; and ***reclassify locally produced pharmaceuticals***, locally produced ***textbooks*** and locally manufactured ***agricultural machinery and tools*** as ***exempt supplies***.	Entity & Rate (Chapters 7 & 8) Supply (Chapter 6)

A) **Amendments to VATA 1998 (Act 546)**			
Amend-ment	**Date**	**Preamble**	**Comments**
2. An Act to ***revise and consolidate*** the laws relating to …			
VAT Act, 2013 (Act 870)	30th April, 2013	… the imposition of the value-added tax and provide for related matters.	Comprehen-sive revamp of the VAT regime
An Act to amend the Value Added Tax Act, 2013 (Act 870) to …			
VATAA, 2015 (Act 890)	10th April, 2015	…to introduce a ***flat rate mechanism*** for accounting for tax payable for the supply of ***immovable property*** by estate developers; to establish the GRA ***General Refund A/c***; to ***exempt pharmaceutical and selected active ingredients and inputs*** for the manu-facture of pharmaceuticals, ***paper for the production of exercise books and textbooks***; and ***mild carbon steel*** for the manufacture of ***machetes*** from the tax and to provide for related matters	Introduced the "combo" ***VAT Flat Presumptive regime that also has small-entity income tax obligations; changed the VAT refund provision to a scheme for all taxes.***
VATAA, 2015 (Act 904)	30th December, 2015	… to increase the ***monetary threshold for registration*** under the Act and to **increase the percentage** of tax revenue required to set aside for the GRA ***Gen-eral Refund Account***.	Increase in the VAT registration threshold
Amend-ment	**Date**	**Preamble**	**Comments**
VATAA, 2017 (Act 948)	5th April, 2017	… to classify the supply of ***financial services, domestic transportation of passengers by air and supply of immov-able property by a real estate developer as exempt supplies***, to give legal back-ing to a ***VAT Flat Rate Scheme*** that will facilitate collection of VAT on the sup-ply of goods in the ***distribution chain*** and to provide for ***related matters***.	Reversal of the initiative to bring non-core financial services and services relat-ed to property into the VAT base.

A) **Amendments to VATA 1998 (Act 546)**			
Amend-ment	**Date**	**Preamble**	**Comments**
VATAA, 2017 (Act 954)	29th December, 2017	… to remove the tax on ***stakes in the National Lotto***, to provide for the ***with-holding from the payment of VAT*** to registered Value Added Tax traders, and to provide for ***related matters***.	Reversal of the policy to streamline the gambling sector to conform to basic VAT rules
VATAA, 2018 (Act 970)	31st July, 2018	… to revise the Value Added Tax ***rate to twelve and a half per cent*** to provide for ***related matters***.	
VATAA, 2018 (Act 980)	28th December, 2018	… to ***zero-rate*** the VAT on the supply of ***locally manufactured textile***s and to provide for ***related matters***.	Expansion of domestic zero-rating in lieu of exemptions
VATAA, 2019 (Act 1005)	28th December, 2019	… to provide exemptions from the payment of VAT on ***imports of plant & machinery*** designed specifically for use in the automobile industry and ***kits imported*** by an automobile ***manufacturer or assembler*** registered under the Ghana Automobile Manufacturing Development program & on ***management fees*** for private equity, venture capital, and mutual funds; and for related matters.	Expansion of the VAT exemption base to new manufacturing sectors.

Appendix Table 8.2

VAT (Amendment) Act, 2000 (Act 579)

Schedule 1A inserted in Act 546

3. The principal enactment is amended by the insertion after Schedule 1 of a new Schedule 1A as follows:

SCHEDULE 1A—ACTIVE INGREDIENTS FOR ESSENTIAL DRUGS

Item			
1	Aluminum Hydroxide powder	18	Ibuprofen Powder
2	Amoxycillin Trihydrate Powder	19	Indomethacin Powder
3	Amoxycillin Trihydrate Compacted	20	Liver Extract
4	Ampicillin Trihydrate Powder	21	Mebendazole Powder
5	Ampicillin Trihydrate Compacted	22	Metronidazole Powder
6	Acetyls alicyclic Acid (Aspirin)	23	Metronidazole Benzoate Powder
7	Codeine Phosphate Powder	24	Oxy-Tetracycline Hel Powder
8	Chloramphenicol Levo Powder	25	Acetaminophen Powder (Parac-etamol)
9	Chloramphenicol Palmitate Powder	26	Penicillin V Potassium Powder
10	Chlordiazepoxide Hcl Powder	27	Piperazine Citrate Powder/ Crystals
11	Chloroquine Phosphate Powder	28	Prednisolone Powder
12	Chlorpheniramine Maleate Powder	29	Sulfamethoxazole Powder
13	Cloxacillin Sodium Powder	30	Sulfathiazole Powder
14	Diazepam Powder	31	Phthayl Sulfathiazole Powder
15	Diphenhydramine Hcl Powder	32	Tetracycline Hel Powder
16	Ferric Ammonium Citrate Powder/ Crystals	33 34	Trimethoprim Powder Gelatin Capsule Shells
17	Hemoglobin Powder		

Appendix Table 8.3

Schedule 1(A) of VAT (Amendment) Act 670, 2004

Schedule 1 to Act 546 amended. The Value Added Tax Act, 1998 (Act 546) as amended is further amended

a) ***by the substitution for item 12 of Schedule 1 of the following:***

"12. Medical Supplies and Services—Pharmaceuticals
i. Medical Services
ii. Pharmaceuticals

a. Essential drugs as listed under Chapter 30 of the Harmonized Commodities Classification Code 1999, *produced or supplied by retail in Ghana*

b. Active ingredients specified in Schedule 1A for essential drugs

c. Imported special drugs determined by the Minister for Health and approved by Parliament as specified in Schedule 1B.

b) ***By the substitution of Schedule 1A of the following:***

SCHEDULE 1A—ACTIVE INGREDIENTS FOR ESSENTIAL DRUGS

Item		Item	
1	Aluminum Hydroxide Powder	34	Gelatin Capsule Shells
2	Amoxycillin Trihydrate Powder	35	Flucloxacillin Compacted/Powder
3	Amoxycillin Trihydrate Compacted	36	Albendazole Powder
4	Ampicillin Trihydrate Powder	37	Griseofulvin Powder
5	Ampicillin Trihydrate Compacted	38	Diclofenac Sodium Powder
6	Acetylsalicylic Acid (Aspirin)	39	Nifedipine Powder
7	Codeine Phosphate Powder	40	Glibenclamide Powder
8	Chloramphenicol Levo Powder	41	Metformin Powder
9	Chloramphenicol Palmitate Powder	42	Quinine Sulphate Powder
10	Chlordiazepoxide Hel Powder	43	Ciprofloxacin Powder

11	Chloroquine Phosphate Powder	44	Propranolol Powder
12	Chlorpheniramine Maleate Powder	45	Artesunate Powder
13	Cloxacillin Sodium Powder	46	Doxycycline Compacted/Powder
14	Diazepam Powder	47	Sulphadoxine Powder
15	Diphenhydramine Hcl Powder	48	Pyrimethamine Powder
16	Ferric Ammonium Citrate Powder/Crystals	49	Methylsalycylate Powder
17	Hemoglobin Powder	50	Theophylline Powder
18	Ibuprofen Powder	51	Phenobarbitone Powder
19	Indomethacin Powder	52	Magnesium Hydroxide Powder
20	Liver Extract	53	Salbutamol Powder
21	Mebendazole Powder	54	Erythromycin Powder
22	Metronidazole Powder	55	Promethazine Powder
23	Metronidazole Benzoate Powder	56	Folic Acid Powder
24	Oxytetracycline Hcl Powder	57	Amodiaquine Powder
25	Acetaminophen Powder	58	Isoniazid Powder
26	Penicillin V Potassium Powder	59	Thioacetazone Powder
27	Piperazine Citrate Powder/ Crystals	60	Rifampicin Powder
28	Prednisolone Powder	61	Ferrous Salt Powder
29	Sulfamethoxazole Powder	62	Reserpine Powder
30	Sulphathiazole Powder	63	Frusemide Powder
31	Phthalylsulphathiazole Powder	64	Bisacodyl Powder
32	Tetracycline Hcl Powder	65	Ergometrine Maleate Powder
33	Trimethoprim Powder	66	Cimetidine Powder

- *by the substitution of Schedule 1A of a new Schedule 1B as follows:*

SCHEDULE 1B—ACTIVE INGREDIENTS FOR ESSENTIAL DRUGS

Item		Item	
1	Acetylcysteine Inj. 200mg/ml	34	Metformin Tablet, 500mg
2	Aminophylline Injection, 250mg/10ml	35	Metformin Tablet 850 mg
3	Antileprosy Pack (Clofazimine Tablet, 100mg: Dapsone Tablet), 50mg	36	Nifedipine Capsule, 10mg

4	Antirabies immunoglobulins Inj. 1000IU/mg (Bovine)	37	Nifedipine Capsule, 5mg (slow release)
5	Antirabies immunoglobulin Inj. (Human)	38	Nifedipine Tablet, 10mg (slow release)
6	Anti-snake venom, Polyvalent Inj.	39	Nifedipine CapsuleTablet, 20mg (slow release)
7	BCG Vaccine Injection	40	Oxygen (Medicinal Gas) Inhalation
8	Carbamazepine Tablets, 200mg	41	Phenytoin Inj. 50mgml
9	Chlorpromazine Tablet, 100mg	42	Phenytoin sodium Tablet, 100mg
10	Chlorpromazine Tablet, 25mg	43	Poliomyelitis Vaccine Oral solution
11	Chlorpromazine Tablet, 50mg	44	Pyrazinamide Suspension, 125mg/ml
12	Diagnostic Strips - Glucose	45	Pyrazinamide Suspension, 500mg/ml
13	Diagnostic Strips – Multipurpose	46	Quinine Inj. 40mg/ml in 5 ml
14	Diagnostic Strips – Protein	47	Quinine Tablet, 300 mg
15	Diagnostic Tablets – Glucose	48	Rabies vaccine Injection
16	Diagnostic Tablets – Ketones	49	Rifampicin + Isoniazid Suspension, 75gm+50mg
17	Diphtheria + Pertussis + Tetanus vaccine Injection	50	Rifampicin + Isoniazid Tablet, 150gm+100mg
18	Ethosuximide Syrup 250mg/5ml	51	Salbutamol Inhaler, 200 dose 100mcg/metered dose
19	Ethosuximide Tablet, 250mg	52	Salbutamol Nebulizer Solution, 5mg/ml as sulphate
20	Glibenclamide Tablet, 5mg	53	Salbutamol Sulfate Inj. 50mcg/ml
21	Glyceryl Trinitrate Sublingual Tablet 500mg	54	Salmeterol Inhaler, 120 doses 25mcg/metered dose
22	Haloperidol Inj. 50mg	55	Streptomycin Inj. 1 gm
23	Hepatitis B Vaccine Injection	56	Tetanus Immunoglobulin Injection, 2501U/ml
24	Hydralazine Inj. 20mg/Ampoule	57	Tetanus Vaccine Injection, 401U/5ml
25	Imipramine Tablet 25 mg	58	Tetracycline Eye Ointment 1% 5 gm
26	Isoniazid + Thioacetazone Tablet, 300 + 150mg	59	Timolol Maleate Eye Drops 0.5%

27	Insulin Isophane Inj. 100 units/ml 10 ml	60	Tuberculin (PPD) Injection
28	Insulin Lente Inj. 100 units/ml 10ml	61	Valproate sodium capsule, 200mg
29	Insulin soluble, 100 units/m/10m	62	Valproate sodium syrup, 200mg/5ml
30	Isoniazid Tablet 6mg	63	Yellow fever vaccine injection 20 doses
31	Ivermectin Tablet, 6mg	64	Yellow fever vaccine injection 10 doses
32	Measles Vaccine Injection	65	Zidovudine + Lamivudine Tablet, 300mg + 150mg
33	Meningococcal Vaccine Injection	66	All other anti-retroviral drugs approved for use in Ghana

Chapter 9

VAT POLICY REVIEW-2: ZERO-RATED AND RELIEF SUPPLIES [SCHEDULES 2 AND 3]

1. Introduction

After the coverage of exemptions (Schedule 1), ***this chapter*** continues the evaluation in **Part III** on amendments, with a focus on the ***zero-rated*** (Schedule 2) and ***relief*** (Schedule 3) supplies. Summaries of VATA 870 elaborate further on the scope of zero-rating of exports. The gist of Chapter 7 is the expansion of zero-rating to domestic supplies and several non-conventional reliefs, with outcomes that include ***complex upstream, midstream and downstream distortions*** to the value addition chain.

Adherence to the ideal VAT under the unique *Invoice-Credit VAT mechanism* facilitates its efficiency, buoyancy, compliance, and administration. Hence, ***countries must revert to a simple and broad-based tax structure*** that assigns the general consumption tax to VAT, with complementary income tax (i.e., revenue and investment incentives), excise duty (i.e., punitive) and import duty or tariff (i.e., protection) regimes.

2. Ideal VAT Invoice-Credit Method

This paragraph repeats the ideal VAT Invoice Credit method in Table 9.1, which is compared later with the relatively more complex policies and outcomes from the expanded exemption, relief and zero-rating structures—including the zero-rating of domestic supplies and benefits to end-users. *The "ratios" are based on the ex-VAT values* and refer to the proportions of Value Added (VA) along the value chain.

Table 9.1: Ideal VAT regime [all entities registered]

Ideal VAT regime [All Registered]								
Business entity	**Value ex-VAT**	**Value Added**	**Output VAT**	**Input VAT**	**Net VAT**	**Price [tax plus]**	**Comments**	**Ratios**
Importer	1000	1000	175		175	1175	All the entities in the value chain are registered to charge Output VAT and claim ITC.	35.7
Manufacturer	800	1800	315	175	140	2115		28.6
Wholesaler	600	2400	420	315	105	2820		21.4
Retailer	400	2800	490	420	70	3290		14.3
Consumer	2800				490	3290		100.0
Rate [standard]		17.5%						

Table 9.1 repeats and shows the ideal ***outcomes as*** total ***value added*** (GH₵ 2,800), tax ***revenue*** and ***burden*** (GH₵ 490), and ***final consumer price*** (GH₵ 3,290).

3. Original zero-rated supplies: Schedule 2 (s36 of VATA 1998 [Act 546])

Section 3 covers the original VATA 1998 (Act 546) exclusions while Section 4 covers the amendments that expanded the scope of supplies (including domestic zero-rating) and end-users (from the Head of State and diplomats to the pharmaceutical, agricultural and manufacturing) sectors. Schedule 2 of VATA 1998 (Act 546) covers the application of a non-positive zero (0) rate of tax (instead of the) to supplies under Section 15, which notes as follows—

> *"**Output tax shall be at zero (0)** on the supply of the goods and services specified in Schedule 2 to the Act".*

The following summarizes the provisions under the ***VAT and customs laws or Acts with respect to zero-rating***—with the original law having a very simple structure and target.

- The ***loading of vessels or ships and aircraft stock is done under customs supervision*** and law and is strictly for consumption on board, hence they are viewed as exports.
- The full VAT refund under the ITC mechanism puts the country in a competitive position because ***the country does not export local or domestic taxes.***

The impact of all domestic VAT charged is neutral because the ITC claim for ***VAT paid on taxable inputs is offset against a zero-input VAT—leading to a VAT refund claim.*** As Table 9.2 notes, Schedule 2 has two (2) items only and the zero ***(0) rate does not apply to domestic supplies***—implying ***that the reliefs are similar to exemptions.***

Table 9.2: Zero-rated items (s1 Schedule 2)

Item	Description	Comments
1	Export of taxable goods and services	The two items refer to only exports or supplies of goods and services leaving the country.
2	Goods shipped as stores on vessels and aircrafts leaving the teritories of Ghana	

Table 9.3 shows the impact of zero-rating exports on the VAT burden and zero-rating under the invoice-credit ITC method.

Table 9.3: Exports of domestic output

Exports [zero-rated]: Retail exporter stage								
	Business entity	Value ex-VAT	Value Added	Output VAT	Input VAT	Net VAT	Price [tax plus]	Comments
	1	2	3	4	5	6	7	8
			2+[{b/f}]	(3xf3)		(4 - 5)	(3 + 4)	
a	Importer	1000	1000	175		175	1175	B2B [ITC]
b	Manufacturer	800	1800	315	175	140	2115	B2B
c	Wholesaler	600	2400	420	315	105	2820	B2B
d	Exporter	400	2800	0	420	**(420)**	2800	B2B
e	Foreign Entity	2800				0	2800	B2C [VAT is neutral]
f	Rate [standard]		17.5%		Exports	0%		

4. Reviews of VATA 1998 (Act 546): [Domestic] Zero-rated supplies

Schedules 2 of both Act 546 (original) and Act 870 (revamped) refer to zero-rating and not exemptions (Schedule 1) or reliefs (Schedule 3). The ***amendments and repeals*** of zero-rated supplies in specific sections of VATA 1998 (Act 546) resulted in ***domestic zero-rating.*** The original provision is shown in Table 9.4 below.

Table 9.4: Zero-rated [domestic] supply items (s1 Schedule 2)

Item	Description	Comments
Original: VAT Act 1998 *(Act 546)*—Original		
1	Export of taxable goods and services	The two items refer to only supplies of goods and services leaving the country
2	Goods shipped as stores on vessels and aircraft leaving the territories of Ghana	

Amendments and repeals: exemptions and zero-rating of domestic supplies in various amendment laws and provisions include the following two (2) major legislation.

a. ***VATAA, 2006 (Act 696):*** the ***amendment*** states the following:

"***Schedule*** 2 to Act 546 amended… The VAT Act, 1998 (Act 546) referred to as the "principal enactment is ***amended in Schedule*** 2 by the insertion after Item 2 of the following new items" (see Table 9.4 below).

b. ***VATAA 2008 (Act 765):*** This amendment ***adds to VATAA 696,*** as explained further in Table 9.4 below:

"***The Second (2nd) Schedule*** to Act 546 amended … (6): The principal enactment is ***amended*** in Second Schedule by the ***addition of Item No. 5***". Table 9.5 summarizes the amendments 1 and 2 in VATAA 2006 (Act 696) and VATAA 2008 (Act 765).

Table 9.5: Amendment—zero-rated [domestic] supplies (Schedule 2)

<table>
<tr><th>Item</th><th>Description</th><th>Comments</th></tr>
<tr><td colspan="3">Original: VAT Act 1998 (Act 546)—Amendments</td></tr>
<tr><td colspan="3">1st Amendment: VAT (Amendment) Act 2006 (Act 696)</td></tr>
<tr><td colspan="3">An Act to amend the VAT Act, 1998 (Act 546) to zero-rate locally produced textbooks, exercise books, locally manufactured agricultural machinery and implements or tools for related matters.</td></tr>
<tr><td>3</td><td>Locally produced textbooks and exercise books</td><td rowspan="2">Introduced zero-rating for domestic supplies of manufacturing inputs of final goods in the VAT legislation</td></tr>
<tr><td>4</td><td>Locally manufactured agricultural machinery and other agricultural implements or tools.</td></tr>
<tr><td colspan="3">2nd Amendment: VAT (Amendment) Act 2008 (Act 765) ---note 1</td></tr>
<tr><td colspan="3">An Act to amend the VAT Act, 1998 (Act 546) to zero-rate locally produced pharmaceuticals and to provide for related matters</td></tr>
<tr><td>5</td><td>Locally produced pharmaceuticals as determined by the Minister for Health and approved by Parliament</td><td>Extension of zero-rating to domestic supplies at the distribution stage</td></tr>
</table>

Note 1: The second amendment (VATA 2008 [Act 765] is discussed further below).

Multi-subject amendment [VATAA 2008 (Act 765): it is important to note that this law does not deal exclusively with the zero-rating of supplies or end-users. The provisions of the entire Act are summarized below.

Section 1 states that the Commissioner may ***refund excess ITC*** due for specified agricultural supplies relating to the following ***Schedule 1 Items***—

- Item 2: Animals, livestock and poultry ***imported*** for breeding purposes.
- Item 3: Animal product in its raw state [***produced in Ghana***].
- Item 4: Agricultural and aquatic food products in ***their raw state.***
- Item 5: Seeds, bulbs, roots, and other forms of ***propagation*** [of edible fruits, nuts, and vegetables.

Section 2 relates to **registration**: the power of the Commissioner-General to enforce compliance where voluntary compliance fails.

Section 3 substitutes ***Item 12*** of Schedule 1 (exempt supplies), as shown in Table 9.6, for ***"zero-rating"***.

Table 9.6: Amendment: VATAA 765, Section 3, Item 12

VAT AMENDMENT ACT, 2008 (ACT 765)			VAT ACT, 1998 (ACT 546)		
Section 3, Schedule 1				Section 3, Schedule 1	
The 1st Schedule to the principal enactment is amended			Original Act to be amended & Schedules		
Item #	**Item**	**Description**		**Item**	**Description**
a) by the ***substitution*** for Items No. 12 and description of			***Substitution of Item 12***		
12	Medical supplies & Services	(a) Medical Services	12	Medical supplies & services–pharmaceuticals	Essential drug list and medical supplies determined by the Minister for Health and approved by Parliament
	Pharmaceuticals	(b) Pharmaceuticals:			
		(i) Essential drugs as listed under Chapter 30 of the HS Classification Code, 1999, supplied by retail in Ghana			
		(ii) Imported special drugs determined by the Minister for Health and approved by Parliament as specified in First Schedule A			

Section 3 also amends (or adds to) ***Item 14*** of Schedule 1 (exempt machinery supplies), as shown in Table 9.7, by changing its status to ***"zero-rated" supplies.***

Table 9.7: Amendment: VATAA 765, Section 3, Item 12

VAT AMENDMENT ACT, 2008 (ACT 765)		
Section 3, Schedule 1		
The 1st Schedule to the principal enactment is amended		
Item #	**Item**	**Description**
(b) by the ***addition*** of a new description (e) under Item No. 14		
14	Machinery	Machinery, apparatus, appliances and parts thereof, designed for use in
		a) agriculture, veterinary, fishing and horticulture
		b) industry
		c) mining as specified in the mining list and dredging; and
		d) railway & tramway
	Machinery (New)	*e) agriculture (excluding locally manufactured agricultural machinery & other agricultural implements or tools).*

VAT ACT, 1998 (ACT 546)		
Section 3, Schedule 1		
Original Act to be amended		
Item #	**Item**	**Description**
Addition to Item 14		
14	Machinery	Machinery, apparatus, appliances and parts thereof, designed for use in
		a) agriculture, veterinary, fishing and horticulture
		b) industry
		c) mining as specified in the mining list and dredging; and
		d) railway & tramway

- ***Continuation of VATA 765 repeals and amendments:*** The amendments to ***VATA 2008 (Act 765)*** also dealt with Appendix 1 (Exemptions), which was discussed in Chapter 6. The remaining sections 4 to 7 are summarized below.
- ***Section 4: First Schedule A to Act 546 repealed:*** The principal enactment is amended by the repeal of *First Schedule A*—as shown in ***Appendix Table* 6.1 [Chapter 6]**.
- ***Section 5: First Schedule B to Act 546 amended:*** The principal enactment is amended in *First Schedule B by the re-numbering of First Schedule B as First Schedule A*—as shown in ***Appendix Table* 6.2 [Chapter 6]**.
- ***Section 6: Second Schedule to Act 546 amended***: The principal enactment is amended in the *Second Schedule by the addition of Item No. 5 … "5. Locally produced pharmaceuticals as determined by the Minister for Health and approved by Parliament"* (see Table 9.4 above).
- ***Section 7: Fifth Schedule to Act 546 amended:*** The ***Fifth Schedule*** to the principal enactment is amended by the addition of a new Form B after Form A. This amendment relates to ***Warrants for Enforcement*** by GRA.

In summary, *Act 765 refers to Schedule 1 (exemptions) that were zero-rated (Schedule 2)*. Typically, the MoF and GRA issue Regulations and Guidance Notes (including changes to the Customs HS Code to enhance compliance with the law.

5. Zero-rated supplies: Schedule 2 (s36 of VATA 870)

Section 4 ended the overview of zero-rating (Schedule 2) under VATA 1998 (Act 546) and as ***background to the VAT Act 2013 (Act 870***—which Act represents a ***comprehensive overhaul of VAT policy, legislation, and administration.*** It overturns most of the VAT Act 546 amendments, including definitions in ***Schedule 2, Item 1*** while separating the zero-rating of goods ***(Schedule 2, Item 2)*** from that of services ***(Schedule 2, Item 3)***. **Supply of goods—*Section 2 (Schedule 2)*** covers the following categories of exports of goods—with the rental and charters typically falling under the "special" supplies rules or category in the literature.

- ***Exports (s2[1]):*** A supply of goods where the supplier has entered the goods for export pursuant to the Customs Act, 2015 (Act 891) and the goods have been exported from the country by the supplier.
- ***Trans-shipment (s2[2]):*** A supply of goods where the Commissioner-General (CG) is satisfied that the goods have been exported from the country by the supplier without having been used in the country after the supply was entered, except as necessary for or incidental to, the export of the goods.
- ***Rental and charter (s2[3]):*** A supply under a rental agreement, charter party or agreement for chartering, where the goods are used exclusively in an export country.
- ***Ship or vessel store (s2[4]):*** Subject to Item 1 (4) of this Schedule, a supply of goods shipped as stores on foreign-going vessels or foreign-going aircraft leaving the territories of Ghana and going to a destination in an export country.
- ***Supplies of services***—Section 2 (Schedule 2): As discussed earlier, ***zero-rated supplies*** were ***covered*** under Section 15 (Schedule II) of the original VATA 1998 (Act 546) but VATA 870 expands further on this provision.
- ***Free zone developer or enterprise (s2[5]):*** A supply to a free zone developer or free zone enterprise, requires that they provide satisfactory documentation that its operations and the

procedure for acquisition of the supply satisfy the requirements of the Free Zone Act, 1995 (Act 504).

- *Going concern (s2[6]):* A supply of goods as ***part of the transfer of a taxable activity, as a going concern,*** by one *taxable person* to another *taxable person,* if

    a. Section 19 [cancellation of registration] and s19(4)(18) [notice of cancellation in respect of turnover] are satisfied; and

    b. the notices, including the details of the transaction, required by regulations are provided to the CG.

- ***Tourists and similar persons (s2[7]):*** The Minister may, by Regulations, provide for the zero-rating of exports of goods by tourists and similar persons, under such terms and conditions as the Minister shall specify. Take note of the additional explanations in Box 7.1.

Box 7.1 Some comparisons between VAT 870 and VATA 546

Compared to the explicit rendition in VATA 870, VATA 546 (Section 15) ***implicitly*** allowed for zero-rating of ***Item 3 (rental and charters), Item 5 (free zone operations)***, and ***Item 7 (tourists and similar persons),*** where Ghana is the origin of the supply. Items 5 and 7 are ***administered at points of entry and exit*** (i.e., air, land, and sea) by the Customs Division of GRA. Also, note that ***Item 6 (transfer of going concern)*** was treated as an ***exempt supply*** (Item 19) under the original VAT Act 1998 (Act 546).

- *Non-exports (s2[8]):* VATA 870 explicitly explains conditions that lead to declaring a "non-exports". An activity or supply cannot be ***considered exported*** unless
- immediately being put on board the conveyance for export, the goods are produced to the Commissioner of Customs for examination;
- on demand by the Commissioner, the exporter provides samples of the goods as may be required for testing or any other purpose;
- the person in charge of the conveyance for the export or any other person that the person in charge may authorize for the purpose, certifies on the document on which the goods are entered that the goods have been received on board; and

- particulars of the goods are included in the cargo manifest of the conveyance.

Table 9.8 shows the general effect of applying the standard VAT rate at the final stage of the value-addition chain until the goods are exported by a VAT-registered supplier and the rate changes to zero (0).

Table 9.8: Zero-rated exports

Zero-rated supply [exports & specified domestic supply]							
Business entity	**Value ex-VAT**	**Value Added**	**Output VAT**	**Input VAT**	**Net VAT**	**Price [tax plus]**	**Comments**
Importer	1000	1000	175		175	1175	All entities register and charge Output VAT (zero [0] for exports and specified domestic supplies) and claim ITC.
Manufacturer	800	1800	315	175	140	2115	
Wholesaler	600	2400	420	315	105	2820	
Export/Domestic	400	2800	0	420	(420)	2800	
Consumer	2800				0	2800	
Rate [standard]		17.5%		Zero-rated		0%	

The outcome is a ***refund of Input VAT*** after the offset of a zero (0) amount of Output VAT against an Input VAT of 420—with no VAT burden transferred to foreign consumers.

- ***Re-importation (s2[9]):*** A supply of goods shall not be considered as exported from this country if the supply has been or will be re-imported to the country by the suppliers. Ordinarily, ***re-importation*** was treated ordinarily under the Customs Act 2015 (Act 896).

  In general, goods for ***reimportation*** are "entered" as such, under the import rules, by the Customs Division of GRA without the payment of VAT since they are tracked after the prior re-export declaration. Refunds or credits may result where the Division requires a deposit at the time of the temporary export.

a. **Supply of services (Schedule 2[s3]):** The following rules apply to zero-rating the supply of services—

- ***Land and improvements to land (s3[1]):*** A supply of services directly in connection with land or any improvement to *land situated outside* the country.

- ***Personal property (s3[2])***: A supply of services directly in respect of *personal property situated outside* the country at the time the services are rendered.
- ***Consumption outside Ghana (s3[3])***: A supply of services to the extent that the *services are consumed elsewhere* than in the country.
- ***Intellectual property (s3[4]):*** A supply of services comprising the filing, prosecution, granting, maintenance, transfer, assignment, licensing or enforcement of any *intellectual property rights for use outside* the country.
- ***Freight and insurance (s3[5]):*** A supply of freight and insurance directly attributable to the export of goods.

  Note that under the ***"reverse charge" rules*** for consultancy and other professional services, the VAT-registered (domestic) ***recipients of taxable imported services*** charge Output VAT from non-resident and non-registered experts. The registered person then deducts any related Input VAT before paying the net VAT to the tax office.

b. *VAT Refunds:* the ***main challenge*** in applying zero rates to domestic supplies in developing states is the inefficient VAT refund processes that are the result of inadequate Budget provision.

The lack of adequate budget funds delays refund payments to registered persons with excess credits. However, the zero rating at the import stage is similar to the old waiver or deferral or "ring" methods under the Sales Tax regimes that VAT replaced.

6. Relief supplies: VATA 2013 (Act 870), Section 38 (Schedule 3)

Besides the registered manufacturers (Schedule 3[6]) below, the conventional reliefs often apply to a narrow range of organizations or persons who are not usually registered for VAT and, therefore, tend to be end-users or beneficiaries of a taxable supply. Schedule 3 of VATA 2013 (Act 870) applies the relief supply provision to the following—

- ***Office of Presidents (Schedule 3[1]):*** Ghana follows the example of exempting these high executive officers and offices from payment of direct and indirect taxes in many countries.

- *Diplomats (Schedule 3[2])*: Subject to Item 4 (i.e., reciprocity), a supply for the official use of any Commonwealth or Foreign Embassy, Mission or Consulate.
- *Diplomats (Schedule 3[3]):* Subject to Item 4 (i.e., reciprocity), a supply for the use of a permanent member of the Diplomatic Service of any Commonwealth or foreign country that is exempted by Parliament from the payment of customs duties.
- *Reciprocity (Schedule 3[4])*: The relief provided in Items 2 and 3 of this Schedule applies only if a similar privilege is accorded by the Commonwealth or foreign country to the Ghana representative in that country.
- *International agencies (Schedule 3[5])*: A supply for the use of an international agency or technical assistance scheme where the terms of agreement made with the Government and approved by Parliament include exemption from domestic indirect taxes.
- *Emergency relief items (Schedule 3[6]: VAT-registered manufacturers* for raw materials at importation, subject to the condition that:

    i. the manufacturer is a member in good standing of the Association of Ghana Industries;

    ii. the manufacturer has submitted all previous tax returns and paid the tax, penalties, and interest from previous tax periods, if any;

    iii. the CG is satisfied that the manufacturer has met the conditions in sub-paragraphs (i) and (ii) of this paragraph and other compliance requirements of this Act and has listed the manufacturer in a register published by the CG with a validity period of twelve months effective from 1st January of each year;

    iv. the imported raw materials will be applied solely and exclusively for the manufacturing operations of the relief beneficiary.

Table 9.9 shows the ***impact of exemptions that effectively zero-rate the importation of raw materials by registered manufacturers*** of the Association of Ghana Industries (AGI) and pharmaceuticals. Since the zero rating implies that the import VAT is only substantively deferred upstream, subsequent taxable transactions along the value chain recapture the full amount of the VAT (c490) under the ideal method.

Table 9.9: Zero-rating imported raw materials

Category 4: Zero-rating importation of raw materials for specified manufacturers									
Business entity	Value ex-VAT	Value Added	Output VAT		Input VAT		Net VAT	Price [tax plus]	Comments
			Taxable	Exempt	Allowed	Denied			
Mfg/Imports	1,000	1,000	0	0	0	0	0	1,000	End-user VAT beneficiary (Manufacturer): exempt raw material supplies
Mfg/Others	800	1,800	315	0	0	0	315	2,115	
Wholesaler	600	2,400	420	0	315	0	105	2,820	
Retailer	400	2,800	490	0	420	0	70	3,290	
Consumer	2,800						490	3,290	
Rate [standard]		17.5%	Zero-rating (imported raw materials)				0%		

The *effect is neutral*, as compared to the Ideal VAT Invoice-Credit method outcomes because the zero-rating takes place "upstream" at an early stage of the value addition process. The total input VAT that is waived is recaptured, without cascading at subsequent B2B stages where the standard Output VAT rate applies until the final B2C stage.

To re-emphasize, the implementation of the tax law, regulations or practice notes often follows procedures for reliefs that include:

- ***upfront exemption***—the waiver of VAT on eligible supplies is granted upfront; or
- ***refunds***—the beneficiary pays the tax upfront and applies for a refund.

Another basic requirement is the ***registration*** of the beneficiary and relief interest with the tax agency, which then issues an identification for the purposes.

7. Original VATA 546: Relief supplies—Section 17 (Schedule 3)

Schedule 3 of VATA 1998 covers the ***relief from Output VAT to specified natural and legal persons*** under Section 17, which notes as follows—

> *"There shall be relief from the tax on taxable supply to the* ***individuals, organizations and businesses*** *specified in Schedule 3 to this Act".*

As Table 9.10 shows, the original VATA Schedule 2 (based on Section 17) gave reliefs from Output VAT to specific end-users of all supplies and during emergencies.

Table 9.10: Relief items (s 17 Schedule 3)

Item	Description	Comments
Original: VAT Act, 1998 (Act 546)		
1	President of the Republic of Ghana	
2	For the official use of any Commonwealth or Foreign Embassy, Mission or Consulate (relief applies only to VAT on imported goods)—*subject to Note below.*	These reliefs to Diplomats fall under the Vienna Convention. Some diplomatic institutions challenge the restriction relating to imports.
3	For the use of a permanent member of the Diplomatic Services of any Commonwealth or Foreign country, exempted by Parliament from the payment of Customs Duties (relief applies only to VAT on imported goods)—*subject to Note below.*	
4	For the use of an international agency or technical assistance scheme where the terms of the agreement made with the Government include exemption from domestic taxes.	The Minister for Finance and the affected Ministry often sponsor these through Cabinet.
5	Emergency relief items approved by Parliament.	

Provided that, with regard to items 2 and 3 of this Schedule, a similar privilege is accorded by such Commonwealth or Foreign Country to the Ghanaian representative in that country.

a. ***Methods of implementation:*** in practice, tax agencies administer the ***waiver of, or credit for, VAT on imports or domestic "relief" supplies*** along the following alternative or complementary administrative processes:

- ***waiver of import VAT*** at the point of entry by the customs authorities, in line with the import tariff schedule, for supplies brought in for the benefit of these individuals (President and Diplomats) and institutions (Diplomatic Missions);
- ***waiver or exempt certificates*** to these individuals and institutions, which registered entities use as the basis for waiving the Output VAT;
- ***payment and refunds or credits,*** whereby the beneficiary uses the certificate to apply for a refund of the VAT paid (not waived) on eligible supplies; and

- ***upon sale or transfer for non-privileged use***: VAT is calculated and paid, usually on open market value (OMV) or re-assessed by Customs at the time of sale—after taking account of wear and tear from using the asset.

  Normally, the risk of cascading is minimized since the supply does not re-enter the value chain, where ***any irrecoverable VAT*** would have resulted in cascading. The general policy implication is an exemption or zero-rating of domestic supplies or imports.

b. ***Addition to the original list of relief items:*** Table 9.11 shows the amendment that ***extended the relief privilege to domestic entities***. A further extension for ***"raw materials"*** applied to ***manufacturers*** who ***are registered with the Association of Ghana Industries (AGI)***.

Table 9.11: New relief items

Amendment: VAT (Amendment No.2) Act 2004 (Act 671)		
Item	**Description**	**Comment**
"Schedule 3 of the VAT Act, 1998 (Act 546) amended (s2): Schedule 3 of the principal enactment is amended by the addition of the following items		
2	VAT-registered ***manufacturers*** for ***raw materials at importation***, subject to the conditions that: (i) the ***manufacturer is a member of in good standing*** of the Association of Ghana Industries; (ii) has ***submitted all previous tax returns*** and paid the tax, penalties and interest from previous tax periods; (iii) the *Commissioner is satisfied* that the manufacturer has ***met the conditions*** in subparagraphs (i) and (ii) of this paragraph and other compliance requirements of this Act and has listed the manufacturer in a register published by the Commissioner with a validity period of 6 months effective 1st January of each year; (iv) the ***imported raw materials will be applied solely and exclusively*** for the manufacturing operations of the relief beneficiary.	The footnote introduces the concept of reciprocity that was typically applied to diplomatic privileges in tax laws. In principle, this would require ratification by the Parliaments of Ghana and those of other States.

The amendment in VATAA 2004 (Act 671) is retained in Section 38 of VATA 2013 (Act 870) in Schedule 3, Item 7. The policy results in a ***cash-flow advantage*** to beneficiaries but the zero-rating of domestic VAT supplies could lead to ***refund claims that suffer from***:

- weak administrative and enforcement processes; due to
- inadequate budget provision for refunds; and therefore
- non-payments of refund claims that effectively result in higher prices, due to treating the irrecoverable Input VAT as costs.

As noted in many Chapters, these distortions in the VAT structure and administration will affect the efficiency of VAT operations and complicate compliance.

8. Policy review: mixed taxable, exempt, zero-rated, and relief supplies

The expansion of ***exempt and relief supplies as domestic zero-rating*** makes VAT regimes complex to administer and enforce. Tables 7.12 and Table 9.13 show two (2) sectors with different value addition ratios and mixes of exempt, relief, and zero-rated supplies. They are combined in Table 9.13 to show the combined effect on costs, revenues and prices.

a. ***Category 1: exempt manufacturing and retail stages:*** The ***exempt*** supplies in Table 9.12 occur ***midstream*** (manufacturing) and ***downstream*** (retail) while ***upstream*** supplies at the import and wholesale stages attract the standard 17.5 per cent rate.

Table 9.12: Category 1 exemption at manufacturing and retail stages

Category 1: Partial midstream [mfg] & downstream [retail] partial supplies											
Business entity	Value ex-VAT	Value Added	Output VAT		Input VAT		Net VAT	Price [tax plus]	Comments	Sector ratios	
			Taxable	Exempt	Allowed	Denied				S1	S2
Importer	250	250	44	0	0	0	44	294	Supplies made midstream (mfg) and downstream (retail) are exempt and denied ITC	25%	75%
Manufacturer	***520***	***814***	***0***	***142***	***0***	***44***	***0***	***814***		65%	35%
Wholesaler	330	1144	200	0	0	0	200	1344		55%	45%
Retailer	***240***	***1584***	***0***	***277***		***200***	***0***	***1584***		60%	40%
Consumer	1340						244	1584		51%	49%
Rate [standard]		17.5%									

b. ***Category 2: exempt midstream (manufacturing and wholesale) and downstream zero-rated (retail) supplies:*** Table 9.13 shows these different policies.

Table 9.13: Category 2 exemption (manufacturing) and zero-rating (retail)

Category 2: Partial downstream [retail] zero-rated supply											
Business entity	Value ex-VAT	Value Added	Output VAT		Input VAT		Net VAT	Price [tax plus]	Comments	Sector ratios	
			Taxable	Exempt	Allowed	Denied				S1	S2
Importer	750	750	131	0	0	0	131	881	All supplies are taxable at pre-retail (17.5%) & retail zero rate (0%)	25%	75%
Manufacturer	280	1,030	180	0	131	0	49	1,210		65%	35%
Wholesaler	270	1,300	228	0	180	0	47	1,528		55%	45%
Retailer	***160***	***1,460***	***0***	***0***	228	***228***	***(228)***	1,460		60%	40%
Consumer	1,460						0	1,460		51%	49%

c. ***Category 3: Combined—exempt, zero-rating, and standard-rated supplies:*** Table 9.14 shows the combined results of the mixed supplies for Categories 1 and 2.

Table 9.14: Category 3: Combined Cat. 1 & 2 supplies

Consolidated: Exempt midstream (Cat. 1) plus zero-rated downstream (Cat. 2) supplies											
Business entity	Value ex-VAT	Value Added	Output VAT		Input VAT		Net VAT	Price [tax plus]	Comments	Sector ratios	
			Taxable	Exempt	Allowed	Denied				S1	S2
Importer	1,000	1,000	175	0	0	0	175	1,175	Consolidation of registered entities making mixed taxable, exempt & zero-rated supplies	25%	75%
Manufacturer	800	1,844	180	142	131	44	49	2,024		65%	35%
Wholesaler	600	2,444	428	0	180	0	247	2,871		55%	45%
Retailer	400	3,044	0	277	228	428	(228)	3,044		60%	40%
Consumer	2,800						244	3,044		51%	49%
Rate [standard]		17.5%			Exempt		0	(Nil)			

The outcomes from these complex policies are compared to the ideal invoice-credit VAT outcomes: consumer price of GH₵ 3044 (GH₵ 3290) and tax burden and fiscal revenue of GH₵ 490 (GH₵ 244)—with the reductions attributed to the zero-rating policy that will result in additional ITC or refund claims.

9. VATA 810 and minimizing the complexity in VAT exclusions

Apart from the amendments noted in ***Box 7.1 (Paragraph 5)*** above, with respect to domestic zero-rating, prior to the comprehensive

VAT review **VATA 2013 (Act 870)**, Ghana's Parliament had passed ***VATAA 2010 (Act 810)*** to address various issues that include—

- increasing the threshold for registering small entities that cannot keep adequate records;
    - limiting the application of the ***VFRS to certain supplies***, as specified below; and
    - ***reverting to the original exempt (Schedule 1) status*** for agricultural and pharmaceutical products that were ***changed to domestic zero-rating and reliefs (Schedules 2 and 3)***—as summarized in Box 7.2 above.

Table 9.15 shows the revised VATA 810 provision that restored exempt provisions for supplies that had been zero-rated or given relief status.

<table>
<tr><th colspan="4">Table 9.15: Application of VFRS [3 per cent] to specified supplies</th></tr>
<tr><td colspan="4"></td></tr>
<tr><th>Section</th><th>Heading</th><th>Description</th><th>Comments</th></tr>
<tr><td colspan="4">VAT (Amendment) Act, 2010 (Act 810); An Act to amend the VAT Act, 1998 (Act 546) to revise and expand the coverage of the threshold for registration; and re-classify locally produced pharmaceuticals, locally produced textbooks and locally manufactured agricultural machinery and tools as exempt supplies.</td></tr>
<tr><td colspan="4">Section 3 of Act 546 amended</td></tr>
<tr><td>1</td><td rowspan="2">Rate of Tax</td><td>(1) The VAT Act, 1998 (Act 546) as amended and referred to in this Act as the principal enactment is further amended in this Section by the substitution for subsection (2) of</td><td rowspan="2">Section 5 refers to Schedule 1 of the amended VATA 1998 (Act 546). Section 5(b) refers to "locally produced" textbooks, pharmaceuticals, and agricultural machinery (see below).</td></tr>
<tr><td>2</td><td>(2) A person to whom subsection (1)(b) of section 5 applies shall account for the VAT payable under this section at a flat rate of 3% calculated on the value of the taxable supply.</td></tr>
</table>

10. Conclusion

Typically, in comparison with the Ideal Invoice-Credit VAT mechanism, exemptions and reliefs result in multiple taxation or cascading which, when added to the cost build-ups of businesses, increase the tax burden and price. The less distortionary waivers or exclusions applied at the final distribution stage only or zero-rate domestic relief supply.

However, compared to exemptions, the ***zero-rating of domestic supplies results in refunds*** that may be compromised by complicated VAT administration and compliance in countries that have weak tax agencies and refund processes. The most active pharmaceutical sector in Ghana and the Ghana Manufacturer's Association (GMA) express dissatisfaction with cascading from midstream reliefs or waivers. This has led to several unconventional amendments that made Ghana's original VAT regime less ideal (Schedule 1 to Schedule 3).

The changes in the exemption rules in this Chapter, together with the VAT registration threshold rules (Chapter 9) and VAT structure (Chapter 8), made it complex to administer and comply with the amended VAT Act. Unfortunately, the reversal of many of these distortions in the comprehensive rewriting of the VAT Act in 2015 suffered a serious setback with the reverse amendment from 2017 to 2020.

The expansion of "zero-rated" and "exempt" policies undermines the tax effort and leads to shortfalls in revenue targets. This is because cascading results in higher costs and consumer prices, which makes tax administration and compliance complex and gives rise to tax evasion and avoidance.

Chapter 10

VAT POLICY REVIEW—3: DISTORTIONARY IMPACT OF LEVIES ON VAT BASE AND STRUCTURE

1. Introduction

As compared with the other forms of collecting expenditure or consumption taxes, this chapter continues with the focus on the VAT Invoice Credit or Input Tax Credit (ITC) method, which makes ***VAT policy, administration and enforcement or compliance relatively efficient and effective.*** This chapter discusses practical difficulties in implementing policy changes to the VAT base and structure that often lead to significant distortions. To restate, the main attributes of the ITC method include—

- ***registration:*** all eligible ***entities*** making ***taxable supplies*** must register, charge VAT, and claim ITC or tax paid on inputs related to taxable supplies;
- ***tax base:*** as a general consumption tax, the VAT base is broader than those of other indirect taxes, which makes it a major source of generating revenues; and
- ***tax structure:*** the non-revenue objectives of the tax regime are often assigned to other taxes—such as excise duty (punitive) and tariffs or customs duties (protection).

2. Levies distort the structure of VAT

The distortion of the VAT regime caused by the reversal of several policies in VATA 870, which was designed to improve its efficiency, is manifest in fundamental changes to the VAT structure that sets aside the credit and refund schemes as the basis for enforcing compliance. In this regard, the focus of Chapter 8 is on the

- reintroducing parallel ***sales and service taxes*** that the VAT replaced, including the ***Communications Service Tax (CST) and other levies*** on the supplies of goods and services—which total levies, other than VAT or excise duty, have now exceeded ten (10), as at the end of FY 2022;

- injecting ***excise duty-type "straight" levies*** into the indirect tax structures—this being the new name for the original VAT-based GETFund Levy and NHIL regimes that allowed registered entities to claim input tax credit (ITC) and refunds for purchases of taxable supplies or inputs;
- applying income tax-type ***presumptive*** and ***withholding*** tax tools to VAT, even though the invoice-based ITC is fundamentally a withholding or compliance tool; and
- adding a lower or ***sub-standard VAT rate*** of 3 per cent, called ***VAT Flat Rate Scheme (VFRS),*** on retailers and, for a short period, wholesalers of goods in Chapter 9.

Traditionally, the withholding and presumptive income tax regimes are used to enforce the law and facilitate compliance by small entities in large informal sectors or economies. In Ghana, as with most developing states, the reasons for these distortions include—

- stopping revenue administration reforms, namely the Revenue Modernization Project (Phase II)—which was being implemented alongside the expenditure reforms under the Ghana Integrated Information Management Information (GIFMIS) project;
- Phase I included a review of all fiscal and some banking legislation as well as the merger of the Internal Revenue Service (IRS) and VAT Service (VATS)—as the Domestic Tax Revenue Division (DTRD) of the Ghana Revenue Authority (GRA) in 2009;
    - particularly, the adverse effect on the ***reorganization*** of operations; ineffective ***integrated training programs*** for the staff of the two former independent agencies, alongside the Customs Division that replaced the Customs, Excise and Preventive Services (CEPS); and
    - the delay in implementing a comprehensive ***automation*** agenda for the integrated VAT and income tax functions under GRA's Domestic Tax Revenue Division (DTRD).

A focus on these original goals of the GRA reorganization or revenue modernization programs would have improved the tax policy, structure and compliance methods. The benefits of administration reforms include ***staff development and re-design of operations that include significant automation.***

3. Political-economy reasons for VAT rate increases and earmarking

Originally, the Ghana Education Trust Fund (GETFund) Levy, the National Health Insurance Levy (NHIL) and, much later, the Ghana Infrastructure Investment Fund (GIIF) were often classified under Ghana's ***"earmarked" funds.*** Under their original and VAT laws, they were ***"collected as VAT"*** at 2.5 per cent each and with full right to ITC and refunds.

These *de facto* increases in the 10 per cent VAT rate and subsequent "earmarking" to special funds were partly manoeuvres by the NDC and NPP governments to bring the VAT regime to a ***fiscally sustainable range of 15 per cent to 20 per cent*** in many countries. They added 7.5 per cent to the original 10 per cent VAT rate from 1998. This resulted in ***the entire 17.5 per cent being eligible for ITC claims and refunds.***

Recall that, upon suspension of the VAT initiative in 1995, the 17.5 per cent rate was reduced to 10 per cent, as part of the strategies to facilitate its reintroduction in 1998 [reference Part I, Chapter 2] and Part V, Chapters 13 and 14]].

Table 10.1 shows the impact on ***costs, tax burdens and consumer prices*** of introducing VAT at 17.5 per cent before its cancellation in 1995. This was based on the first VAT law, namely, the VAT Act 1994 (Act 496).

Table 10.1: Initial introduction of VAT at 17.5 per cent rate in 1994

Introduction at 17.5 percent							
Entity	**Value Added**	**Cumm. Value**	**Output VAT**	**Input VAT**		**Net VAT**	**Consumer Prince**
				Allowed	**Denied**		
Importer	1000	1000	175	0	0	175	1175
Manufacturer	800	1800	315	175	0	140	2115
Wholesaler	600	2400	420	315	0	105	2820
Retailer	400	2800	490	420	0	70	3290
Consumer	**2800**					**490**	**3290**
Standard Rate	**17.5%**						

Table 10.2 shows the effect of reducing the VAT rate from the initial ***17.5 per cent to 10 per cent*** to facilitate the reintroduction of the VAT in 1998.

Table 10.2: Effect of the reintroduction of VAT at a 10 per cent rate

Introduction at 10 percent							
Entity	Value Added	Cumm. Value	Output VAT	Input VAT		Net VAT	Consumer Prince
				Allowed	Denied		
Importer	1000	1000	100	0	0	100	1100
Manufacturer	800	1800	180	100	0	80	1980
Wholesaler	600	2400	240	180	0	60	2640
Retailer	400	2800	280	240	0	40	3080
Consumer	**2800**					**280**	**3080**
Standard Rate	**10%**						

Table 10.3 shows the effective difference in reducing the VAT rate from ***17.5 per cent to 10 per cent*** to neutralize the perceived impact of VAT on consumer prices and inflation to facilitate the reintroduction of the VAT in 1998.

Table 10.3: Differences between the rates at 17.5 per cent and 10.0 per cent

Comparison of outcomes							
Rates	Value Added	Cumm. Value	Output VAT	Input VAT		Net VAT	Consumer Prince
				Allowed	Denied		
17.5% rate	400	2800	490	420	0	490	3290
10.5% rate	400	2800	280	240	0	280	3080
Difference	**0**	**0**	**210**	**180**	**0**	**210**	**210**

As the outcomes show, the expedient reduction in VAT rate lowers the ***tax burden*** (GH₵ 490 to GH₵ 280 = Gh210) and consumer ***price*** (GH₵ 3290 to GH₵ 3080 = GH₵ 210). However, this is also the amount of VAT revenue that was lost to the state and which made the reduction *fiscally unsustainable.*

The main **problem that prompted the earmarking strategy was the VAT protests** that led to the suspension of the tax in 1995. Yet, apart from known operational hiccups in developing countries, ***earmarking did not affect the invoice-credit mechanism rule until the conversion of GETFund and NHIL to "straight" levies.*** The straight levy policy nullified the collection of the Statutory Funds "as though they were a VAT" because it barred registered entities from claiming ITC and refunds on taxable inputs or purchases.

4. Earmarking net VAT proceeds as GETFund Levy, NHIL and GIIF

Given the VAT introduction challenges and the ***need to anchor the VAT rate on a realistic fiscal base,*** the NDC and successive governments used the "earmarking" as (a) expedient means of raising the initial rate of 10 per cent to the more realistic 17.5 per cent; but (b) doing so in three (3) incremental and separate steps of 2.5 per cent each.

The outcome is the passage of laws to assign or "earmark" the revenue increments for purposes of education (i.e., GETFund in 2000), health insurance (i.e., NHI in 2003) and commercial infrastructure (i.e., GIIF in 2014). The remaining sessions discuss these policy issues and their implementation by GRA, in the order in which they were introduced.

a. Ghana Education Trust Fund (GETFund)

The Scheme is set up under the Ghana Education Trust Fund (GETFund) Act, 2000 (Act 581) but collection and substantial parts of funding are embedded in the VAT laws, namely, the VATA 1998 (Act 546), as amended by the VAT (Amendment) Act, 2000 (Act 579). This Act was also replaced with the VAT Act, 2013 (Act 870)—and, also, as amended to date.

- ***Nature of Fund:*** the purpose is to establish a Fund to finance education; provide for the management of the Fund; and to provide for related matters. The Board of Trustees
    - has a ***corporate identity,*** perpetual succession and common seal (s4);
    - has the ability to enter into contracts and acquire, purchase and hold movable and immovable property; and
    - can convey, assign and transfer any movable or immovable property or any interest vested in the Trust.

The Board of Trustees includes a representative of the Ministry of Finance and Commissioner-General of GRA.

- ***Objectives of the Fund:*** The objects of the Fund under the GETFund Act, 2000 (Act 581), Section 2), which are reproduced in Table 10.4, have no reference to the design or oversight of tax policy and administration.

Table 10.4: Objects of the Fund

GETFund Act 2000 (Act 581)	
Section 2: Object of the Fund	
Section	**Description**
2(1)	The object of the Fund is to provide finance to suplement the provisionof the education at all levels by Government.
2(2)	For the purposes of attaining this object, the monies from the Fund are to be expended as follows:
(a)	to provide financial support to the agencies and institutions under the Ministry of Education, through the Ministry, for the development and maintenance of essential facilities and infrastructure in public educational institutions, particularly, in tertiary institutions;
(b)	to provide supplementary funding to the Scholarship Secretariat to grant scholarships to gifted but need students for studies in the second-cycle & accredited tertiary institutions in Ghana;
(c)	to contribute monies from the Fund towards the operation of student loans schemes for students in accredited tertiary institutions through loan scheme mechanisms and agencies, approved by the minister;
(d)	to provide through the National Council of Tertiary Education, grants to tertiary institutions;
	(i) to train brilliant students as members of faculties;
	(ii) to undertake research & other academic programmes of relevance to national development; and
	(iii) to provide monies to support such other educational activities and programmes for the promotionof education as the Minister in consultation with the Board may determine.

- *GETFund Levy:* The main source of inflows for the Fund is the VAT, as stated in the VAT (Amendment) Act, 2000 (Act 579) which, as Table 10.5 shows, was passed within 14 months of the charging of VAT from 1998/99.

Table 10.5: VAT as the Source of Funds for GETFund

Section	Heading	Description	Comments
VAT (Amendment) Act, 2000 (Act 579)			
Section 3 of Act 546 amended			
1	The VAT Act, 1998 (Act 546) referred to in this act as the "principal enactment" is amended		Increase is ***dedicated to GETFund*** which is collected as though it were a VAT, subject to ITC rules
3	Rate of Tax	in Section 3 by the substitution for "10 per cent" of "12.5 per cent"	

- ***Sources of Funds:*** The GETFund Act, 2000 (Act 581) shows the entire sources from which the Trust generates or receives its funds, including the ***amount that GRA collects as VAT and pays to the Trust Fund within 30 days of collection.*** Under the various VATA, taxpayers file by the last working day of the month that follows the imposition of the VAT. Table 10.6 shows the entire sources from which the Trust receives its funds.

Table 10.6: The Sources of funding for the GETFund

Section 3: Sources of money for the Fund		
Section	**Description**	**Comments**
3	The sources for the money of the Fund are as follows:	
(a)	an amount of money, equivalent to two and one half percent out of the prevailing rate of the VAT to be paid by the GRA to the Fund or such percentage not being less than two and one half percent of the VAT rate, as Parliament may determine	The most relevant provision of the GETFund Act relating to the "earmarking" of VAT.
(b)	such other money as may be allocated by Parliament for the Fund;	The Trust Fund's other sources of financing
(c)	money that accrues to the Fund from investment made by the Board of Trustees of the Fund;	
(d)	grants, donations, gifts and other voluntary contributions of the Fund; and	
(e)	other monies or propertyat may in the manner become lawfully payable and vested in the Board of Trustees for the Fund.	

The Fund is clearly ***designed to rely on inflows from a tax source, which tax predated the Trust and, therefore, did not form part of the mandate of the Board*** and management for implementation of social goals.

- ***Payment of VAT collected to GETFund***: In practice, it is MOF that pays (through the Controller and Accountant-General), the share of "net VAT" (i.e., Output VAT less ITC and Refunds) generated by GRA to the GETFund and NHIA. Table 10.7 shows the provision under which the Ministry and GRA are required to make the payments.

Table 10.7: Payment of monies collected

Section 4: Bank account for the Fund		
Section	**Description**	**Comments**
1	Monies of the Fund shall vest in the Board of Trustees and shall be paid into bank accounts that shall be opened by the Board with the approval of the Accountant-General.	Authority over funds
2	The GRA shall, within 30 days of receipt of VAT revenue pay directly into the bank account opened under subsection (1) the proportion of the VAT revenue htat is required to be paid into the Fund under Section 3(a).	The most relevant provison of the GETFund Act relating to payment of amounts collected.

The administration of refunds and credits may require auditing and recovery of unpaid VAT. It makes the provision for payment within 30 days ambiguous since, in principle, GRA can only pay after making the relevant adjustments for credits, refunds and non-payment.

b. National Health Insurance Levy (NHIL

As with the Ghana Education Trust Fund (GET Fund), the National Health Insurance Authority (NHIA) was also set up under the NHI Act 2003 (Act 650), as a body corporate with a Board of Directors. Its replacement law, NHI Act, 2012 (Act 852), was meant to consolidate the NHIS, remove administrative bottlenecks, introduce transparency, reduce corruption, and make the scheme more effective to govern.

Subsequently, the NHI (Amendment) Act, 2018 (Act 971) and VATAA 2017 (Act 948) made further changes to the NHI Act 2012 (Act 852). The Chapter also discusses further changes made to this approach and other Sections of NHI Act 852 by VAT (Amendment) Act, 2017 (Act 948). The extracts used (and in Appendix 8.1) are substantially based on the relevant VAT and NHI levy provisions in NHIL Acts 852 and 971.

Imposition of the levy: Unlike the GETFund levy, where the rate is imposed under the VAT (Amendment) Act 2000 (Act 579), the rate of NHIL was originally imposed by the substantive NHIL Act 852. Indeed, the approach of the Act seems to repeat certain conventional VAT rules and definitions to make the levy appear as a standalone levy. Table 10.8 shows how Section 47 (1) of NHI Act 2012 (Act 852) is used to impose the levy and define the scope, time and place of supply rules in similar terms as those of the VAT.

Table 10.8: Imposition of the NHIL

Section 47: Levy on supply of goods and services		
Section	**Description**	**Comments [Act 630 [2003])**
47(1)	There is imposed by this Act, a National Health Insurance Levy charged at the ***rate of two and half percent***, calculated on	Same wording as s86(1) of Act 630 (2003)
	a) ***each*** supply of goods and services made or provided in Ghana;	Same wording as s86(1)[a-c] except for "each" replacing "every". Rules more elaborate in VATA 2013 (Act 870).
	b) ***each*** importation of good, and	
	c) supply of an imported service	
	unless otherwise exempted in this Act or under the Regulations.	
47(2)	The levy is payable at the time the goods and servies are supplied or imported.	Same as s86(2) of Act 630.
47(3)	For the purposes of the NHIL, the provisions on supply of goods and services in the enatment that establishes the revenue or collection agency charged with responsibility for the collection of this levy by the Minister responsibole for Finance shall apply.	Same as s86(3) of Act 630 (2003). By legislation, this is the Ghana Revenue Authority (GRA).
47(4)	The Minister responsible for Finance may by Legislatiive Instrument amend the rate of the levy specified in subsection (1).	Not part of NHIL, 2003 (Act 630).

- ***Supply rules:*** Also, compared with the GETFund law which defers to the VAT Act for its ***supply rules***, the NHIL Act 2012 (Act 852) had its "supply" rules in the VAT rendition. They are similar to, but less elaborate than, those in the VAT Act 2015 (Act 870).
- ***Exceptions to the supply rules:*** Similarly, as Table 10.9 shows, the NHIA Act contains its own exclusions from, or exceptions to, the "supply" rules that are also less elaborate than those contained in the VATA 2013 (Act 870).

Table 10.9: Exceptions to the general supply rules

Sections 48 to 51: Other "supply"provisions		
Section	**Description**	**Comments**
48	**Exempt supply of goods and services**	Similar to Section 87 to Section 89 of NHIL Act, 2003 (Act 630). The provisions and schedules are similar to those in the VATA 2013 (Act 870), as amended.
	A supply in respect of any of the matters set out in Part One of the Second Schedule is exempt from the levies imposed under s47	
49	**Zero-rated supply of goods and services**	
	A supply in respect of any of the matters set out in Part Two of the Second Schedule is zero-rated as regards the levy under s47.	
50	**Relief from the Levy**	
	Relief from levy There is granted by this Act, relief from the payment of the levy to the individuals,organizations and in respect of the matters specified in Part Three of the Second Schedule.	

- ***Repeal of provisions:*** As Table 10.10 shows, the separate exceptions in the NHIL 2012 (Act 852) were repealed in the ***VAT (Amendment) (No; 2) Act, 2017 (Act 948).***

Table 10.10: Consequential amendment to Act 852.

Consequential VAT Amendment to NHIL Act, 2012 (Act 852)		
Section	**Description**	**Comments**
VAT (Amendment) Act, 2017 (Act 948)		
5	**The National Health Insuracne Act 2012 (Act 852) is amended by**	The purpse of the amendment is to promote efficient administration and compliance by aligning the NHIL Act 852 to that of the VATA 870.
(a)	the substitution for section 48, of	
	"Exempt supply of goods and services	
	48. A supply in respect of any of the matters set out in the First Schedule of the VAT Act, 2013 (Act 870) is exempt from the levies imposed under Section 47".	
(b)	the substitution for section 49, of	
	"Zero-rated supply of goods and services"	
	49. A supply in respect of any of the matters set out in the Second Schedule of the VAT Act, 2013 (Act 870) is zero-rated as regards the levy imposed under section 47."	
(c)	the substitution for section 50, of	
	50. There is granted by this Act, relief from the payment of the levy to the individuals, organizations and in respect of the matters specified in the Third Schedule of the VAT Act, 2013 (Act 870)."	
(d)	the deletion of the Second Schedule.	

- ***Collection and payment of levy:*** Table 10.11 completes the summary with Sections 51 and 52 on the ***collection and payment*** of the levy. Note that the Section 51 provisions have been ***amended by the NHA (Amendment) Act, 2018 (Act 971)***. It is also important to take note of the paramount reference to the GRA Act, 2009 (Act 791), which Authority was established as the apex body for the tax and customs institutions.

Table 10.11: Collection and Payment of Levy

Section 51 and 52: Collection and Payment of Levy		
51	**Collection of the Levy**	
51(1)	The levy shall be collected by the revenue or collection agency determined by the Minister responsible for Finance	Similar to Section 90 of NHIL Act 2003 (Act 870). By the substantive legislation, GRA collects the levy, even as "straight" levy
51(2)	The GRA Act, 2009 (Act 791) shall apply with the necessary modifications in the collection of the Levy	
52	**Payment of Levy into the Fund**	
52(1)	The Minister responsible for Finance shall within 30 day after the collectionof the levy cause the levy to be paid directly into the Fund and furnish the Minister responsible for Health and the Authority with evidence of the payment	Similar to Section 91 of NHIL Act 2003 (Act 870). By the substantive legislation, GRA collects the levy, even as "straight" levy
52(2)	The Minister responsible for Finance shall present to Parliament every six months a report on payment of levies into the Fund	

c. Ghana Infrastructure Investment Fund (GIIF)

The preamble to the Ghana Infrastructure Investment Fund (GIIF) Act, 2014 (Act 877), which was established on 15th August 2014, defines the ***purpose*** of the Fund as follows—

"An Act ***wholly owned*** by the Republic of Ghana to ***mobilize, manage, coordinate and provide financial resources for investments*** in a ***diversified portfolio*** of infrastructure projects in Ghana for national development and to provide for relevant matters".

Table 10.12 cites Section 1 of the GIIF Act to show the ***"body corporate"*** nature of the Fund and as having ***"perpetual succession"***.

Table 10.12: Corporate body status of GIIF

Ghana Infrastructure Investment Fund Act, 2014 (Act 877)		
Section & Items	**Description**	**Comments**
1	**Establishment of the Fund**	
(1)	There is established by this Act, a Fund to be known as the Ghana Infrastructure Investment Fund (GIIF)	Note the emphasis in the Preamble that states clearly that the Fund is ***"wholly owned by the Republic of Ghana"***.
(2)	The Fund is a ***body corporate*** with perpetual succession and a common seal, may sue and be sued and has in all respects the powers of a body corporate.	

- ***Objectives of the Fund:*** Section 2(1) **repeats these objectives *verbatim*** while Section 2(2), in sub-items (a) to (j) further elaborates on these ***objectives in detail***. In essence, the Act seeks to establish a Sovereign Wealth Fund (SWF), to pursue viable infrastructure investment projects for the development of the country. The relevant extract is shown in Table 10.13

Table 10.13: Objective of GIIF*Powers of the Board & Independence of the Fund:* Table 10.14 cites Section 3 of the GIIF Act in relation to the ***powers of the Board,*** which falls into three categories as follows: ***establish subsidiaries or affiliates***; acquire and dispose of ***assets and investments in various*** forms; and ***borrow*** to achieve the goals and purposes of the Fund. Section 4 ***makes the Fund independent*** in pursuit of its goals but subject to the Act and accountability to the Minister.

Table 10.14: Powers of the GIIF Board

Ghana Infrastructure Investment Fund Act, 2014 (Act 877)	
Section & Items	**Description**
Powers of the Board	
3	The Fund shall have the power to
(a)	Create sub-funds, ***affiliates or subsidiaries*** in ***any jurisdiction*** in furtherance of the object of the Fund;
(b)	Invest in, purchase, maintain, divest from, sell or otherwise realize ***assets and investments*** of any kind; and
(c)	Borrow and raise money, on its partnership with or through its affiliates, from domestic and international markets.
Independence of the Fund	
4 (1)	Except as otherwise provided in this Act, the ***Fund shall be independent*** in the performance of its functions
4(2)	The Fund shall be ***accountable to the Minister*** on the achievements of its objectives and compliance as set out in the Act and the guidelines of the Fund.

- ***Sources of Funds:*** Table 10.15 shows the ***specific and original sources from which the Fund*** derives its resources under the GIIF Act. The two main sources are as follows—
    - ***2.5 per cent of net VAT collection*** under the VAT Act, 2013 (Act 870); and
    - an amount not exceeding 25 per cent of the annual allocation to the Annual Budget Funding Amount (ABFA) under the Petroleum Revenue Management Act (PRMA), 2011 (Act 815).
- ***Increase in VAT rate (2.5 per cent) under GIIF Act:*** The GIIF Act specifically refers to the VAT Act in relation to ***rate and collections*** but ***did not amend the VAT Act 870.*** Hence, the GIIF Act is ***deemed to be the source of the 2.5 per cent increase*** until the first amendment of Act 870 was the VAT (Amendment) Act 2014 (Act 890). Hence, this amendment ***increased the de facto pre-straight levy rate to 17.5 per cent***—VAT (12.5 per cent), GETFund (2.5 per cent), NHIL (2.5 per cent) and GIIF (2.5 per cent).

Table 10.15: Sources of Funds for GIIF (ref: VATA 870)

Ghana Infrastructure Investment Fund Act, 2014 (Act 877)		
Section & Items	**Description**	**Comments**
5 (1)	**Sources of money for the Fund**	
(a)	an amount of money equivalent to two-and-one-half percentage points of the existing Value Added Tax revenue	Refers to ***but does not amend*** the Value Added Tax Act, 2013 (Act 870)
(b)	*an amount of money not exceeding twenty-five per cent of the Annual Budget Funding Amount* ***(ABFA) to be applied to amortization and direct*** *infrastructure expenditure.*	ABFA is part Petroleum Revenue Management Act [PRMA] 2011 (Act 815).
(c)	repayment inflows of money on-lent by the Ministry of Finance to government ministries, departments and agencies or state-owned enterprises, for capital project or infrastructure development;	
(d)	proceeds from the disposal of state-owned equity investments;	
(e)	grants, donations, gifts and other voluntary contributions to the Fund;	
(f)	fees or other money earned by the Fund in pursuance of its functions under this Act;	*Effective immediate date: GIIF Act, 2014 (Act 877)*
(g)	money that accrues to the Fund from investments made by the Fund;	
(h)	money borrowed and raised from the local and international capital markets or its affiliates;	
(i)	money that may become lawfully payable to the Fund or any other property that may become lawfully vested in the Board for the Fund; and	
(j)	any other money that the Minister with the approval of Parliament determines to be paid into the Fund.	
5 (2)	(2) The sources of monies under paragraphs (a) and (b) of subsection (1) designated for the Fund shall be due for payment into the Fund from 1st January 2015.	The effective date for the flow of Funds

- ***Administration of GIIF as a Statutory Fund:*** Under Section 6 (1) of the GIIF Act, the Board shall set up a Bank Account into which the Fund shall pay in amounts received. As Table 10.16 notes, however, in Section 66 (2) the Minister for Finance is also required to transfer the amounts due from VAT and

ABFA collection into the GIIF's Bank account in line with the conventional method used for other "earmarked" or Statutory Funds such as the DACF, NHIL and GETFund.

Table 10.16: Bank Account of the Fund

Ghana Infrastructure Investment Fund Act, 2014 (Act 877)		
Section & Items	**Description**	**Comments**
Bank Account of the Fund		
6 (1)	The Monies for the Fund shall vest in the Board and shall be paid into a bank account opened for the purpose by the Board with the approval of the Minister	
6 (2)	The Minister shall, not more than thirty (3) days following the end of each month, pay directly from the Consolidated Fund, into the bank account opened under subsection (1), the proportions of the VAT revenue and Annual Budget Funding Amount (ABFA) required to be paid into the Fund under Sections 5(a) and 5(b) respectively.	

- *Advisory Committee:* The GIIF corporate oversight differs from other mainstream State-Owned Enterprises that are also corporate entities because it has an Advisory Committee in addition to the Board of Directors. The Memorandum to the Bill explains the purpose of the Advisory Committee in Clause 21 of the Bill as follows—

  "The Advisory Council is to advise the Board within the confines of national policy guidance on infrastructure investment. In the discharge of its duties, the Advisory Council is to observe the independence of the Board."

Table 10.17 reproduces the sections of the Act that deal with the establishment of the Advisory Committee and its functions.

Table 10.17: Advisory Committee

Ghana Infrastructure Investment Fund Act, 2014 (Act 877)	
Section & Items	**Description**
Establishment of an Advisory Council,	
20 (1)	There is established by this Act, an Advisory Committee for the Fund comprising the following members:
(a)	a chairperson who is the Minister responsible for Finance,
(b)	the Governor of the Bank of Ghana (BOG),
(c)	the Director General of the National Development Planning Commission (NDPC), and
(d)	two other persons from the private sector, one of whom is a woman.
20 (2)	The members of the Advisory Committee shall be appointed by the President in accordance with Article 70 of the Constitution.
Functions of the Advisory Committee	
21 (1)	The Advisory Committee shall advise the Board within the confines of national policy guidelines on infrastructure investment.
21(2)	The Advisory Committee shall, in the discharge of its duties, ***observe the independence of the Board.***

- ***Other sections relating to the Advisory Committee:*** these are covered under the following Sections: tenure of office of members of the Advisory Committee (s21); tenure of office of members of the Advisory Committee; meetings of the Advisory Committee (s23); and disclosure of interest (24).
- ***Sections on administrative, financial and miscellaneous provisions***: the final parts of the Act include Chief Executive Officer (CEO) and functions (s25-26); Appointment of other staff (s27); Accounts and audit (s28); Annual report and other reports (s29); Investment Policy Statements, codes of practice, regulations and internal guidelines (s30); Indemnity (s31); Regulations (s32); and Interpretation (s33).
- **Appendix ...** reproduces (other Sections of) the GIIF Act for easy reference. The Table of Contents of the Act is shown in Table 10.18 below.

Table 10.18: Arrangement of Sections

Ghana Infrastructure Investment Fund Act, 2014 (Act 877)			
Arrangement of Sections			
Section		**Sectiion**	
Establishment of GIIF		**18**	Administrative expanses of the Fund
1	Establishment of the Fund	**19**	Tax exemption
2	Object of the Fund	**Advisory Committee**	
3	Powers of the Fund	**20**	Establishment of Advisory Committee
4	Independence of the Fund	**21**	Functions of Advisory Committee
5	Sources of money for the Fund	**22**	Tenure of office of members of the Advisory Committee
6	Bank account of the Fund	**23**	Meeting of the Advisory Committee
7	Head Office & branches of the Fund	**24**	Disclosure of interest
The Board and Management of the Fund		**Administrative, financial and miscellaneous provisions**	
8	Governing body of the Fund	**25**	Chief Executive Officer
9	Functions of the Board	**26**	Functions of Chief Executive Officer
10	Duties and liabilities of members of the Board	**27**	Appointment of other staff
11	Tenure of office of non-executive members	**28**	Accounts and audit
12	Meetings of the Board	**29**	Annual report and other reports
13	Disclosure of interest	**30**	Investment Policy Statements, codes of practice, regulations and internal guidelines
14	Establishment of committees	**31**	Indemnity
15	Allowances	**32**	Regulations
16	Disbursement from the Fund	**33**	Iterpretation
17	Application for funding		

- ***Effect on VAT structure or mechanism:*** *In principle, as Table 10.19 shows, the VAT-registered entities could charge the GIIF Output VAT (under Section 5(1)(a)* and pay the net amount to GRA under the original GIIF Act, 2014 (Act 877). Under the old "earmarked" funds arrangement, GRA then transferred the amount due to the GIIF Secretariat, as it did with the GETFund Levy and NHIL

Table 10.19: VAT [10%] & GIIF [2.5%] under VAT credit mechanism

VAT & VAT as separate taxes [under credit mechanism]									
Item	**Entity**	**Value Added**	**Total VA**	**Output VAT**		**Input VAT**		**Net VAT**	**VAT + Price**
				VAT	**GIIF**	**VAT**	**GIFF**		
a	Importer	1000	1000	100	25	0	0	125	1125
b	Manufacturer	800	1800	180	45	100	25	100	2025
c	Wholesaler	600	2400	240	60	180	45	75	2700
d	Retailer	400	2800	280	70	240	60	50	3150
e	Consumer	2800						350	3150
	Rates	**VAT**	10.0%		**GIFF**	2.5%		**Total**	12.5%

Reversal of use of GIIF proceeds: From 2017 until 2021, sections 5(1)(a) and 5(1)(b) of the GIIF Act were repealed by the ***Earmarked Funds Capping and Realignment Act, 2017 (Act 947)***. Consequently, the proceeds from the 2.5 per cent collection were paid directly into the Consolidated Fund. However, the GIIF (Amendment) Act, 2021 (Act 1063) has ***reversed the earmarking under 5(1)(a)*** relating to the payment of the proceeds of 2.5 per cent VAT to GIIF. Hence, the VAT flows revert to Table 10.19 above.

5. VAT and Earmarking of Funds

In principle, **as de facto VAT measures--in all but name,** and until their conversion to **"straight" levies**—registered entities could claim the GETFund and NHIL paid on **taxable inputs** (i.e., purchases and expenses) as **ITC or refunds**. It is important to emphasize that the conversion and blocking of the ITC and refund rights did not affect the GIIF levy.

- ***VAT without "earmarked funds:*** Table 10.20 repeats the outcomes of the ***ideal VAT "invoice-credit"*** rule on consumer prices and revenues at 10 per cent, assuming the 17.5 per cent, without the combined 7.5 per cent rate for GETFund Levy, NHIL and GIIF.

Table 10.20: VAT without Earmarked Funds as VAT

Value Added Tax [VAT] Introduced at 10 percent								
Item	Entity	Value Added	Total VA	Output VAT	Input VAT	Net VAT	VAT + Price	Comments
a	Importer	1000	1000	100	0	100	1100	Shows the impact of VAT introduction in 1998/99 on tax burden and consumer prices.
b	Manufacturer	800	1800	180	100	80	1980	
c	Wholesaler	600	2400	240	180	60	2640	
d	Retailer	400	2800	280	240	40	3080	
e	Consumer	2800				280	3080	Single tax rate and impact of VAT on prices and tax burden
f	Standard rate	10.0%						

The outcome is that the VAT regime continues to be efficient at a lower rate of 10 per cent, with a tax burden of GH₵ 280 that is exactly equal to 10 per cent of VAT of GH₵ 2,800 and a consumer price of GH₵ 3,080. While these result in a lower tax burden, they failed to meet the revenue or fiscal needs of the government, hence the increases.

- ***Combined NHIL, GETFund levy and VAT***: As the combined Table 21, shows, the assumption underlying the original GETFund Levy, NHIL and GIIF levy (at 2.5 per cent each) was to collect them as if they were a VAT in an efficient manner.

Table 10.21: Standard VAT and GETFund Levy and NHIL as *de facto* VAT

GETFund/NHIL as VAT														
(Assumes that NHIL and GETFund are charged on invoice value)														
Item	Entity	Value Added (ex-Tax)	Total Value Added	Input VAT [Allowed]			Output Tax			Net Payments			VAT/Levy-inclusive Price	Comments
				VAT	GF/NHIL Levies	Total	VAT	GF/NHIL Levies	Total	Net VAT	Net Levies	Total		
	1	2	3	4	5	6	7	8	9	10	11	12	13	14
a	Importer	1,000	1,000	0	0	0	125	50	175	125	50	175	1175	
b	Manufacturer	800	1,800	125	50	175	225	90	315	100	40	140	2115	Regime before the decoupling of NHIL and GETFund Levy as "Straight" Levies
c	Wholesaler	600	2,400	225	90	315	300	120	420	75	30	105	2820	
d	Retailer	400	2,800	300	120	420	350	140	490	50	20	70	3290	
e	Consumer	2,800								350	140	490	3290	Consumer pays VAT/Levies
f	Standard rate	12.5%	GETFund	2.5%	NHIL	2.5%	GF+NH	5%	Total VAT rate		17.5%			
g			Total GETFund/NHIL		Ratios:	Allowed	100%		Denied		0%		Taxable & exclusion ratios	

The combined tax rate of 17.5 per cent consists of (a) the core VAT rate of 10 per cent; and (b) an additional 7.5 per cent for the earmarked funds: 2.5 per cent each for NHIL, GETFund Levy and GIIF. Yet, collectively, they had an ideal invoice-credit outcome, with a tax burden of GH₵ 490 and a final price of GH₵ 3,290 on a VA base of GH₵ 2,800.

- ***Levies as allocation of "earmarked" VAT revenue:*** In terms of ***fiscal management***, the GETFund Levy, NHIL and GIIF laws, whether in a GIIF or Straight Levy context, result in significant ***"earmarking"*** of total VAT revenues. The ***budget allocations*** of the net amount (i.e., Output VAT less ITC/refunds) are made to satisfy specific economic goals that include

    - social sector intervention programs, namely, education and health; and
    - infrastructure development or boosting the capital budget fund.

As noted in the ensuing sections, this relatively efficient general consumption tax process continued until the conversion of the NHIL and GETFund Levy to ***"Straight" levies***, without recourse to the conventional ITC (as with the CST).

- ***Political economy***: the ***"earmarking" strategy*** made it easy to ***increase the rate but made the original VAT mechanism efficient*** by (a) allowing the levies or taxes for the GETFund (2000), NHIL (2003), and GIIF (2014) to be charged as VAT; and (b) allocating the net VAT to the Funds under the "Formula" approved by Parliament. The other forms of earmarking of levies and revenues include—
  - ***DACF allocation:*** the earmarking from 2000 to 2019 was the same as the other most significant decentralization policy, the District Assemblies Common Fund (DACF), which is based on payment of a percentage of total revenues, not below 5 per cent (except petroleum taxes) under the 1992 Constitution.
  - ***Earmarking of petroleum revenues:*** Ghana pools all mid-stream and upstream tax and non-tax petroleum revenues into the Petroleum Holding Fund (PHF) under the Petroleum Revenue Management Act (PRMA), 2011 (Act 815).

  These are distributed annually by formula into the Stabilization and Heritage Funds as well as the Annual Budget Funding Amount (ABFA) and the National Oil Company (NOC) budget.
- ***Internally*-Generated Funds (IGF):** Other examples include fees and charges such as the Internally-Generated Funds (IGFs) under the Fees and Charges, 2009 (Act 793) as amended and repealed annually with the Budget—currently, Fees and Charges (Miscellaneous Provisions) Act, 2022 (Act 1080)—and subject to annual change as Legislative Instruments (LIs).

6. Conversion of GETFund Levy and NHIL to "Straight" Levies

The conversion of the GETFund Levy and NHIL to ***"Straight" levies, without recourse to ITC and refunds*** but still reflected on VAT invoices, affects the efficient administration of, and compliance with, Ghana's general tax policy and consumption or expenditure regimes.

- ***Imposes excessive tax burden:*** The outcome of the denial of ITC or refund is that registered entities will pass the tax on as part of their input costs and prices in business (B2B) or consumer (B2C) transactions.

- ***Weakens ITC administration:*** The denial of ITC results in cascading because of the higher consumer prices from multiple taxation while the higher tax burden also makes it difficult to administer the tax, due to the complexity of tax returns and apportionments.
- ***Weakens compliance:*** the incentive for taxpayers to issue VAT invoices, which gives rise to the ITC "self-policing" attribute and "audit trail" attributes—due to effective "cross-checking of VAT purchases and sales invoices.

The right to offset Input VAT paid on purchases and expenses against Output VAT on sales in business-to-business (B2B) transactions minimizes "cascading" and multiple taxation. Hence, the treatment of the statutory funds as VAT is efficient since, when applied uniformly, the Invoice-Credit method *separates (a) the collection of VAT from (b) its "earmarking" or allocation as a separate fiscal exercise.*

Box 8.1 shows a summary of the legislation and policy that separates (a) the combined 12.5 per cent for VAT and GIIF—for which ITC and refunds are still allowed; and from (b) the combined five (5) per cent Straight Levy (i.e., NHIL and GETFund Levy), for which ITC and refund are denied. The ensuing paragraphs discuss the implications of this decoupling for VAT-registered businesses or entities.

The policy which decouples and disallows ITC for GETFund Levy and NHIL paid on inputs is a major distortion—which decision was taken under a mistaken expectation of getting higher revenues from multiple or cascading tax regimes. A summary of the legislation and examples are shown in Tables 8.22 to 8.25.

- ***GETFund (VATAA 970 {2018}): Denial of ITC/Refund for "Straight" Levies:*** Table 10.22 reproduces the ***VATA 970 provision that decoupled the GETFund Levy from the VAT*** structure and renamed them as ***"Straight Levies"***.

Box 8.1: Summary of Policy Changes to NHIL/GETFund from VAT to "Straight" Levies

VAT Rate: VAT (Amendment) Act, 2018, Act 970 revises the VAT rate from 15%, including GETFund and NHIL, to a 12.5% Standard rate that will be the only amount that will be subject to Output and Input VAT.

National Health Insurance (Amendment) Act, 2018, Act 971: The Act separates the NHI Levy (NHIL) from VAT and with the NHIL component no longer subject to input tax credit (ITC) or refund. The goods on which the VAT flat rate is imposed are not subject to the Levy but provides for the Revenue Administration Act, 2016, Act 915 to remain applicable under GRA, which is responsible for its collection. The National Health Insurance (Amendment) Act, 2015 (Act 888) has been repealed.

Ghana Education Trust Fund (Amendment) (GETFund) Act, 2018, Act: the Act converts the 2.5% GETFund portion of the current VAT rate into a levy that will not be subject to input tax deductions. The Act provides that the Levy is applicable on (a) he supply of goods and services made in the country other than exempt goods and services; (b) the import of goods or services other than exempt imports

According to the Act, the Levy is not applicable to exempt individuals and organizations and goods that are subject to the VAT flat rate.

Table 10.22: Decoupling of GETFund Levy /NHIL, as "Straight" Levies

<table>
<tr><th colspan="4">VAT (Amendment) Act, 2018 (Act 970)</th></tr>
<tr><th>Section</th><th>Item</th><th>Description</th><th>Comments</th></tr>
<tr><td colspan="4">"Section 3 of Act 870 amended</td></tr>
<tr><td colspan="3">The Value Added Tax Act, 2013 (Act 870), is amended in section 3 by the substitution for the subsection (1) of</td><td rowspan="4">The provision that decoupled the GETFund [2.5%] and NHIL [2.5%] from the VAT structure--as so-called "Straight Levies". Substantive VAT rate reduced to 12.5 percent.</td></tr>
<tr><td>(1)</td><td>Rate of Tax</td><td>Except as otherwise provided in this Act, the rate of the tax is twelve and a half percent and is calculated on</td></tr>
<tr><td></td><td>(a)</td><td>the value of the taxable supply of the goods or services; or</td></tr>
<tr><td></td><td>(b)</td><td>the value of the import</td></tr>
</table>

- ***NHILA, Act 971 {2018}—Denial of ITC/Refund for Straight Levies***: Table 10.23 reproduces the ***NHILA 971 provision that decoupled the NHIL from the VAT*** structure and renamed them as ***"Straight Levies"***.

Table 10.23: Decoupling of GETFund Levy /NHIL, as "Straight" Levies

Table 8.22: Decoupling of GETFund Levy /NHIL, as "Straight" Levies

VAT (Amendment) Act, 2018 (Act 970)			
Section	**Item**	**Description**	**Comments**
"Section 3 of Act 870 amended			
The Value Added Tax Act, 2013 (Act 870), is amended in section 3 by the substitution for the subsection (1) of			The provision that decoupled the GETFund [2.5%] and NHIL [2.5%] from the VAT structure--as so-called "Straight Levies". Substantive VAT rate reduced to 12.5 percent.
(1)	**Rate of Tax**	Except as otherwise provided in this Act, the rate of the tax is twelve and a half percent and is calculated on	
	(a)	the value of the taxable supply of the goods or services; or	
	(b)	the value of the import	

- ***Illustration of Straight levy as VAT-inclusive tax instrument:*** Table 10.24 assumes that all registered entities charge Output VAT (with the levies) and claim ITC at all stages of the import-to-distribution chain. In essence, the ***levies were "imposed as though they were VAT"***. It separates the ***efficiency of the VAT policy*** from the allocation of the net proceeds of the levies to achieve specified fiscal socio-economic goals.

Table 10.24: GETFund Levy and NHIL as part of VAT structure

All Entities registered: GF&NHIL part of VAT regime (pre-2018);										
Entity		Value Added (ex-Tax)	Total Value Added	Input VAT (ITC allowed)			Output VAT	Net VAT	VAT + Price	Comments
				VAT	*G-Fund & NHIL*	Total				
	1	2	3	4	*5*	6	7	8	9	10
			(2+{3-r1})	5xfc	*5xg5*	4 + 5	6 x fc	6 - 4	2 + 7	VAT-registered entities offset NHIL & GETFund [*de facto* VAT] as Inputs VAT against the Output VAT.
a	Importer	1000	1000	0	*0*	0	175	175	1175	
b	Manufacturer	800	1800	125	*50*	175	315	140	2115	
c	Wholesaler	600	2400	225	*90*	315	420	105	2820	
d	Retailer	400	2800	300	*120*	420	490	70	3290	
e	Consumer	2800						490	3290	Consumer bears taxes
f	Standard rate	12.5%	GETFund	2.5%	NHIL	2.5%	GF+NHIL	5.0%		
g	Total VAT rate	17.5%	Total GETFund/NHIL		Ratios:	VAT	71.4%	GF/NHIL	28.6%	(Apportionment)

- Achieving "ideal" VAT outcomes: the tax burden of c490 and consumer price of c3,290 on a cumulative value added (VA) of c2,800 produces the most efficient or non-distortionary outcomes. This treatment of the ***NHIL and GETFund, as VAT-inclusive tax instruments,*** has the same result as the Ideal VAT benchmark.

To reiterate, the approach requires all business entities to register, charge Output VAT, claim ITC, and pay the difference (Net VAT) to the revenue agency or allow a credit to be carried forward or make a refund where the claim is negative.

- ***Denial of ITC for GETFund Levy and NHIL levies:*** The guidelines released by GRA on the "straight" levies follow the conventional VAT rule of ***adding irrecoverable input VAT and other non-VAT indirect taxes*** such as excise duty, tariffs, and property tax to costs or expenses. The irrecoverable ***"straight levy"*** *is added to the costs before the computation of VAT at the reduced rate of 12.5 per cent.*

Cascading eliminates any benefits from reducing the VAT rate and, further, could make tax evasion and avoidance pervasive. Table 10.25 shows the effect of (a) decoupling the GETFund Levy and NHIL as "straight levies"; (b) denying the right to ITC and refunds; and (c) adding the unclaimed levies as cost along the value addition chain.

Table 10.25: ITC denied for GETFund Levy and NHIL

ITC disallowed for GETFund and NHIL										
			Input VAT/Levy		Output VAT/Levy					
Entity	Value Added (ex-Tax)	Total Value Added	VAT (Allowed)	G-F/ NHIL (Denied) (5% i.e 2.5% +2.5%)	GETFund/ NHIL (5% i.e 2.5% +2.5%)	Total Value + GETFund/ Levy	VAT	Payment: VAT/Levy	VAT + Price	Comments
		A	B	C	D	E = A + D	F= E*12.5%	G = (F+D)-B	H = A + G	Registered entities cannot offset GETFund & NHIL as ITC against Output VAT. They become cost
Importer	1000	1000	0	0	50	1050	131	181	1181	
Manufacturer	800	1850	131	50	93	1943	243	204	2185	
Wholesaler	600	2543	243	93	127	2670	334	218	3003	
Retailer	400	3070	334	127	153	3223	403	223	3626	
Consumer	2800		Allowed	Denied			0	826	3626	
Standard Rate	12.5%	GETFund	2.5%	NHIL	2.5%	GF+NHIL	5%			
Total VAT Rate	17.5%	Total GETFund/NHIL		Ratios:	Allowed:	100%	Denied:	100%		(Apportionment)

Irrecoverable input tax paid by registered entities increases consumer price (GH₵ 3626 instead of GH₵ 3290) and tax burden (GH₵ 807 instead of GH₵ 490). This is a significant distortion of the VAT regime and the minimum default exemption position.

Finally, the conversion of NHIL and GETFund Levy to Straight Levies may result from inadequate budgetary provisions for paying refunds for exports that are taxed at a zero rate, thus increasing the price of exportable domestic products and making them less competitive.

7. Communications Services Tax (CST)

The Communications Services Tax (CST) Act, 2008 (Act 754) imposed a "tax of 6 per cent of the charge for the ***use of the communication service***". The CST (Amendment) Act, 2013, (Act 864) was "to clarify the scope and coverage of the tax and to provide for related matters". Other amendments to the CST Act are the CST (Amendment) Act, 2019 (Act 998) and the CST (Amendment) Act, 2020 (Act 1025).

- ***Nature of CST***: CST is still a ***sector-based*** indirect or consumer tax which, originally, was "***payable by consumers*** for the use of communication services provided, by telecommunications companies classified as Class 1 license holders under the Legislative Instrument 2003 (LI 1719)".

    - ***CST base:*** the base includes the provision of a service through a communications system for the transmission or routing of signals or a combination of these functions.
    - ***Persons liable to pay CST:*** payable together with the communications service charge to communications service providers by consumers of the service. The tax, interest, and penalties are payable to GRA and, further, into the Consolidated Fund.
    - ***Earmarking CST for youth employment programs:*** *20 per cent of the tax collected* is dedicated to specified youth employment programs—a budget ***earmarking and allocation*** after collection and payment.

The definition of communication services includes the provision of a service through a communications system for the transmission or routing of signals or a combination of these functions.

- ***CST as a turnover tax:*** In principle, CST is a ***superfluous general consumption tax*** since the original VATA 1998 repealed the Service Tax laws that existed before 1998 (Acts 500 and 529). The *6 per cent CST imposed in section 3 is concurrent with the 17.5 per cent VAT*—which, until the "straight" (NHIL/GETFund Levy) levy amendment, was non-distortionary as *de facto VATs.*

The apparent use of ***CST to replace import duties*** on cell phones is another flawed policy argument since the purpose of tariffs is to protect local industries while the VAT is a general consumption tax that is designed to be neutral. Hence, it makes it difficult or uncompetitive to develop the local electronics industry that will not be competitive

Hence, unlike the original NHIL and GETFund Levy, the CST was enacted as an *excise- or turnover-type indirect tax rather than a consumption tax*, with no VAT ITC or refund benefits in the CST Act 754 for businesses that also register to charge the VAT.

- ***CST administration by GRA***: The CST Act 754 places the administration of VATA under the Ghana Revenue Authority (GRA)—specifically, its Domestic Tax Revenue Division (DTRD).
    - ***Responsibility: Section 4(1)*** notes *"the Authority is responsible for the administration and management of the tax and shall collect and account for the tax and any interest and penalty paid under the relevant tax laws)".*
    - ***Consolidated Fund: Section 4(2)*** *"Subject to section 5, the Commissioner-General of GRA shall pay the tax collected together with any interest and penalty into the Consolidated Fund".*
    - ***Earmarking: Section 5*** also notes that *"At least, 20 per cent of the revenue generated from the tax shall be used to finance the national youth employment program".*
    - ***Alignment to VATA (Sections 6 to 14)*** completes the administration of CST with alignments to VATA 546, as amended, and VATA 546—as repealed or amended.
    - ***Filing and payment (s6 & s7):*** the provisions, including penalties, as administered by the CG, are consistent with the VATAs.
    - ***Recovery of tax, interest or penalty (s8 & 10)***: empowers the CG, including applications to the courts, to collect any unpaid amounts relating to tax, interest and penalty. Section 9 relates to restraint for liability, in accordance with a court order, while Section 10 deals with recovery under liquidation.
    - ***Records, related matters, offences and penalties (s11):*** these are cross-referenced to the VATA, with appropriate modifications, where necessary.

- ***Objections & appeals (s12):*** these are cross-referenced to relevant parts of VATA 546, as amended and repealed.
- ***Evidence in proceedings (s13)***—relates to certificates issued, photocopies furnished, and statements made by the CG as evidence in court proceedings.

The remaining section of the Act deals with other administrative issues such as ***powers*** and ***directives*** of the Minister and CG (s14); ***regulations*** (s15); and ***interpretation*** (s16). Note that many of these original tax administrative provisions are covered by the Revenue Administration Act 2016 (Act 915) for direct and indirect taxes.

- ***CST (Amendment) Act, 2013 (Act 864):*** As noted, the CST Act 754 was amended by the CST (Amendment) Act, 2013, (Act 864) ***"to clarify the scope and coverage of the tax and to provide for related matters"***.
    - ***Imposition of CST (Section 1):*** The CST Act contains its own imposition, unlike the GETFund Levy and GIIF which were ***originally*** designed to increase in the standard VAT rate. Table 10.26 shows the CST as a tax on electronic and communication services.

Table 10.26: Imposition of CST

<table>
<tr><th colspan="3">Communications Service Tax (Amendment) Act, 2013 (Act 864)</th></tr>
<tr><th>Section</th><th>Description</th><th>Comments</th></tr>
<tr><td colspan="3">Section 1 of Act 754 amended</td></tr>
<tr><td>1</td><td>The CST Act, 2008 (Act 754) referred to in this Act as the principal enactment is amended by the substitution of</td><td rowspan="5">Sections that relate to the base for imposition of the CST</td></tr>
<tr><td></td><td>Imposition of CST</td></tr>
<tr><td></td><td>1(1) There is imposed by this Act a tax to be known as CST to be levied on charges payable by a user of an electronic communications service other than private electronic communications services.</td></tr>
<tr><td></td><td>1(2) The tax shall be levied on electronic communications services supplied by service providers;</td></tr>
<tr><td></td><td>1(3) For the purposes of this section, the supply of any form of recharges shall be considered as a charge for usage of electronic communications service</td></tr>
</table>

- ***Structure and Base of CST (Section 2):*** Table 10.27 reiterates that the CST is a standalone excise or turnover tax, with the *registered communications provider being responsible for collecting and paying the tax* on services rendered to beneficiaries.

Table 10.27: Persons liable to register and charge CST

Communications Service Tax (Amendment) Act, 2013 (Act 864)		
Section	**Description**	**Comments**
Sections 2, 3 and 8 of Act 754 amended		
2	The principal enactment is amended by the substitution for section 2 of	
	Persons liable to pay the tax	
	2(1) The tax shall be paid together with the electronic communications service charge payable to the service provider by the user of the service.	Definition of taxpayer
	CST is due & payable on any supply of electronic communications services (Act 775) by vendors, even if not registered to charge the CST ***(paraphrased)***	Time of payment

- ***Base of tax and invoicing (Sections 3 & 4):*** Table 10.28 emphasizes that the base of the CST is the amount charged for specified communication services.

Table 10.28: Base of tax and invoicing

Communications Service Tax (Amendment) Act, 2013 (Act 864)		
Section	**Description**	**Comments**
	Bases of the tax and invoicing	
3	The principal enactment is amended in s6(1) by the substitution for "communications service provider" of "service provider".	
4	The principal enact is amended in s8 by the substitution of s8(2):	
	(2) A tax on a bill or invoice is recoverable as tax from the issuer, whether or not	Recovery of tax (CST) consistent with other tax law definitions
	a) tax is chargeable on the electronic communications service usage; or	
	b) person is authorized to provide services under Act 775 (2008)	

- ***Administration of CST under GRA (Section 5 to 7):*** as Table 10.29 shows, at the time of passing the original law, the VAT Service was charged with collection and accounting for the tax. The GRA Act 791 now makes the Domestic Tax Revenue

Division (DTRD) responsible for these functions. As discussed in Chapter 10, the tax processes are also subsumed in the Revenue Administration Act (RAA) 915 that are discussed in Part IV [Chapters 10-12].

Table 10.29: Administration of CST

Administration of CST under GRA		
Section	**Description**	**Comments**
Sections 11, 12 & 14 of Act 754 amended		
5	The principal enactment is amended by the substitution for section 11 of	
	Application of VAT Act 546 to the tax	
	(11) Section 29 and 30 and Part XII of the VAT Act, 1998 (Act 546) apply to the management of the CST with the necessary modifications	s29 Records & s30 Assessment
6	The principal enactment is amended by the substitution for section 12 of	
	Objections and appeals	
	(12) Sections 54 and 55 of the VAT Act, 1998 (Act 546) apply to matters of objections and appeals related to the tax.	s54 Objection & s55 Appeal to Court
7	The principal enactment is amended by the substitution for ***section 14***	
	MOF & MOC collaboration with respect to monitoring (base for tax & revenue) & physical access to the facility; and addition of new subsections 5 (refusal to provide access), 6 (the monitoring mechanism will not cover calls) & 7 (objections).	Compliance with, and enforcement of, the VAT & CST laws

- ***Amendments and interpretation (Sections 8 and 9):*** Section 8 amends Section 16 of the CST Act and defines the "charge for communications usage" as
    - the amount chargeable by a service provider for electronic communications service usage, ***other than the VAT and the National Health Insurance Levy;***
    - where the charge for electronic communications service usage is ***for money consideration,*** the amount of the consideration but excluding the amount of VAT and the National Health Insurance Levy;

- where the charge is ***partly for money consideration, the open market value (OMV)*** excluding the VAT and the National Health Insurance Levy; and
- in the case of promotion, protocol, personal use, bonus, gift and similar supplies, the charge shall be the OMV excluding VAT and NHIL".

These provisions bring the "consideration" for the supply of communications services within the general provisions of the VAT Act—but without recourse to ITC. The ensuing Table 10.30 reproduces the interpretations in detail.

Table 10.30: Changes to Interpretations in Act 754

<table>
<tr><th colspan="3">Interpretation</th></tr>
<tr><th>Section</th><th>Description</th><th>Comments</th></tr>
<tr><td colspan="2">Section 16 of Act 754 amended</td><td rowspan="8">Clarification of the meaning of various terms, including consistency of use in VAT and GRA Acts</td></tr>
<tr><td>8</td><td>The principal enact is amended in section 16</td></tr>
<tr><td>(a)</td><td>(a) by the substitution for the interpretation of</td></tr>
<tr><td>i[a]</td><td>charge for electronic service usage, excluding VAT & NHIL;</td></tr>
<tr><td>i[b-d]</td><td>usage charge in relation to money consideration and open market value (OMV) under the VAT Act 546;</td></tr>
<tr><td>ii.</td><td>communication service of electronic communications services.</td></tr>
<tr><td>iii.</td><td>service provider under Act 775, 2008 and LI 1991, 2011</td></tr>
<tr><td>(b)</td><td>[i] closed user group service; [ii] Commissioner-General under GRA Act 791; [iii] Court in relation to electronic communications; electronic communications network; and interconnection; [iv] open market value; [v] private electronic communications service; [vi] supply; and [vii] user & value-added service.</td></tr>
</table>

- ***Impact of CST and other taxes:*** This section shows the ***full implications of imposing the VAT on CST-inclusive costs because of the denial of ITC.*** GRA requires the VAT, GETFund Levy and NHIL to be imposed on the CST-inclusive amount. It is important to note that, unlike CST, ITC is allowed for GETFund Levy and NHIL paid because they were *de facto* VATs before their conversion to "Straight" Levies.

- Table 10.31 shows the impact of the denial of ITC for CST while it is allowed for GETFund Levy and NHIL—*before their reclassification "Straight" levies.*

Table 10.31: ITC *Allowed* for NHIL/GETFund Levy [*de facto VATs* but Disallowed for CST

ITC Allowed for Pre-Straight Levy GETFund & NHIL											
Entity	Value Added (ex Tax)	Total Value Added	Output VAT/Levies/CST			Input VAT/Levies/CST			Net VAT	VAT + Price	Comments
			VAT/GIIF	NHIL/GET Fund	CST	VAT/GIIF	NHIL/GET Fund	CST			
Importer	1000	1000	133	53	60	0	0	0	246	1246	Registered entities
Manufacturer	800	2046	271	108	123	133	53	60	317	2362	cannot offset CST as
Wholesaler	600	2962	392	157	178	271	108	123	348	3310	ITC, compared to
Retailer	400	3710	492	197	223	392	157	178	361	4071	NHIL and GETFund as
Consumer	2800					Allowed	Allowed	Denied	1271	4071	*de facto* VATs
VAT/GIIF	12.50%		GF/NHIL	5%		CST	6%		Total	23.50%	
Ratios	Allowed		74.50%			Denied	25.50%				

The denial of ITC for CST results in distorted outcomes: the final price of GH₵ 4071 instead of GH₵ 3290 and a tax burden of GH₵ 1271, compared to GH₵ 490 under the Ideal VAT. Table 32 presents another scenario where, as input taxes and levies, the CST and Straight Levies (i.e., GETFund and NHIL) are denied as refunds or ITC.

Table 10.32: ITC disallowed for Straight levies (GETFund Levy & NHIL) and CST

ITC disallowed for GETFund, NHIL and CST									
Entity	Value Added (ex Tax)	Total Value Added	Output VAT/Levy		Input VAT/Levy		Net Tax	VAT + Price	Comments
			VAT/GIIF	NHIL/GF & CST	VAT/GIIF	NHIL/GF & CST			
Importer	1000	1000	139	113	0	0	252	1252	entities
Manufacturer	800	2052	286	232	139	113	378	2430	cannot offset
Wholesaler	600	3030	422	342	286	232	479	3509	GetFund &
Retailer	400	3909	544	442	422	342	564	4473	NHIL as ITC
Consumer	2800				Allowed	Denied	1673	4473	against
VAT/GIIF	12.50%		GF+NHIL	11.00%		Total Taxes	23.50%		
Ratios:	Allowed	53.20%		Denied	46.80%	(Apportionment)			

The *combined "straight" levies with CST,* both without ITC, lead to *more distorted outcomes*: the final price of GH₵ 4473 instead of GH₵ 3290 and tax burden of GH₵ 1673, compared to GH₵ 490.

- ***Increase and reversal of CST rate:*** Parliament passed the ***CST (Amendment) Act, 2019*** (Act 998), as part of the policies in the 2019 Mid-Year Review of the Budget. It increased the CST rate from 6 per cent to 9 per cent, as it applies to charges for the use of electronic communications services.

  The ***taxable supply base*** for CST continues to be the *service value **excluding** VAT, GETFund Levy, and NHIL.* However, this is clearly difficult for taxpayers to track and comply with since, at various times, there were policies such as the application of the VFRS for large retailers and wholesalers as well as VAT withholding.

A year later in August 2020, with the rate increase being unpopular, Parliament passed the **CST (Amendment) Act, 2020, Act *1025 to reduce the rate to 5 percent*** with effect from September 15, 2020. The Act also continued to provide for a minimum of 20 per cent of the revenue generated to be earmarked to the national youth employment program. The ***direct tax impact is the downward and upward changes*** in the CST tariff rates, tax burden, distortions from cascading, and consumer prices.

8. Proliferation of Levies—Worsening the VAT Regime Distortion

Some of these *ad hoc* or special taxes and levies resemble ***excise duties,*** which, unlike ***tariffs,*** are neutral between the supply of domestic and imported goods. The common approach is to make several amendments and repeals to the substantive VAT or other acts which significantly alter the objectives and structures of the ideal VAT and other major tax handles. These distortions are made on socio-economic, political, and technical grounds.

Recall as discussed in Chapter 1 that the original VAT Act, 1994 (Act 486) repealed a significant number of (a) service taxes collected by the then Internal Revenue Service (IRS); and (b) sales tax collected by the then Customs, Excise and Preventive Services (CEPS). A major benefit is the ***right of all registered entities to claim ITC and refunds***—which replaced the relatively selective deferral or "ring" mechanism. In essence, ***the spate of recent levies in Ghana that block these rights reverts to relative retrogressive steps*** that make the VAT regime inefficient by stunting revenues while increasing costs, prices and tax burdens.

Tables 8.33 to 8.35 summarize the path to the most distortionary policy measure that changed the de facto VAT-like GETFund and NHIL to "straight levies and very formally blocks the right to ITC and refunds for VAT-registered entities. Table 10.32 specifically refers to the NHIL, the first of the taxes that are usually referred to as "Statutory" funds.

Table 10.33: Summary—Conversion of NHIL to "Straight" Levy

Current (GIIF) & Past VAT-Based ("Straight") Levies [GETFund and NHIL)					
SN	**Tax/Levy**	**Legislation**	**Rates(s)**	**Tax Base**	**Comments**
A) National Health Insurance Levy (NHIL)					
1	**National Health Insurance Levy (NHIL)**	NHI Act, 2003 (Act 630), Sections 86 to 91	***Two-and-half percent (2.5%)***	Same taxable & relief basis as VAT, including right to ITC & refunds	Charges the ***Minister for Finance to designate the agencies that collect the goods and services taxes to charge the NHIL.*** These Acts had their own taxable, exempt & relief schedues as VAT
2		NHI Act, 2012 (Act 852), Sections 47-52			
3		NHI (Ammendment) Act, 2015 (Act 888)		s1(3) The Levy is ***not subject to an input tax credit (ITC)***	Aligns the exemptions for land, buldings & construction as well as financial services to the VAT Act 2013 (Act 870)
4	**NHIL as *Straight Levy***	NHI (Ammendment) Act, 2018 (Act 971)		Conversion of NHIL to "Straight" Levy	Preamble: "An Act to convert the NHIL into a Levy which is ***not subject to the input-output metbod of computation*** and to proide for related matters

Table 10.34 shows two (2) other Statutory Funds, with the GETFund being converted to a "Straight" levy, without ITC or refunds while the GIIF retains those attributes.

Table 10.34: Summary—GETFund and GIIF levies

Current (GIIF) & Past VAT-Based ("Straight") Levies [GETFund and NHIL)					
SN	**Tax/Levy**	**Legislation**	**Rates(s)**	**Tax Base**	**Comments**
(B) Ghana Education Trust Fund (GETFund)					
6	**GETFund Levy**	Ghana Education Trust Fund , 2000 (Act 581)	***Two-and-half percent (2.5%)***	Taxable supply base of net VAT base	Section 3: "An amount of money, equivalent to 2.5% out of the ***prevailing rate of the VAT*** to be paid by GRA to the Fund ..."; ***without ITC/refunds***
7	**GETFund as Straight Levy**	Ghana Education Trust Fund (Amendment) (GETFund) Act, 2018, Act		Taxable supply base of net VAT base	As with NHIL, the "straight" levy provision ***excludes ITC/refunds*** rights to registered taxpayers
(C) Ghana Infrastructure Investment Fund (GIIF)					
8	**Ghana Infrastructure Investment Fund (GIIF)**	GIIF Act, 2014 (Act 877) & GIIF Act, 2021 (Act 1063)	***Two-and-half percent (2.5%)***	Taxable supply base of net VAT base	The GIIF Levy substantively increased the VAT rate to 17.5% and earmarked for "self-financing" commercial projects; ***allows ITC/refund privileges*** to registered entities.

In contrast with the preceding summaries, Table 10.35 covers (a) the VAT Flat Rate Scheme (VFRS) which represents both a levy (without the right to ITC/refunds) and (b) a policy distortion that compromises the ITC/refund structure with a VAT withholding that misses the essence of input VAT payment by registered entities as having an inherent withholding feature.

Table 10.35: The distortionary potential of VFRS and VAT withholding

D) Other VAT-Based Structural Measures (VFRS & VAT Withholding)					
SN	**Tax/Levy**	**Legislation**	**Rates(s)**	**Tax Base**	**Comments**
9	**VAT Flat Rate Scheme (VFRS)**	Various ***(Chapter 9-- VAT small-entiry schemes)*** of VAT Book	Three percent (3%) sub-standard VAT rate	Calculated on the value of the supply ***after all other taxes have been added*** excluding the VAT	A distortionary small entity VAT that was worsened by extension to large retailers and wholesalers until FY 2022. Operates alongside the conventional annual VAT turnover threshold.
10	**VAT Withholding**	VAT Act, 2017 (Act 954) s3 (Amendment of s47 of VAT Act 870)	Seven percent (7%)	Taxable VAT output; buyer issues VAT Withholding Certificate (VWC) to supplier for ITC credit/refund purposes	Applies the ***income tax type withholding rules to VAT***; seems superfluous since Input VAT is inherent "withholding" that is offset against Output VAT. Hence may result in cashflow problems for registered entities (selected by CG)

Table 10.36 covers the imposition of separate general consumption taxes in addition to the VAT on an apparent "new economy" which, given the all-inclusive definition of "taxable supplies" could have me embedded in the VAT regime more efficiently. In an austerity context, the e-Levy was presented as having a significant potential to resolve the nation's current challenges that has driven a reluctant government back into an IMF Program.

Table 10.36: Communication/electronic sector "new economy" taxes

Communications Sector Levies					
SN	**Tax/Levy**	**Legislation**	**Rates(s)**	**Tax Base**	**Comments**
11	**Communications Service Tax (CST)**	CST Act, 2013 (Act 864) & CST Act 2019 (Act 998)	Five percent (5%)	Calculated on the charge for the use of communications service before calculating the VAT on the service charge	A sector-based turnover tax expenditure or consumption tax on imports and domestic supplies that does not allow for ITC claims for the tax paid on inputs by registered businesses.
12	**Electronic Transfer Levy (elevy)**	Electronic Transfer Levy Act, 2022 (Act 1075) & ETLA, 2023 (Act 1089)	One percent (1%)	Is calculated on the amount of money that is being transferred electronically	Imposes a levy on specified electronic money transfers

Table 10.37 is both contemporary (i.e. FINSEC and Growth & Sustainability Levy) as well as structural (i.e. Temporary Import Duty and National Fiscal/Stabilization Levy). As noted earlier, Ghana has used the latter two (2) to effect corrections in the context of IMF Programmes—with clear "sunset clauses". Following the apparent long-term nature of the ESLA and COVID-19 Fund (see later), Parliament appears to have imposed such clauses in the recent levies that it passed (FY2021 and FY2023).

Table 10.37: Structural adjustment levies

Structural Adjustment (Austerity) Levies					
SN	Tax/Levy	Legislation	Rate(s)	Tax Base	Comments
13	FINSEC Levy	FINSEC Act 2021 (Act 1067)--***subject to review at the end-FY2024***	Five percent (5%)	Calculated on profit before (regular) tax under the Income Tax Act 2015 (Act 896)	This is a levy to be paid by only banks (other than rural and community banks) and without recourse to exemption, tax holiday etc provisions in any direct or indirect tax enactment
14	Growth and Sustainability Levy	GSL 2023, (Act 1095) for ***FY2023 to 2025 (payable at end of each quarter)***	Category 1 (5%); Category 2 (1%); Category 3 (2.5%) of ***Profit before Tax***	Calculated on profit before tax	Imposes a levy on companies operating in selected sectors and falling in specified categories
15	Temporary Import Duty	Imposed by all Governments since ERP/SAP era at ***low rates (e.g., 2-3 percent)*** on imports (CIF + other taxes) by GRA specified imports. Typically, they were ***subject to a 2-3 year sunset clause***.			
16	National or Fiscal Stabilization Levies	This was the direct tax equivalent of the temporary import duty which was also imposed on selected sectors, typically financial, telecommunications etc., sectors as part of austerity or stabilization programs			
17	COVID-19 Health Recovery Levy (CHRL)	COVID-19 Health Recovery Levy (CHRL), 2021 (Act 1068)	One percent (1%)	Calculated on the Value of taxable supply under VAT	The levy is applied as a straight levy, and VAT-registered businesses cannot reclaim the levies paid on inputs. .
18	Pollution & Sanitation Levy	Energy Sector Levies (Amendment) Act, 2021, (Act 2021)	GHS 0.10p per litre of petrol & diesel	Calculated on the cost of a litre of petrol & diesel purchased	his levy takes the form of an excise tax since it is imposed on specific products (i.e petrol & diesel).

9. VAT Withholding Agent Scheme

The Chapter ends with the VAT Withholding Agent Scheme that was enacted under the **VAT (Amendment) (No. 2) Act, 2017 (Act 954).** This policy change also adds to the complexity of VAT administering and compliance that underlie VAT principles, laws and rules. The VATAA 954 that was passed in 2017, with an effective date of May 1, 2018., applies to non-registered VAT entities. It became effective on May 1, 2018.

9.1 Comparison of VAT and income tax withholding

This tax policy appears to ***imitate the income tax withholding schemes*** on incomes such as salaries, dividends, and contracts. In principle, the ***Input VAT claimed as ITC*** by registered entities is ***a form of withholding*** until its offset leads to a credit or refund when the taxpayer files a VAT Return. It is important to take note of the following conceptual points.

- ***Withholding responsibility:*** In both cases of income tax and VAT, ***eligible entities*** perform the withholding responsibilities on behalf of the revenue authority. The income tax withholding is often on employee emoluments (e.g., PAYE), dividends, and the value of a contract or supplies—while the VAT withholding applies to payments due to sellers of taxable VAT supplies.
- ***VAT withholding is discriminatory:*** The income tax withholding is an obligation of all registered entities that do not have a tax clearance certificate (TCC). In contrast, as noted later, the VAT withholding is selective because it applies to ***specified entities*** that only make taxable supplies to standard-rated VAT entities that do not possess a VAT credit certificate (VCC).
- ***Scope of income tax withholding***: The employees and other taxpayers who are subject to income tax withholding are allowed a credit offset for the amount withheld at the time of filing a tax return. This may lead to a tax credit or refund, prior to which they are deemed to suffer a cash flow disadvantage that is the price for an effective and popular compliance tool for fiscal authorities in all countries.
- ***Withholding on supplies:*** While the income tax withholding is an obligation of ***all registered entities***, the VAT withholding is collected by ***selected registered entities*** in selected sectors only. Further, income tax applies to both ***taxable and non-taxable*** supplies while the VAT is withheld on only ***taxable*** supplies. In contrast, all ***selected VAT-registered and non-registered entities in the VWH list*** are required to be withholding agents for GRA.
- ***Incidence of tax:*** Ultimately, upon filing, income tax withholding is used to offset the direct tax liability or obligation of employees and business entities. As an indirect tax mechanism, the VAT withheld initially reduces the payment that would have been received by the buyer until they can present the relevant VAT returns.

An input VAT is an upfront ***payment*** until the filing of VAT returns and claim of ITC or refunds after their offset against the Output VAT. The compliance value of VAT clearance certificates attests to relatively inefficient VAT administration, given the intrinsic enforcement value of audit trails and invoice cross-matching features of VAT regimes.

9.2 Appointment of VAT Withholding Agents

The Commissioner-General (CG) of GRA may *appoint specified institutions and entities as* ***"withholding" agents*** to ***withhold 7 per cent of Output VAT*** on the chargeable amount due to other registered ***entities*** and remit the amount to GRA. Table 10.38 shows the relevant provisions of the VAT (Amendment) Act, 2017 (Act 954).

Table 10.38: Appointment of VAT Withholding Agents

<table>
<tr><td colspan="4">VAT (Amendment) Act, 2017 (Act 954)</td></tr>
<tr><td>Section</td><td>Item</td><td>Description</td><td>Comments</td></tr>
<tr><td colspan="4">“Section 47A to 47C inserted</td></tr>
<tr><td>3</td><td>Tax payable for tax period</td><td>The principal enactment is amended by the insertion after section 47 of:</td><td rowspan="3">The Commissioner appears to have latitude in the appointment of a "withholding" agent.</td></tr>
<tr><td colspan="3">Appointment of VAT Withholding Agent</td></tr>
<tr><td>47A</td><td colspan="2">The Commissioner-General may in writing appoint a VAT</td></tr>
</table>

- ***Distortion of tax structure:*** The VAT withholding scheme worsens the *distortion from other schemes* such as VFRS, CST, Straight and other levies. These show in multiple taxation and cascading, cashflow constraints as well as high administrative and compliance costs.
- ***Duties withholding agents*** Table 10.39 shows the duties and scope or coverage of Withholding Agents under the law—notably zero-rated suppliers, such as exporters with refund claims as well as government and other VAT-registered entities. It appears to give significant room for the Commissioner-General to determine the number of VAT withholding agents.

Table 10.39: Duties and scope of withholding agents

<table>
<tr><td colspan="4">VAT (Amendment) Act, 2017 (Act 954)</td></tr>
<tr><th>Section</th><th>Item</th><th>Description</th><th>Comments</th></tr>
<tr><td colspan="4">“Section 4A to 47C inserted</td></tr>
<tr><td colspan="3">Duties of a VAT Withholding Agent</td><td rowspan="9">The VAT-inclusive price is subject to "withholding" by the purchaser at the time of payment; similar to the withholding rule under the Income Tax Act.</td></tr>
<tr><td>47B</td><td colspan="2">A VAT Withholding Agent shall</td></tr>
<tr><td>(a)</td><td colspan="2">withhold from the payment to a registered VAT trader, seven (7) percent of the taxable output value of standard rated supplies; and</td></tr>
<tr><td>(b)</td><td colspan="2">at the time of making payment for the standard rated supplies, <u>issue a Withholding VAT Credit Certificate</u> in the form prescribed by the Commissioner-General to the supplier.</td></tr>
<tr><td colspan="3">Scope of VAT Withholding Agent</td></tr>
<tr><td>47C</td><td colspan="2">The scope of a VAT Withholding Agent shall include:</td></tr>
<tr><td>(a)</td><td colspan="2">VAT registered entities whose supplies are zero-rated; and</td></tr>
<tr><td>(b)</td><td colspan="2">selected Government and other VAT registered entities.</td></tr>
</table>

- ***Discretionary nature of VAT withholding regime:*** The ***VAT withholding*** policy is ***discretionary, selective, and discriminatory***—given factors such as the following:
    - obliging ***only specific GRA-appointed "purchasers"***, called ***VAT withholding agents,*** to ***deduct the tax withheld from the amount due*** to the "supplier"; and
    - resulting in liquidity challenges for only taxpayers that make ***standard rate*** suppliers even though the VFRS of 3 per cent is also ***deemed to be equal*** to Output VAT less Input VAT.

As Table 10.40 from GRA's website shows, the CG had appointed only 144 VAT withholding agents. The generic and small number of withholding agents among the thousands of entities that are eligible to apply for VAT.

Table 10.40: Appointed VAT Withholding Agents

Sector	Number
Financial institutions	28
Government agencies	36
Petroleum sub-contractors	24
Mining	17
Manufacturing	8
Others (construction)	1
Total number of Agents	**114**

Source: Ghana Revenue Authority (GRA)

In particular, the list of registered withholding agents in Table 10.35 ***excludes large, registered retailers and wholesalers*** since the VAT (Amendment) Act, 2017 (948) had restored and extended the eligibility for the VAT Flat Rate Scheme (VFRS) of 3 per cent on these types of entities. Note further amendment in FY2022.

Table 10.41 shows the obligation for a Withholding VAT Credit Certificate complicates administration and cost of compliance with the measure.

Table 10.41: VAT Withholding Certificate.

<table>
<tr><td colspan="4">VAT (Amendment) Act, 2017 (Act 954)</td></tr>
<tr><td>Section</td><td>Item</td><td>Description</td><td>Comments</td></tr>
<tr><td colspan="4">"Section 48 of Act 870 amended</td></tr>
<tr><td colspan="3">Secton 48 of the principal enactment is amended by</td><td rowspan="3">Deductible input tax (i.e., ITC) is subject to holding a Withholding VAT Credit certificate--which mimics Tax Clearance Certificates under the Income Tax Act.</td></tr>
<tr><td>4 (a)</td><td>Deductible Input Tax</td><td>The insertion after subparagraph (iii) of paragraph (a) of subsection (1) of "(iv) in respect of supplies made in Ghana, the taxable person is in possession of a Withholding VAT Credit Certificate issued under this Act; and</td></tr>
<tr><td>(b)</td><td></td><td>the renumbering of subparagraph (iv) of paragraph (a) of subsection (1) as (v)."</td></tr>
</table>

- ***ITC is a relief for tax paid upfront:*** Though waivers are granted, the cloning of income tax withholding as VAT withholding is not consistent with the ITC process being a tool for relieving the input VAT "embedded" in costs and "withheld" at source. All registered entities offset the Input VAT against Output VAT, unlike single-stage sales tax or VAT addition and subtraction methods.

- ***VCC and grossing-up to avoid cascading:*** The VCC complements the issuing of VAT invoices, and evidence for claiming VAT refunds or credits. To ***avoid cascading, the rule on grossed-up*** amounts minimized the cashflow situation of the "supplier". A GRA exploratory note explains that, in filing the monthly VAT returns

  - the ***"supplier"*** [who receives 7 per cent less than the Output VAT charged from the ***"purchaser"***] ***must use 10.5 per cent*** (i.e., 17.5 less 7 per cent) of Output VAT as the basis for ITC offsets; while
  - the ***"purchaser"*** files the regular VAT return with a ***special VAT withholding return*** and pays the ***net VAT and withheld amount to GRA***; and
  - Section 48(1)(iv) also allows an ITC for the amount deducted if the supplier has in possession a WH-VAT credit certificate—a cumbersome compromise that minimizes the cashflow implications for businesses.

The amounts withheld are payable to GRA with a ***Withholding VAT Return***—in addition to the regular VAT Return that now shows a net payment comprising ***Output VAT less Input VAT and amounts withheld***. Table 10.42 shows the effect of the VAT invoice-credit method and ***the "net-of-net ITC" effect of the GRA Directive***—in an ***ideal VAT*** situation where all entities are registered.

Table 10.42: Ideal VAT Withholding (3 Agents on VA chain)

Ideal VAT Withholding Scheme [without VFRS]										
	Entity	Value ex Tax	Taxable Value	Output VAT	Input VAT	Total Payment			Price [tax plus]	Comments
						VAT Withheld	Net VAT	Total		
a	Importer	1000	1000	175	0	70	175	245	1245	Withholding agent
b	Manufacturer	800	1800	189	175	126	14	140	1989	Withholding agent
c	Wholesaler	600	2400	252	189	168	63	231	2652	Withholding agent
d	Retailer	400	2800	490	252	0	238	238	3290	Sales to non-registered
e	Consumer	2800				364	490		3290	
VFRS	3%	Standard	17.5%	VAT Withholding		7.0%	VAT "offset" rate		10.5%	

The outcome in Table 10.37 is the same as the Ideal Invoice-Credit VAT, with a consumer price of GH₵ 3290 and tax burden of GH₵ 490—without the cascading effect of large VFRS wholesalers and retailers.

- ***An ideal credit offset makes VAT withholding neutral:*** since the ***effective*** Output VAT rate is reduced to 10.5 per cent for VAT Withholding Agents, the ***withholding seems***
    - ***neutral to the consumer price and tax burden;***
    - to result in ***cashflow advantage*** to withholding agents ("purchasers") who pay later to GRA in an ensuing month; and
    - to result in ***negative cashflow*** consequence for the "seller" who pays the lower Output VAT after the same period. It is important to note that the "seller" could also be a withholding agent
- ***VAT Withholding Certificate:*** The "purchaser" requires the supplier to show a VCC to avoid withholding—thus imitating the TCC under income tax rules. Where this condition is met, there will be no withholding while, in contrast, the supplier can claim a "credit" for the amount withheld upon filing the VAT returns. Given the small number of withholding agents, the other large number of "suppliers" continue to make non-withholding supplies that complicate administration.
- ***VAT withholding and straight levies:*** It is necessary to note that the effective ***10.5 per cent is based on a standard VAT rate of 17.5 per cent, including the "straight" levies*** (i.e., NHIL and GETFund Levy) that no longer form part of the VAT base and are excluded from ITC claims. Hence, if the withholding rate is retained at ***7 per cent,*** then the ***offset ratio should reduce to 5.5 per cent.***
- ***Additional VAT Withholding Returns:*** As shown in Table 10.43, the requirement to file a separate VAT Withholding Return adds to the complexity of administration and compliance. It may be ideal to include it in the substantive VAT return, along with the creditable ITC that could lead to a refund.

Table 10.43: VAT Withholding Returns

VAT Withholding Returns			
VAT (Amendment) Act, 2017 (Act 954)			
Section	**Item**	**Description**	**Comments**
"Section 48 of Act 870 amended			
5	Section 52 of the principal enactment is amended by the addition of subsection (9)		Deductible input tax (i.e., ITC) is subject to holding a Withholding VAT Credit certificate--which mimics Tax Clearance Certificates under the Income Tax Act.
(9)	**Submission of tax return and date of payment of the tax**	Despite subsection (4) and (5), a VAT Withholding Agent shall not later than the 15th day of the month immediately following the month to which the returns relate	
(a)		submit to the Commissioner-General, returns relating to the VAT withheld under Section 47B for each period in accordance with the prescribed form; and	
(b)		pay the amount withheld for each period to the Commissioner-General	

9.3 VAT Withholding and VFRS

As noted earlier, the list of GRA VAT Withholding Agents ***does not include taxable retailers and wholesalers*** since the VATAA, 2017 (948) restored the VFRS, with the following implications for the VAT regime—

- ***Sub-standard rate:*** application of a flat 3 per cent on supplies made by retailers and wholesalers to the taxable value of the supply as a proxy for the difference between the Output and Input VATs.
- ***Denial of ITC:*** VFRS does not allow registered retailers and wholesalers to deduct taxes paid on inputs under the ITC scheme.
- ***Conventional threshold:*** the law exempts other entities with turnover below the conventional turnover threshold from charging Output VAT and claiming ITC.

Table 10.44 shows the combination of Withholding and application of the VFRS. The outcome is a slightly higher consumer price (GH₵

3292 compared to GHȻ 3290) and tax burden (GHȻ 492 compared to GHȻ 490).

Table 10.44: Regular VAT/GIIF, Withholding and VFRS schemes

VAT Withholding Scheme: with VFRS											
Entity	Value ex Tax	Taxable Value	Output VAT	Input VAT		VAT Payments				Price [tax plus]	Comments
				Allowed	Denied	Paid	Offset	Net VAT	Total		
Importer	1000	1000	175	0	0	70	0	175	245	1175	W-agent: 17.5% O-VAT
Manufacturer	800	1800	315	175	0	126	70	140	196	2115	W-agent: 10.5% O-VAT
Wholesaler	600	2715	81	0	315	0	126	81	(45)	2796	VFRS-registered: VAT withholding as cost
Retailer	400	3196	96	0	81	0		96	96	3292	
Consumer	2800					196	196	492	492	3292	
VFRS	3%	Standard	17.5%	VAT Withholding		7.0%	VAT "offset" rate		10.5%		

- ***Regular VAT/GIIF, withholding, VFRS, and straight levy schemes:*** The GETFund Levy and NHIL are decoupled from the VAT regime as ***"straight" levies*** and excluded from ITC claims or mere budget allocations of VAT under the respective Formulae. Table 10.45 shows the complexity of complying concurrently with the regular VAT/GIIF and Straight levies. The consumer price increases to GHȻ 3531, compared to GHȻ3290.

Table 10.45: VAT Withholding and Straight Levies

VAT, VAT Withholding regime & "Straight(s)" Levies [GET-Fund & NHIL]														
Entity	Value (ex-Tax)	Taxable Value	Output VAT/Levy		Input VAT/Levy			Total Payment					Price (tax plus)	Comments
			VAT	Straight Levy	Allowed	Denied		VAT Withheld		Net VAT	Straight Levies	Total		
						VAT	Levy	Paid	Offset					
Importer	1000	1000	131	50	0	0	0	74	0	131	50	255	1181	Withholding Agent
Manufacturer	800	1981	260	99	131	131	50	146	74	129	99	447	2340	Withholding Agent
Wholesaler	600	2940	88	0	0	260	99	0	146	0	0	146	3029	VFRS
Retailer	400	3429	103	0	0	88	0	0	0	0	0	0	3531	VFRS
Consumer	2800							219	219	260	149	847	3531	
Standard Rate	12.50%	VFRS	3%	S-Levies	5%	VAT Withholding			7%		VAT "offset" Rate		5.5%	

- ***VAT, VFRS, VAT Withholding, Straight Levy and CST regimes:*** The last example adds the CST, which has the same effects as a Straight Levy or Excise Duty, to the VFRS and VAT Withholding regimes. Needless to say, it worsens the multiple taxation and cascading effects further.

As Table 10.46 shows, the joint effect of the CST on the general or overall consumption tax regime is that consumer price increases to GH₵ 4215 (compared to GH₵ 3290) and the tax burden to GH₵ 1528 (compared to GH₵ 490).

Table 10.46: VAT Withholding, Straight Levies & CST

Entity	Value (ex-Tax)	Taxable Value	Output VAT/Levy			Input VAT/Levy				Total Payment						Price (tax plus)	Comments
			VAT	Straight Levy	CST	Allowed	Denied			VAT Withheld		Net VAT	Straight Levies	CST	Total		
							VAT	Levy	CST	Paid	Offset						
Importer	1000	1000	139	53	60	0	0	0	0	78	0	139	53	60	330	1252	Withholding Agent
Manufacturer	800	2052	286	109	123	139	139	53	60	160	78	146	109	123	616	2570	Withholding Agent
Wholesaler	600	3170	101	0	190	0	286	109	123	0	160	0	0	190	350	3460	VFRS
Retailer	400	3860	123	0	232	0	101	0	190	0	0	0	0	232	232	4215	VFRS
Consumer	2800									238	238	286	162	605	1528	4215	
Standard Rat	12.50%	VFRS	3%	S-Levies	5%		VAT Withhd		7%		VAT "offset" Rate		6%				

10. Energy Sector Levies Act (ESLA)

This chapter ends with analyses of the Energy Sector Levies Act (ESLA) that looked harmless as a proposition to resolve some temporary problems, notably the accumulation of arrears from three principal sources. Unfortunately, ESLA is likely to remain with the country for a longer time than the envisaged three (3) to five (5) years, as a temporary tax.

10.1 Why ESLA is harmful and risky

It can be concluded with certainty that Ghana should not look to ESLA ***as a solution to the country's current fiscal challenges,*** given its greater potential to worsen the distortions to the fiscal and tax structures. The reasons include the following—

- its appearance as excise duty and, as such, the lack of inherent credit offset, deferral and duty drawback features of a VAT, excise duty or tariff regime;
- its embeddedness in the cost of production and distribution costs as well as prices makes it burdensome for consumers and non-conducive for pushing a competitive external trade agenda for the nation—not even in an African Continental Free Trade Area (AfCFTA) context;

- the biggest risk is seeing ESLA as a fiscal solution and increasing or adding to the levies on which it is built as well as extending the period for its elimination; and
- since it adds to costs exponentially, it worsens the "cascading" that is associated with an inefficient VAT regime.

Ghana has had temporary direct and indirect tax regimes that it relies on during periods of austerity or restructuring and ESLA is also a poorer substitute for the budget for fiscal buffers and stabilization funds that are integral to the Petroleum Revenue Management Act (PRMA). In short, the country's plan for recovery should depend on comprehensive and structurally sound revenue, expenditure, borrowing and debt measures that exclude or phase out ESLA as soon as possible.

10.2 Purpose and Origin of ESLA

ESLA was designed to tackle peculiar challenges that faced the nation between 2008 and 2015—and, therefore, the levies were to last 3 to 5 years only. These challenges include—

- the consequences and aftermath of the global financial crisis, which resulted in credit crunch and economic difficulties for all categories of countries;
- the disruption in gas supply to Ghana and other countries from Nigeria through the West African Gas Pipeline (WAGP);
- coincidentally, Ghana had to buy crude oil at a globally exorbitant price above US$100 per barrel to generate domestic power;
- associated difficulty in passing on the full cost and price to consumers led to non-payment and accumulated subsidy costs; and
- the significant budget or expenditure overruns that resulted in the accumulation of arrears to public sector workers under the derailed "single spine pay policy (SSPP)".

By late 2015, there was a significant slump in commodity prices, including crude oil, that worsened the fiscal situation, because of shortfalls in the flow of petroleum revenues into the Petroleum Holding Fund (PHF) under the Petroleum Revenue Management Act (PRMA). Consequently, upon the recommendation of the Cabinet, Parliament passed the Energy Sector Levies Act, 2015 (Act

899) to enable the country to move away from borrowing heavily on domestic and external financial markets to clear arrears.

Table 10.47 summarizes the levies that were imposed under the original ESLA law and the first ESL (Amendment) Act 2017 (Act 946).

Table 10.47: Levies imposed under ESLA 899 and reduction under ESLA 956

Energy Sector Levies Act (ESLA)								
Levies or Taxes [1]								
SN	**Legislation**	**Energy Debt Recovery Levy**		**Road Fund Levy**	**Energy Fund Levy**	**Price Stabilization Levy**	**Public Lighting Levy**	**National Electrification Scheme**
1	ESL Act 2015 (Act 899)	Ghp3 per litre on Marine Gas Oil iro TOR debt recovery	Ghp3 per litre on Marine Gas Oil iro TOR debt recovery	Ghp40 per litre on Petrol and Diesel	Ghp1.0 per litre on petrol, kerosene, diesel & fuel oil	Ghp12 per litre on petrol; Ghp10 per litre on diesel; Ghp100 per kg on LPG	5% per price of Kwh of electricity charged on all categories of consumers	5% per price of kWh of electricity charged on all categories of consumers
		Ghp37 per kg on LPG in iro (a) forex under-recovery; Ghp5 per kg (b) power generation & infrastructure support; Ghp28 per kg (c) TOR debt recovery-Ghp4						
2	**ESL (Amendment) Act, 2017 (Act 946)**						3 kgper price of kWh of electricity charged on all categories of consumers	2% per price of kWh of electricity charged on all categories of consumers

The shortfall also made it possible to reduce the pump and utility prices while having ***sufficient cushion to impose a levy*** that could be used to pay the accumulated arrears and debt to the energy sector. It was passed with a policy, not legislative, "sunset" clause, in anticipation of taking the levy off before another uptick in the price.

Surprisingly, as Table 10.48 above shows, in a popular move, the new administration surprisingly reduced some of the levies, under the ESL (Amendment) Act, 2017 (Act 946), because it had called ESLA a "nuisance tax". However, as Table 10.43 shows, instead of tapering the rates off towards elimination, the government started a round of levy increases and additions as well as indirect extension of the maturity dates through the issuing of ESLA Bonds that were based on collateralizing the ESLA flows.

Table 10.48: Increases and additions to the ESLA levies

Energy Sector Levies Act (ESLA)						
Levies or Taxes [2]						
;islation	Energy Debt Recovery Levy	Road Fund Levy	Energy Fund Levy	Price Stabilization Levy	Public Lighting Levy	National Electrification Scheme
ESL (Amendment) Act, 2019 (Act 997)	***Ghp49 per litre on petrol & diesel*** iro (a) forex under recoveries of Ghp5 per each litre; (b) power generation & infrastructure support of Ghp36 per litre; (c) TOR debt recovery Ghp8 per litre; Ghp3 per litre on MGO; Ghp4 per liter on Fuel oil; Ghp 41 per kg on LPG consisting	Ghp48 per litre on petrol & diesel		Ghp16 per litre on petrol; Ghp14 per litre on diesel; & Ghp14 kg on LPG		
ESL (Amendment) Act, 2021 (Act 1064).	Ghp20 per litre on petrol and diesel; Ghp18 per kg of LPG (Note: new Section 5A)					

Table 10.49 shows the ***purpose of each of the levies*** under the original ESLA 2015, (Act 899), which include the (a) Energy Debt Recovery Levy; (b) Road Fund Levy; (c) Price Stabilization and Recovery Levy; (d) Energy Fund Levy; (e) Public Lighting Levy; and (f) National Electrification Levy. The Table also shows the ***administrative arrangements*** for their collection, beneficiary agencies, and the setting up of specific Funds into which the proceeds from the levies will be paid.

Table 10.49: Goals, responsibilities, and purposes of the levies.

ESLA FUNDS & PURPOSE [1]				
Fund/Levy		Purpose	Collecting Agency	Payment To
Energy Sector Levies Act, 2015 (Act 899)				
1	**Energy Debt Recovery Levy**	To facilitate the debt recovery of the Tema Oil Refinery, downstream petroleum sector foreign exchange under recoveries and power generation infrastructure support	Ghana Revenue Agency (GRA)	(a) Energy Debt Service Account and (b) Power and Infrastructure Support Sub-Account
2	**Road Fund Levy**	To support road maintenance	GRA	Road Fund
3	**Energy Fund Levy**	To support Energy Commission activities	GRA	Energy Commission
4	**Price Stabilization and Recovery Levy**	To be used as a buffer for under-recoveries or subsidies to stabilize petroleum prices for the consumer	National Petroleum Authority (NPA)	Price Stabilization and Recoveries Account
5	**Public Lighting Levy**	To support payment of energy consumed by traffic/street lights, public light and highways; to support investment and maintenance of traffic lights/street lights, public lights and hiways by MMDAs; amd to cater for replacement of street lights destroyed by hit and run motor vehicles	Electricity Company of Ghana (ECG), NEDCO and other suppliers of electricity	Ministry of responsible for Power & Electricity Distribution Companies, *and power generation & infrastructure support Sub-Account*
6	**National Electrification Scheme**	To provide funding support for national electrification programme to iprove access to electricity	ECG, NEDCO and other suppliers of electricity	**National Electrification Fund;** *Power Generation and Infrastructure support Sub-Account*

Table 10.50 shows changes to the purposes and responsibilities of the *ESL (Amendment) Act, 2017 (Act 946)*. They involve slight changes to the scope of collection and beneficiaries.

Table 10.50: Changes in collection and beneficiary institutions

	ESLA FUNDS & PURPOSE [2]			
	Fund/Levy	**Purpose**	**Collecting Agency**	**Payment To**
Energy Sector Levies (Amendment) Act, 2017 (Act 946)				
7	**Public Lighting Levy**	To support payment of energy consumed by traffic/street lights, public light and highways; to support investment and maintenance of traffic lights/street lights, public lights and hiways by MMDAs; amd to cater for replacement of street lights destroyed by hit and run motor vehicles	ECG, NEDCO, *VRA* and other suppliers of electricity	Ministry responsible for Power and Electricity Distribution Companies
8	**National Electrification Scheme**	To provide funding support for national electrification programme to iprove access to electricity	ECG, NEDCO, *VRA* and other suppliers of electricity	National Electrification Fund

Finally, ***Table 10.51*** shows a similar change in the depository account for the Energy Debt Recovery Levy, under ***ESL (Amendment) Act 2019 (Act 997***.

Table 10.51: Change in deposit account for Energy Debt Recovery Levy

	ESLA FUNDS & PURPOSE [3]			
	Fund/Levy	**Purpose**	**Collecting Agency**	**Payment To**
Energy Sector Levies (Amendment) Act, 2019 (Act 997)				
9	**Energy Debt Recovery Levy**	To facilitate the debt recovery of the Tema Oil Refinery, downstream petroleum sector foreign exchange under recoveries and power generation infrastructure support	Ghana Revenue Authority (GRA)	(a) *Energy Debt Service Account* and (b) Power and Infrastructure Support *Sub-Account*
10	**Road Fund Levy**	To support road maintenance	GRA	Road Fund
11	**Price Stabilization and Recovery Levy**	To be used as a buffer for under-recoveries or subsidies to stabilize petroleum prices for the consumer	National Petroleum Authority (NPA)	Price Stabilization and Recoveries Account

Table 10.52 shows the addition of a new Sanitation and Pollution Levy and change in the scope of objectives for the Energy Debt Recovery Levy, under ***ESL (Amendment) Act, 2021 (Act 1064)***

Table 10.52: Changes in existing, and addition to, Levies.

ESLA FUNDS & PURPOSE [4]				
	Fund/Levy	**Purpose**	**Collecting Agency**	**Payment To**
Energy Sector (Amendment) Act, 2021 (Act 1064)				
12	**Energy Debt Recovery** Account	s1 [new5(A)] There is imposed by this Act, an Energy Sector Recovery Levy	GRA	
		s3 Moneys in the Energy Sector Recvoery Account shall be used to support the payment of *(a) capacity charges in the energy sector; and (b) energy sector bills including support for Feedstock*		s2 [new s5(A)] The Minister shall cause to be opened and maintained, the *"Energy Sector Recovery Account"* for the purpose of receiving moneys realized from the Energy Sector Recovery Levy
13	**Sanitation & Pollution Account**	Monies in the Sanitation & Pollution Account shall be used to	GRA	Energy Sector Recovery Account
	5B(1) There is imposed by this Act, a Sanitation and Pollution Levy on specified petroleum products	(a) improve air quality in urban areas of the country and combat pollution; (b) design, construct and re-engineer solid and liquid waste treatment & disposal facilities including compost production facilities, recycling facilities, landfill sites, medical and other specialized waste treatment facilities; (c) construct sanitation facilities to accelerate the eliminationm of open defecation; (d) support disinfectation, disinfection and fumigation of public spaces, schools, lorry partks, health centres and markets, and (e) provide dedicated support for the maintenance and management of major landfill sites and other waste treatment plants and facilities across the country.		Sanitation and Pollution Levy Account

11. Conclusion

Ghana introduced the ***VAT Invoice-Credit method to replace various turnover, sales and services tax*** regimes it had until the late 1990s. The purpose was to broaden the general consumption tax base and make its administration and compliance more efficient and effective. However, since the VAT reintroduction in 1998 and, despite a major revamp in VATA 2013 (Act 870), the VAT regime base and structure, including its small-entity registration schemes, have been distorted significantly again.

These add to the ***inefficiencies from expanding the exempt domestic supplies and*** blocking its unique ITC feature, thus making the input taxes "cascade", and increasing costs along the value addition chain. The upstream and midstream exemptions on the chain resulted in the most adverse effect on tax burdens and consumer prices.

The ***zero-rating of domestic supplies, in lieu of exemption,*** worsened the situation further because of inefficient ITC and refund processes that led to huge arrears and delayed payments to registered taxpayers. These non-taxable supply policies that restrict the exemption to "goods produced locally" also made the VAT regimes resemble a tariff or customs duty and excise duty.

Further, the VAT regime is going through a ***significant jolt*** with the decoupling of the GETFund Levy and NHIL regimes as ***so-called "straight levies"*** that worsen the negative effects of the CST regime on the indirect tax structure. The distortions increase "cascading" and do not seem to improve fiscal revenues because the complexity encourages tax evasion and avoidance.

Finally, as discussed in the next Chapter, ***until a recent amendment that affects large wholesalers***, the blocking of VAT paid on inputs became a feature of the 3 per cent sub-standard VFRS charged as Output VAT by all wholesalers and retailers of goods. Similarly, the ***cash flow for taxpayers worsened with the VAT withholding*** that mimicked the income tax withholding, despite the ITC process itself being the outcome of VAT withheld on input costs.

The chapter also draws attention to the need to take steps to make the ESLA levy short-lived and temporary, as originally intended. Its collateralization and subsequent addition to the debt default saga will make this objective difficult to achieve—yet, the alternative of the levies increasing the cost of production and consumer prices will also encourage tax evasion and avoidance as well as not make the tax regime efficient.

Chapter 9 completes Part III on the ***adverse changes to the Ideal VAT regime that excluded small entities with a given annual turnover from registering for VAT***. Various amendments to VATA 546 and VATA 870 extended this exclusion under the VFRS regime to medium and large retailers and wholesalers of goods. Part IV [Chapters 10 to 12] shifts the discussions to VAT administration and compliance while the final Part V [Chapters 13 and 14] discusses the political economy of VAT.

Appendix Chapter 10

Appendix Table 10.1

Extract:

National Health Insurance Act, 2012 (Act 852)

Levy on supply of goods and services

47. (1) There is imposed by this Act a National Health Insurance Levy charged ***at the rate of two and a half per cent calculated*** on (a) each supply of goods and services made or provided in Ghana; (b) each importation of goods, and (c) supply of an imported service, unless otherwise exempted in this Act or under the Regulations.

(2) The levy is payable at the time the goods and services are supplied or imported.

(3) For the purposes of the National Health Insurance Levy, the provisions on the supply of goods and services in the enactment that establishes the revenue or collection agency charged with responsibility for the collection of this levy by the Minister responsible for Finance shall apply.

(4) The Minister responsible for Finance may by Legislative Instrument amend the rate of the levy specified in subsection (1).

Exempt supply of goods and services

48. A supply in respect of any of the matters set out in Part One of the Second Schedule is exempt from the levies imposed under section 47.

Zero-rated supply of goods and services

49. A supply in respect of any of the matters specified in Part Two of the Second Schedule is zero-rated as regards the levy under section 47.

Relief from levy

50. There is granted by this Act "relief" from the payment of the levy to the individuals, organizations and in respect of the matters specified in Part Three of the Second Schedule.

Collection of the Levy (as amended by Act, 971)

51. (1) The Ghana Revenue Authority is responsible for the collection of the Levy.

(2) The Revenue Administration Act, 2016 (Act 915) applies to the administration of the Levy.

(3) The Value Added Tax Act, 2013 (Act 870) applies with the necessary modifications to the collection of the Levy

Payment of Levy into the Fund

52. (1) The Minister responsible for Finance shall within thirty days after the collection of the levy cause the levy to be paid directly into the Fund and furnish the Minister responsible for Health and the Authority with evidence of the payment.

(2) The Minister responsible for Finance shall present to Parliament every six months a report on the payment of levies into the Fund.

Appendix Table 10.2

<table>
<tr><th colspan="4">National Health Insurance Levy</th></tr>
<tr><th colspan="4">NHIL (Amendment) Act, 2018 (Act 971)</th></tr>
<tr><th>Section</th><th>Item</th><th>Description</th><th>Comments</th></tr>
<tr><td colspan="4">“Section 47 of Act 852 amended</td></tr>
<tr><td rowspan="2">1</td><td colspan="2">the “principal enactment” is amended in section 47 by the substitution for subsection (3) of</td><td rowspan="3">The NHIL is no longer deductible in the VAT Calculation</td></tr>
<tr><td>(3)</td><td>The Levy is not subject to an input tax deduction.</td></tr>
<tr><td></td><td>(4)</td><td>Any goods on which the Value Added Tax Flat Rate is imposed is not subject to the levy.”</td></tr>
</table>

Amendment Act 971

Section 47 of Act 852 amended

The National Health Insurance (Amendment) Act, 2018, Act 971, introduced some modifications to Sections 47 and 48 of the principal enactment. The primary change in this amendment is that the Levy is no longer eligible for input tax deduction and any goods on which the Value Added Tax Flat Rate is imposed is not subject to the levy.

Furthermore, this amendment repealed the National Health Insurance (Amendment) Act, 2015 (Act 888)

Chapter 11

VAT POLICY REVIEW 4: VAT SMALL-ENTITY MEASURES

1. Introduction

This chapter ends Part III with a recall that the purpose of allowing ***registered entities*** under the VAT Invoice Credit method to claim Input Tax Credit (ITC) is to make the ***VAT system efficient*** *as* well as facilitate ***its administration and compliance***. It requires entities making ***taxable supplies*** to ***register, charge Output VAT, and claim ITC*** relating to taxable purchases and expenses.

Hence, registered entities are allowed to set off the Input VAT against the Output VAT in ***business-to-business (B2B)*** transactions to ***eliminate or reduce multiple taxation and cascading of costs***. The exception to this rule is the provision that prevents small business entities that ***do not make a given annual amount of turnover or sales from registration.***

2. Summary of the Small-Entity Legislative Changes

This chapter ends the VAT policy and legislative reviews [Part III] with repeals and amendments to the VAT turnover threshold that disqualifies small entities from registration. VAT laws typically exclude small business entities from VAT registration to improve administration and compliance. Again, Table 11.1 draws attention to the redenomination of the value of the cedi from July 1, 2007

> **Box 9.1: Currency Redenomination**
>
> This chapter refers to the registration threshold amount in several places. Recall that the change in the sign of the currency—***Cedis (¢),*** compared to ***Ghana cedis (***GH¢***)***—is the result of ***redenominating the currency by slashing four zeros in the old cedi-to-dollar value from Gh¢ 10,000 to Gh ¢1 from July 1, 2007.***

The rationale, as with presumptive taxation under the income tax regimes, is that these entities operate in large numbers in the ***informal sectors*** and ***cannot keep proper records to meet most tax obligations***. The section summarizes, in chronological order, the trend of small-entity registration under VAT.

- ***Original small-entity provision:*** The ***main anomaly*** in the original ***VAT Act, 1998 (Act 546)*** is to restrict the ***ineligibility*** to register, ***based on the c200m threshold*** to ***"retailers of goods"***— thereby, excluding small entities in other sectors of the economy.
- ***Lowering of VAT registration threshold***: the ***VAT Act, 2001 (Act 595)*** lowers the threshold ***from ¢200m to ¢100m,*** which continues to apply to only ***"retailers of goods".*** Potentially, it ropes in more small entities that cannot keep proper records.
- ***VAT Flat Rate Scheme (VFRS):*** this provision under the ***VAT (Amendment) Act, 2007 (Act 734)*** imposes an obligation on ***"a taxable person who is a 'retailer of goods'",*** to charge Output VAT at a ***sub-standard flat rate of 3 per cent.***
- ***Application of threshold to all sectors:*** the ***VAT (Amendment) Act, 2010 (Act 810)*** is ***notable*** for making ***all small "taxable persons",*** not just retailers of goods eligible. It also increased the limit to ***GH¢90,000*** (i.e., new currency unit [Ghana cedis {GH₵}).
- ***VFRS and turnover within GH₵10,000 and GH₵90,000: VAT Act, 2010 (Act 810)*** also has a second provision that makes ***any person*** with turnover ***below Gh¢90,000 but above GH¢10,000*** eligible to register and charge the VFRS rate of 3 per cent.
- ***Reversal to restrict threshold to "wholesalers and retailers of goods"***; in a political-economy move, the VFRS was restored under the ***VAT (Amendment) Act, 2017 (Act 948),*** with a worsened anomaly that covers ***"wholesalers and retailers of goods".***
- ***Repeal of the extension of threshold to "wholesalers of goods"***; the anomaly in VAT Act 948 above was mitigated under the ***VAT (Amendment) Act, 2021 (Act 1072)*** to apply the threshold to only ***"retailer of goods"***—and, at an increased threshold amount of ***GH¢500,000***

The VAT (Amendment) Act 2022 (Act 1087) increased the VAT rate from 12.5 per cent to 15 per cent (i.e., without the Straight Levies of 5 per cent) but kept the VAT (Amendment) Act 2021 (Act 1072) proviso that applied the ***VFRS rate of 3 per cent for "retailers of goods"*** with "taxable supplies ***not less than GH₵200,000 but not exceeding Gh¢500,000***".

It must be noted that the provision ***did not apply to*** "the supply of any form of power heat, refrigeration or ventilation is as a supply of goods" under the VAT Act 2013 (Act 870). Also, recall that the change in the sign of the currency from ***Cedis (¢)*** to ***Ghana cedis*** (GH¢) is the result of the ***currency redenomination*** that slashed the four zeros in the old cedi-to-dollar equivalent from Gh¢ 10,000 to Gh ¢1 from July 1, 2007 (Box 9.1).

3. Original threshold under VAT Act, 1998 (Act 546)

The ensuing summaries show extracts of the ***small-entity VAT provisions*** in the VAT Act, 1998 (Act 546).

- ***Rate of tax (section 3)***—"Except otherwise provided in this Act, the ***rate of the tax*** shall be 10 per cent calculated on the value of the taxable supply of the goods, services or import";
- ***Taxable person (section 4)***—"A ***taxable person*** is a person registered under section 5 of this Act".
- ***Registration as a taxable person (section 5)***— **(1)** a person is registrable as a taxable person if he is a person who makes a taxable supply of goods or services and, ***in the case of a retailer of goods***"

Table 11.1 shows the annual turnover threshold and related quarterly proportions that serve as signals for new and unregistered entities to determine their obligations to register.

Table 11.1: Original VATA 1998 (Act 546) Registration Threshold Provision

Section	Heading	Description	Comments
Original VAT Act, 1998 (Act 546)			
5(1)	Registration of Taxable person	A person is registrable as a taxable person if he is a person who makes taxable supply of goods or services and ***in the case of a retailer of goods*** he is a person whose business turnover exceeds--	At reintroduction in 1998, compared with the failure in 1995, the registration threshold was set deliberately high to eliminate the like nuisance element of roping in too many small entities into the VAT net.
		a) c200 million over a 12 month period; or	
		b) c150 million over a nine month period; or	
		c) c100 million over a six month period; or	
		d) c50 million over a three month period.	
		whichever is realized earliest	

- ***Application to small-entity "retailers of goods":*** this ***restriction is not conventional*** since, in practice, the ***threshold does not apply to small entities in other sectors.*** Hence, as discussed later, the VFRS (sub-standard rate) imposed in 2007 on "retailers of goods" continued to aggravate this distortion.

- ***Table 11.2*** repeats the outcomes of the ***ideal invoice-credit VAT regime,*** including a consumer price of GHȻ 3290 and a tax burden or fiscal intake of GHȻ 490.

Table 11.2: Ideal Invoice-Credit VAT method

Exemption under conventional threshold							
Entity	Value Added (ex-Tax)	Cumm. Value Added	Output VAT	Input VAT		Net VAT	Consumer Price
				Allowed	Denied		
Importer	1000	1000	175	0	0	175	1175
Manufacturer	800	1800	315	175	0	140	2115
Wholesaler	600	2400	420	315	0	105	2820
Retailer	400	2800	490	420	0	70	3290
Consumer	2800					490	3290
Standard rate	17.5%						

- Table 11.2 is a way of comparing the ideal outcomes with subsequent Tables that show (a) the ***non-registration of small entities*** that are ***"retailers of goods";*** (b) extension of the "threshold" rule to ***"wholesalers of goods"***; (c) introduction of the ***sub-standard rate*** called ***VAT Flat Rate Scheme (VFRS)*** and (d) subsequent ***removal of the emphasis on the "supply of goods".***

In contrast, Table 11.3 shows a situation where the retailer (of goods) (a) has an annual turnover below c200 million; (b) is ineligible to register; (c) cannot charge Output VAT; and therefore (d) denied the right to ITC or refunds.

Table 11.3: Exemption of "retailers of good" Invoice Credit VAT method

Exemption: conventional [low Ghc10,000] threshold							
Entity	Value Added (ex-Tax)	Cumm. Value Added	Output VAT	Input VAT		Net VAT	Consumer Price
				Allowed	Denied		
Importer	1000	1000	175	0	0	175	1175
Manufacturer	800	1800	315	175	0	140	2115
Wholesaler	600	2400	420	315	0	105	2820
Retailer	400	3220	0	0	420	0	3220
Consumer	2800					420	3220
Standard rate	17.5%			Exempt		na	

- ***The outcomes*** are (i) a consumer price of Gh ¢3290; and (b) a tax burden of GH₵ 490 results from the entire value-added chain, which are the ***same as the Ideal VAT regime outcomes.*** This is because of the ***assumption*** that, even at the final stage, small non-retail entities can meet all VAT obligations—register and file tax returns that show Output VAT as well as ITC or refunds, net VAT (or refund claim).
- ***Benefits of non-registration of small entities:*** The difference of Gh¢ 70 in Table 11.3 is equal to the VAT on value added of GH₵ 400 at the standard rate of 17.5 per cent downstream. It is acclaimed to have benefits, such as the following—
  - ***eases compliance (recordkeeping)***: removes a ***"nuisance" factor*** by excluding small or "petty" retailers or traders from the VAT base since they cannot keep elaborate records;
  - ***lowers administration cost:*** eases GRA's cost of operations by ***focusing its scarce resources on the medium and large entities*** that can comply more easily as well as generate the largest share of value-added and revenue; and
  - ***enhances social intervention policy:*** since many see VAT as regressive, the ***lower price favours low-income persons*** who buy from small retail outlets and traditional markets.

While the ***policy may not produce ideal invoice-credit VAT outcomes,*** it reduces administration and compliance costs, due to the ***downstream exclusion of small entities*** from registration. Box 9.2 briefly discusses the political-economy underpinnings of the VAT cancellation saga.

4. Lower VAT Threshold (for "retailers of goods")—VAT (Amendment) Act, 2001 [Act 595])

The purpose of using the VAT (Amendment) Act 595 to alter the VAT Act 546 (1998) was to reduce the existing ***threshold (and quarterly values) in half*** from the annual value of ***c200 million to c100 million***—with continued application to only "retailers of goods". Table 11.4 shows the relevant section of VATAA 2001 (Act 595) with the currency in the old cedi values before the redenomination (see Box 9.1).

Box 9.2: Political-economy context:

The restriction to "retailers of goods" is associated with the difficulties in introducing the VAT regime in 1995 and, therefore, subsequent suspension of the initiative.

- ***Initial VAT registration threshold:*** after Ghana's disruptive VAT period (1993 to 1995), under VAT Act, 1994 (Act 486), the number of taxpayers registered increased at the time of its re-introduction in 1998, despite the increase in the threshold—due to enhanced public education, additional training, and automation of programs and processes.
- ***Practical administration:*** the general view is that a high threshold removes many small entities in the informal sector from the VAT base to enhance compliance—such small entities also pay only presumptive income taxes. Hence the increase in threshold raises the important of sound administration—both in design and implementation.
- ***Adjustment of real value:*** the limit must increase and be adjusted annually to a real cedi value of about of US$100,000—which implies a doubling of the threshold in the medium term. Contrary to this objective, the VAT registration threshold was rather decreased in subsequent legislative amendments.

The *recourse to a relatively higher registration threshold* is cited among the policies that facilitated the re-reintroduction of VAT in 1998. Given that it helped in achieving that goal, the reduction in the VAT threshold amount and, as discussed in the next session, addition of a sub-standard rate of VAT may seem baffling.

Table 11.4: Decrease in VAT registration threshold for *retailers of goods*

<table>
<tr><th>Section</th><th>Heading</th><th>Description</th><th>Comments</th></tr>
<tr><td colspan="4">VAT (Amendment) Act, 2001 (Act 595)</td></tr>
<tr><td colspan="3">The VAT Act, 1998 (Act 546), as amended, is further amended as follows—</td><td rowspan="7">The amendment lowers the annual VAT registration threshold for retailers of goods, contrary to the intention at the time, of increasing thresholds to the equivalent of US$100,000. The amendment also triggered the distortion of VAT rules for small entities—adding to those of reliefs and exemptions (discussed earlier).</td></tr>
<tr><td rowspan="6">5(1)</td><td>Registration as a Taxable Person</td><td>A person is registrable as a taxable person if he is a person who makes taxable supplies of goods or services and in the case of a retailer of goods, he is a person whose business turnover exceeds</td></tr>
<tr><td></td><td>• ¢100 million over 12 months; or</td></tr>
<tr><td></td><td>• ¢75 million over 9 months; or</td></tr>
<tr><td></td><td>• ¢50 million over 6 months; or</td></tr>
<tr><td></td><td>• ¢25 million over 3 months,</td></tr>
<tr><td></td><td>whichever is realized earliest.</td></tr>
</table>

As noted earlier, the ***lowering of the VAT threshold*** is inconsistent with best practice: the ***periodic increase in, or indexation of, the VAT threshold amount,*** which is a common practice in both advanced and developing states. The following bullets ***summarize other notable explicit and implicit policy outcomes of changing the law on small entities.***

- *Lower threshold:* Ghana moved further away from the contemporary VAT trend in using the VATA Act 2001 (Act 595) to ***lower the VAT registration threshold*** from ¢200 million to ¢100 million—in the old currency.
- *Application to retailers of goods:* as with the old law (Act 546), the reduced threshold amount continued to apply to ***only "retailers of goods"*** at the distribution or final stage of the value addition chain—as illustrated in various Tables.
- *Other small entities:* All ***non-goods retail small entities,*** continued to charge Output VAT and claim ITC or refunds while their ***counterpart small retail entities were denied*** this benefit of the Invoice-Credit VAT mechanism.

A further implication, patently unrealistic, is that ***all other small VAT entities*** in the manufacturing, agricultural services and other sectors can navigate the ITC mechanism because they can keep adequate accounting records and file the VAT returns.

5. VAT Sub-standard Rate—VAT Flat Rate Scheme (VFRS I)

A major ***policy change*** occurred with the use of the ***VAT (Amendment) Act, 2007 (Act 734)*** to amend the small-entity VAT registration provision under VATA 1998 [Act 546]). As Table 11.5 shows, this amendment introduced a ***three per cent (3%) sub-standard rate, the VAT Flat Rate Scheme (VFRS)*** for ***"retailers of goods"***—without recourse to ITC or refunds.

Table 11.5: VFRS-1 reproduced from VATAA 2007 (Act 734)

Section	Heading	Description	Comments
VAT (Amendment) Act, 2007 (Act 734)			
Section 24 of Act 546 amended			
1	The VAT Act, 1998 (Act 546), as amended and referred to in this Act as the principal enactment is ***further amended in sub-section 24*** by the insertion after subsection (6) of subsection (6a):		The addition of sub-section 6(a) ***blocks the right to ITC for retailers under the VFRS*** (see also comments against Section 3 below
24	Credit for deductible input tax	(6a) A taxable person to whom subsection (2) of Section 3 applies ***does not qualify for an input tax deduction or tax credit***".	
Section 3 of Act 546 amended:			
2	**The principal enactment is amended in Section 3 by the insertion of sub-section (2)**		
3	Rate of Tax	(2) Unless otherwise directed by the Commissioner in writing, a ***taxable person*** who is ***a retailer of goods*** shall account for the Value Added Tax payable under this section at ***a flat rate of 3%*** calculated on the value of the taxable supply".	Note applies to (a) a taxable person (ref. s4); and (b) a retailer of goods. Since the registration threshold remains (s5), the amendment applies to registered [medium/ large] retailers only

Section 76 of Act 546 amended			
3	**The principal enactment is amended by the insertion after the interpretation of "VAT" of):**		
76	Interpretation (VFRS)	"VAT Flat Rate Scheme" means a VAT collection and accounting mechanism that ***applies a marginal tax percentage representing net VAT payable*** to the value of taxable goods supplied".	The VFRS is deemed to represent the difference between Output VAT and Input VAT, hence the denial of ITC

The VFRS amendments resulted in ***further complications*** for the VAT administration, compliance, structure and policy—which required ***retailers of goods with turnover below c100 million to charge a final 3 per cent sub-standard VAT rate.***

- ***Retailers of goods (1):*** since the amendment does not refer to the threshold of C100 million, it is assumed that retailers of goods with turnover ***below GH₵ 100 million*** were still ineligible to charge ITC and claim ITC or refunds.
- ***Retailers of goods (2):*** the remaining retailers with turnover ***above GH₵ 100 million*** must ***charge VAT at the sub-standard 3 per cent but cannot claim ITC or refunds;***
- ***Other retailers of goods:*** as in Act 546, ***all retailers making taxable above c100,000*** must register, charge Output VAT and claim ITC or refunds.

The addition of a ***VAT sub-standard rate*** is among other policy measures such as the straight levy, VAT withholding and blocking of ITC that have adversely affected the VAT regime in Ghana and continue to make it inefficient, less buoyant, and more difficult to comply with or administer.

6. Application of VAT *Threshold to all Sectors*

Among other provisions, the policy of applying the registration threshold to only ***"retailers of goods"*** was changed with the passage of the ***VAT (Amendment) Act 2010 (Act 810),*** which ***applied its eligibility to all entities and sectors.*** Secondly, the Act ***increased the value of the thresholds,*** which as ***Box 9.1*** notes, was before Ghana redenominated its currency and changed the sign of the currency from Cedis (¢) to Ghana Cedi (GH ¢).

> **Box 9.21 Redenomination of local currency (as GH₵)**
>
> As noted in Box 1, Ghana redenominated its currency on July 1, 2007, by truncating approximately ¢10,000.00 to Gh¢1.00 and the US dollar, also at about $1.00. Hence, while significantly higher, the revised threshold values discussed in the next paragraphs are stated in thousands of Ghana cedis (Gh¢) and not millions of cedis (i.e., not preceded by Ghs.).

Table 11.6 covers the obligation of all eligible small entities to register and charge the VFRS rate of 3 per cent to all sectors of the economy.

Table 11.6: Extract of VFRS Scheme from VATAA 2010 (Act 810)

Section	Heading and Description	Comments
Amendments relating to small-entity supplies		
VAT (Amendment) Act, 2010 (Act 810)		
An Act to amend the VAT, 1998 (Act 546) to revise and expand the coverage of the ***threshold for registration***; and re-classify locally produced pharmaceuticals, locally produced textbooks and locally-manufacture agricultural machinery and tools as exempt supply.		
Section 3 of Act 546 amended		
1(1).	The VAT Act, 1998 (Act 546) as amended and referred to this Act, as the principal enactment, is further amended in Section 3 by the ***substitution*** for subsection (2) of	
(2)	A person to whom ***subsection (1)(b) of section 5 applies*** shall account for the VAT payable under this section at a ***flat rate of 3%*** calculated on the value of the taxable supply.	

- **Section 1(2)**: the section covers the obligation of small entities to ***charge a sub-standard flat rate of 3 per cent*** without recourse to ITC—amends Section 3 of VATA 546) and ***refers to section 5 (below),*** which defines the ***bracket*** for the small entities that are affected by the amendment.

Table 11.7: VFRS issues reproduced from VATAA 2010 (Act 810)

Section	Heading and Description	Comments
Section 5 of Act 546 amended		
Amendments relating to small-entity supplies		
2.	The VAT Act, 1998 (Act 546) referred to in this Act as the principal enactment is amended in Section 5 by the ***substitution*** for subsection (1) of **"Re-registration as a taxable person** 1) A person is ***registrable as a taxable person*** if that person is a person who makes a taxable supply of goods or services and has a business ***turnover that exceeds—*** • GH₵ 90,000 over twelve months; • GH₵ 67,500 over nine months; • GH₵ 45,000 over six months; or • GH₵ 22,500 over three months— whichever is achieved earliest."	**Increase** *in the VAT registration threshold* but in terms of the ***re-denominated currency, the Ghana cedi (GH₵)***—which may make the amounts ***seem to be relatively lower.***
	2) A person whose ***business turnover is below GH₵ 90,000 but exceeds GH₵ 10,000*** over twelve months or a proportionate part thereof is ***registrable*** as a taxable person and shall ***charge and account for the tax*** as provided under sub-section (2) of section 3 of this Act."	Introduces ***2 threshold levels for small entities***—below GH₵ 10,000 (non-registered, ***all entities***) & GH₵ 10,000 to GH₵ 90,000 ***(3% registered entities)***

It is necessary to re-emphasize the following implications of the various amendments in VAT (Amendment) Act **2010 (Act 810)**—

- **Section 2(1):** involves an upward revision of the ***VAT registration threshold*** *(in the* ***redenominated cedi*** *currency)* with the relevant quarterly apportionments that assist with compliance—amends Section 5 of VATA 546).
- **Section 2(2)**: applies the ***VFRS, within a bracket of Gh¢ 10,000 to Gh ¢ 90,000,*** to all small entities, not just retailers of goods, that must ***charge the 3 per cent sub-standard VAT rate without recourse to ITC***—also amends Section 5 of VATA 546.
- ***Turnover below GH₵ 10,000:*** These entities are precluded from charging both the standard and sub-standard VAT rates and, hence, cannot claim ITC or refunds. They must add any Input VAT to their costs and prices for all supplies.

The ensuing Tables show the practical impact of the various issues discussed above, notably from the perspective of business-to-business (B2B) costs, tax burden, and consumer prices. Table 11.8 begins with the ***Ideal VAT invoice-credit method and its outcomes.***

Table 11.8: Larger retailers registered to charge VAT (17.5 per cent)

Retailer charges standard 17.5 percent rate							
Entity	Value Added (ex-Tax)	Cumm. Value Added	Output VAT	Input VAT		Net VAT	Consumer Price
				Allowed	Denied		
Importer	1000	1000	175	0	0	175	1175
Manufacturer	800	1800	315	175	0	140	2115
Wholesaler	600	2400	420	315	0	105	2820
Retailer	400	2800	490	420	0	70	3290
Consumer	2800					490	3290
Standard rate	17.5%						

- ***In contrast, Table 11.9*** shows the obligation under VAT Act 810 to charge Output VAT at 3 per cent but without ITC for ***VFRS-registered entities within the special band of GH₵ 10,000 and GH₵ 90,000.***

Table 11.9: Final stage *eligible* entities under 3 per cent VFRS rate

VFRS Downstream 3% turnover [Ghc10,000 to Ghc90,000] range							
Entity	Value Added (ex-Tax)	Cumm. Value Added	Output VAT	Input VAT		Net VAT	Consumer Price
				Allowed	Denied		
Importer	1000	1000	175	0	0	175	1175
Manufacturer	800	1800	315	175	0	140	2115
Wholesaler	600	2400	420	315	0	105	2820
Retailer [VFRS]	400	3220	97	0	420	97	3317
Consumer	2800					517	3317
Standard rate	17.5%			VFRS		3.0%	

The outcomes result in ***more cascading*** because (a) the entity charges 3 per cent VAT (GH₵ 97) on cumulative value-added, which (b) includes blocked GH₵ 420 Input VAT under VFRS; which (c) adds to the final consumer price of GH₵ 3317.

- ***Exclusion of entities with turnover below GH₵ 10,000:*** Table 11.10 shows that these entities can neither charge Output VAT nor claim ITC. However, subject to the Commissioner-General's approval, they may exercise ***the voluntary registration option*** that was not affected by the amendment.

Table 11.10: Lower [below GHC 10,000] small entity threshold

Exemption: conventional [low Ghc10,000] threshold							
Entity	**Value Added (ex-Tax)**	**Cumm. Value Added**	**Output VAT**	**Input VAT**		**Net VAT**	**Consumer Price**
				Allowed	**Denied**		
Importer	1000	1000	175	0	0	175	1175
Manufacturer	800	1800	315	175	0	140	2115
Wholesaler	600	2400	420	315	0	105	2820
Retailer	400	3220	0	0	420	0	3220
Consumer	2800					420	3220
Standard rate	17.5%			Exempt		na	

It gives the ***default (downstream) exempt outcomes***: lower tax burden (Gh¢420), the consumer price of Gh¢3220 and the difference (Gh¢ 3290 less Gh¢ 4220 equals Gh¢70 or the tax on value added of Gh¢400)—even though the denied Input VAT (GHC 420) is added to costs.

- ***Voluntary registration***: the VFRS amendments did not repeal the ***voluntary registration clauses under Section 13 of the VAT Act 2013 (Act 870) and Section 5(10) of the VAT Act 1998 (Act 546)***. At the same time, the 3 per cent VFRS scheme appears to be mandatory and, thereby, takes the option for voluntary registration from those clusters of small entities—which came into force under the VAT Act 2010 (Act 810).

It is important to note that the VAT (Amendment) Act, 2010 (Act 810) also relates to two other unrelated issues, including—

(i) deletion of Section 25(1) (1b)—relating to "a refund under subsection (1) shall be made to the taxable person where the excess remains outstanding for a continuous period of three (3) months or more", which implies prompt refund payment under Section 25(1)(a); and

(ii) amendments to the obstruction of officers as well as Schedule 1 (Exemptions) and Schedule 2 (zero-rating).

These zero-rating, exemption and relief topics are dealt with in the relevant chapters of the book. Finally, it also deals with the revocation of Legislative Instrument LI 1817—The Ghana Investment Promotion Centre (Promotion of Tourism) Instrument 2005 (LI 1817).

7. Registration Threshold and Reviews under VAT Act, *2013* (Act 870)

The passage of VATA 2013 (Act 870) was a ***comprehensive review*** that went beyond the amendments that took place from 1998 to 2013. Since an earlier chapter reviews the Act fully, the ensuing sections are limited to the discussion of the ***restoration of the conventional small-entity VAT registration provisions*** under Section 6 of the law.

- ***Bringing the VFRS scheme to an end:*** It is necessary to note that the small entity provisions in VATA 2013 (Act 870) ***did not refer to the VFRS scheme***—effectively adopting the ***conventional registration threshold, without "retailers of goods".***
- ***Apply the threshold to all sectors***: Consequently, VAT Act 870 continued to apply the threshold to small entities in all sectors—following the VAT Act 810 initiative.
- ***Increasing the VAT threshold following comprehensive review:*** The policy reviews include an ***increase in the annual amount of the VAT registration threshold*** from GH₵ 90,000 under VATA 810 to GH₵ 120,000. The specific provisions of Section 6 of the law are shown in **Table 11-13.**

Table 11.13: Increase in the VAT threshold

VATA 2013 (Act 870)—Registration		
Registration requirement		
Section	**Description**	**Comments**
6(1)	Except otherwise provided in this Act, a person who is engaged in a ***taxable activity and is not registered*** for tax purposes shall register if	To demonstrate progress in the administration of VAT, the law ***does not refer to "retailers of goods"*** among the registration requirements—which started with VATAA 810.
(a)	at the end of ***any period of 12 or less months***, the person made, during that period, ***taxable supplies exceeding GH₵ 120,000***; or	
(b)	at the ***end of any month***, there are reasonable grounds to expect that that person will make taxable supplies in the ***next 12 or less months exceeding GH₵ 120,000.***	
(2)	Despite subsection (1), a person shall register if	
(a)	At the end of ***any period of 3 months***, the person made during that period, ***taxable supplies exceeding GH₵ 30,000***; and	
(b)	There are reasonable grounds to expect that the total value of ***taxable supplies*** made by that person during that period and to be made during the ***next consecutive nine months, will exceed GH₵ 120,000.***	
ss (7) to (6)	These refer to the powers of the ***Commissioner-General to register a person compulsorily*** and the obligation of taxpayers to register formally and comply with the provisions of the law.	

- ***Sustaining the increase in VAT Threshold:*** the enactment of VATAA (No. 2), 2015 (Act 904), as shown in ***Table 11.14***, was a ***conscious movement towards "indexation"*** of the annual turnover threshold. As noted, this is a common practice that is ***often linked to the rate of inflation*** or other business and economically relevant factors.
- ***Monthly proportions:*** the amendment (section 2[b]) has the ***normal proportional monthly estimates*** that can also prompt a registration, provided they indicate that the taxpayer will exceed the threshold by the end of the 12 months.

8. Increase in VAT Threshold—VAT (Amendment)(No.2) Act, 2015 (Act 904)

This amendment of the VAT Act, 2013 (Act 870) continued to increase the VAT threshold for all business entities. The policy of increasing the level of registration is consistent with aligning it to macroeconomic factors that, notably, include inflation.

Table 11.14: Further Increase VAT Threshold Level

VATAA (No. 2) 2015 (Act 904)		
Section 6 of Act 870 amended		
The VATA2013 (Act 870), referred to in this Act as the principal enactment, is amended in Section 6		
Section	**Description**	**Comments**
1(a)	by the ***substitution*** for subsection (1) of	A further increase in the ***VAT threshold amount***, consistent with the ***"indexation"*** to realistic values or amounts. As noted, this is often linked to the ***rate of inflation***, which may not necessarily be in the same ratio.
	"(1) Except as otherwise provided in this Act, a person who is engaged in a ***taxable activity*** and is ***not registered*** for tax purposes shall register if	
	a) at the ***end of any period of 12 or less months***, the person made, during that period, taxable supplies ***exceeding GHȻ 200,000.***	
	b) at the end of any month, there are reasonable grounds to expect that that person will make taxable supplies in the ***next 12 or less months exceeding GHȻ 200,000.***	
	c) at the end of any month, there are reasonable grounds to expect that that person will make taxable supplies in the next 12 or less months ***exceeding GHȻ 200,000.***".	
(b)	by the ***substitution*** for subsection (2) of	
	"(1) Despite subsection (1), a person ***shall register if***	
	(a) At the end of ***any period of 3 months,*** the person made, during that period, taxable supplies ***exceeding GHȻ 500,000.***	
	(b) There are reasonable grounds to expect that the total value of taxable supplies made by that person ***during that period*** and to be made during the ***next consecutive 9 months*** will ***exceed GHȻ 200,000.***".	
2	Section 57 of Act 870 ***amended***	
	"(1) The Minister shall set aside an amount not more than ***6 per cent of the total revenue collected*** under this Act and any other enactment administered by the Commissioner-Genera, in an account designated as the ***GRA Refund Account***"."	The policy was to increase the amount to cater for ***all (not just VAT) refunds.***

- ***Non-small entity provision (retention for VAT/tax refunds):*** VATAA 904 is also an important tax policy provision (Section 2) that increased the proportion of revenue collected that ***GRA could retain to meet refund claims for all taxes—not just VAT***. Nonetheless, ***VAT remained the main impetus***, given the regular nature of refunds to the effective implementation of VAT, notable for taxpayers who are exporters.

Table 11.15 reiterates in numerical terms that, in principle, ***small entity non-registration lowers the consumer price***, with the difference of GH₵ 90 also being the reduction in the tax burden for the consumers.

Table 11.15: Conventional VAT Registration Threshold

Exemption: conventional threshold							
Entity	Value Added (ex-Tax)	Cumm. Value Added	Output VAT	Input VAT		Net VAT	Consumer Price
				Allowed	Denied		
Importer	1000	1000	175	0	0	175	1175
Manufacturer	800	1800	315	175	0	140	2115
Wholesaler	600	2400	420	315	0	105	2820
Retailer	400	3220	0	0	420	0	3220
Consumer	2800					420	3220
Standard rate	17.5%			Exempt		na	

- The ***proportional amount of tax relief is the lowest*** because the value added at the final distribution stage is also the lowest. In many instances, the small retailer of goods or service providers in this state buy their goods for resale or for rendering services from larger retailers—instead of wholesalers.

9. Application of VFRS to Wholesalers—VAT (Amendment) Act, 2017 (Act 948)

Following this effort at devising a common regime for small entities, the decision to use of VAT (Amendment) Act 2017 (Act 948) to extend the small-entity scheme to ***wholesalers of goods is very unconventional*** for both direct and indirect tax policy.

- ***Application of the threshold rule to non-small entities:*** The purpose of amending VAT Act, 2013 (Act 870) to extend the VFRS to ***"wholesalers of goods"*** is non-conventional since, in principle, they are usually large entities that can keep proper tax records.

- "The VAT Act, 2013 (Act 870), referred to in this Act as the "principal enactment", is amended in section 3—

  (a) by the ***substitution*** for subsection (2) of

  "(2) A taxable person who is a ***"retailer or wholesaler of goods"*** shall account for the VAT payable under this section at a ***flat rate of three (3) percent,*** calculated on the value of the taxable supply.", and

  (b) the ***insertion*** of subsection (2), of

  "(3) Subsection (2) does not apply to the supply of goods specified under section 27."

Section ***27 of VAT Act 2013 (Act 870) defines as*** "The supply of any form of power, heat, refrigeration or ventilation is a supply of goods".

- ***Reversal of Act VAT Act 810 and VAT Act 870:*** the essence of VAT Act 810 was to apply the threshold to a***ll entities and also increase the qualifying annual and quarterly threshold amounts*** for registering to charge VAT and claim ITC. Hence, VAT Act 948 had ***two (2) major anomalies,*** namely,

  - reversal of the restriction that applied the VAT registration threshold to ***only "retailers of goods"*** **between 1998 and 2010; and**

  - making it worse by extending a "small-entity" policy to ***"wholesalers of goods"*** that should keep proper records.

Note that this ***major shift in policy*** after the comprehensive repeal of VAT Act 546 by the VAT Act 2013 (Act 870) and the use of VAT Act 810 to ***increase the threshold significantly*** (in terms of the redenominated currency).

Finally, it must be noted that many countries adopt the conventional approach of applying the registration threshold to all small entities making taxable supplies (of goods and/or services) to lower compliance and administration costs.

10. Summary of the Impact of VRFS

Initially, the ***VAT Flat Rate Scheme (VFRS)*** applied the lower VAT sub-standard rate of 3 per cent to only ***"retailers of goods"*** until the addition of ***wholesalers of goods*** under the ***VAT (Amendment) Act, 2017 (Act 948).*** This meant that larger entities that can keep both income tax and VAT records, file returns and be accountable for all tax obligations.

- ***Retailers:*** prior to the VAT Act 810, ***retailers of goods*** that operate below the VAT conventional or VFRS threshold are not obliged to register and cannot charge VAT or claim ITC. The larger retailers must register and meet all VAT obligations.
- ***Wholesalers:*** from 2017 to 2021, ***all wholesalers of goods,*** whether large or small, were added to the VFRS and were required to ***charge VAT at the flat 3 per cent sub-standard rate*** (without recourse to ITC/refund).
- ***Manufacturers:*** in principle, small manufacturers with taxable supplies below the registration threshold were ineligible to register for VAT—neither can they charge VAT nor claim ITC'
- ***Service providers***: as with small manufacturers, the small service providers are ineligible to register for VAT—they can neither charge VAT nor claim ITC.

Hence, for a ***long period from 1998 to 2010,*** Ghana did not apply the general threshold registration policy to all small entities that supplied both goods and services. It was only after the enactment of the VAT (Amendment) Act, 2010 (Act 810) that this common practice became a feature of the country's VAT regime. The following is a summary of some complications and options under the current small-entity VAT registration or non-registration regime in Ghana.

11. Modified [Presumptive] Tax: Income Tax Act (ITA) 2015 (Act 896)

The ***Modified Taxation Scheme*** under Section 1[5], Schedule (2) of ITA 2015 (Act 896) allowed ***the VAT threshold and 3 per cent sub-standard rate to apply to the presumptive income tax regime.*** As noted later, this move appears to have been ***reversed in 2017*** and replaced with the VFRS II, as discussed in earlier sections.

The ***Income Tax Act (ITA) 896 (s1[5], Schedule II*** has two ***Modified Tax*** options, namely (a) ***Presumptive Tax*** scheme (***3 per cent)***; and

(b) ***Modified Cash*** accounting scheme that aims at simplifying the overall tax compliance for small taxpayers.

- The passage of ***ITA 896 in 2015 occurred after VATAA 2010 (Act 810) and VATA 2013 (Act 870) had restored the conventional threshold for all taxpayers*** and started to ***index the amount against inflation.***
- ***Concurrent with the modified taxation provisions in ITA 2015 (Act 896),*** Parliament passed ***VATAA 2015 (Act 904)*** to adjust the VAT threshold to the GH₵ 200,000 value used for the ***presumptive income tax in the ITA.***

Hence, the ***main policy added*** to the small-entity VAT option is the effort to ***integrate the small-entity income tax and VAT presumptive tax rules*** with reference to the threshold values and VAT sub-standard (3 per cent) rate.

- ***Principles of modified taxation***: these include non-registration for VAT under the specified turnover values. Table 11.16 to Table 11.20 reproduce the ITA 896 provisions—to represent the ***principles*** underlying the modified taxation (presumption tax and cash basis).

The provisions assume that SMEs conduct business on a ***"cash basis" with minimal or no records***—at best on a ***"semi-accrual" basis***—rather than on a full "accrual" accounting basis.

Table 11.16: Modified Tax Principles and Presumptive Tax Scheme

Income Tax Act, 2015 (Act 896): Section 1(5), Schedule 2			
Modified Taxation (Section 1[5])			
Schedule	**Item**	**Description**	**Comments**
1	**Principles of modified taxation**		**Section 1(5):** Income tax payable by an individual with respect to assessable income from a business may be subject ot the modified taxation rules set out in the 2nd Schedule
	The Schedule modifies the taxation of eligible resident individuals by		
	a) imposing a presumptive tax on individuals that only have income from the businesses specified in paragraphs 3 and 4; and		
	b) applying a modified cash basis in calculating income from the businesses specified in paragraph 5.		

- ***Presumptive tax scheme***: Recall again that at the time ITA 896 was passed, VATA 870 had abolished VFRS (with its GH₵ 10,000 second-tier VAT registration threshold) and replaced it with a conventional GH₵ 120,000 annual turnover threshold.

Table 11.17 bridges the gap between the two amounts, ***resulting in a unified VATA [threshold] and small-entity regime [presumptive] income tax scheme.***

Table 11.17: Modified Taxation (Presumptive Tax Scheme)

Income Tax Act, 2015 (Act 896): Section 1(5), Schedule 2			
Schedule	**Item**	**Description**	**Comments**
2	**Presumptive Taxation**		
2(1)	a) the chargeable income of a resident individual for a year of assessment consists exclusively of income from a business;		Income tax bases
	b) the income is exclusively from sources within Ghana; and		
	c) the invidual		
	(i) is not registered for VAT purposes and has an annual turnover of not more than Ghc 20,000 from the business, computed as an average of the turnover for 3 consecutive years ending in the year of assessment; or		Cross-reference to VAT registration threshold criteria.
	(ii) has an annual turnover of more thatn Ghc20,000 from the business and is not required to register for VAT purposes.		
2(2)	For purposes of subparagraph (1c) where the average turnover of an individual is not available for the period specified, the CG may determine how the turnover is to be calculated.		Power of CG determine qualification to register

- ***Integrating VAT and income tax presumptive schemes***: Despite the policy to integrate, the lower ITA threshold of GH₵ 20,000 Schedule II, Par. 2(1)[c{i}] appears to show a continuing policy ambivalence with VFRS.
- It implies ***eligibility to pay income tax under the regular or instalment options under ITA*** FOR small entities with turnover between GH₵ 20,000 and the VAT registration threshold of GH₵ 120,000;
- It enhances the GH₵ 10,000 and GH₵ 90,000 bracket under VATAA 2010 (Act 810) and the upper limit of GH₵ 120,000 under VATA 2013 (Act 870).
- ***Power of Commissioner-General (CG):*** Where the application of the rules is unclear, the CG has the power to issue an enforceable ruling on presumptive tax.
- ***Exclusion of specific taxpayers and sectors from presumptive income tax***: As Table 11.18 shows, Schedule II [Paragraph 3] of ITA 896 restricts the entities that appear capable of keeping records from registering for the presumptive tax.

Table 11.18: Specific exclusions from income tax presumptive scheme

Income Tax Act, 2015 (Act 896): Section 1(5), Schedule 2			
Schedule	Item	Description	Comments
3	Exclusions from presumptive tax		
3(1)	The following are excluded from Presumptive taxation under paragraph 4 & 5, even if they meet the requirements of paragraph 2 (above):		
	an individual who (a) has a professional qualification; (b) is engaged in a regulated business, with a high profit or turnover ratio; (c) has more than 1 business; (d) has a business with more than 1 business outlet; and (e) in a partnership; & (e) elects to disapply pars 4 & 5 for a year of assessment.		Income tax regulations
3(2)	where a person elects to disapply paragraphs 4 and 5 shall not apply to that individual for that year of assessment and the following 5 years of assessment		

- ***Presumptive tax (income and turnover bases)***: Given that VATA 870 does not impose a sub-standard rate, Table 11.19 appears to imply a compromise in having a ***single 3 per cent rate or presumptive assessment*** to fulfil both VAT and income tax obligations.

Table 11.19: Presumptive tax (income and turnover bases)

Income Tax Act, 2015 (Act 896), Schedule 2		
Schedule	**Item & Description**	**Comments**
2(4)	**Presumptive tax (based on instalments)**	
	Where presumptive taxation is under par. 2(1) (c)(i), the tax payable for a year of assessment under s1(1)(a) is the total of instalments payable by that individual for a year of assessment under Section 121.	The individual is not registered for VAT; and an annual estimate of tax is payable quarterly
2(5)	**Presumptive tax (based on turnover)**	
	Where presumptive taxation is under par 2(1) (c)(ii), the tax payable for a year of assessment under s1(1)(a) is 3 per cent of the turnover of the business, where the turnover is more than Ghc20,000 but does not exceed Ghc120,000	Introduced a sub-standard rate & 2nd quantitative registration band.

- ***Modified cash basis:*** As summarized in Table 11.20, ITA 896 (Schedule II, Par. 6(1) taxpayers with turnover below the VAT registration threshold limit of GH₵ 120,000 ***can apply to use the basic cash (other than accrual) accounting option.*** The other option under Paragraph 6(2) is based on assessable income tax, not turnover. Paragraph 6(3) enumerates exceptions that specify ineligible business activities.

Table 11.20: Modified cash basis (with VAT Overlap)

Income Tax (Amendment) Act, 2015 (Act 902), Schedule 2		
Second Schedule to Act 896 amended		
Schedule	**Item & Description**	**Comments**
2	The principal enactment is amended in the Second Schedule	
	(a) by the substitution for paragraph 5 of	
	Presumptive tax based on turnover	
5	Where presumptive taxation applies to an individual, as referred to in paragraph 2(1)(c)(ii), the tax payable by the individual for a year of assessment under section 1(1)(a) I is three (3) per cent of the turnover of the business, where the turnover is more than Ghc20,000 but does not exceed Ghc200,000 and	Adjustments reflect similar changes in the VAT Act 2013
	(b) by the substitution for paragraph 6(1)(b) of	
	Modified cash basis	
6(b)	"The turnover of that individual does not exceed Ghc200,000, calculated using the modified cash basis.	Adjustments reflect similar changes in the VAT Act 2013

12. Increase in Registration Threshold [VATA 870 and ITA 896]

The revision in the threshold values is to ***compensate for inflation since 2013 (VATA 870)*** and to bring the real value of the threshold to the equivalent of US$50,000. As discussed in Table 11.19 and Table 11.21 below, given the ***policy decision to integrate the small entity income tax and VAT regimes,*** Parliament passed the ***complementary VAT (Amendment) Act, 2015 (Act 904) and ITA (Amendment), 2015 (Act 902).***

- *VAT (Amendment) Act 2015 (Act 904):* The Act increased the registration threshold values to GH₵ 200,000 as the basis for registration, charging Output VAT, claiming ITC, and paying Net VAT. The provisions are summarized in Tables 9.21 and Table 11.22.

Table 11.21: Increase in Conventional VAT Turnover Threshold

VAT(Amendment) Act, 2015 (Act 904)			
Registration: Section 6, VAT Act, 2013 (Act 870) amended			
Section	**Item**	**Description**	**Comments**
6(1)	**Registration requirement**	Except as otherwise provided in this Act, a ***person*** who is ***engaged in a taxable activity and is not registered*** for tax purposes shall register if	Taxable Activity isdefined in Section 5
(a)	at the ***end of any period of 12 or less months***, the person made, during that period, ***taxable supplies exceding*** two hundred thousand Ghana Cedis ***(Ghc200,000)***; or		Ghc200,000 taxable supplies for any period of 12 months or less)
(b)	at the ***end of any month***, there are reasonable grounds to expect that that ***person will make taxable supplies*** in the ***next 12 or less months exceeding*** two hundred thousand Ghana Cedis ***(Ghc200,000)***		Ghc200,000 (taxable supplies at the end of any periods)

Table 11.22 shows the VATAA 2013 provisions or guidance on monthly and quarterly turnover amounts that indicate a potential obligation to register.

Table 11.22: Monthly and Quarterly indicative amounts

VAT (Amendment) Act, 2017 (Act 948)			
Registration: Section 6, VAT Act, 2013 (Act 870) amended			
Section	**Item**	**Description**	**Comments**
6(2)	**Registration requirement**	Despite subsection (1), a person shall register if	Monthly and quarterly rules
(a)	at the end of any period of ***three (3) month*** s, the person made, during that period, taxable supplies ***exceeding fifty thousand Ghana cedis (Ghc50,000***); and		Ghc50,000 (taxable supplies end of any period of 3 months)
(b)	there are reasonable grounds to expect that the total value of taxable supplies made by that person during that period and to be made during the ***next consecutive nine (9) month*** s will exceed ***two hundred thousand Ghana Cedis (Ghc200,000)***.		Ghc200,000 (taxable supplies during the next consecutive 9 months)

- ***Income Tax (Amendment) Act, 2015 (Act 902):*** Table 11.23 shows the small-entity presumptive and modified cash adjustments that complement VATAA 2015 (Act 904).

Table 11.23: Presumptive tax amendment (ITAA, 2015 (Act 902) based on turnover.

Income Tax Act, 2015 (Act 896): Section 1(5), Schedule 2			
Second Schedule to Act 896 amended			
Schedule	**Item**	**Description**	**Comments**
2	The principal enactment is amended in the Second Schedule		
	(a) by the substitution for paragraph 5 of		
	Presumptive tax based on turnover		
5	Where presumptive taxation applies to an individual, as referred in paragraph 2(1)(c)(ii), the tax payable by the individual for a year of assessment under section 1(1)(a) is three (3) percent of the turnover of the business, where the turnover is more than Ghc20,000 but does not exceed Ghc200,000; and		Adjustments reflect similar changes in VATA 2013.
	(b) by the substitution for paragraph 6(1)(b) of		
	Modified cash basis		
6(b)	"the turnover of that individual does not exceed Ghc200,000 cedis, calculated using the modified cash basis.		Adjustments reflect similar changes in VATA 2013.

13. VAT and Earmarked Funds, Straight Levies, and VFRS

The options discussed so far group VAT entities under various ***standard, substandard, and zero rates as well as liberal exempt provisions and levies,*** which include a mix of turnover taxes and excise duties. They worsen the adverse effects of blocking ITCs and refunds for VAT-registered entities. Table 8.20 illustrates the complex outcome of imposing various standard and sub-standard rates in addition to other schemes that block ITC and refunds.

- ***VAT, "Straight" Levies (GETFund Levy /NHIL) and VFRS:*** Table 8.19 is complex because it adds ***large wholesalers and retailers*** to the 3 per cent VFRS regime—even though they ***operate above the conventional turnover threshold.*** Their inclusion in the VFRS without recourse to ITC claims, was discussed earlier in this and other chapters.

Table 8.19: VAT, Straight Levies (GETFund Levy /NHIL) and VFRS

Mixed VFRS 3% (wholesale/retail); VAT/GIFF 12.5% (importer/manufacturer); Straight Levies (5 percent)											
ITC denied for Straight Levies (GETFund & NHIL) and VFRS											
			Output VAT/Levy			Input VAT/Levy					
Entity	V-A (ex-Tax)	Total V-Added	GF/NHIL	Total Value + GETFund/Levy	VAT/GIIF	GF/NHIL	Total Value + GETFund/ Levy	VAT/GIIF	Net VAT	Final Price	Comments
		A	B	C=(A+B)*5%	D=C*12.5%						
Importer	1000	1000	50	1050	131	0	0	0	181	1181	ITC: VAT/GIIF allowed; GF/NHIL denied
Manufacturer	800	1850	93	1943	243	50	1050	131	204	2054	
Wholesaler	600	2785	NIL	2785	84	NIL	NIL	NIL	84	2869	ITC: VFRS & GF/NHIL(Straight levies) denied
Retailer	400	3269		3269	98	NIL	NIL	NIL	98	3367	
Consumer	2800								567		
											Note (VFRS): any size of retail or wholesale entity cannot claim ITC
Rates	VAT/GIIF	12.50%			VFRS	3%			GF/NHIL	5%	
	Allowed				Denied				Denied		

To stress, ***any Input VAT that is denied as ITC is added to cost*** by registered entities which, ultimately, increases consumer prices. Hence, Table 8.19 leads to a higher consumer price of GH₵ 3,367 (compared to GH₵ 3,290) and tax burden of GH₵ 567 (compared to GH₵ 490) because of the multiple denials of ITC [i.e., Straight Levy and VFRS] that aggravates the cascading and a high tax burden.

Table 8.20: Complex standard, substandard, straight levy, VFRS & exempt regimes

Mixed VFRS 3% (wholesale/retail); VAT/GIFF 12.5% (importer); Straight Levies (5 percent); conventional exempt (manufacturer)											
ITC denied for Straight Levies (GETFund & NHIL) and VFRS											
			Output VAT/Levy			Input VAT/Levy					
Entity	V-A (ex-Tax)	Total V-Added	GF/NHIL	Total Value + GETFund/ Levy	VAT/GIIF	GF/NHIL	Total Value + GETFund/ Levy	VAT/GIIF	Net VAT	Final Price	Comments
Importer	1000	1000	50	1050	131	0	0	0	181	1231	ITC allowed but zero
Manufacturer	800	1981	NIL	NIL	NIL	50	1050	131	0	1981	Exempt no ITC
Wholesaler	600	2581	NIL	NIL	77	NIL	NIL	NIL	77	2659	VFRS no ITC
Svc Provider	400	3059	153	3212	401	0	0	0	554	3613	Standard
Consumer	2800								813	3613	
Rates	VAT/GIIF	12.50%		VFRS	3%	GF/NHIL	5%	Exempt	N/A		
	Allowed			Denied							

The complexity leading to a higher consumer price (GH₵ 3613 compared to GH₵ 3290) and tax burden (GH₵ 813 compared to GH₵ 490) continues because of the worsening of cascading and denial of ITC from various distortionary policies [i.e., Straight Levy, VFRS and exempt].

- ***VAT, Straight Levies (GETFund Levy/NHIL), VFRS and exports:*** The discussions to this point show that the ***original VFRS*** applied to only small (retail) entities. Secondly, for example, service providers at various points on the value addition chain may be ineligible to register because their sales fall below the annual threshold. An overall point is that cascading arises when registered entities are not able to secure VAT invoices to claim ITC.

  Indeed, as Table 8.21 shows, exporters fall victim to the complex structures that worsen the VAT regime. While they may register and charge VAT at a zero rate, the right to credit or refund is blocked if the purchaser (e.g., a VFRS wholesaler) is not registered or the commodity is exempt or not taxable.

Table 8.21: ***VAT, Straight Levies (GETFund Levy/NHIL), VFRS II and exports***

VFRS II; mix 3 percent, 17.5 percent & zero-rated regimes											
Mixed standard/sub-standard rates, VFRS & export VAT structure											
Entity	V-A (ex-Tax)	Total V-Added	Output VAT/Levy			Input VAT/Levy			Net VAT	Final Price	Comments
			GF/NHIL	Total Value + GETFund/Levy	VAT/GIIF	GF/NHIL	Total Value + GETFund/Levy	VAT/GIIF			
Importer	1000	1000	50	1050	131	0	0	0	181	1181	ITC allowed for VAT/GIIF;
Manufacturer	800	1850	93	1943	243	50	1050	131	204	2054	disallowed for GF/NHIL
Wholesaler	600	2785	N/A	N/A	84	N/A	N/A	N/A	84	2869	VFRS; ITC disallowed
Exporter	400	3269	163	3432	0		0	0	163	3432	Zero-rated; ITC allowed but no
Consumer	2800								632	3432	VAT invoice from wholesaler for
											ITC claim
Rates	VAT/GIIF	12.50%		VFRS	3%	GF/NHIL	5%	Zero-rated	0		
	Allowed				Denied			Allowed			

The outcomes of a final price of ***GHȻ 3432 (compared to GHȻ 3290) and tax burden of GHȻ 632 (compared to zero [0])*** may generate fiscal revenues, provided it does not also lead to tax evasion and avoidance. These ***outcomes make Ghana's exports or external trade non-competitive*** in foreign or destination markets. Since zero rating is globally common, countries implementing it provide relief for exports while Ghanaian exports cede the VAT advantage to competing states.

14. Conclusions

The VFRS was a major but not necessarily consistent with invoice-credit VAT method best practice since it has an equally major distortionary impact on the VAT regime—notably, its extension to larger wholesalers and retailers, which element has since been reversed. The effort at correction led to the restoration of the conventional VAT threshold regime, with the passage of ***VAT 2013 (Act 870)***.

A second effort was made to implement a ***single small-entity VAT and presumptive income tax regime*** by making the VAT threshold the basis for a single 3 per cent rate for VAT and income tax commitments for small entities. Despite the merits of VATA 870, a VAT amendment in 2017 restored VFRS I and was extended to all ***wholesalers and retailers, with no recourse to ITC.***

The distortion worsened with the decoupling of ***NHIA and GETFund levies*** from the VAT base, as ***"straight" levies***—also without recourse to ITC. It calls for an update of the GRA VFRS Guidelines since this policy ***increases the number of "excise-type"*** **taxes and levies increase cascading and multiple taxation.**

Countries apply the ***flat rate or presumptive tax regimes*** to the informal sector ***small entities*** that cannot keep adequate income tax and VAT records. However, with the policy change, larger entities that registered and charged the standard 17.5 (or 12.5) per cent VAT rate and claimed VAT ITC had to comply with the VFRS without that privilege. Consequently, input costs increase because VFRS (a) blocks ITC without (b) repealing the conventional threshold; and (c) continues to cover all service providers and manufacturers.

These policy measures make the VAT structure, administration and compliance complex and increase the tax burden and consumer prices. They promote tax evasion and avoidance and have virtually no significant boost to fiscal revenues since 2017. The inefficiencies arising from a dual VFRS and conventional regime undermine the use of the VAT threshold to simplify tax compliance among registered and non-registered entities.

Appendix Table 11.1

Income Tax Act [ITA], 2015 (Act 896) Section 1[5]
Second (2nd) Schedule—Modified Taxation

Section	Heading	Description	Comments
Income Tax Act, 2015 (Act 896)—s1[5], 2nd Schedule			
Second Schedule [Modified Taxation]			
Principles of modified taxation			
1.	This Schedule modifies the taxation of eligible resident individuals by:		
(a)	imposing a ***presumptive tax*** on individuals that only have income from the businesses specified in paragraphs 3 and 4; and		
(b)	applying a ***modified cash basis*** in calculating income from the businesses specified in paragraph 5.		
Presumptive taxation			
2 (1)	Presumptive taxation applies where—		
(a)	the ***chargeable income*** of a ***resident individual*** for a year of assessment consists exclusively of income from a business;		
(b)	the income is ***exclusively from sources within Ghana***; and		
(c)	the individual (i) is ***not registered for Value Added Tax (VAT)*** purposes and has an ***annual turnover of not more than twenty thousand cedis (GH₵ 20,000)*** from the business, computed as ***an average of the turnover for 3 consecutive years*** ending in the year of assessment; or (ii) has an ***annual turnover of more than twenty thousand cedis (GH₵ 20,000)*** from the business and is ***not required to register*** for Value Added Tax (VAT) purposes.		
(2)	For purposes of sub-paragraph (1)(c), where the average turnover of an individual is not available for the period specified, the Commissioner-General may determine how the turnover is to be calculated.		
Exclusion from presumptive tax			
3(1)	The following ***individuals are excluded from presumptive taxation*** under paragraphs 4 and 5, even if they meet the requirements of paragraph 2:		
(a)	an individual who has a professional qualification;		
(b)	an individual who is engaged in a business prescribed by regulations that has a high profit-to-turnover ratio;		
(c)	an individual who has a business with more than one business;		
(d)	an individual who has a business with more than one business outlet;		

(e)	an individual in a partnership; and
(f)	an individual who elects to disapply paragraphs 4 and 5 for a year of assessment.
(2)	Where ***an individual elects*** to disapply paragraphs 4 and 5, shall not apply to that individual for that year of assessment and the following five years of assessment but that individual may qualify for modified cash basis taxation under paragraph 6.
Presumptive tax on instalments	
4	Where ***presumptive taxation*** applies to a***n individual*** as referred to in paragraph 2(1)(c)(i), the tax payable by that individual for a year of assessment under section 121.
Presumptive tax based on turnover	
5	Where ***presumptive taxation applies to an individual*** as referred to in paragraph 2(1)(c)(ii), the tax payable by that individual for a year of assessment under section 1(a) is ***three (3) per cent of the turnover of the business***, where the turnover is more than twenty thousand cedis ***(GH₵ 20,000)*** but does ***not exceed*** one hundred and twenty thousand cedis ***(GH₵ 121,000).***
Modified cash basis	
6(1)	The ***modified cash basis*** under sub-paragraph (2) applies where
(a)	The ***assessable income*** of a resident individual for ***a year of assessment*** from all businesses conducted by that individual consists exclusively of income from sources in the country; and
(b)	The turnover of that individual does ***not exceed one hundred and twenty thousand cedis (GH₵ 120,000),*** calculated using the modified cash basis.
(2)	Where the ***modified cash basis*** applies as referred to in sub-paragraph (1), the income of an individual from a business for a year of assessment shall be calculated—
(a)	According to ***the standard rules*** for calculating income from a business; and
(b)	Using the ***modified cash basis*** of accounting.
(3)	For the purpose of ***sub-paragraph (2)(b)***, sections 17, 21(4), 25, 26 and 31 do not apply to the calculation of the income of an individual from a business for a year of assessment.
(4)	In this Schedule, ***"turnover for a business for a year"*** means the amount derived from the business during the year that is required to be included in calculating income from the business under section 5(2)(a), (i)(ii) and (vii) only.

Date of Assent: 1st September, 2015

Appendix 9.2

GHANA REVENUE AUTHORITY (GRA)

Practice Note on

The Application of VAT Flat Rate Scheme (VFRS) under The Value Added Tax Act, 2013 (ACT 870)

Practice Note Number: IDT/017/001

Date of Issue: 12/05/2017

Contents

6. Tax Law

This Practice Note applies to the supply of goods by a taxable person who is a retailer or a wholesaler and it is based on Section 3(2) of the Value Added Tax Act, 2013 (Act 870) as amended by VAT (Amendment) Act, 2017 (Act 948).

7. Interpretation

In this Practice Note, the word 'Act' means the Value Added Tax Act, 2013 (Act 870) as amended. Definitions and expressions used in this Practice Note have the same meaning as they are in the Act.

- ***VAT Flat Rate Scheme:*** A VAT Flat Rate Scheme (VFRS) is a VAT collection and accounting mechanism under which a registered taxpayer who is a retailer or wholesaler of goods applies a marginal VAT&NHIL rate of 3% on the value of taxable goods supplied. The marginal rate of 3% represents the net VAT payable and is the difference between the output tax and the input tax of a wholesaler or retailer if the taxpayer were operating the Standard Rate Scheme.

Thus, it should be noted that the VFRS is ***an alternative to the invoice-credit (or input-output) method*** of VAT accounting.

- *Retailing and Wholesaling of Goods "Definition of Terms"*
    - ***Retail:*** To sell by small parcels, and not in the gross. To sell in small quantities.
    - [Case law examples: State vs Lowenhaught, 11 Lea (Tenn.) 13; Bridges vs. State, 37 Ark, 224; McArthur vs. State, 69 Ga. 444; Com vs Kimball, 7 Mete (Mass.) 308] - ***(Black's Law Dictionary)***
    - ***Retailer:*** A person or business selling goods to the public as against a person or business selling to another business for resale - ***(Black's Law Dictionary)***
    - ***Wholesale:*** To sell by wholesale is to sell by large parcel, generally in original packages, and not by retail - ***(Black's Law Dictionary)***
    - ***Wholesaler:*** A person or company purchasing large amounts of stock from several producers and then reselling to retailers - ***(Black's Law Dictionary).***

The Integrated Compliance Information System (ICIS) dictionary also defines Retailing and Wholesaling as follows:

- *"**Retailing:*** As defined by the ICIS Dictionary, Retailing is the resale (sale without transformation) of new and used goods mainly to the public for personal or household consumption or utilization.

  This includes retailing by shops, department stores, stalls, mail-order houses, door-to-door salespersons, hawkers and peddlers, consumer cooperatives, auction houses etc."

- *"**Wholesaling:*** As defined by the same dictionary, wholesale is the resale (sale without transformation) of new and used goods to retailers, industrial, commercial, institutional or professional users, or to other wholesalers. The major characteristic of wholesalers is that they physically assemble, sort and grade goods in large lots, break bulk, repack and redistribute in smaller quantities."

The definitions ***above also apply to importers*** who ***either resell*** their goods to retailers (in which case they should be classified as wholesalers) or to consumers directly (in which case they should be classified as retailers). In either case, they are obliged by the (amendment) Act 948 to charge VAT/NHIL at 3% on their taxable supplies. Such importers will, however, continue to pay VAT/NHIL at importation at the standard rate of 17.5 per cent.

- The Purpose of this Practice Note

  This practice note is to ***give clarity to the provisions of the law on the supply of goods*** by retailers and wholesalers as provided for in ***section 3(2) of the VAT Act, 2013 (Act 870) as amended,*** and to bring about consistency in the administration of the Act. It is also intended to ***address administrative and operational challenges*** that may arise from the interpretation and scope of the VAT Flat Rate Scheme.

- **Application of this Practice Note**
- *Scope and coverage of the VAT Flat Rate Scheme*
- The VFRS is ***restricted to wholesalers and retailers of taxable goods and does not cover manufacturers, service providers, etc.*** as provided for by section 3(2) of VAT Act) 870 as amended by VAT (Amendment) Act, 2017 (Act 948) viz: A ***taxable person***

who is a retailer or wholesaler of goods shall account for the Value Added Tax payable under this section at a ***flat rate of 3%*** calculated on the value of the taxable supply.

- It covers the ***supply of all taxable goods,*** except the supply of any form of power, heat, refrigeration or ventilation (see section 1 (b) of VAT (Amendment) Act, 2017 (Act 948).
- All other provisions relating to the supply of goods under the VAT Act, 2013 (Act 870) and L.I. 2243 shall apply appropriately to the VFRS, ***except the right to deduct input tax***: VFRS operators are, therefore, ***not entitled to input tax credit*** as provided for in section 48(7A) of Act 870 as ***amended*** by VAT Act 948 as follows:

  "A taxable person to whom subsection (2) of section 3 applies does not qualify for an input tax deduction in respect of a supply of goods".

- ***Wholesalers and retailers*** of taxable goods who are currently registered to operate the Standard Rate Scheme (SRS) are to be ***automatically converted*** to the VFRS.
- ***Some features of the VFRS:*** The ***VFRS is differentiated from the standard VAT scheme*** by the under-listed features:
  - It has a ***marginal tax rate of 3 per cent*** applied to the value of the taxable supply of goods.
  - It ***does not allow input tax credit*** i.e. VFRS operators shall not be entitled to input tax claims.
  - It is ***restricted to only wholesalers and retailers*** of taxable goods.
  - Taxpayers operating the VFRS shall issue a ***simplified VAT/NHIL invoice.***
- **Mechanics of the VFRS**

The VFRS applies a ***marginal tax percentage of 3 per cent*** on the value of taxable goods supplied. The marginal tax percentage ***represents the net VAT rate*** on the value of the taxable goods supplied. The VFRS ***does not therefore allow recovery of input tax.***

- ***Illustration 1: Computing the VAT payable under the VFRS GH₵***
  - Cost price of item - 100.00

- Input Tax (17.5%*100) - 17.50
- Value Added (10% *117.50) (i.e., margin & other overheads)-11.75
- Taxable Value (a+b+c) - 129.25
- Output tax @ 3% Flat Rate - 3.8
- VAT/NHIL payable (i.e., 3% Flat Rate) - 3.88
- Cost to Consumer (tax inclusive) (d+f) - 133.13

- ***Illustration 2: Extracting the Tax from the Inclusive Amount:*** Normally, VAT-registered taxpayers prefer to quote the final prices of their wares (i.e., price to the consumer) at their tax-inclusive values. It would therefore not be uncommon for VFRS operators to do the same. To obtain the tax from the tax-inclusive value of an item sold under the VFRS therefore, the ***VFRS fraction (3/103)*** is applied to the tax-inclusive amount. Therefore, for the ***VFRS tax inclusive*** amount of (GH₵ 133.13) above,

  The tax = (= 3/103 x GHÂ¢133.13) = (= GHÂ¢3.88)

  - ***Illustration 3 Splitting the Tax Amount into VAT & NHIL:*** It should be noted that the 3% marginal Flat Rate consists of both VAT and NHIL.
    - To obtain VAT from the tax amount, the fraction 6/7 is applied to the tax amount. Therefore,
      - VAT = (GH₵ 3.88 x 6/7) = GH₵ 3.33)
      - To obtain the NHIL from the tax amount, the fraction 1/7 is applied to the tax amount. Therefore,
      - NHIL = (GH₵ 3.88x1/7) = (GH₵ 0.55)

- ***Migration of Taxpayers to VFRS***

VAT/NHIL certificates of registration issued under the standard VAT scheme are still valid.

- To operate the ***special retail schemes,*** taxpayers already on a particular scheme should immediately apply to the Commissioner-General to get the initial authorisation regularised.

- Taxpayers granted the dispensation to ***use their own invoices*** (including computer-generated invoices, electronic cash register etc.) to adjust their systems to reflect the new rate and ***apply to*** the Commissioner-General for approval.
- VFRS taxpayers are required to ***submit/file monthly VFRS returns***. A special return form has been designed for this purpose, copies of which may be obtained from the GRA website or the nearest GRA office.
- Taxpayers are required to submit all ***outstanding VAT Returns relating to the Standard Rate Scheme*** prior to their migration to the VFRS to their respective tax offices.
- Taxpayers are also required to pay up all Outstanding VAT liabilities owed to the Commissioner General to avoid Interest & Penalties.
- Migrated taxpayers having ***outstanding VAT credit balances*** with the Commissioner General which are a result of input taxes on unsold stocks of goods, are to ***recover such credits*** as part of their cost build-up to the selling prices of the unsold stocks of goods.
- Ghana Revenue Authority will ensure that the said ***balances represented by the unsold stock*** are reflected in subsequent declarations by VRFS operators.
- All fully used Commissioner General's ***SRS VAT invoice booklets*** should be kept at the taxpayer's business premises for future audit purposes by authorised officers of GRA.
    - ***Partly used*** SRS VAT invoice booklets should also be sent to taxpayers' respective local tax offices for review. These would be returned to taxpayers after the review for keeps.
    - ***Unused Commissioner General's SRS VAT invoice*** booklets should be sent to the Taxpayer's local tax office to be replaced with VFRS invoices at NO COST.
- ***Situations where a Taxpayer is involved in a separate supply of Goods and Services***

  A taxpayer whose business operations span more than one sector (e.g., wholesale, Retail, Service or Manufacturing) and whose *supply of goods as retailer or wholesaler constitutes a separate and distinct supply from the other supplies* as anticipated by section 23 of the Act and Regulation 51 of the VAT Regulation, 2016 L.I. 2243, is required to account for the tax separately and file separate returns in respect of the wholesale/retail of goods (under the VFRS) and the other supplies (under the SRS).

Illustration: XYZ Motors sells (retails or wholesales) automobiles and also operates a motor vehicle servicing and repair shop on the same premises.

The operations of the *part of the business which sells vehicle parts are separate and distinct from the servicing and repairs section.* In other words, no part of the supply (sale of a motor vehicle or servicing and repairs of automobiles is incidental to the other.

In that case, the retail and wholesale parts of the business will be accounted for at the 3 % flat rate whereas the servicing and repairs portion will be accounted for under the SRS (at 17.5%). XYZ Motors will have to file ***separate returns*** in respect of the two schemes; SRS and VFRS.

- ***Treatment of Agency Fees Charged to Manufacturers or Producers by Their Agents for Distribution of Their Goods***

  In some instances, manufacturers/producers appoint agents to distribute or market their goods. Such agents charge a commission as consideration (either monetary such as a percentage of sales made, or the equivalent in goods) for the service rendered for the principal. Such commissions or agency fees are taxable at the standard rate of 17.5 per cent (%).

- ***Return Forms***

  Taxpayers of the nature discussed under item 4.5 above have the distinct obligation of accounting for SRS and VFRS supplies separately and as such filing separate monthly returns for the two schemes they operate. For purposes of filing in respect of VFRS, a new return has been designed (and attached, herewith, as Appendix I) for use by such taxpayers, as well as those who will be registered for or migrated to operate the VFRS.

- ***Record-Keeping Requirements***

  In order to facilitate the conduct of compliance activities by GRA, VFRS taxpayers are expected to maintain the required records in line with the relevant provisions of the VAT Act, 2013

(Act 870), as amended, and the VAT Regulations, 2016 (L. I. 2243).

- ***Effective Date of Implementation***

  The effective date of implementation of the (amendment) Act (Act 948) is June 1, 2017.

Appendix Table 3

VAT (Amendment) Act 2010 (VATAA (Act 810)

Table 11.6: VAT Flat Rate Scheme I [VFRS-1]

<table>
<tr><th>Section</th><th>Heading</th><th>Description</th><th>Comments</th></tr>
<tr><td colspan="4">VAT (Amendment) Act, 2010 (Act 810)</td></tr>
<tr><td colspan="4">An Act to amend the VAT, 1998 (Act 546) to revise and expand the coverage of the threshold for registration; and re-classify locally-produced pharmaceuticals, locally-produced textbooks and locally-manufacture agricultural machinery and tools as exempt supplies.</td></tr>
<tr><td colspan="4">Section 3 of Act 546 amended</td></tr>
<tr><td>1.</td><td colspan="3">The VAT Act, 1998 (Act 546) as amended and referred to in this Act as the principal enactment is further amended in Section 3 by the substitution for subsection (2) of</td></tr>
<tr><td>(2)</td><td colspan="2">A person to whom subsection (1)(b) of section 5 applies shall account for the VAT payable under this section at a <u>flat rate of 3%</u> calculated on the value of the taxable supply.</td><td></td></tr>
<tr><td colspan="4">Section 5 of Act 546 amended</td></tr>
<tr><td>2.</td><td colspan="2">The VAT Act, 1998 (Act 546) referred to in this Act as the principal enactment is amended in Section 5 by the substitution for subsection (1) of
"Re-registration as a taxable person
(1) A person is registrable as a taxable person if that person is a person who makes a taxable supply of goods or services and has a business turnover that exceeds
• GHC 90,000 over twelve months;
• GHC 67,500 over nine months;
• GHC 45,000 over six months; or
• GHC 22,500 over three months
whichever is achieved earliest."
(1) A person whose business turnover is below GHC 90,000 but exceeds GHC 10,000 over twelve months or a proportionate part thereof is registrable as a taxable person and shall charge and account for the tax as provided under sub-section (2) of section 3 of this Act."</td><td></td></tr>
<tr><td colspan="4">Section 25 of Act 546 amended</td></tr>
</table>

3.	Section 25 of the Principal enactment is amended by the deletion of subsection 1(b).	
Section 62 of Act 546 amended		
4.	Section 25 of the Principal enactment is amended by the substitution for section 62 of "Obstruction of Officer of the Service 62. A person who (a) obstructs the Commissioner or an Officer authorized by the Commissioner in the performance of functions under this Act; (b) assaults or refuses to grant access to that person's premises to the officer in the performance of functions; (c) breaks into any premises sealed under the warrant of the Commissioner; or (d) interferes with any property on which a warrant of distress has been executed commits an offence is liable on summary conviction to a fine of not less than 100 penalty units or more than 800 penalty units or 3 times the amount of tax or revenue involved, whichever is higher or to a term of imprisonment of not more than 5 years or both."	
First Schedule of Act 546 amended		
5.	**First Schedule** to the principal enactment is amended	
(a)	by the substitution for Item No.12 if "**12. Transportation** includes transportation by bus and similar vehicles, train, boat and air but excludes haulage and vehicle hiring"	
(b)	By the insertion after Item 24 of "***25. Pharmaceuticals*:** Locally produced pharmaceuticals as determined by the Minister for Health and approved by Parliament, ***25, Textbooks*** Locally produced pharmaceuticals as determined by the Minister for Health and approved by Parliament.	

	26. Agricultural machinery Locally manufactured agricultural machinery and other agricultural implements and tools."	
Second Schedule of Act 546 amended		
6.	The principal enactment is amended in the 2nd Schedule by the deletion of items numbered 3, 4 and 5	
L.I. 1817 revoked		
7.	The Ghana Investment Promotion Centre (Promotion of Tourism) Instrument 2005 (L.I. 1817) is hereby revoked	
8.	Section 25 of the principal enactment is amended by the deletion of sub-section (1)(b)	

Date of Assent: 31st December, 2010

PART IV

POLITICAL ECONOMY OF VAT

Chapter 12

ERP/SAP ERA RATIONALIZATION OF TAX POLICY AND INSTRUMENTS

1. Introduction

Under the National Revenue Secretariat (NRS) that preceded both the Revenue Agencies' [Governing] Board (RAGB) and the Ghana Revenue Authority (GRA), Ghana undertook several reforms of the tax structure. These involved semi-autonomy from the civil service to the income tax and customs agencies as well as assigning specific revenue and non-revenue goals to the various direct and indirect tax handles or instruments.

The initial action was the transfer of oversight of tax and customs operations from the Ministry of Finance (MOF) to NRS. The Secretariat led the semi-autonomy granted IRS and CEPS as well as various legislation on organization, policy and operations were taken through Cabinet and Parliament. The key elements include the following—

- **1985 to 2002:** as discussed in various chapters, there were reforms of the organization, systems and processes under the semi-autonomous tax-type Internal Revenue Service (IRS) and the Customs, Excise and Preventive Service (CEPS)—and, with the introduction of VAT, the VAT Service (VATS) in 1995;
- **2002 to 2009:** replacement of the three (3) supervisory Boards of Directors for IRS, CEPS and VATS a single Revenue Agencies' [Governing] Board—and, earlier, ministerial responsibility for agencies reverting to MOF
- **2009 to date:** setting up an apex-style executive structure in the form of Ghana Revenue Authority (GRA); merger of IRS and VATS as GRA's Domestic Revenue Tax Division (DTRD) and changing CEPS to GRA's Customs Division (CD); and
- **2016 to date:** consolidation of the common elements of direct and indirect administration and enforcement under a uniform Revenue Administration Act (RAA), 2016 (Act 915); and its overlap with VAT administration.

The NRS (and semi-autonomous IRS, CEPS and VATS), tax policy and downstream tax administration reforms were part of the macro-fiscal reforms under the Economic Reform Program (ERP) or Structural Adjustment Program Secretariat (SAP) reforms discussed in the next and final chapter. This was the case with several monetary, financial, public financial management and real sector reforms that were undertaken in the 1980s and 1990s.

2. Tax policy and tax structure reforms

As regards tax policy, the ERP/SAP reforms included a major rationalization of the revenue and non-revenue goals of the individual direct and indirect tax instruments. The reforms occurred in two (2) stages and continue to have non-revenue goals that include investment incentives, protection, and social intervention (e.g., progressive income tax rates, exempt supplies punitive regimes etc).

- **1985 to 1993:** the proper delineation of direct (i.e., income and property) tax from the indirect (consumption and protective) taxes as well as streamlining their foreign or external components, notably, import duty or customs regime; and
- **1993 to 2000:** the setting up of a VAT Project office to improve the general consumption tax regime, comprising sales and service taxes, resulted in the launch of the current VAT regime that dominated this period, suffered an early setback but has remained in existence for over 20 years.

The main elements of the structural changes are ***streamlining*** the ***revenue and non-revenue goals*** of the direct and indirect tax instruments, with the introduction of the VAT being its last episode for the era. As a comprehensive consumption tax instrument, VAT has a primary revenue focus and ***replaced the sales and service taxes*** under CEPS and IRS.

3. Fiscal framework

Tax policy, legislation and administration have fiscal, budget, and macroeconomic contexts that are ***based on the framework used to prepare the annual and multi-year Budget***.

- *Budget cycle:* The budget is the ***estimate or projection*** of revenues, expenditures and deficit or fiscal balances, borrowing or financing and the debt stock as the main elements.

- ***Revenues***: tax revenue is the substantive element of total revenues, with the other high-level components being non-tax revenues and grants.
- ***Expenditures***: the state uses the total revenues it generates to meet its total expenditure commitments that, at a high level, include—
    - ***recurrent expenditure:*** typically spent on the current fiscal year's recurring costs in the annual budget;
    - ***capital expenditure:*** these "project" or "programme" costs are multi-year and developmental and, hence, go beyond the current year;
- ***Budget deficit (fiscal balance):*** the strength of revenues determines the fiscal gap (i.e., deficit or fiscal balance) or difference between revenues and expenditures—with ***arrears*** being the difference between the deficit and fiscal balance.
- ***Financing (borrowing):*** in principle, the fiscal balances give the amount of government ***borrowing from domestic and external or foreign sources***—typically through loans and sales of government securities called treasury bills and bonds.
- ***Debt stock:*** the annual debt stock increases or decreases by a net amount which is the ***difference*** between the annual borrowing and the annual debt repayment or amortization.

The multi-year (3-year) "rolling" budget, which includes the current year's budget, is called the Medium-Term Expenditure Framework (MTEF) even though it covers projections of revenues, expenditures, and financing. Table 12.1 shows the fiscal framework in compact form.

Table 12.1: Overall Fiscal and Budget Framework

GHANA: OVERALL FISCAL FRAMEWORK [BUDGET CLASSIFICATION]			
High-level: revenue, expenditure, deficit & financing			
ITEMS	HEADING	CATEGORY	POLICY OBJECTIVES/COMMENTS
1	Revenues & grants		Tax & non-tax revenues & grants
1.1		Domestic revenue	Tax & non-tax revenues
1.2		Grants	Budget support from donors
2	Expenditures	Expenditure	Total exenditures
2.1	Recurrent expenditure		Current budget year expenditures
2.2	Capital expenditure		Multi-budget year expenditure
3	Budget Deficit	Revenue less expenditure	Usually negative
3.1	Routine arrears		Recurs annually
3.2	Exceptional arrears		Do not recur & may be multi-year
3.3	Discrepancy		Fiscal correction due to errors
4	Fiscal balance	Budget deficit plus arrears	Usually negative ()
5	Financing		Borrowing to finance budget deficit (3)
5.1	Foreign		Borrowing from outside Ghana
5.2	Domestic		Borrowing within Ghana
5.3	Other		Domestic or foreign
5.4	Ghana Petroleum Funds		PRMA statutory funds (negative)

4. Elements of Revenue

VAT is a consumption and one of several direct and indirect taxes that countries use to raise revenues to meet their budget needs. The main high-level elements of revenues include—

- ***total revenues:*** at the apex of the framework, this includes domestic revenue (i.e., tax and non-tax revenues) and grants or aid;
    - ***domestic revenues:*** these comprise tax and non-tax revenues, including social security and other tax revenues—with GRA taking the lead in mobilizing the domestic revenues discussed earlier; and
    - ***grants or aid:*** these include the external (i.e., non-domestic) financial resources that the multilateral and bilateral institutions, including foreign governments and their agencies, give to support the budget.

Table 12.2 summarizes the high-level and downstream classification of the domestic revenues and grants or aid (from development partners and institutions).

Table 12.2: High-level Sources of Total Revenue and Grants

GHANA: TAX & NON-TAX REVENUES [BUDGET FRAMEWORK]					
ITEMS	HEADING	CATEGORY	SUB-CATEGORY	SUB-ITEM	POLICY OBJECTIVES
1	**Revenue & grants**				Total revenues
1.1		Domestic revenue			Local sources of income
1.1.1			Tax Revenue		Tax (direct/indirect) & Non-Tax Revenues
1.1.1.1				*Taxes on Income & Property*	Direct taxes
1.1.1.2				*Taxes on Domestic Goods & Svcs*	Indirect [domestic] taxes
1.1.1.3				*International Trade Taxes*	Indirect [foreign] taxes
1.1.2			Social contributions		SSNIT contributions to NHIL
1.1.3			Non-Tax Revenues	*Income and fees*	Part is Internally-Generated Funds (IGF)
1.1.4			Other revenues	*Taxes, incomes & fees*	Exceptional & non-reccurent
2		Grants/Aid	Foreign income or budget support other than loans		Mostly from multilateral & bilateral sources

5. Tax revenues—direct taxes on income and property

Table 12.3 is a summary of the direct taxes or taxes on income and property, which is the first major category of tax and domestic revenues.

Table 12.3: Taxes on Income and Property

GHANA: TAX & NON-TAX REVENUES [BUDGET FRAMEWORK]			
A] Tax Revenues: Direct Taxes [Taxes on Income and Property]			
ITEMS	CATEGORY	SUB-CATEGORY	POLICY OBJECTIVES
1	**Taxes on Income & Property**		Revenue and non-revenue goals
1.1	Personal income tax [PIT]		Tax on income of employees [PAYE]
1.2	Self-employed tax		Tax on profit of non-corporate entities
1.3	Company income tax [CIT]		Tax on profit of coporate entities
1.3.1		o/w Petroleum CIT	Petroleum sector element of CIT
1.4	Other direct taxes		Mainly royalties
1.4.1		o/w Royalties from oil	Part of PRMA (oil/gas) revenues
1.4.2		o/w Royalties from minerals	
1.5	National Fiscal Stabilization Levy		Originally, a temporary tax handle for managing austerity and fiscal crisis
1.6	Airport tax		Tax on airline travel ticket
1.7	SSNIT Contribution to NHIL	NHIL is an indirect tax but SSNIT contribution is on employee salaries	

5.1 ***Revenue goals for instruments:*** The ***Income Tax Act (ITA), 2015 (Act 896)*** imposes taxes on (a) business profits—sole proprietorships, partnerships and companies; (b) employee salaries and allowances; and (c) rent or capital gains from disposing of property.

- ***Personal income tax (PIT):*** The *PIT rates for employment and unincorporated businesses are graduated or progressive* as a social intervention tool—to alleviate the burden of tax on low-income persons and do the opposite for high-income earners.
    - ***PAYE withholding:*** Employers withhold PIT in advance in a scheme called Pay-As-You-Earn (PAYE) that conforms to a guidance table published by GRA.
    - ***PAYE offset:*** The amount withheld can be offset or credited against the total tax liability due from all the owner's or partner's sources of income.
- ***Self-employed tax:*** imposed on the profits made by unincorporated businesses called sole proprietorships and partnerships—with the individual owners or partners being obliged to add their share of profit to other incomes for tax purposes.
    - ***Rate of tax:*** the schedule for PIT and self-employed tax rates are the same and follow a graduated bracket scheme whereby the margin of income and tax rate increase as the total income increases.
- ***Corporate income tax (CIT):*** the CIT rate on the profits of companies is typically flat but, with other features of the structure (e.g., deductible expenses and tax base), may be varied or adjusted to give fiscal incentives (e.g., attract investment) to businesses.
- ***Rent tax:*** this is the tax paid on the rental or lease of property, usually fixed property, at a separate flat rate or as an addition to personal or corporate income.
- ***Capital gains tax (CGT):*** the CGT on profit from selling tangible or intangible property may be (a) a separate flat rate; or (b) form part of the base of taxable PIT or CIT income—often, with exceptions made for disposal of domestic residence.
    - ***Rates of tax:*** unlike the graduated rates in marginal income brackets, the ***CIT, rent and CGT*** are often flat rates—with lower rates applied for specific tax policy goals (e.g., infant industry or rural location).

- *Special taxes:* these are exceptional to the regular tax regime and address specific fiscal goals such as austerity program tools. They include the temporary import duty and National (Fiscal) Stabilization Levy which Parliaments enact with "sunset" clauses for specific periods.

5.2 *Non-revenue goals of direct tax regime:* The CIT and PIT/ self-employed elements are the material source of the central government's revenues but all the direct and indirect taxes serve non-revenue goals.

- *social intervention programs:* these include the use of the PIT/ self-employed taxes for reliefs (e.g., progressive and exempt tax rate regime);
- *tax incentives:* use of CIT measures to attract investments, including accelerated depreciation, preferential rates, tax credits, exemptions, tax holidays etc.);
- *austerity measures:* since the 1990s, the use of temporary taxes (i.e., National or Fiscal Stabilization Levy) and indirect tax measures (e.g., temporary import duty) as counter-cyclical tax handles for austerity, including IMF, programs;
- *punitive taxes:* as noted earlier, countries use excise taxes to counter the effect of certain products that impose burdens on society—health (e.g., tobacco and alcohol) and environmental (petroleum products) hazards;

Countries now prepare to manage various domestic and global financial or non-financial crises. In addition, besides its Stabilization Fund, Ghana's Parliament passed the ESLA to resolve the serious fiscal crisis in the banking, energy, road and health (COVID-19) sectors.

6. Indirect taxes [goods and services]

These are taxes on consumption or expenditures that add to the cost of production or sales and, thereby increase the prices that consumers pay for goods and services. The tax laws impose indirect taxes under several tax legislation and with different policy objectives.

- *General and specific consumption or expenditure legislation* that covers both permanent and temporary or "earmarked" tax instruments.

    - *Value Added Tax (VAT) Act, 2013 (Act 870)* in relation to the imposition of the most comprehensive general consumption tax.
    - **Ghana Education Trust Fund (GETFund), 2000 (581) was originally enacted as though it were a VAT but later changed to the so-called "Straight" levy.**
    - **National Health Insurance Act (NHIL) Act, 2003 (Act 650): also originally enacted as though it were a VAT but later changed to the so-called "Straight" levy.**
    - *Communications Service Tax (CST) Act, 2008 (Act 754),* which is a specific services sector (communications) consumption or expenditure tax.
- *Customs Act, 2015 (Act 891)* regarding the imposition of tariffs or customs duties and charges—under the ECOWAS Common External Tariff.
- **Excise Duty Act**, *2014* (**Act** *878),* which is the law for imposing various commodity-based consumption or expenditures that society considers harmful.

In addition, there are varieties of excise-type and turnover-type levies under various laws, as summarized in Chapter 8. Table 12.5 shows the main indirect tax handles from these laws, followed by a discussion of their policy and operational relevance.

Table 15.3: Indirect Taxes on Domestic Goods and Services

GHANA: TAX & NON-TAX REVENUES [BUDGET FRAMEWORK]			
B] Tax Revenues: Indirect Taxes [Taxes on Goods & Services]			
ITEMS	CATEGORY	SUB-CATEGORY	POLICY OBJECTIVES
2	Taxes on Domestic Goods & Services		Indirect [domestic] taxes
2.1	Excise duties		Punitive tax on harmful products; alcohol, tobacco, petroleum etc (goods only)
2.1.1		Excise duty (non-petroleum)	
2.1.2		Petroleum tax	
2.1.2.1		o/w Energy Fund Levy	
2.1.2.2		o/w Road Fund Levy	
2.2	Value Added Tax (VAT)		General consumption/expenditure tax
2.2.1		Domestic VAT	Levied on goods and services
2.2.3		External VAT	
2.3	National Health Insurance Levy		Sector consumption tax (special levy) on goods

2.3.1		Customs collection	
2.3.2		Domestic collection	
2.4	Communications Service Tax		Sector consumption tax (on services)
3	**International Trade Taxes**		**Non-neutral indirect [foreign] taxes**
3.1	*Import duty*		Protection & revenue goals (goods only)
3.2	*Export duty*	o/w Cocoa	Special levy on only cocoa exports

- ***Some specific indirect revenue tools:*** the following explains the policy rationale for these indirect taxes which, as with the direct taxes, are used to achieve various revenue and non-revenue goals.

    - ***Customs duty or tariffs:*** since the burden of tariffs falls on only imports, they "protect" local businesses from external competition. Similarly, countries implement various "drawback" measures to avoid exporting their domestic taxes.

    - ***Excise duty:*** the tax burden for these punitive taxes falls on harmful (e.g., tobacco and alcohol), luxurious, and environmental products (e.g., petroleum) supplies—in a ***neutral*** manner than import duties that increase the prices for imported products only.

    - ***Value Added Tax (VAT):*** the design of VAT on "all-inclusive" rules, with narrow exemptions or reliefs —and, in some cases, the use of sub-standard and zero rates on specified supplies—aims at neutrality and maximizing revenues.

    - ***Import duty or tariffs:*** while they generate significant amounts of revenue, import duties or tariffs are also protective or discriminatory because they apply to only imported goods.

- ***Special taxes:*** some special direct and indirect taxes are not part of the permanent tax handles. The ***indirect tax*** aspects include—

    - ***earmarked taxes:*** the main "earmarked" taxes are the GETFund Levy and NHIL, which until 2018 when they became "straight levies", were 2.5 per cent "top-ups" each of the VAT rates; others include the CST, road fund; IGFs etc.

    - ***temporary taxes:*** these include the temporary import duties that Parliament passes to complement the National (or Fiscal) Stabilization Levy to raise revenues to counter domestic and external pressures such as the fall in commodity crisis;

- *singular goals: the Energy Sector Levies Act (ESLA)* was enacted in November 2015 as a levy on petroleum pump prices to resolve the energy and banking sector arrears that resulted in a non-performing loan (NPL) crisis.

The *specific ESLA levies* are the Energy Debt Recovery Levy (EDRL), Public Lighting Levy (PLL), National Electrification Scheme Levy (NESL)—also called the Self-Help Electrification Levy (SHEP)—and Price Stabilization and Recovery Levy (PSRL).

- *Non-revenue goals:* In summary, indirect taxes have non-revenue generation goals but are key to generating revenues for the state.
    - *Protection*: import duties generate revenues but, as noted, other import duties or tariffs discriminate against imports and, therefore, protect local businesses. This is because they are not neutral and affect only taxable imports or supplies.
    - *Punishment:* a primary fiscal role of excise duties is to impose indirect taxes on harmful products such as petroleum, tobacco, alcohol, and sugary products—in addition to some goods that countries classify as luxuries.
    - *Specific fiscal or economic goals:* the state uses indirect taxes such as ESLA and temporary import duties to implement austerity programs, including those arising from the domestic or exogenous crisis.

7. Non-Tax Revenues and Grants

The difference between tax and non-tax revenues is that taxes are compulsory payments which *do not relate to any direct benefits* of goods or services from the state. In comparison, the fees and user charges that form the bulk of non-tax revenues are discretionary. Table 12.6 shows specific details of non-tax revenues, as they appear in the national budget.

Table 12.6: Non-Tax Revenues and Grants

GHANA: TAX & NON-TAX REVENUES [BUDGET FRAMEWORK]			
C] Non-Tax Revenues/Grants:			
ITEMS	**CATEGORY**	**SUB-CATEGORY**	**POLICY OBJECTIVES**
1	Income & fees (Retention/IGF)		NTR less MDA/MMDA transfers
2	Other lodgements:		From miscellaneous sources
2.1	Fees & charges		MDA/MMDA sources
2.2	Oil/gas:		PRMA revenue sources
2.2.1		*Dividends, interest, profits*	
2.2.2		*Surface rentals/PHF interest*	
2.2.3		*Gas receipts*	
2.3		On-lent facilities	Income from government properties
2.4		Licences	
2.5		Sale of shares	
3	Energy Sector Levy Act (ESLA)		
3.1		Energy Debt Recovery Levy	o/w Public Lighting, National Electrification
3.2		Price Stabilization &Recovery	
4	Grants		
4.1		Project grants	Usually tied to capital budget
4.2		Program grants	Usually tied to recurrent budget

- ***Nature of non-tax revenues***: The charges and fees that generate non-tax revenues are often linked to direct benefits of goods and services provided by central and sub-national governments (SNGs) to the beneficiaries.
- ***Types of fees and charges:*** the fees and charges that accumulate to become non-tax revenues include the following—
    - ***user fees:*** usually, this is a generic term used for services that MDAs and MMDAs render to citizens—the typical example being one-time or renewable fees paid for operating licenses (e.g., to trade or process a permit).
    - ***charges:*** governments classify these as part of fees but related to payments made in exchange for the supply of tangible goods or property.
    - ***incomes:*** these are earnings (i.e., price or profits) made by MDAs and MMDAs for selling physical items to citizens, an example being the sale of bound Tariff Classification for goods.

  - *levies:* these have features of taxation since they may be paid compulsorily, in whole or in part for services that are not related to goods or services.
- *Grants or aid:* grants or aid represents direct external inputs to the budget above and they are typically from multilateral and bilateral sources, including institutions such as the World Bank and national development institutions such as USAID or DFID.

8. SNG (MMDA or Assembly) revenues and transfers

Currently, the main sources of revenues for Metropolitan, Municipal, and District Assemblies (MMDAs) or Assemblies, as Ghana calls its SNGs, are derived from the constitution, legislation and budget transfers. There are constitutional and legislative limits on the extent to which an MMDA may borrow.

- *DACF or transfers:* the MMDAs get most of their revenues from the District Assemblies Common Fund (DACF)—a Constitutional mandate to distribute a given percentage of non-oil revenues to MMDAs.
- *Other GOG transfers:* the central government also places the approved employees of the Assemblies on the national budget, in addition to paying some recurrent and capital expenditures of the assemblies.
- *Property tax*: this is a tax an Assembly imposes on tangible commercial and household assets (mainly buildings), using an official valuation of the asset and rates that the Assemblies authorize by Resolution.
  - *User fees and charges:* the fees and charges that MMDAs pass by Resolution include penalties and they are levied on diverse goods and services supplied within the official or specified local area of the Assembly.
- *Loans or bonds:* the Assemblies may borrow to finance their capital and recurrent but only with the express approval of the Minister of Finance.

Parliament uses a legal "Formula" that it reviews annually to allocate the DACF to the Assemblies. Besides some Cabinet-recommended allocations, the Assemblies determine the method of use of the DACF in their annual Budget.

9. Expenditure Framework

The central government taxes finance expenditures for MDAs and MMDAs on the national budget. As with revenues, it is important to distinguish between the GOG and MMDA or Assembly expenditures.

- *Central or GOG expenditure budget:* Table 12.7 shows the recurrent and capital expenditure items for the central government.
- *MMDA (SNG) expenditure budget*: the MMDA expenditure items mirror those of GOG and they are financed from both GOG and MMDA resources.

The Consolidated Budget, called the Composite Budget, is similar to the General Government Budgets in some countries. Table 12.7 shows the economic classification of expenditures used in Ghana's annual budgets and MTEF.

Table 12.7: Recurrent expenditure components [Budget]

GHANA: OVERALL FISCAL FRAMEWORK [BUDGET CLASSIFICATION]			
Recurrent and capital expenditures			
ITEMS	**HEADING**	**CATEGORY**	**POLICY OBJECTIVES/COMMENTS**
1	Recurrent expenditure		Current budget year expenditure
1.1		Compensation	Wages, salaries & social contribution
1.2		Use of goods & services	Expenditures on MDA/MMDAs
1.3		Interest payments	Component of debt service
1.4		Subsidies	Mainly water, electricity & petroleum
1.5		Transfers	Grants to other government units
1.6		Social benefits	SSNIT employer payments etc
1.7		Other Expenditures	Non-routing, non-recurring
2	Capital expenditure		Multi-year budget items
2.1	Domestic-financed	Identified by the source of funds, mainly loans	Different types of development projects in sectors
2.2	Foreign-financed		

- *Expenditure components:* a brief description of the components of the recurrent and capital expenditures in Table 12.7 includes the following—
  - *Recurrent expenditures:* These are expenditures spent in the current fiscal year and, in principle, recur and lapse at the end of the year—with provision for carrying forward, *relatively unpaid* minor commitments or arrears.

- ***Compensation:*** includes salaries, wages and allowances paid to civil and public servants in MDAs and MMDAs and pensions, gratuities and social security contributions paid by GOG (as an employer) on their behalf.
- ***Use of goods and services:*** these are the expenditures for running government offices and consist mainly of purchases of goods (e.g., stationary, batteries, etc.) and services (e.g., electricity, transport etc.).
- ***Interest payments:*** the amount charged annually as interest or income to lenders of domestic and foreign loans that the government contracts as part of financing—which, together with the amortization under financing, equals debt service.
- ***Subsidies:*** these payments are the difference between market and controlled or official prices for goods and services, mainly utilities (i.e., electricity) and petroleum products provided by state-owned enterprises (SOEs).
- ***Social benefits:*** these are similar to subsidies but are specific with respect to lifeline consumers of electricity and transfers for social protection, particularly, for low-income and vulnerable persons.
- ***Grants to other government units:*** these are lump-sum or itemized payments to departments and agencies "on-budget" or as allocations of "earmarked" funds to statutory funds such as GETFund Levy, NHIL and Road Fund.
- ***Other recurrent expenditures:*** some of these items are *ad hoc* and often lapse within a specified number of fiscal years—a prime example being the banking and energy sector spending related to the Energy Sector Levies Act (ESLA).

The largest items of recurrent expenditures are compensation and interest payments, which take a substantial proportion of tax and total revenues. ***Ghana's budget is also reputed to be among the most "earmarked" among many countries.***

- ***Capital expenditure:*** As noted, capital expenditures define the use of budget resources over multiple fiscal years or periods. The categories by source of funding include—
    - ***Domestic-financed projects:*** unlike the use of treasury bills (T-Bills) to finance the liquidity needs of governments, GOG uses medium-term bonds with 3-year and 5-years plus duration to finance development.
    - ***Foreign-financed projects***: the sources of financing are external, often from development partners (DPs) and commercial entities, with loans and grants from bilateral and multilateral sources.

A related budget classification of capital expenditures is ***programme and project loans*** that associate the latter with capital expenditure (e.g., roads, power plants etc.,) and the former with recurrent expenses (e.g., compensation; use of goods and services).

10. Budget Deficit or Fiscal Balances

The difference between the total Revenue and Expenditure (Item 3 of Table 15.1) is the Budget Deficit (or Surplus, in principle), which is brought forward as the Fiscal Balance on a Commitment basis. Table 15.8 shows the Fiscal Balance I plus conventional commitments or arrears and the Fiscal Balance II which adds exceptional arrears and discrepancies.

Table 12.8: Deficit and Fiscal Balances (I & II)

GHANA: FISCAL BALANCES [BUDGET FRAMEWORK]			
Budget Deficit, Arrears, Discrepancies and Fiscal Balances			
ITEMS	**CATEGORY**	**SUB-CATEGORY**	**POLICY OBJECTIVES**
1	Budget Deficit (b/f) = Overall Balance (Commitment)		The net of ***CASH*** revenue & expenditures
1.1	Add: unpaid bills (routine)	Net Arrears	Occur routinely for unpaid capital and recurrent warrants (bills) at end-year.
2	Overall Balance (Cash I)	Fiscal balance (narrow)	
2.1	Add: exceptional items	Often non-recurring	Invariably, these expenditures are linked to domestic & external fiscal crisis
2.2	Add: discrepancies	Net negative or positive	
3	Overall Balance (Cash II)	Fiscal balance (broad)	Includes all ***COMMITMENTS*** or arrears

Table 15.8 is on an ***all-inclusive approach*** that adds both routine and exceptional expenditures and commitments in showing different levels of fiscal deficiency.

- ***Budget deficit:*** this is on a ***cash basis*** and shows the difference between actual cash received and cash paid during the fiscal year. It shows the fiscal deficiency at first and on a very narrow basis.
- ***Fiscal balance I (narrow)***: the ***cash-based budget deficit plus arrears or commitments*** of recurrent (e.g., unpaid fuel or stationery bought on credit) and capital (e.g., work-in-progress [WIP] for road works) expenditures is the fiscal deficiency at a second level.
- ***Fiscal balance II (broad)***: The Fiscal Balance I plus discrepancies (i.e., errors) and exceptional commitments (e.g., utility or fuel subsidy, bank and energy sector arrears (due to gas/ crude shortage or high price etc.) gives the third level of fiscal deficiency.

It is necessary to note that the exceptional (e.g., divestiture receipts) and discrepancy items can be positive. Secondly, in principle, the budget deficit and fiscal balances can be positive but even the deficit on a narrow basis does not occur in developing countries. Further, the all-inclusive approach ensures that GOG accounts for all expenditures (and receipts), thereby giving a true reflection of the level of borrowing and debt.

11. Finance or borrowing

Table 12.9 shows that GOG must finance the budget or fiscal balances from domestic and foreign sources since it does not raise sufficient revenues to pay for expenditures. Given that the domestic financial markets in developing countries such as Ghana are not sufficiently large, they rely heavily on foreign multilateral and bilateral institutions as well as commercial banks to finance the deficit.

Table 12.9: Financing of budget deficit and fiscal balances

GHANA: FISCAL BALANCES [BUDGET FRAMEWORK]			
Financing of budget deficit and fiscal balances			
ITEMS	**CATEGORY**	**SUB-CATEGORY**	**POLICY OBJECTIVES**
1	Overall Bal (Cash II) = Financing		
2	Foreign financing (net)	Loans & Bonds	Stock market and bank borrowing
2.1	Borrowing	New debt	
2.1.1	o/w: Project Loans	Concessional and non-concessional (or commercial)	Mainly to finance the annual and multi-year development or capital budget
2.1.2	Program Loans		
2.1.3	Sovereign Bond		
2.2.	Amortization	Debt repayment	Borrowing less amortization = Net Debt
3	Domestic financing (net)	Bills and Bonds	Stock market and bank borrowing
3.1	Banking	Mainly commercial banks	Part of OMO and GFIM (Stock Exchange)
3.1.1	o/w: Bank of Ghana (BOG)	Advances	Up to 5% of prior-year total revenues
3.1.2	Commercial Banks	OMO & Stock Exchange (primary & secondary markets)	
3.2	Non-banks	Other financial institutions and entities (e.g., SSNIT)	
3.3	Other domestic		

It is important to take note of the Sovereign Bond element in Table 12.9, as a source of borrowing from stock exchanges, equity funds etc., by the lower and upper middle-income countries (MICs) that are being weaned of concessional financing and grants.

- ***Sources of funds:*** these from domestic and external sources which, in both cases involve multilateral (e.g., World Bank), Bilateral (e.g., official state agencies), stock exchanges and money market (e.g., bond markets), and banks (Central Banks [BOG], Development Banks, EXIM, and commercial banks).
- ***Debt instruments:*** these are typically short-term (e.g., treasury bills) and medium-to-long-term (e.g., bonds) loans from the sources described above.

As Table 12.9 shows, the net borrowing or difference between borrowing (Item 2.1) and amortization or debt repayment (item 2.2) is what increases or reduces the stock of public debt from prior years.

12. Public Debt Stock

The composition of Debt reflects the sources of borrowing and types of instruments discussed above. As a Lower Middle-Income Country (L-MIC), Ghana is no exception to the sovereign bond loan phenomenon which, without a solid debt repayment strategy, is leading to widespread risk of debt distress and some defaults in countries that are transitioning to MIC status—but remain substantive developing states.

Table 12.10: Public Debt Classification

Classification of Gross Public Debt		
Items	**Description**	**Comments**
1	**Total Public Debt**	The Total Public Debt and its components as measured at the end of each fiscal year.
1.1	*External Debt*	
1.2	*Domestic Debt*	
2	**External Debt**	Portion of public debt secured from outside the country, showing the source of the funding
2.1	*Multilateral*	
2.2	*Bilateral*	
2.3	*Commercial*	
3	**Domestic Debt**	The componet of public debt secured from local sources. Most marketable are traded on the Stock Exchange while the non-marketable are held by BOG and other institutions or entities
3.1	*Marketable:*	
3.1.1	*Short-Term Instruments*	
3.1.2	*Medium-term Instruments*	
3.2	*Non-Marketable*	
3.3	*Standard Loans*	

13. Conclusion

This Chapter shows that VAT is one of several direct and, particularly, indirect tax revenues as well as non-tax revenues and grants that countries rely upon to finance their budget deficits or fiscal balances. However, due to its wider tax base, VAT plays a significant role as the "money" spinner for budgets.

Further, the design of VAT must be efficient, with few exemptions on technical or social intervention grounds, to make it the tax with the widest base among the "consumption" or "expenditure" taxes. Hence, tax handles such as the CST and levies that operate without a right to ITC or VAT compromise the efficiency of VAT regimes.

The collection of VAT also occurs at multiple stages along the value-addition chain, unlike most income and expenditure taxes that employers and businesses collect officially on behalf of the revenue or tax authorities. Indeed, tax offices collected the sales and service taxes that VAT replaced which were also collected at single stages.

In some instances, the "ring mechanism" was applied to turnover and, excise taxes to ensure that businesses do collect the tax at multiple stages—through a suspension of the tax due on inputs. However, in all instances, the invoice-based input tax credit (ITC) method remained superior in avoiding "cascading" and multiple taxation that results in high tax burdens and consumer prices.

Despite its strength, the Input Tax Credit (ITC) method performs well with efficient credit and refund processes, particularly, for zero-rated exports. Despite this important fiscal or revenue "spinner" role of VAT regimes, Ghana's VAT has become the most politicized and mutilated. This is the result of unorthodox schemes such as the VAT Flat Rate Scheme (VFRS) and the conversion of the GETFund Levy and NHIL into so-called excise-type "straight" levies. They confuse the revenue and non-revenue goals that the ERP/SAP restructuring of tax handles achieved from the 1980/90s.

The most devastating effect of both schemes is the denial of ITC for medium and large businesses, with the consequences being cascading, higher tax burdens and consumer prices without the benefit of higher revenue because of tax evasion and avoidance. Indeed, the GRA Practice Note on both schemes specifically emphasizes that the input tax denied should be added to the cost or value addition before calculating the VAT.

Chapter 13

POLITICAL ECONOMY OF VAT: VAT AND MACROECONOMIC REFORMS

1. Introduction

The Value Added Tax (VAT) replaced the Sales Tax regime on imports and, domestic supplies at the manufacturing stage. There was a complementary Service Tax regime further midstream and downstream on selected services. As taxes on consumption expenditure, with only the method of collection to differentiate, both were key to fiscal performance. Indeed, the introduction of ***VAT was a critical element of the fiscal*** component of the 1980/90s Economic Recovery Program (ERP) or Structural Adjustment Program (SAP).

Under the old consumption tax regime, sales and service tax collection were at single stages while VAT is at multiple stages—along the production-distribution or *value-addition* chain. The old Customs, Excise and Preventive Service (CEPS) charged and collected both the domestic and import Sales Tax while the Internal Revenue Service (IRS), though a direct tax institution, was responsible for the Service Tax regime—because of the proximity of its larger number of offices, than CEPS, to the service providers.

The Value Added Tax Act (VATA), 1995 (Act 498) and, at reintroduction after the cancellation of the initial attempt, VATA, 1998 (Act 546), were administered by a newer third agency, the VAT Service (VATS). Consequently, VATS collected the domestic VAT (and excises) while CEPS maintained its responsibility for the external (import and export) VAT. Hence, the IRS became an agency for only the direct taxes on income and property.

Under the Ghana Revenue Authority (GRA) Act, 2009 (Act 971), which ***changed the structure of tax administration fundamentally in Ghana***, CEPS became the Customs Division (CD) of GRA while an integrated Domestic Tax Revenue Division (DTRD) of the Authority took over IRS and VATS. A third Support Services Division (SSD) combines the separate support activities for IRS, CEPS and VATS. Further, an integrated Board of Directors also took over the functions of the three previous Boards while the administration of direct and indirect taxes now falls under a single Revenue Administration Act (RAA), 2016 (Act 915).

VAT was ***part of the comprehensive reforms*** that rationalized the direct and indirect tax regimes. The pillars of the ***direct tax*** on incomes and property are the Corporate Income Tax (CIT) and Personal Income Tax (PIT) while the pillars of the ***indirect tax*** on consumption or expenditures are Excise Duty, VAT, and Import Duty. Ghana's ***non-tax revenues*** are mainly fees and charges. The reforms in ***property tax*** as well as some local fees and charges were part of the decentralization program that changed the local or sub-national government (SNG) structure to Metropolitan, Municipal and District Assemblies (MMDAs).

In a ***fiscal*** context, the reforms also related to ***expenditure policy and administration*** geared towards attaining sustainable ***budget deficits and public debt*** through better management of expenses, arrears and borrowing or financing. The ***fiscal, monetary, financial, and real sector reforms*** were part of the overall macroeconomic reforms called ERP/SAP, which placed Ghana firmly among the wave of "market-oriented" macroeconomic reforms called the "Washington Consensus", led by the International Monetary Fund (IMF) and the World Bank.

2. VAT and ERP/SAP

Ghana went through ***severe social, political and economic stress*** from the late 1960s to the early 1980s—after the overthrow of Ghana's 1st Republic civilian administration in a *coup d'état* in 1966 and a long period of alternating military and two (2nd and 3rd) Republican civilian administrations.

- ***Macroeconomic instability and SAP/ERP:*** The 1970s through to the early 1980s were a period of social and economic instability, with the situation stabilizing and improving after the launch of ERP/SAP in 1983 by the last military government, the Provisional National Defence Council (PNDC). The PNDC also promulgated the 1992 Constitution and formed the National Democratic Congress (NDC) won the 1992 elections and formed the first civilian government under the 4th Republic that has lasted into the 21st century.
- ***VAT, ERP/SAP, and transition politics:*** The ***planning*** for VAT introduction as well as its ***suspension*** and ***reintroduction*** from

1993 to 1999 was the last major reform under ERP/SAP. The period overlapped with the 1996 elections and ended with the NDC's defeat in the 2000 elections by the New Patriotic Party (NPP). VAT was embroiled in major transitions: end of military rules; promulgation of the 1992 Constitution; switch to multi-party civilian rule under the NDC and NPP; and end of ERP/SAP from 1983 to 2000.

- ***VAT and the adverse view of IMF Programs:*** After the ERP/SAP, Ghana continues to rely on IMF programs to manage the economic crisis, notably the fall in commodity crisis from exogenous and environmental factors. The reforms continue with grant and loan support from the World Bank, African Development Bank (AfDB), development partners (DPs) and financial institutions. The reforms led to substantial inflows from grants and loans—with the latter source leading to the declaration of HIPC (Heavily-Indebted Poor Country) in the first half of the 2000s.

Hence, while the ERP/SAP was a major structural and transformational national initiative, it has also been linked with the intermittent IMF austerity Programs for correcting domestic and exogenous shocks. This is also the context in which many Ghanaians came to associate VAT with ERP/SAP and the unrest in the transition to civilian rule under the 4th Republic's 1992 Constitution.

3. Economic decline before ERP/SAP

Ghana's post-independence economic narrative starts with a strong state-led policy under the 1st Republic. This defined real sector production and extensive social intervention policies but with space for significant private sector activities, particularly, in agriculture (as a global leader in cocoa production). Then followed the mix of state-led and market-led rules, as the nation moved from civilian rule (2nd and 3rd Republics) to intermittent military rules for about two decades. The mixed domestic fortunes and external or global shocks that help explain the importance of, and rationale for, ERP/SAP include the following—

- ***Political upheavals:*** As summarized later, the overthrow of Dr. Kwame Nkrumah's regime under the 1st Republic marked the start of the alternation between two (2) civilian administrations under the 2nd and 3rd Republics and five (5) military administrations. It culminated in a difficult transition to civilian rule under the 4th Republican 1992 Constitution. Since then, Ghana has sustained civilian power under five (5) administrations that continue to alternate between the National Democratic Congress (NDC) and the New Patriotic Party (NPP).

- ***Natural factors:*** Ghana suffered from periodical natural and environmental disasters in the 1970s/80s. The inadequate rains resulted in severe droughts, bushfires and the destruction of forests which led to low agricultural output from cocoa and other cash-crop production, based largely on subsistence or peasant farms. Apart from the effect on food supplies the drought affected the flow and level of water in the Volta River and led to power shortages from the Akosombo Dam which was the main source of power supply at the time.

- ***Economic decline:*** The decline in economic fortunes was predictable and felt by the citizenry as low food shortages led to higher prices. The fiscal deficit and non-payment of subsidies led to rationing and long queues for basic goods and services, which extended backwards from the distribution stage to the farmgate and fuel stations. Indeed, this led to a strong social intervention element of SAP.

  The fall in cocoa and gold prices and their exports affected BOG's foreign currency reserves, the value of the cedi as well as import and consumer prices. Indeed, the justification for the *coup d'états* that toppled the 2nd and 3rd Republic governments included inflation and high prices, fast depreciation and devaluation of the cedi, shortages of basic consumer goods, and overall harsh economic situation.

- ***Fiscal deterioration:*** The fall in output results in less taxes but static or rising expenses, widening budget deficits, higher borrowing, and rising public debt. The inability of the government to support, mainly subsidies, to farmers, households and businesses (including state-owned enterprises) during the 1970s and 1980s led to a mass exodus of qualified and unqualified Ghanaians to Nigeria, Southern Africa, Europe, the US and other major global centres.

- ***Effect on real and other sectors:*** The real sector meltdown affected fiscal, financial and monetary management, with banks recording high non-performing loans (NPLs) that were "ring-fenced" in a "bad bank" called Non-performing Asset Recovery

Trust (NPART). The Bank of Ghana (BOG), which had to be recapitalized itself, struggled with sufficient foreign exchange reserves to support imports, debt service and other payments,

As noted, this situation put significant pressure on the value of the currency and domestic prices. Indeed, these factors led to several IMF austerity programs to support the overall ERP/SAP agenda, with extensive structural reforms in the fiscal, financial, monetary, and real sectors. The fiscal reforms led to major drastic reviews of tax policies, instruments or tax handles, and administration, including the use of VAT as the tool with a clear goal of widening the tax base to increase revenues.

4. Elements of ERP or SAP

As detailed below, the ERP/SAP framework included comprehensive fiscal, monetary, financial, real sector, and social intervention policies and measures. The goals of the programs—often designed with technical assistance from the IMF, World Bank, African Development Bank (AfDB), DPs, and other institutions—were to correct, stabilize, and transform the entire economy. The background was the problems discussed above.

- **Fiscal reforms:** The macro-fiscal reforms aim at complementing the overall macroeconomic reforms, with a focus on how the government generates its revenues, spends, borrows and manages the public debt to achieve its developmental objectives, including social intervention goals.
    - *Tax policy:* The first element of the fiscal reforms was the revenue or tax modernization programs that the NRS started and implemented in 1984. In addition to rationalizing the tax and customs or tariff structures discussed above, NRS initiated the ***domestic revenue reforms*** that led to the ***"semi-autonomy"*** and ***"revenue authority"*** concepts that were discussed in detail in Part IV.
    - *Tax administration:* The autonomy concept consisted of removing the two (2) revenue agencies (IRS and CEPS) from the core civil service in 1986—a notion that many African countries have implemented. Other aspects include legislation reviews, staffing under the GRA reforms, and revamping of operations, including enhanced automation of tax collection and compliance or enforcement processes.

- ***Budget and expenditure management:*** The opposite of the revenue reforms was improved budget and expenditure management to achieve sustainable outcomes. The reforms focused on streamlining the ***"activity-based"*** budget framework and improving its information technology (IT) platform, under a comprehensive *Public Financial Management Review Project (PUFMARP)*.
- ***Process reforms:*** Other elements were improved budget preparation, implementation (financial accounting), control, and monitoring processes—with secondary programs for payroll, commitment, and arrears/contract management. PUFMARP was replaced with the current Ghana *Integrated Public Financial Management Information System (GIFMIS)* while budgeting has shifted from the ***"activity-based"*** framework to ***"Program-Based Budgeting (PBB)"***.

To reiterate, the goal of fiscal reforms is generating sufficient domestic revenues to support a prudent and manageable expenditure and budget deficit or fiscal balance. The ultimate macro-fiscal outcome of an improved ***public financial management (PFM) framework*** includes planned borrowing to achieve sustainable public debt (i.e., domestic and external debt) levels. Hence, the design of administrative processes to support these policies tends to be organized along the policy elements above.

- ***Domestic revenue mobilization (DRM):*** rationalizing the goals of direct and indirect taxes—including VAT replacing sales and service taxes; and revenue administration reforms to achieve (a) new organizational setups—such as Ghana Revenue Authority (GRA); and (b) taxpayer self-assessment or voluntary compliance and automated processes involving registration, collection; filing and payments, and enforcement.
- ***Expenditure or budget reforms***: enhancing MDA/ MMDA processes for (a) forecasting and ceilings, (b) arrears and contracts to avoid budget overruns; (c) resource allocation for better outputs and outturns in strategic plans and programs; (d) treasury and cash management (Treasury Single Account [TSA]); and (e) financial accounting reporting).
- ***Borrowing and debt management:*** the two parts of overall debt management are (a) developing debt instruments to facilitate borrowing for short, medium, and long-term on domestic and

external capital markets; and (b) adopting and monitoring market strategies and plans to ensure sustainable debt limits, including debt payment schedules.

The administration reforms require an effective IT platform; an elaborate coding and classification of organizations (i.e., cost centres); economic and functional classification, including programs; and chart of accounts (COA) for all revenues (receipts and incomes), expenditures (expenses), assets and liabilities.

- ***Monetary sector reforms:*** These cover monetary policies and measures under various programs that the Bank of Ghana (BOG) led, in collaboration with MOF. As the government's banker and custodian of domestic and foreign resources and assets, the recapitalization of BOG enabled it to perform its regulatory role effectively and supervise the implementation of the necessary structural reform measures in the monetary and financial sectors.
    - ***Foreign exchange management:*** restoration of foreign exchange reserves to manage the inflows of foreign currency to support imports more sustainably; stabilization of the value of the local currency (cedi) in relation to major international currencies; streamlining foreign currency trading more formally in banks; and transforming the large informal and parallel "black market" into better-organized forex bureaus.
    - ***Price stability and inflation:*** prior to the reforms, BOG policy affected pricing adversely through excessive deficit-financing, which aggravated the effects of droughts and bushfires on cocoa exports; and led to shortages of domestic supply and imports of goods and services. The escalating domestic prices put inflation and high consumer prices at the centre of BOG's monetary policy; and led to its ***"inflation targeting"*** strategy that uses interest rates and another tool to guide the thrust of BOG's monetary policy to date.
- ***Financial sector reforms:*** Besides strengthening the central bank, the SAP/ERP reforms were key to the non-performing loan (NPL) and recapitalization strategy that aimed at revitalizing commercial banking and establishing new or strengthening existing regulatory institutions in the country.

- ***Revitalization of commercial banking:*** the banking sector was laden with significant non-performing loans (NPLs); the turnaround came with the creation of a "bad bank", under the Non-Performing Assets Recovery Trust (NPART) to take over the liability owed to depositors and to allow for the revival of the financial sector.
- ***Establishment of financial sector Regulators:*** the reforms during the period also resulted in setting up or strengthening Regulatory institutions such as the Securities and Exchange Commission (SEC) and the National Insurance Commission (NIC).
- ***Development of the domestic capital market:*** the Ghana Stock Exchange (GSE) was set up during the period to be at the forefront of resource mobilization, financing, and trading or exchange of financial instruments among buyers and sellers.
- ***Private financial markets:*** the era saw the start of the SEC's issuance of operational licenses to private equity, mutual and other funds and brokerage and insurance firms. They complemented the commercial banks in mobilizing the savings that support the private and public sectors.

The latest financial market reforms from 2015 include a primary dealer plan to support flotations (through the Book Building method) and trading of medium-term GOG instruments, as part of the Ghana Fixed Income Market (GFIM) started in 2015. This has restricted the BOG's role in issuances to short-term liquidity instruments (e.g., Treasury Bills and 1 and 2-year notes) through the traditional Open Market Operations (OMO) auctions.

5. Reorganization of the Structure of Government

To ensure proper accounting and reporting of resources, the medium-term plan, strategic plan, programs and budgets use a uniform ***classification and coding or Chart of Accounts (COA) framework.*** The ***functional and economic classifications*** formed part of the Public Financial Management Program ***(PUFMARP)*** reforms in the 1990s and were revamped in 2010 as the Ghana Integrated Financial Management Information System *(GIFMIS)*.

- **Functional classification:** This heading groups the "functions" of the state into "sectors" for *(a)* ***central government*** bodies called Ministries, Departments, and Agencies (MDAs) and

*(b) **counterpart sub-national governments_(SNGs)*** called the Municipal, Metropolitan, and District Assemblies (MMDAs). This broad classification guides the preparation of the annual budget and medium-term plans.

- ***Administration sector:*** These MDAs, which perform the core oversight functions, include the executive (i.e., Office of Government Machinery and Presidency); other arms of the state (i.e., Legislature and Judiciary); and Constitutional Bodies (e.g., Audit Service) and Commissions (e.g. Public Services Commission).
- ***Economic sector:*** This cluster of MDAs oversees the implementation of vital long-term developmental policies and operations and the judicious use of budget resources sectors that cover energy, agriculture, industry, and trade. Some of them (e.g., energy) operate with significant budget outlays in the infrastructure sector.
- ***Infrastructure sector:*** This sector is notable for its significant developmental budget outlays on projects that include roads and highways, transport (i.e., harbours, ports, and railways), works and housing, and communications.
- ***Social sector:*** These include significant but soft infrastructure (e.g., education and health) and social intervention (e.g., social welfare, civic education, and chieftaincy and culture). The education and health sectors take significant recurrent and capital budget resources.
- ***Public safety:*** These MDAs also have significant budget outlays and include defence, interior, and security has large budget outlays in agencies such as the Armed Forces (i.e., military, police, navy, and air force) and other security apparatus.

MOF and the Ministry of Local Government and Rural Development (MLGRD) are part of the Administration Sector, with the latter supervising all the SNGs or MMDAs. The functional classification is based on IMF's Government Finance Statistics (GFS) which utilizes the UN's Classification of the Functions of Government (COFOG) for government activities.

- ***Economic classification:*** The ***economic classification*** shows the types of (a) ***revenues*** that GOG mobilizes; and (b) the

expenditures or spending to which it allocates the revenues, through the annual budgets to MDAs and MMDAs to perform their ***functions, programs, projects or activities***.

- ***Revenue classification:*** This section deals with the classification of <u>*revenues*</u> while the remaining sections cover *expenditures, commitments or arrears (under accrual or semi-accrual processes), financing or borrowing, and public debt management.*
    - ***Direct taxes***: these are imposed on incomes and property as (a) personal income tax (PIT) on salaries, wages and allowances; and profits earned by self-employed persons and partners; and (b) corporate income tax (CIT) on profits made by artificial persons or businesses.
    - ***Indirect taxes***: these are imposed on (a) import duties or tariffs on only imported goods; (b) value added tax (VAT) on all taxable supplies of goods and services, sold locally or imported; (c) excise duties and special levies, as punitive taxes on only luxurious and harmful supplies such as petroleum, tobacco, alcohol and luxury vehicles.
    - ***Property taxes***: these are classified into two groups (a) rent tax collected by GRA as a direct tax for the central government; and (b) property tax collected by virtue of ownership by MMDAs at the sub-national level.
    - ***Non-tax revenues:*** fees and charges are not imposed compulsorily but paid by beneficiaries for the goods and services they receive from the central government or MMDAS (e.g., vehicle texting, location of businesses on streets that require cleaning, death and birth certificates).

The ERP and SAP rationalized the objectives of these sources in the 1980/90s to define their policy objectives properly, namely revenue generation and other non-revenue goals (e.g., protection of local firms, punishment, business incentives, social intervention etc.).

- ***Expenditure classification:*** These classify the purposes for which governments meet the spending commitments of MDAs and

MMDAs. In many instances, the allocations or classifications specify the beneficiaries.

- ***Compensation*:** these payments to public sector employees are (a) ***salaries and wages*** made in return for rendering services; and (b) ***allowances*** that are negotiable secondary payments that may vary among the employees.
- ***Interest payments*:** these refer to the annual costs or charges for loans to finance recurrent or capital expenditures; it does not refer to the repayment of the principal amount of the loan called amortization (under financing below).
- ***Recurrent (goods and services)***: these are annual payments for running public offices that derive their spending amounts from the budget and include expenses such as transportation, cleaning, stationery, servicing meetings, and printing.
- ***Capital expenditure*:** the payments for infrastructure or development projects and programmes, usually from loans because of revenue shortfalls that lead to deficits. They include planned borrowing for major projects that take multiple years to construct or complete.

- ***Arrears or commitment:*** these are end-year unpaid or outstanding payments for recurrent and, in principle, capital costs to be financed from undisbursed loans that MDA/MMDAs accrue at the end of the fiscal year. They are shown as the "net" amount between the current and preceding years but the principle is to show them as ledger records of the balances, new costs and payments under semi/partial or full accrual accounting rules.
- ***Financing or borrowing:*** governments borrow in short-term (liquidity) and medium-to-long-term (loan) markets to finance the shortfall between the annual or multi-year revenues and expenditures, called the *budget deficit or fiscal balance*. In principle, the difference can be a budget *surplus* when revenue exceeds expenditures.
  - ***Amortization and debt management:*** Amortization refers to the repayment of the principal amount of loans taken in prior years—as part of the debt management process that countries set up to make their borrowing efficient. The

concept of ***debt service*** involves the payment of interest and principal amounts due.

Collectively, the compensation, payments for goods and services, and interest paid are also called ***current or recurrent expenses*** since their benefits are often exhausted in a single fiscal or financial year—compared to ***capital expenditures*** that have multi-year benefits.

6. VAT and the "pain" of ERP/SAP austerity programs

At the time of the introduction of VAT in 1995, ERP/SAP was a decade old and its ***structural aspects*** were taking root. However, its occasional *austerity element* was also taking a big toll on citizens This was due to the ***counter-cyclical*** measures that Ghana and other countries used to ***correct and realign the economy*** after domestic (e.g., drought) or external (e.g., fall in commodity prices) shocks.

Hence, ERP/SAP also defined the ***political-economy*** aspects that the opposition used to court support in the transition from military to constitutional (multi-party) rule.

- ***VAT—a structural pillar of tax reforms:*** VAT was part of the ***structural reforms*** that rationalized the tax regime—with clear revenue increase and expenditure containment measures. By 1990, the public had started to join the debate on the formulation and promulgation of the 1992 Constitution. However, within this context, VAT became a major economic issue for the opposition in the campaign for the 1996 elections.
- ***Common causes of austerity measures:*** The *austerity measures* are due to (a) *domestic factors* such as droughts, bushfires, and excess fiscal burden of subsidies and other social intervention programs; and (b) *external shocks* such as the US sub-prime interest rates saga that started the Global Financial Crisis in 2008; slump in BRIC demand, notably China, and fall in crude oil prices in 2014; and the COVID-19 virus pandemic that has led to a global lockdown in 2020.
- ***Economic consequences:*** The consequences include (a) economic and social events or factors that lead to a fall in productivity and demand in advanced and emerging market economies; (b) related fall in demand for primary commodity imports (in reverse, primary commodity exports from developing states);

and (c) glut in supply leading to continuous fall in commodity prices.

- ***Effects of crisis***: The sequence ends with falling foreign exchange inflows that reduce central bank reserves and put pressure on financing exports and currency values; a downturn in productivity and economic stability and growth; and a shortfall in tax revenues that result in higher budget deficits, borrowing, and rapid rise in the public debt.

- ***VAT and corrective measures:*** Taxes feature prominently among the *temporary* fiscal tools used to make corrections in austerity programs. The *direct tax tool* is the fiscal stabilization levy, as a top-up of the corporate income tax (CIT) rate while the *indirect tax equivalent* is the temporary import duties. Some of the corrections are *structural*, such as excise duties that are classified as special petroleum tax on petroleum products.

  Another major corrective tax is in two separate 2.5 per cent *proxy VAT rate increases* (i.e., GETFund Levy and NHIL), in which net revenue is dedicated to education and health programs. The conversion of GETFund Levy and NHIL to so-called *"straight" levies* came with an ill-advised move to deny VAT ITC to registered entities.

- ***Delay in introducing VAT:*** The general view is that Ghana should have introduced VAT in the mid-1980s under ERP/SAP, with the major macroeconomic, monetary, fiscal, and real sector reforms. This meant that PNDC should have taken immediate action on the HIID study and positive recommendations in 1988 and aligned the VAT reforms more firmly with the other direct and indirect tax reforms mentioned earlier.

7. ERP/SAP, VAT and Governance

The 4th Republic under the 1992 Constitution has brought about the longest spell of civilian governments to date since the attainment of political independence from the United Kingdom (UK) in 1957. However, it is only the two (2) pre-independence local political traditions that have been alternating power.

- ***Military and civilian administrations before the 4th Republic:*** In practice, *all governments in Ghana ran a largely mixed economy* while its political parties professed policies that tilted towards the left (state-led) or the right (free market).

- ***Liberal leaning***: as practised in immediate post-independence or 1st Republic, with the state being dominant in sector development and, in general, the use of national resources in annual budgets for variable objectives such as sports and social intervention.
- ***Conservative leaning***: as amplified during the short-lived 2nd Republic, it steers affairs towards a market-based economy—although the citizens of developing countries have a higher expectation of the role governments play in improving living conditions.

Table 13.1 shows various civilian and military rules in a political-economy context of the discussions in this chapter.

Table 13.1: Period from 1st Republic and Military Rules

Ghana: post-colonial and mix civilian [1st to 3rd Republic] and military governments				
Period	**Government**	**Leader**	**Nature**	**Comments**
1st Republic				
1957 - 1966	Convention Peoples' Party (CPP)	Osagyefo Dr Kwame Nkrumah	Civilian	1st Republic: Ghana attained political indepedence under the CPP from (UK) in 1957; status of a Republic in 1960. State-led and redistributive economic policies
Military rule				
1966 - 1969	National Liberation Council (NLC)	Gen. Kotoka & Lt. Gen. Ankrah	Military	1st Military Rule: professed [?] to stopping the country from creeping further into a dictatorship
2nd Republic				
1969 - 1971	Progress Party	Dr. K. A. Busia	Civilian	2nd Republic: restored civilian rule with market-oriented economic policies
Military rule				
1971 - 1979	National Redemption Council (NRC)	Gen. Acheampong & Gen. Afrifa	Military	2nd Military Rule: Dissatisfaction with social and economic conditions: mixed economic policies
1979 -1979	Armed Forces Revolutionary Council (AFRC)	Flt Lt. J. J. Rawlings	Military	3rd Military rule: stop social and economic injustice; execution of top military officers
1983 - 1992	Provisional National Defence Council (PNDC)	Flt Lt. J. J. Rawlings	Military	4th Military Rule: major economic reforms under Economic Recovery Program (ERP) or Structural Adjustment Program (SAP) during IMF/World Bank-led Washington Consensus era
3rd Republic				
1979 - 1983	Peoples National Party (PNP)	Dr. Hilla Limann	Civilian	3rd Republic: restored civilian rule under state-led and redistributive policy orientation

- ***Last military regime and the launch of ERP/SAP:*** The launch of ERP/SAP under the last PNDC military rule was initially left-leaning but later led to a significant paradigm shift to a market economy. The main reason is the search for solutions during the Washington Consensus era to the instability and turmoil of coups, public protests, and harsh living conditions that defined the post-1966 era.

- All the governments up to the 1985 ERP/SAP under the PNDC and NDC faced accelerated or sharp declines in the economy. It was also the context in which Ghana launched its VAT project and reform.
- Ghana became prominent in the Washington Consensus era in the 1980s and 1990s under an IMF and World Bank view of global and market-oriented economic policies and principles.
- It started the use of IMF Programs to stop the decline of the economy; achieve steady growth from 1983 to date; and added corrective austerity measures to reverse setbacks and crises.
- Given its left-of-centre orientation, the PNDC had several social intervention programs, notably the launch of the Program of Adjustment to Mitigate the Social Cost of Adjustment (PAMSCAD) as part of the ERP-SAP initiative.

Ghana's participation in these reforms was successful in ending the oscillation and decline in growth and continued use of IMF programs by the civilian governments to make corrections to the periodic economic setbacks. Table 13.2 shows the alternation of power between the NDC and the National Patriotic Party (NPP) under the 4th Republic.

Table 13.2: ERP/SAP governance and afterwards

Ghana: post-colonial civilian [4th Republic] governments				
Period	**Government**	**Leader**	**Nature**	**Comments**
Ghana: 4th Republic governments				
1983 - 1992	Provisional National Defence Council (PNDC)	Flt Lt. J. J. Rawlings	Military	4th Military Rule: major economic reforms under Economic Recovery Program (ERP) or Structural Adjustment Program (SAP) during IMF/World Bank-led Washington Consensus era
1992 - 2000	National Democratic Congress (NDC 1)	Flt Lt. J. J. Rawlings	Civilian	4th Republic: restoration of Civilian Rule, continuatin of ERP/SAP, 1st tax modernizatin program, and introduction of VAT
2001 - 2008	National Patriotic Party (NPP 1)	Mr. J.A.K. Kuffuor	Civilian	4th Republic: market-oriented policies; discovery of oil in commercial quantity; and amendmenr=ts that changed VAT structure

2009 - 2012	National Democratic Congress (NDC 2)	Prof. J. E. A. Mills	Civilian	4th Republic: transition to MIC & petroleum production status; 2nd tax modernization program and review of VAT legislation
2012 - 2013	National Democratic Congress (NDC 2)	Mr. J. D. Mahama	Civilian	4th Republic: consolidation of MIC/petrol economy status; review of economy and new VAT legislation
2016 to 2020	National Patriotic Party (NPP 2)	Mr Nana A.D. Akuffo-Addo	Civilian	Launch of expansive social intervention policies and reversal of VAT policies in new legislation

8. VAT policy, structure and legislation

This section summarizes the events that led to the passage of two (2) substantive VAT laws, namely VAT Act, 1994 (Act 498) and VAT Act, 1998 (Act 546)—prior to the more recent revamp under VATA 2015 (Act 870). In 1988, the Harvard Institute for International Development (HIID) issued a feasibility report to back a ***two-stage*** VAT introduction.

This launch was delayed until 1993 when Crown Agents assigned full-time, short-term, and peripatetic experts to help the VAT Project prepare for the VAT launch in 1995.

- **Pre-VAT and VAT structure:** VAT replaced the ***single-stage domestic and import Sales Tax*** under Customs, Excise and Preventive Service (CEPS) and Service Tax under Internal Revenue Service (IRIS). Table 13.3 summarizes the laws that covered the narrow-based and less buoyant sales and service taxes, replacing them with a comprehensive VAT with an unambiguous revenue goal, and suspension of the latter because of the public protests.

Table 13.3: Pre-VAT tax regime legislation

VAT Acts: Important Milestones				
Items	**Pre-1994 Legislation**	**Tax Instrument**	**Features**	**Comments**
1	**Pre-VAT Consumption Tax Laws**			
1.1	Customs, Excise and Preventive Service (Management Act),	Sales Tax	Single (manufacturing/import) tax on goods; "ring" as input tax relief	Restricted in scope and eligibility to be GRA tax agent
	Income Tax Decree,	Service Tax	Tax on selected professional	
2	**1st VAT law (introduction)**			
2.1	Value Added Tax Act 1994 (Act 486)	VAT	Original VAT Act (repealed)	Introduced VAT for the first time; not much change

3	**VAT suspension, pre-VAT restoration, transition**			
3.1	CEPS (Management) (Amendment) Act, 1995 (Act 500)	Sales Tax	Restored previous sales tax	Made old sales tax effective till 1998/99
3.2	Service Tax Act, 1995 (Act 501)	Service Tax	Restored previous service tax; kept the VAT Service also in suspension	Transition laws between period of VAT introduction and reintroduction
3.3	Service Tax Act, 1995 (Act 529)	Service Tax/ organization	Reversed VATS suspension; under IRS, VAT honoured VAT obligations for the 3 months that VAT was effective	

- **Strength of VAT mechanism:** VAT is necessary for fiscal and macroeconomic stability since it has a ***wider base*** under an "all-inclusive" rule or design whereby, all supplies of goods and services by registered entities are taxable, unless specifically exempted. Further, the VAT ***invoice-credit and ITC*** processes make the VAT ***self-policing*** since the purchaser needs the VAT invoice as proof for the ITC claim. Under the invoice credit and ***Input Tax Credit (ITC)*** mechanism, registered entities can set off the VAT on purchases (Input VAT) against the VAT on sale (Output VAT).

- **VAT introduction:** Ghana ***launched the VAT Project in 1993*** with funding from the United Kingdom (UK) Government's Department for International Development (DfID) and technical assistance (TA) from UK Crown Agents. The VAT Service that took over from the Project launched the VAT in March 1995 but it was not successful. After continuing protests, the Government withdrew the VATA 546 through Parliament after only ***three and half months*** of implementation.

- **Suspension of VAT implementation:** VAT became a tool for the opposition in the 1996 election campaign; agitation against economic reforms; certain provisions of the proposed 1992 Constitution; and alleged increase in consumer prices. Parliament passed three (3) laws to ***"suspend"*** and reintroduce the VAT between 1995 and 1998: CEPS (Management) (Amendment) Act 500 (1995) and Service Tax Act 501. They restored the collection of the old sales tax by CEPS and the Service Taxes by the IRS.

- **VAT organization and administration:** The Government used the new VAT law in 1994 to set up the VAT Service (VATS) to charge and collect the domestic VAT while CEPS continued to collect the import VAT. The transition laws (a) restored the old sales and service tax regimes under CEPS and IRS; and (b) allowed the VATS staff under IRS to mob issues relating to the cancellation of the 3-month-old VAT.
- **Re-introduction of VAT:** The "suspension" ended in 1996 after the elections and preparations re-started again and led to a successful reintroduction in 1998/99. Despite the "suspension", the amendment laws were helpful since they ***preserved the right of registered entities to claim ITC and refunds*** for the three and half months of the VAT. This became a major selling point for the reintroduction since the entities were able to compare the benefits of VAT to the old sales and service taxes.

9. Amendments, rate increases, and levies:

The NDC 1 ***planned, introduced, cancelled, and reintroduced VAT*** between 1993 and 1998 before losing power in 2000. Upon taking office in 2001, the first NPP 1 government passed many ***VAT amendments, including certain laws that complement the VAT regime***. The laws include (a) *de facto* VAT rate increases by 2.5 per cent each in 2000, 2007, and 2015 (i.e., from 10 per cent to 17.5 per cent); and (b) assignment of the net proceeds to the social sector and investment programs:

- *Ghana Education Trust Fund (GET-Fund):* the NDC 1 administration increased the VAT rate from 10 per cent to 12.5 per cent and dedicated the net proceeds to the Ghana Education Trust Fund (GETFund).
- *National Health Insurance Levy (NHIL):* the NPP 1 government also increased the VAT rate from 12.5 per cent to 15 per cent and dedicated the net amount to the National Health Insurance Scheme (NHIS).
- *Ghana Infrastructure Investment Fund (GIIF):* NDC 2 applied the proceeds from another rate increase, from 15 per cent to 17.5 per cent, to the Ghana Infrastructure Investment Fund (GIIF).
- *Exemption and other amendments:* these related mainly to non-taxable (i.e., exempt and relief) and zero-rated supplies but with some relating to administrative provisions.

- ***VATA revamp:*** in 2013, GOG replaced and updated the entire VAT Act 1998 (Act 546) with the VAT Act 2013 (Act 870)—but with reversals in 2017 under the new government.

Table 16.4 summarizes the main VAT legislation, with some of their characteristics.

Table 16.4: Pre-VAT tax regime legislation

VAT Acts: Important Milestones				
Items	**Pre-1994 Legislation**	**Tax Instrument**	**Features**	**Comments**
4	**2nd VAT law (re-introduction)**			
4.1	VAT Act, 1998 (Act 546)	VAT	Reintroduction of VAT (replaced in 2013)	The Act was used to reintroduce VAT successfully
4.2	GETFund Act, 2000	VAT	VAT rate increase by 2.5 percent; net proceeds dedicated to education sector	GETFund levy is *de facto* VAT; allocation of net proceeds is budgetary allocation
4.3	NHIL Act, *2008 (Act ...)*	VAT/Levy	VAT rate increase by 2.5 percent; net proceeds dedicated to health sector	NHIL levy is *de facto* VAT; allocation of net proceeds is budgetary allocation
4.4	VAT Act, 1998 (Act 546)	VAT	Reintroduction of VAT (replaced in 2013)	The Act was used to reintroduce VAT successfully
4.5	VATA 546 Amendments		Various, often distortionary, amendments	Various distortionery policy changes
5	**3rd VAT law (comprehensive review)**			
5.1	VAT Act, 2013 (Act 870)	VAT	Comprehensive review of entire VAT Act	First major review pf VAT since enactment of Act 546
5.2	VATA 870 Amendments		Various, often distortionary, amendments	Various distortionery policy changes

- **Complementary VAT and "Straight Levy" legislation:** In their original forms, the GET-Fund, NHIS and GIIF taxes or levies were treated as *de facto* VAT rate increases, with due right to ITC for VAT on taxable inputs. The GIIF continues in VAT and budget allocation forms but the NPP government converted the GET-Fund and NHIL to excise-type "straight" levies in 2018, without recourse to ITC claims by registered entities. These GET-Fund and NHIL changes and expansion of exemptions resulted in major distortions to the original VAT.

10. Conclusion

Ghana's VAT experience was unique in many respects: it involved the suspension of a major tax initiative against the background of many successful macroeconomic and fiscal reforms; Ghana became the third country to cancel or suspend a VAT plan; and timing a major initiative at a time significant political transitions.

Even though the reintroduction of VAT has been eventually successful, the frequent changes in VAT policy and structure have created instability in the application by tax officials and registered entities. The changes are often due to industry lobby and political considerations.

There is no reason for the situation to persist since VAT has developed into a major source of revenue, based on known fiscal rules, in more than 100 countries that are advanced, middle-income, and developing country status. Some changes are fundamentally flawed, such as the conversion of a general consumption expenditure tax regime, such as VAT, to an excise-type instrument that denied ITC to registered entities.

It is important for the Government to protect and sustain the basic structure of tax instruments, notably VAT, personal and corporate income tax, excise, and tariffs—with the strengthening of property tax at the SNG level. In tandem, there must be a strengthening of the systems and processes in local tax offices.

Ghana and other African states have attained Lower Middle-Income Country (L-MIC) status in the last one-and-a-half decade. Based on this World Bank per capita income classification, ***Africa is "stratified" as fragile, developing and MIC states,*** which require enhanced MIC tax administration and policy structures. This is required to generate sufficient domestic revenues to replace the inevitable loss of access to concessional loans and grants or aid from multilateral institutions such as the World Bank [WB] and African Development Bank [AfDB] as well as other bilateral sources.

Their inability to replace the concessional sources of revenue appropriately has led to capital market exposures, public debt distress, difficulty in servicing costly debt, and inability to counter domestic and global financial and real sector crises—the most recent being the COVID-19 pandemic. In a crisis context, the MIC states that they do not have fiscal buffers of their own and have difficulty in accessing fiscal largesse such as budget support and debt relief or even deferment. This is a wake-up call for Africa to improve its domestic resource mobilization and enhance its budget buffer, borrowing and debt management.

Index

U

V

W

Z

www.ingramcontent.com/pod-product-compliance
Lightning Source LLC
LaVergne TN
LVHW020653110826
845149LV00012B/1975

* 9 7 9 8 9 9 3 9 1 6 2 9 3 *